CRICKET
ENCYCLOPEDIA

GUINNESS
CRICKET
ENCYCLOPEDIA

A L A N   R U S T A D

Published in Great Britain by
Guinness Publishing Ltd,
33 London Road, Enfield, Middlesex

Cover design by AdVantage Studios

Text design and layout by John Rivers

Typeset in Helvetica by
Ace Filmsetting Ltd, Frome, Somerset

Printed and bound in Great Britain by
The Bath Press, Bath, Avon

'Guinness' is a registered trademark
of Guinness Publishing Ltd

A catalogue record for this book
is available from the British Library

ISBN 0-85112-650-2

C O N T E N T S

PREFACE

THIS ENCYCLOPEDIA HAS BEEN TWO years in the making and I thought the hard part would be knowing where to start. Not a bit of it. The hard part was knowing where to stop.

Cricket is now a twelve months of the year game and it seems hardly a day goes by without a Test or one-day international taking place somewhere. Inevitably, keeping on top of what is going on in the farthest-flung parts from Auckland to Zimbabwe is never easy.

I am aware too that statistics can become out of date almost before the word processor has had time to churn them out. However, every effort has been made to keep information as up to date as possible and our printing deadline of 20 March 1995 has enabled the book to cover almost all of the 1994/95 winter season.

Recent years have not been happy ones for English cricket. Another Ashes defeat, coming after a similar 3–1 drubbing in the West Indies the previous winter, has left critics examining the very core of the game. Too much county cricket of a mediocre standard, elderly selectors out of touch with modern thinking, and players who look upon the game merely as a means of earning a living have all been cited as causes of the current malaise.

Yet the problems facing cricket go further than just the domestic game in England. Ball-tampering, the use of third umpires with modern technology, and allegations of match-fixing all suggest that world cricket is in turmoil. Against this background, I hope this encyclopedia presents an honest and accurate look at days gone by as well as affairs of the moment.

I have tried to present a balance between profiles of players, coverage of international and grass-roots cricket, and the history of the game. There is only so much room so my apologies if your favourite player or subject is not included.

Much midnight oil has been burned on this project and I owe a big debt of gratitude to my wife and family who must often have wondered whether the effort would ever be worthwhile.

I must thank many friends and cricket officials who have helped provide me with much valuable background information. In particular my thanks

Alan Rustad was born in Surrey and educated at Malvern College in Worcestershire. He began his journalistic career on the Surrey Herald newspaper before joining BBC Radio Merseyside where he worked on both news and sport.

He joined HTV in Wales as a reporter and went on to become senior presenter of the nightly news programme. During his time with HTV he presented a wide range of programmes including sport, current affairs and documentaries.

Alan is a keen follower of all sports, particularly cricket and golf, and has played for Surrey Young Cricketers. He now lives in the home of Welsh cricket, Glamorgan, with his wife and three children.

go to Charles Richards and Stephen Adamson at Guinness Publishing for taking on this project and giving me so much support.

My final thank you must go to my late father. It was his patience and encouragement over many hours of bowling in the back garden that introduced me to a wonderful game. I hope some of that enthusiasm comes over in the following pages.

ABDUL QADIR

Pakistan

Born 1955
Punjab, Lahore and Habib Bank

ABDUL QADIR WAS A LEG-spin and googly bowler who presented problems to the very best batsmen in the world.

Second only to Imran Khan in the number of Test wickets for Pakistan, he averaged 3.5 wickets per Test, no mean achievement for a spin bowler. With his bouncy action, his spin was hard to pick, and on his day he was a true match-winner.

His performances in domestic cricket brought him his first Test appearance against England at Lahore in 1977/78. Then his 6 for 44 at Hyderabad helped to dismiss England for just 191.

His tour of England in 1978 was disappointing as he was dogged by injury. But four years later he proved to be the star attraction, taking 57 wickets in 12 matches, with ten wickets in three Tests.

Back home in 1982/83 he took 22 wickets in three Tests against Australia and became the first bowler to take 100 wickets in a Pakistan season. The following year his 18 Test wickets were the deciding factor in Pakistan's first series win against England.

Qadir inflicted further misery on English batsmen in 1987/88, taking 30 wickets in the three-Test series which Pakistan won. He made his last Test appearance in 1990.

First Class Career:
Wickets – 897. Average 23.43

Test Match Career:
Tests – 67
Wickets – 236. Average 32.80

ADELAIDE

THE ADELAIDE OVAL, HOME of the South Australian Cricket Association (SACA), is rightly regarded as the most attractive Test venue in Australia. Set in parkland, from it one can see the spire of nearby St Peter's Cathedral, while to the north there are the peaks of the Lofty Mountains.

Its name, the Oval, is thought to have come from a former Surrey member who went to live in Australia

Abdul Qadir's leg-spin wizardry was the scourge of international batsmen. England's were on the receiving end of his best Test figures, 9–56 in the first innings at Lahore in 1987/88.

in about 1860. It is very much an oval, with long straight boundaries and very much shorter ones square of the wicket.

As with other Test grounds in Australia there has been much improvement recently, with the new Creswell Stand opened in 1989/90 costing A$8.5 million. It includes corporate hospitality suites, an air-conditioned restaurant and better facilities for the media.

Although able to hold about 40,000 spectators, the Adelaide Oval has had less than half the Tests of Sydney and Melbourne, despite staging its first as far back as 1884/85. But with a smaller population than the other two cities, it can never expect to attract the same numbers.

Adelaide was the scene of Don Bradman's first first-class century in 1927. He also made the highest score ever seen on the ground – 369 for South Australia against Tasmania in 1936.

The ground also saw the climax to the Bodyline affair, with injuries to Australian players Bill Woodfull and Bert Oldfield in the third Test against England. The Saturday of the match saw 50,000 cram into the ground.

CURTLY AMBROSE

West Indies

Born 1963
Leeward Islands and Northamptonshire

AT SIX FEET SEVEN INCHES tall, Curtly Ambrose is probably the most hostile fast bowler in cricket today. He follows in a long line of fine West Indies 'quicks' over the past 25 years and rates among the very best of them.

Like all good fast bowlers, Ambrose has the ability to turn a game within a few overs. In the third Test against England at Trinidad in 1993/94, with the visitors set just 194 to win, he single-handedly tore through the top and middle order as England were reduced to 40 for 8 at close of play on the fourth day.

Ambrose took 6–24 in the innings, 11–48 in the match.

Bowling from such a height, he naturally achieves great bounce. Although not a great swinger of the ball, he has a rhythmical run-up and bowls with great accuracy, a fact

Eyes blazing in triumph, arms pumping in celebration, Ambrose claiming another victim. The West Indies fast bowler reached 200 Test wickets, in his 46th match, at a lower average than any other bowler.

The Recreation Ground at St John's, Antigua, pictured in 1994 during the historic Test in which Brian Lara made his record 375.

regularly borne out by his economical figures.

Not surprisingly given his height, this giant from Antigua was a natural basketball player and nearly opted to play the game in the United States.

But he was persuaded to try cricket by, among others, former West Indies pace bowler Andy Roberts, and in 1987/88, in his first full season in domestic cricket in the West Indies, Ambrose took a record 35 wickets at an average of 15.51.

He also made his Test debut against Pakistan in April, but it was an unhappy start, the West Indies suffering their first home defeat for ten years.

That summer he enjoyed a more successful first tour of England, taking 22 Test wickets as the West Indies inflicted a 4–0 defeat on the home side.

Since then he has become West Indies' leading bowler. His best figures are 8 for 45 against England at Bridgetown in 1991, including a spell of five wickets in five overs.

In 1992/93 he took 7 for 25 against Australia, his seven wickets coming at a cost of just one run off 32 balls. It helped dismiss Australia for 119 after they had been 85 for 2. His captain, Richie Richardson, said it was the best spell of fast bowling he had seen.

Ambrose took 33 wickets in that series, a record for the West Indies against Australia, at an average of 16.42.

In England, his performances have helped improve the fortunes of Northamptonshire. He took a wicket with his first ball on his championship debut against Glamorgan in 1989, and has played in two NatWest finals.

First Class Career:
Wickets – 651. Average 20.40

Test Match Career:
*Tests – 48
Wickets – 219. Average 21.07*

ANTIGUA

THE ANTIGUA RECREATION Ground at St John's is the most recent addition to the Test match circuit in the West Indies. It hosted its first Test in 1980/81 against England.

It was a fitting reward for an island that has produced some of the West Indies' greatest players in recent years, among them Viv Richards, Andy Roberts and Richie Richardson.

The island itself is well situated to host top-class cricket, with a fine airport to aid communications. Not far from the ground is the sea, a jail – providing a ready supply of labour for the preparation of the pitch – and a hotel and casino.

That first historic Test ended in a draw, but at least the local supporters were cheered by Richards, who scored a fine century. It came just two days after his wedding, for which it seemed the whole island turned out.

The pitch at the Recreation Ground is a good batting strip on which bowlers have to toil hard to gain any reward.

But the ground also lives up to its title. While it may now be a Test match venue, it is still used by the population at large for non-sporting events such as carnivals, calypso contests and political rallies.

JOHN ARLOTT

THERE HAVE BEEN MANY great writers and broadcasters on the game of cricket, but perhaps no one ever combined both quite as brilliantly as John Arlott.

For years he was the voice of cricket, with his famous Hampshire burr being a favourite subject for showbiz and amateur impersonators alike. You could listen to a

THE GUINNESS

commentary from Arlott and be given not just the detail of what was happening on the pitch, but the full tapestry of the crowd, the ground, and the many other things that make up a game of cricket.

During his lifetime, as some of the commentary on BBC Radio's Test Match Special became a little too 'jokey' for some tastes, Arlott provided the serious appreciation of the game. His love of cricket always shone through.

Born in Basingstoke in 1914, Arlott became a policeman in 1934 and had eleven years in uniform. During that time he would write in a freelance capacity for the BBC, which eventually led him to a producer's job there in 1945.

The chance to broadcast on cricket occurred soon after, and there followed the start of a long writing career too, most notably for *The Guardian* newspaper.

He also developed a great love of wine and would regularly write with as much passion on this subject as he would on cricket.

He was much respected by those playing the game, and always looked upon his presidency of the Cricketers' Association (from 1968 until his death) as a great honour. He also played a leading role in bringing the talented South African Basil D'Oliveira to England.

Life was not always kind to Arlott. He lost his eldest son James in a road accident at the age of 21 and then in 1976 suffered the loss of his second wife Valerie, who was 42.

After his retirement, Arlott moved to Alderney in the Channel Islands. He died in his sleep on 14th December 1991, at the age of 77.

Arlott at the microphone for BBC Radio's Test Match Special at Lord's, in his last match as a commentator. Characteristically spurning any grand exit, he retired from cricket broadcasting by simply handing over to his colleagues as normal.

THE ASHES

AT JUST FOUR INCHES tall, the terracotta urn that contains 'The Ashes' must surely be the smallest, yet most famous trophy in world sport.

For more than a hundred years it has been eagerly contested by the two oldest Test-playing countries. But its origins have always been the subject of much debate.

What is certain is that Test matches between England and Australia began at Melbourne in 1877. England won the first Test on English soil in 1880, but two summers later W.L. Murdoch led Australia to a seven-run victory in a tense match at the Oval. Frederick Spofforth, known as 'the Demon Bowler', was largely responsible for that win, having match figures of 14 for 90.

The defeat hurt English national pride. Mr Reginald Shirley Brooks, a journalist who was the son of the editor of *Punch*, was moved to write a mock obituary that appeared in the *Sporting Times*.

'In affectionate remembrance of English Cricket, which died at the Oval on 29th August 1882, deeply lamented by a large circle of sorrowing friends and acquaintances. R.I.P.

N.B. The body will be cremated and the ashes taken to Australia.'

Three weeks later the Honourable Ivo Bligh, later Lord Darnley, took an England team to Australia with the country demanding he 'bring back the ashes'. England duly won the series by two matches to one.

The Ashes themselves, it is generally believed, came into being when a group of Melbourne ladies, including Miss Florence Rose Murphy, presented Bligh with an urn containing the ashes of a bail used in the third match. Later, Mrs J.W. Fletcher made a small velvet bag, embroidered with gold, to hold the Ashes.

However, at the time of the centenary of the Oval Test match in 1982, evidence was produced that suggested the ashes were actually those of a ball, and were given to the England captain by Sir William Clarke before the Tests in 1883.

Either way, Miss Murphy eventually married Bligh, and on his death in 1927 she gave the Ashes to Lord's, where they remain in the museum irrespective of whichever country holds them. One can also see the bag, the original scorebook of the 1882 tour, and the scorecard of the Oval Test.

The words on the urn are believed to have first appeared in the *Melbourne Punch*. They read :

When Ivo goes back with the urn, the urn,
Studds, Steel, Read, and Tylecote return, return:
The Welkin will ring loud,
The great crowd will feel proud,
Seeing Barlow and Bates with the urn, the urn;
And the rest coming home with the urn.

ASIF IQBAL

Pakistan

Born 1943
Hyderabad, Karachi, Pakistan International Airlines, National Bank and Kent

FOR MANY, ASIF IQBAL personified the very best of Pakistani cricket. He was a charismatic all-rounder – an attractive middle-order batsman who was like lightning between the wickets, and a useful seam bowler.

He was also a determined campaigner for a fair deal for Pakistani cricketers. That led him to become one of the leading figures in the Kerry Packer revolution.

Asif: a fine all-round cricketer who captained both Kent and Pakistan.

He batted at number ten in his first Test for Pakistan, making 41 and 36, and opened the bowling with Majid Khan. Both ultimately became very much better known for their batting.

Asif showed his true potential as a Test batsman when he scored 76 at Lord's in 1967. Later in the series, with Pakistan 65 for 8 at the Oval, he scored a brilliant 146, putting on 190 in 175 minutes with Intikhab Alam – a Test record for the ninth wicket.

His most successful Test season came in 1976/77. Then, in three different series, he scored four centuries. His highest ever Test score was 175 against New Zealand at Dunedin in 1972/73.

In England, he joined Kent in 1968 and scored 1,000 runs in a season six times. He was part of a very successful team, helping the county to Championship, B&H Cup and John Player League honours.

First Class Career:
Runs – 23,375. Average 37.28
(45 centuries)
Wickets – 291. Average 30.15

Test Match Career:
Tests – 58
Runs – 3,575. Average 38.85
(11 centuries)
Wickets – 53. Average 28.33

MICHAEL ATHERTON
England
Born 1968
Cambridge University and Lancashire

NO ONE COULD DESCRIBE Michael Atherton's reign as England captain as uneventful. Disagreements over selection, poor team performances, and personal disciplinary problems have all fallen on the shoulders of a young man seemingly destined to lead his country's cricket team.

From university days Atherton had acquired the nickname 'FEC' (Future England Captain) and he eventually succeeded to the top job for the final two Tests against Australia in 1993.

Taking over a dispirited team from Graham Gooch with the Ashes already lost, he acquitted himself well, and after losing his first match in charge, led his side to victory at the Oval. It was England's first win in 11 Tests, and Atherton was consequently chosen to lead the team in the West Indies.

That tour proved a learning experience for him, with a young side who faced a torrid time. The series was lost 3–1 but it ended on an upbeat note, and the captain wanted to persevere with a youth policy.

The arrival of Ray Illingworth as chairman of the selectors appeared to change that as many of the 'old

A young Mike Atherton in the field for England in 1990. Mischievous readers will no doubt observe an early tendency for the hands to stray towards the pockets!

guard', led by Gooch, returned for the summer series against New Zealand and South Africa.

It was not a happy summer for Atherton personally. He came close to losing his job after he was found to have dirt in his pocket during a match against South Africa at Lord's on a hot and sticky Saturday afternoon.

The captain said it was to keep his

hands dry – but television pictures appeared to show him applying the dirt to the ball. He was fined.

The disastrous Ashes tour of 1994/95, with a squad ravaged by injury, tested the young captain to the limit, yet his own performances with the bat could not be faulted.

A solid opening batsman with a greater range of shots than he sometimes shows, Atherton is a determined and yet relaxed character. Although he does not captain Lancashire, he was a clear favourite to succeed Gooch as England captain ahead of Alec Stewart and Mike Gatting.

A product of Manchester Grammar School, he made an immediate impact in county cricket in 1987 when he became the first batsman for 11 years to score more than 1,000 runs in his debut season.

In 1988 he began a two-year spell as captain of Cambridge University and the following year led the Combined Universities team to the quarter-finals of the Benson and Hedges Cup. That was also the year in which he made his Test debut against Australia at Trent Bridge.

His first major disappointment was quick to follow, however, when he was overlooked for the tour of the Caribbean in 1989/90.

He returned to the England team the following summer and made his highest Test score, 151, against New Zealand at Trent Bridge.

He formed a consistent opening partnership with Graham Gooch at a time when England's middle-order batting was frail, but again fell from favour during the disastrous tour of India and Sri Lanka in 1992/93.

It was perhaps a blessing in disguise. After the Ashes series in 1993 was also lost, Gooch stepped down as captain and Atherton soon brought a change of approach and a new feeling of optimism.

First Class Career:
Runs – 12,399. Average 44.12 (34 centuries)

Test Match Career:
Tests – 45
Runs – 3,324. Average 40.04 (7 centuries)

AUCKLAND

EDEN PARK IN AUCKLAND is New Zealand's premier Test venue, although not the oldest one – that honour goes to Lancaster Park in Christchurch. With rugby being played at Eden Park in the winter, it is an all-purpose sporting venue.

What is now a fine stadium for both sports was at one time a swamp. However, around the turn of the century Eden Park was turned into a sports ground.

Two huge grandstands give plenty of room for spectators. As many as 43,000 attended a one-day game against Australia, and the ground was also well populated for

With grandstands on either side and sweeping terraces at both ends, Eden Park is a venue for Test rugby as well as cricket.

the World Cup matches in 1992.

New Zealand's cricket fortunes have known great highs and lows at Eden Park.

In 1955, England inflicted upon the home side a massive humiliation, dismissing them for just 26, the lowest score in Test cricket.

But a year later the West Indies were beaten by 190 runs to give New Zealand their first victory in Test cricket.

AUSTRALIA

AS THE VENUE FOR THE first ever Test match, Australia has always held a very special place in the history of cricket. The game 'down under' may have undergone many changes, but the attraction of a series against the men in the baggy green caps always draws crowds around the world.

For all the recent upheavals in Australian cricket, it is generally accepted that the structure of the game has been responsible for producing young, competitive players who adapt quickly to the demands of Test cricket.

The initial organisation of Australian cricket was very different from that in England, and it was tours by teams from the Mother Country that led to standards in Australian cricket improving quickly during the latter part of the 19th century.

It has led to a situation today where there is a great sense of competition running through the game right down to club cricket.

First-class matches are played on huge grounds capable of holding numbers of spectators far in excess of anything that can be found in England.

In recent years the Australians' love of 'instant' cricket has led to big attendances for one-day internationals, many being day/night matches with the latter stages played under floodlights. But this has in turn led to a shrinking of crowds for five-day Test matches – a worrying trend which administrators have so far failed to reverse.

Australia has also been the home of several experiments with the game itself in recent years. The latest came during the Ashes tour of 1994/95, with a one-day game between England and Western Australia split into four quarters, both sides batting for 25 overs before going out again to finish off their innings.

Australia's main domestic competition, the Sheffield Shield, has also suffered from the success of one-day cricket, with little interest being shown by the public or television.

Indeed, the 1993 edition of *Wisden* recorded: 'It is a wonder that the Sheffield Shield competition survives, and the players must take credit for their ability to adapt from limited-overs games.'

The competition saw another interesting new development in 1993/94 with three umpires taking part, standing in rotation to avoid fatigue in the hot sun.

Australia is renowned as a country of noisy, sometimes hostile crowds, where the barracking of players is almost as much a sport as the action on the pitch. Most grounds have their areas where the comments are phrased in highly colourful language, none more so than Sydney where the 'Hill' was for years populated by spectators never slow to make their feelings known. But while the Australian spectator will show no mercy to an unfortunate player, his love of a real hero knows no bounds.

Australians have never loved a sporting hero more than the great Sir Donald Bradman, surely the greatest batsman ever to play the game. His records are unparalleled, with a career average of 95 and a Test average of 99. It is hard to imagine a modern-day player coming close to such an achievement.

It was the difficulty countries faced in trying to get Bradman out that led to one of the gravest crises the game has known when the England touring party of 1932/33 used 'bodyline' tactics to restrict him. England called it 'leg theory', but whatever you may choose to call it, it worked – at a tremendous cost.

At one time, with cables being sent backwards and forwards between Australia and London, it looked as if the whole future of Test cricket was in jeopardy, not to mention Australia's place in the Commonwealth. Happily, good relations were eventually restored.

It was all very different from that first Test, held at Melbourne in 1877, in which Australia beat England by 45 runs thanks largely to a century by their opener Charles Bannerman.

For the best part of a century, the Melbourne Cricket Club controlled the affairs of Australian cricket in a manner similar to that of the MCC in England. Initially they underwrote the costs of tours from England and set the game up on a sound footing.

In 1905 a Board of Control took over, after much wrangling among the states. New South Wales and Victoria were the founding members, with Queensland joining a few weeks later, South Australia the following year, Tasmania in 1908 and Western Australia during the First World War.

After the war, cricket in Australia saw another innovation: the eight-ball over. The Australians only reverted to six-ball overs in the 1970s.

Since the Second World War, Australian legislators have had to deal with a number of difficult issues. There were the bowling controversies of the late fifties and early sixties where throwing and dragging caused such heated debate. It brought a premature end to the Test career of fast bowler Ian Meckiff.

Then in the late 1970s the rise of Kerry Packer's World Series Cricket split opinion, with the effects of what was seen as the Board's capitulation to the media magnate's demands still influencing the direction of the game in Australia today. Packer's revolution improved the lot of the very best players, but WSC's elevation of the one-day game over five-day Tests has changed the

St Peter's Cathedral overlooks the Adelaide Oval, headquarters of the South Australian Cricket Association and one of the five main centres of Australian cricket.

appetite of the cricketing public in Australia, although an exciting Test series will still draw healthy crowds.

Verbal insults on the field, commonly termed 'sledging', are prevalent in Australian cricket, putting unwelcome pressure not just on opposition players but on umpires as well.

Yet if cricket is tough in Australia, it is undeniable that in their Institute of Sport Cricket Academy in Adelaide, they have a breeding ground that is the envy of the world.

Run by former wicket-keeper Rodney Marsh, the Academy has already brought such stars as Shane Warne, Michael Slater and Michael Bevan to Test cricket, and it seems this production line will develop significant talent for Australia for many years to come.

AUSTRALIA
V
INDIA

AUSTRALIA HAVE USUALLY enjoyed the upper hand in meetings between these two countries. It took India three series before they recorded their first win, and more than thirty years elapsed before they managed to win a series.

Australia dominated their first meetings in 1947/48, Don Bradman's last home season. Four-nil, with one Test drawn, was the depressing outcome for India, three of Australia's wins coming by an innings. Bradman averaged 178.75 for the series, with Lindsay Hassett's average also in three figures.

Australia had another comfortable series win in India in 1956/57 when they played three Tests after touring England. Richie Benaud in particular revelled on ideal wickets

for a wrist-spinner, taking 23 wickets at 16.86.

The first full series between the two in India came in 1959/60 and in it the Indians finally broke their duck, coming back after losing the first Test to take the second at Kanpur by 119 runs. It was a remarkable achievement after they had batted first on a crumbling wicket and made just 152. But Patel with 5 for 55 and Umrigar with 4 for 27 spun the home side to victory, dismissing Australia for 105 in their second innings.

The 1977/78 series was perhaps the most exciting of all. It all looked so comfortable for Australia when they went 2–0 up with wins at Brisbane and Perth. But against the odds, India hit back to achieve conclusive wins in Melbourne and Sydney, only for Australia to take the series with victory in the final match at Adelaide.

It was not until 1979/80 that India finally won a series. Draws in the first two Tests were followed by an Indian win at Kanpur, Kapil Dev and

Yadav precipitating an Australian collapse after the visitors had been set 279 to win in 312 minutes.

Victory by an innings in the sixth Test at Bombay sealed a memorable triumph for India's captain Sunil Gavaskar, who was top scorer with 123.

In the 1980s honours were shared, and fittingly the most exciting moment came with only the second tie in the history of Test cricket at Madras in 1986/87.

Australia, batting first, scored a massive 574–7 declared and India were set 348 to win on the final day. At 193 for 2 at tea, they looked to have a good chance. They lost Gavaskar and Kapil Dev, but at 331 for 6 they still seemed to have the match won. As Matthews and Bright shared the wickets between them, last-man-in Maninder had three balls to score the winning run, but was lbw to the penultimate ball of the match.

Allan Border then led his team to a crushing 4–0 win at home in 1991/92, with David Boon scoring three centuries in the series.

them when Australia made their first visit to New Zealand. The visitors won by an innings and 103 runs, the home side being dismissed for 42 and 54. It was not until some two years later that the ICC recognised the match as a full Test.

Almost another thirty years were to pass before the two met in Tests again, when New Zealand toured Australia in 1973/74 for a three-match series.

Australia, led by Ian Chappell, were again far too strong, winning the first and third Tests by an innings. Rain caused the second match to be drawn with New Zealand in a commanding position.

That first elusive win for New Zealand came when Australia made the return visit just a month later. At Christchurch, a century in each innings by Glenn Turner and fine bowling from the Hadlee brothers, Dayle and Richard, brought the home side a five-wicket victory. Australia won the next match at Auckland to share the series.

Australia held the upper hand in

the next two series, and then shared the spoils in New Zealand in 1981/82. It was when the countries began playing for the Trans-Tasman Cup in 1985/86 that New Zealand recorded their first series win in Australia.

Richard Hadlee was the man responsible, taking 33 wickets in the three-match series which saw the tourists win by an innings and 41 runs at Brisbane and by six wickets at Perth. Martin Crowe was the bedrock of the batting with a fine 188 at Brisbane.

New Zealand proved this was no fluke by winning the next series at home in 1985/86. Australia though came back to take a three-Test series in 1987/88.

The matches marked Allan

New Zealand skipper Martin Crowe congratulates his Australian counterpart Allan Border on passing Sunil Gavaskar's world record for Test runs during the first Test at Christchurch in February 1993.

Season	Ven	Tests	Winners	Res
1947/48	Aus	5	Australia	4–0
1956/57	Ind	3	Australia	2–0
1959/60	Ind	5	Australia	2–1
1964/65	Ind	3	–	1–1
1967/68	Aus	4	Australia	4–0
1969/70	Ind	5	Australia	3–1
1977/78	Aus	5	Australia	3–2
1979/80	Ind	6	India	2–0
1980/81	Aus	3	–	1–1
1985/86	Aus	3	–	0–0
1986/87	Ind	3	–	0–0
1991/92	Aus	5	Australia	4–0

AUSTRALIA
V
NEW ZEALAND

IT IS QUITE EXTRAORDINARY that Test cricket between these two neighbours did not begin until 1945/46. What makes it all the more interesting is that New Zealand's record in the series is a good one.

The omens did not look good for

Border's achievement in becoming Australia's highest Test scorer, beating Greg Chappell's record. Richard Hadlee took his total of Test wickets to 373, equalling Ian Botham's world record.

The next full series, in New Zealand in 1992/93, was shared, but Australia recorded another series win against their closest neighbours at home in 1993/94.

Season	Ven	Tests	Winners	Res
1945/46	NZ	1	Australia	1–0
1973/74	Aus	3	Australia	2–0
1973/74	NZ	3	–	1–1
1976/77	NZ	2	Australia	1–0
1980/81	Aus	3	Australia	2–0
1981/82	NZ	3	–	1–1
1985/86	Aus	3	N. Zealand	2–1
1985/86	NZ	3	N. Zealand	1–0
1987/88	Aus	3	Australia	1–0
1989/90	Aus	1	–	0–0
1989/90	NZ	1	N. Zealand	1–0
1992/93	NZ	3	–	1–1
1993/94	Aus	3	Australia	2–0

From 1985/86: for the Trans-Tasman Trophy

AUSTRALIA
V
PAKISTAN

AUSTRALIA PLAYED THEIR first Test in Pakistan in 1956/57, on their way home from England, and immediately set a record. On a slow matting wicket at Karachi, only 95 runs were scored on the first day, the fewest ever in a full day's play.

This was largely made up of Australia being dismissed for just 80. They never really recovered and were beaten by nine wickets.

Australia were more of a match when they returned in 1959/60 prior to touring India. Richie Benaud, who himself took eighteen wickets in the three-match series, led his side to a two-nil win, with victories in the first two Tests at Dacca and Lahore. The fourth day's play in the third match at Karachi was watched by US President Eisenhower.

The first three-Test series in Australia in 1972/73 was a whitewash for the home side. The Pakistanis, led by Intikhab Alam, were an unhappy team.

Their next visit was an altogether happier affair, a shared series including their first victory on Australian soil. It was the bowling exploits of Imran Khan, with match figures of 12 for 165, that secured that historic win at Sydney.

Pakistan recorded their first series win at home in 1979/80. Both sides had their World Series Cricket players back, but it was the home team's spinners who dominated the first Test at Karachi, the only match that ever looked like producing a result.

The 1981/82 series in Australia was a generally bad-tempered affair. Australia won it 2–1, but there was a particularly ugly incident between Dennis Lillee and Javed Miandad. Lillee obstructed the Pakistani batsman when he tried to take a run, and Javed then raised his bat in retaliation. Lillee was banned for two one-day matches and fined.

Two years later in Pakistan there was a clean sweep for the home team, with the speed of Imran Khan and the subtle spin of Abdul Qadir proving too much for the Australians.

Since then, the home side has generally won through, although in 1994/95 Pakistan's series win was achieved only after a last-wicket stand of 57 between Inzamam-ul-Haq and Mushtaq Ahmed brought victory in the first Test at Karachi.

Season	Ven	Tests	Winners	Res
1956/57	Pak	1	Pakistan	1–0
1959/60	Pak	3	Australia	2–0
1964/65	Pak	1	–	0–0
1964/65	Aus	1	–	0–0
1972/73	Aus	3	Australia	3–0
1976/77	Aus	3	–	1–1
1978/79	Aus	2	–	1–1
1979/80	Pak	3	Pakistan	1–0
1981/82	Aus	3	Australia	2–1
1982/83	Pak	3	Pakistan	3–0
1983/84	Aus	5	Australia	2–0
1988/89	Pak	3	Pakistan	1–0
1989/90	Aus	3	Australia	1–0
1994/95	Pak	3	Pakistan	1–0

AUSTRALIA
V
SOUTH AFRICA

THE SOUTH AFRICANS took a big step towards establishing themselves in world cricket by boldly inviting Australia to visit them in 1902/03. The Australians were on their way home, having just won a series in England, and were unquestionably a class above their hosts.

Not surprisingly, Australia won two of the three Tests played, but South Africa's fighting spirit made them a much tougher proposition than anyone had imagined.

South Africa's first visit to Australia in 1910/11 resulted in a comprehensive 4–1 win for the home side. The South Africans relied on spin, and without a serious fast bowler they were heavily punished by a strong Australian batting line-up.

They were at least cheered by their first victory on Australian soil, which came at the end of six days' play in Adelaide. In all, 1,646 runs were scored in the match.

The third meeting between the two countries came in England in 1912. A triangular tournament, featuring the home country as well, was held at South Africa's suggestion. The idea was not a success, though – bad weather spoilt many of the games and South Africa were considerably weaker than the other two countries.

The next four series between 1921/22 and 1949/50 resulted in overwhelming Australian victories, with South Africa failing to win a single Test. In 1931/32, Australia won 5–0 on some difficult wickets, with Bradman dominating, scoring 806 runs at an average of 201.50.

The next two series, in 1935/36 and 1949/50, both went to Australia 4–0, with two matches being drawn. The latter series saw the arrival on the scene of a young Australian, Neil Harvey. The 21-year-old left-hander scored 660 runs at an average of 132.00.

Aussie opener Mark Taylor narrowly escapes a caught & bowled chance during the third Test against South Africa at Adelaide in January 1994. Brian Macmillan is the unlucky bowler.

South Africa's third visit to Australia in 1952/53 at last produced a change in fortune.

They went one down, but won the second Test at Melbourne by 82 runs and the final match on the same ground by six wickets, after Australia had scored 520 batting first. The series was shared, 2–2.

However, Australia again proved invincible in South Africa in 1957/58, winning 3–0, the talents of Ken Mackay with the bat and Richie Benaud and Alan Davidson with the ball being decisive.

South Africa finally recorded a victory over Australia on home soil in 1966/67 when Peter van der Merwe's team beat Bobby Simpson's tourists 3–1. This series saw the first appearance on the Test scene of Mike Procter, who took fifteen wickets in three Tests.

South Africa then went one better in 1969/70 when Ali Bacher led his side to a 4–0 series win over a party led by Bill Lawry.

This was a bitter-sweet affair – sweet because the talents of Barry Richards, Eddie Barlow, Graeme Pollock, Peter Pollock and Procter shone through; bitter because this was the final series before the Republic's isolation.

It was over twenty years before the two met again, with South Africa visiting Australia in December 1993. Bad weather ensured the first Test was an anti-climax, but South Africa then went on to win at Sydney by just five runs in a dramatic game. Australia needed just 117 for victory, but fast bowlers Donald and de Villiers ensured a remarkable ending. Australia hit back at Adelaide with victory by 191 runs.

Much interest in the series centred on the South African captain Kepler Wessels. His country's isolation had led him to move to Australia, for whom he played 24 Tests before returning to his homeland in time for their restoration to world cricket.

Honours were again even at 1–1 when the two met in a three-match series in South Africa immediately afterwards. Australia's newest talent, leg-spinner Shane Warne, took fifteen wickets in the series.

Season	Ven	Tests	Winners	Res
1902/03	SA	3	Australia	2–0
1910/11	Aus	5	Australia	4–1
1912	Eng	3	Australia	2–0
1921/22	SA	3	Australia	1–0
1931/32	Aus	5	Australia	5–0
1935/36	SA	5	Australia	4–0
1949/50	SA	5	Australia	4–0
1952/53	Aus	5	–	2–2
1957/58	SA	5	Australia	3–0
1963/64	Aus	5	–	1–1
1966/67	SA	5	S. Africa	3–1
1969/70	SA	4	S. Africa	4–0
1993/94	Aus	3	–	1–1
1993/94	SA	3	–	1–1

AUSTRALIA
V
SRI LANKA

TEST MATCHES BETWEEN Australia and Sri Lanka began in 1982/83, and Sri Lanka have still to record their first victory.

Australia won that first meeting at Kandy by an innings and 38 runs, David Hookes and Kepler Wessels both scoring centuries. Sri Lanka passed 200 in both innings but never really looked like forcing their guests to bat again.

Sri Lanka visited Australia in 1987/88, losing the one Test played, and lost and drew the two Tests scheduled in 1989/90.

The first three-match series between the two was played in Sri Lanka in 1992/93. It turned out to be Australia's first series win on the Indian sub-continent for 23 years.

Yet Sri Lanka had looked set for a famous win in the first Test. They needed just 54 runs for victory off almost 25 overs but then collapsed, losing their last eight wickets for 37 runs to give Australia victory by 16 runs. The home crowd jeered their players at the presentation ceremony.

Sadly, rain was to play a dominant part in producing drawn matches in the other two Tests in the series.

Season	Ven	Tests	Winners	Res
1982/83	SL	1	Australia	1–0
1987/88	Aus	1	Australia	1–0
1989/90	Aus	2	Australia	1–0
1992/93	SL	3	Australia	1–0

AUSTRALIA
V
WEST INDIES

TEST SERIES BETWEEN Australia and the West Indies have produced many memorable moments since matches began in 1930/31. Perhaps the most famous came at Brisbane on 14 December 1960 when a dramatic run-out led to the first ever tied Test. Irrespective of the result, it had been one of the greatest Test matches of all time.

Having entered the Test arena with two series against England, the West Indies found their first tour of Australia in 1930/31 a tough ordeal. Australia won three of the first four Tests by an innings, and the other by ten wickets. The West Indians

Pace bowler Merv Hughes enjoys a fine record in Tests against the West Indies. He even top-scored for Australia with 43 in this match at Adelaide in January 1993.

came back well to win the fifth at Sydney by 30 runs, when rain helped them by bringing extra life to the wicket.

There was a similar result to the next series more than twenty years later, and the first meeting between the two in the Caribbean in 1954/55 again saw Australia dominate, 3–0.

But it was the fourth series in Australia in 1960/61 that really captured the imagination.

The sides had two of the most entertaining captains Test cricket has seen, Richie Benaud for Australia and Frank Worrell for the West Indies. The historic first Test at Brisbane, one of only two tied Tests in the history of the game, set the scene for the series.

The West Indies batted first and thanks to a magnificent century by Sobers made 453. Australia replied with 505, O'Neill making 181. Australia were left with 233 to win after dismissing the West Indies for 284 in their second innings, but it was the visitors who looked to be heading for a comfortable victory when Wesley Hall reduced Australia to 92 for 6.

However, Alan Davidson and Richie Benaud added 134 to take Australia to the brink of victory. Davidson was then run out by Solomon, leaving six needed for victory off the last over.

A leg bye came off the first ball, and Benaud was caught behind off the second trying for the winning runs. A bye to the wicket keeper came off the fourth and another run came next ball when Hall dropped a skier to give Grout a let-off.

Grout was then run out attempting a third run. With the scores tied and with one ball to go, Kline set off for the run that would have meant victory, but Solomon swooped again to score a direct hit, with just one stump to aim at, to dismiss Ian Meckiff.

It was an extraordinary match – and the rest of the series maintained the high level of excitement.

Australia took the second Test at Melbourne by 7 wickets, but the West Indies came back to win the third by 222 runs. A draw followed at Adelaide before Australia

clinched the series with a two-wicket win in the final Test. A world record crowd of 90,800 saw the second day's play.

The West Indies recorded their first series win, 2–1, in 1964/65 but Australia dominated the next three series, their most emphatic triumph coming at home in 1975/76 when Greg Chappell's side recorded a 5–1 win in what was looked upon as an unofficial Test World Championship.

They went one up at Brisbane but West Indies hit back with a convincing innings victory at Perth. However, Australia recovered the upper hand to win the final four Tests thanks to dominating batting by Chappell and Ian Redpath and superb, hostile fast bowling from Dennis Lillee and Jeff Thomson.

That turned out to be Australia's last series win to date. Since then the West Indies have won seven series, with one, in Australia in 1981/82, being tied. For all his great leadership, Australia's Allan Border in four attempts never managed to overcome West Indies teams led by Clive Lloyd, Viv Richards and Richie Richardson.

The sides' most recent meeting in 1992/93 saw the talented young West Indies batsman Brian Lara really come into his own. His 277 at Sydney changed the course of the series as the West Indies, having lost the first Test, stormed back to take the rubber 2–1.

Season	Ven	Tests	Winners	Res
1930/31	Aus	5	Australia	4–1
1951/52	Aus	5	Australia	4–1
1954/55	WI	5	Australia	3–0
1960/61	Aus	5	Australia	2–1
1964/65	WI	5	W. Indies	2–1
1968/69	Aus	5	Australia	3–1
1972/73	WI	5	Australia	2–0
1975/76	Aus	6	Australia	5–1
1977/78	WI	5	W. Indies	3–1
1979/80	Aus	3	W. Indies	2–0
1981/82	Aus	3	–	1–1
1983/84	WI	5	W. Indies	3–0
1984/85	Aus	5	W. Indies	3–1
1988/89	Aus	5	W. Indies	3–1
1990/91	WI	5	W. Indies	2–1
1992/93	Aus	5	W. Indies	2–1

From 1964/65: for the Frank Worrell Trophy

MOHAMMED AZHARUDDIN

India

Born 1963
Hyderabad and Derbyshire

FROM THE MOMENT HE stepped into the cricketing spotlight, the Indian captain Mohammed Azharuddin looked a class player. His progress since making his Test debut has been impressive to say the least.

Azharuddin, like all great batsmen, plays the ball late with plenty of use of the wrists. His timing is rarely less than perfect and he has the necessary concentration to play big innings.

He was just eighteen when he made his first-class debut for Hyderabad in the Ranji Trophy. His Test breakthrough came against David Gower's England touring party in 1984/85.

He scored 110 on his debut at Calcutta, 105 in the next match at Madras, and then 122 at Kanpur. No one else has ever made centuries in his first three Tests.

Despite his prolific scoring at home, he had faced a torrid time in the West Indies and it was not until India's 1989/90 tour of Pakistan that he scored his first Test century outside India.

Early in 1990 he was made captain for India's tour of New Zealand. He has led his country in two series against England, and against Australia, South Africa, Sri Lanka and Zimbabwe.

His highest Test score, 199, came against Sri Lanka at Kanpur in 1986/87. Another big score, 192 against New Zealand at Auckland, was notable for being the highest score by an Indian captain abroad.

First Class Career:
Runs – 11,420. Average 52.87
(39 centuries)

Test Match Career:
Tests – 62
Runs – 4,020. Average 47.29
(14 centuries)

DR ALI BACHER
South Africa

Born 1942
Transvaal

ARON 'ALI' BACHER captained South Africa against Australia in 1969/70 in their final Test series before their expulsion from world cricket. But as an administrator, he did more than anyone to bring about the changes that resulted in South Africa being brought back into the fold.

Bacher worked tirelessly in the seventies and eighties to bridge the gulf between the races in South Africa. His diplomatic skills led to a greater degree of integration in cricket than in other sports, as he developed a close understanding with Steve Tshwete, chief sports spokesman of the African National Congress.

As full-time director of cricket for the white South African Cricket Union, Bacher organised several tours by unofficial 'rebel' teams from England, Sri Lanka, West Indies and

A young Ali Bacher in confident form during his debut series against England in 1965.

Australia, while also working hard to develop youth cricket in the townships.

He became managing director of the United Cricket Board of South Africa, the controlling body formed by the merger of the Cricket Union and the non-white South African Board, and his dream was realised when his country resumed Test cricket in 1992.

As a player, he was a determined, stocky, right-hand middle order batsman, and a fine fielder.

First Class Career:
Runs – 7,894. Average 39.07 (18 centuries)

Test Match Career:
Tests – 12
Runs – 679. Average 32.33

TREVOR BAILEY
England

Born 1923
Cambridge University and Essex

TREVOR BAILEY, NOW known chiefly as a BBC radio summariser, was a fine all-rounder for his university, county and country.

He was given the nickname 'Barnacle' for his often dour batting, although that was a quality England were often glad to make use of. It was not typical of Bailey as a player – he could often make runs quickly and attractively when needed.

THE GUINNESS

As a right-arm fast medium bowler he was of high class, and he was also a first-rate fielder.

His reputation as the man England depended on when the going got rough was well illustrated in the series against Australia in 1953. At Lord's, for example, Bailey batted with Willie Watson for almost the whole of the final day to save the game. His 71 came in four and a quarter hours.

His greatest Test achievement with the ball came against the West Indies at Sabina Park in 1953/54. On a terribly hot day and on a good batting wicket, he took 7 for 34 in 16 overs.

In domestic cricket he performed the double of 1,000 runs and 100 wickets eight times. After retiring from the captaincy of Essex, he went on to become the county's secretary.

First Class Career:
Runs – 28,642. Average 33.42
(28 centuries)
Wickets – 2,082. Average 23.13

Test Match Career:
Tests – 61
Runs – 2,290. Average 29.74
(1 century)
Wickets – 132. Average 29.21

A genuine all-rounder of the highest class for Essex and England, Trevor Bailey represented the county for over 20 years as a player, from 1946 to 1967.

BARBADOS

IT CAN JUSTLY BE SAID that the Kensington Oval at Bridgetown in Barbados is the cricket centre of the West Indies.

Home of the Pickwick Cricket Club, Kensington Oval has three particularly close links with England. It was the venue for the first match by a visiting touring team, the first West Indies v MCC game, and the first West Indies v England Test match.

The Barbados Cricket Association has responsibility for the upkeep and maintenance of the ground. Since the 1970s many

Barbados and its palm trees – not surprisingly, now a favourite destination for those who follow England in Test matches overseas – here plays host to the first ever Test between the West Indies and South Africa in 1992.

improvements have been made, most notably in the provision of new grandstands named after great West Indies cricket heroes, such as the '3 Ws' stand and the Sir Garfield Sobers Pavilion.

Pitches at the Oval have generally favoured the batsmen over the years, usually West Indian ones. However, there was a major turn-up in 1993/94 when England beat the West Indies to end the home side's 59-year undefeated run there.

England were already three down in the series, but the bowling of Fraser and Caddick came as a welcome tonic to the many thousands of holidaying English supporters.

England had last won on the ground in 1934/35 when they recorded a four-wicket win on a muddy pitch. The West Indies managed the highest total of an extraordinary game, just 102.

The crowds in Barbados have a reputation for being quieter than others in the Caribbean, but they are generally considered to be the most knowledgeable.

EDDIE BARLOW
South Africa

Born 1940
Transvaal, Eastern Province, Western Province, Boland and Derbyshire

PUGNACIOUS SUMS UP Eddie Barlow. A fine all-round cricketer, he was always in the thick of the game, whether as a right-hand opening batsman or medium-pace bowler who could make the ball swing considerably.

Barlow was a vital cog in the South African team in the 1960s. He enjoyed a particularly good season in 1963/64, scoring 1,900 runs against Australia and New Zealand at an average of 63.33. The highlight of the tour was his 201 against Australia at Adelaide.

When the scheduled South African tour of England was cancelled in 1970, Barlow played for the Rest of the World in the series that replaced it. He did the hat-trick against England at Headingley in a burst of four wickets in five balls.

In 1976 he joined Derbyshire and in three seasons there brought a greater sense of purpose to the county, taking them to a Benson and Hedges Cup final at Lord's.

After his playing days were over he worked tirelessly to promote South African sport and campaigned for his country's return to Test cricket.

First Class Career:
Runs – 18,212. Average 39.16 (43 centuries)
Wickets – 571. Average 24.14

Test Match Career:
Tests 30
Runs – 2,516. Average 45.74 (6 centuries)
Wickets – 40. Average 34.05

KEN BARRINGTON

England

Born 1930. Died 1981
Surrey

KEN BARRINGTON WAS A true boys' own hero character. As a player and a coach he was always totally committed. But it could be said that it was his dedication and diligence that led to his sad death in 1981 while on tour as assistant manager and coach to the England team in the West Indies.

Barrington made his county debut for Surrey in 1953. An attractive strokemaker, he was awarded his

Barrington hits out for Surrey against the touring Australians at the Oval in 1961. Keeping wicket is his namesake Barrington 'Barrie' Jarman; keeping a close eye on proceedings at slip is the tour captain Richie Benaud.

county cap in 1955 and that summer made his Test debut, albeit not a successful one as he made a duck against South Africa at Trent Bridge.

Dropped after the second Test at Lord's, he determined to become more disciplined, a process that was complete when he returned to the England side in 1959. He became a regular fixture in the team as a solid, dependable batsman as well as a useful leg-spin bowler.

His sheet-anchor role for England was not always appreciated. Against New Zealand he once took seven and a half hours to make 137. He was dropped for public relations reasons, but returned after missing just one game.

A doughty fighter, Barrington was also something of a worrier. He suffered a mild heart-attack at the age of 38 while playing in a double-wicket tournament in Melbourne, and retired from first-class cricket. He became a well-respected Test selector, assistant manager and coach.

He had the total respect of his players, and his death from a heart

attack during the Barbados Test, coming as it did during a fraught tour, was a cruel blow to English cricket.

The following morning before the start of play, many players were in tears as they stood in silence in his memory.

First Class Career:
*Runs – 31,714. Average 45.63
(76 centuries)
Wickets – 273. Average 32.61*

Test Match Career:
*Tests – 82
Runs – 6,806. Average 58.67
(20 centuries)
Wickets – 29. Average 44.82*

BISHEN BEDI

India

Born 1946
Punjab, Delhi and Northamptonshire

BISHEN BEDI WAS ONE OF the greatest slow left-arm spin bowlers of all time. He was also a highly popular character both amongst his fellow cricketers and the public at large.

Wearing brightly coloured patkas, Bedi stood out on any cricket ground. But it was his bowling that really caught the eye. Off a short run, he had everything at his command – changes in pace and flight, and the ability to turn the ball.

He made the first of 67 Test appearances in 1966/67 and took wickets consistently throughout his career. He captained his country on 22 occasions, winning six Tests.

But if he was a friendly character, Bedi was also involved in his fair share of controversy.

He declared India's two innings closed early in protest at intimidatory West Indies fast bowling in Jamaica in 1976, and once objected to two England bowlers wearing vaseline gauzes.

He enjoyed some success with Northamptonshire between 1972 and 1977, twice taking more than 100 wickets in a season. He has

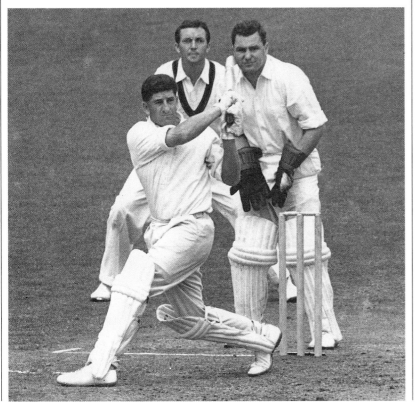

With the famous turban ever present, Bedi, the finest slow left-arm bowler of his era, now coaches India's young cricketers.

passed on the benefit of his experience by coaching Indian players, and is still involved with cricket administration in his country.

First Class Career:
Wickets – 1,560. Average 21.69

Test Match Career:
Tests – 67
Wickets – 266. Average 28.71

ALEC BEDSER

England

Born 1918

Surrey

ALEC BEDSER WAS A member of the successful Surrey Championship-winning sides of the 1950s, played in 51 Test matches for England, and served as a selector for a record 23 years.

Born within minutes of his identical twin brother Eric, Alec Bedser made his county debut in 1939, but it was not until after the Second World War that his career began in earnest.

As a fast-medium bowler, he made an explosive start to his international career, taking eleven wickets in each of his first two Tests against India in 1946.

His success owed much to a model bowling action. His inswinger was his stock delivery, and the leg-cutter, bowled slower, was a fearsome weapon on wet or broken wickets.

Bradman has said that in certain conditions Bedser was the most difficult bowler he faced.

Unlike some modern bowlers, he remained fit and positively enjoyed shouldering the burden of long spells. He simply loved bowling. His batting, while not fluent, was often useful, and he was an effective nightwatchman.

He was very conservative in his attitude to the game – loyal, and with firm beliefs about hard work and clean living. This shone through during his time as a selector.

He joined the committee in 1962 and served as chairman from 1969 to 1981. No one has picked more Test teams, and although as chairman he often had to defend selections to a sometimes hostile press and public, he bore the pressures with good grace and courtesy.

First Class Career:
Wickets – 1,924. Average 20.41

Test Match Career:
Tests – 51
Wickets – 236. Average 24.89

The Second World War held back Bedser's introduction to Test cricket, but with his classic action he was an immediate success.

● THE GUINNESS

RICHIE BENAUD

Australia

Born 1930
New South Wales

NOW KNOWN TO A NEW generation as one of the world's leading broadcasters on the game, Richie Benaud was unquestionably one of the greatest Test captains.

His record of leadership stands comparison with anyone. Taking over at a time when Australian cricket had had to play second fiddle to a resurgent English team in the mid-fifties, Benaud captained his country to series wins against England twice, West Indies and Pakistan.

He was an inspiring leader and a tough competitor, but he never forgot the need to entertain the public and always tried to make Test cricket interesting.

He was principally a leg-spin bowler, who maintained great consistency while at the same time producing a wide variety of leg-breaks, googlies, top-spinners and the flipper, an off-spinning top spinner. He was a forcing lower-middle order batsman and a wonderful close to the wicket fielder, particularly in the gully.

Although he toured England in both 1953 and 1956, it wasn't until 1957/58 in South Africa that he proved himself to be a complete all-rounder, scoring four centuries in his aggregate of 817 runs on the tour. He also took 106 wickets.

Benaud played a major role in recapturing the Ashes when he first led his country in 1958/59, taking 31 wickets in the series. Two seasons later Australia and West Indies staged a memorable series, including a dramatic tied Test.

It was during that series that Benaud first developed the shoulder trouble that was to end his career. However, he led his country one final time to England in 1961 and made a telling contribution as his team held onto the Ashes.

In the fourth Test at Old Trafford, England looked set for victory on 150 for 1, needing little more than another hundred runs to win. But Benaud, bowling into the rough, took 6 for 70 and England were dismissed for 201.

His shrewd tactical brain is now employed in television commentary boxes in Australia and England, helping armchair watchers appreciate the finer points of the game. He also writes for newspapers.

First Class Career:
Runs – 11,719. Average 36.50 (23 centuries)
Wickets – 945. Average 24.73

Test Match Career:
Tests – 63
Runs – 2,201. Average 24.45
Wickets – 248. Average 27.03

With a wry smile and eyes to camera, Australia's captain might be auditioning for the television rôle he later took up with such aplomb. This is Benaud at the start of the 1961 tour to England which saw his team retain the Ashes.

BENSON AND HEDGES CUP

THE SUCCESS OF BOTH the Gillette Cup and the John Player League persuaded the administrators to introduce a third one-day competition to English cricket in 1972.

BENSON AND HEDGES CUP			
	Winners	Runners-up	
1972	Leicestershire	Yorkshire	5 wickets
1973	Kent	Worcestershire	39 runs
1974	Surrey	Leicestershire	27 runs
1975	Leicestershire	Middlesex	5 wickets
1976	Kent	Worcestershire	43 runs
1977	Gloucestershire	Kent	64 runs
1978	Kent	Derbyshire	6 wickets
1979	Essex	Surrey	35 runs
1980	Northamptonshire	Essex	6 runs
1981	Somerset	Surrey	7 wickets
1982	Somerset	Nottinghamshire	9 wickets
1983	Middlesex	Essex	4 runs
1984	Lancashire	Warwickshire	6 wickets
1985	Leicestershire	Essex	5 wickets
1986	Middlesex	Kent	2 runs
1987	Yorkshire	Northamptonshire	Took more wickets
1988	Hampshire	Derbyshire	7 wickets
1989	Nottinghamshire	Essex	3 wickets
1990	Lancashire	Worcestershire	69 runs
1991	Worcestershire	Lancashire	65 runs
1992	Hampshire	Kent	41 runs
1993	Derbyshire	Lancashire	6 runs
1994	Warwickshire	Worcestershire	6 wickets

Amid lengthening shadows at Lord's, traditional scenes at the end of the Benson & Hedges Cup final. Notts supporters rush on to help Eddie Hemmings (left) and Bruce French celebrate victory off the last ball against Essex in 1989.

The problem they faced was how to make it distinctive. The Gillette was a straightforward knock-out, the John Player a straightforward league. In the end they decided on a mixture of both in a new Saturday competition of 55 overs per side.

In that first season, 40 preliminary matches were played in four regional divisions of five teams. The seventeen first-class counties were joined by two Minor Counties XIs and Cambridge University, with Oxford University taking their turn the following year. The top two in each zone contested the quarter-finals when the competition reverted to a knock-out format.

Making the leagues regional reduced travel costs, but it also had the effect of bracketing together some of the best teams.

The strength of the South group for example meant that Kent, the 1971 beaten Gillette Cup finalists, Surrey, the 1971 County Champions, and Essex were all eliminated at the first stage.

The competition has had its controversies. In 1979 the Somerset captain Brian Rose declared his side's innings at 1 for no wicket after just one over of their match against Worcestershire.

His decision exposed a quirk in the points-scoring system whereby if more than two teams finished level on points at the top of the table, the two qualifiers would be decided by the best 'wickets taken to balls bowled' ratio.

Rose decided it was better to lose the game in this manner than to run the risk of running up a worse wickets/balls ratio.

Although not strictly against the rules – not least because no one had ever imagined that a captain would declare in a limited-overs game! – the ploy backfired when the Test and County Cricket Board expelled Somerset from the competition, with Glamorgan taking their place in the quarter-finals.

Kent were the early kings of the competition, winning the cup three times in the first seven years. Leicestershire have also won it three times, while Somerset are the only county to have won it in successive years – 1981 and 1982.

The Benson and Hedges Cup's reputation of being a particularly open event is demonstrated by the fact that in 23 years of the competition, fifteen counties have won it – Durham, Glamorgan and Sussex the only ones to miss out.

There have also been some close finishes, with Middlesex beating Kent by two runs in 1986 and the following year Yorkshire beating Northamptonshire by virtue of having taken more wickets, with the scores tied.

After more than twenty years, it was considered that the early season zonal matches should be dropped and so in 1993 the Benson and Hedges Cup became a simple knock-out competition, with the eighteen first-class counties being joined by Scotland, the Minor Counties, and the Combined Universities. Ireland were added a year later.

But in 1995 the competition returned to the zonal league format with knockout matches from the quarter-final stage.

A universally popular character, umpire Dickie Bird, whose love of cricket seems to know no bounds, in typically cheerful pose.

DICKIE BIRD

NO ONE HAS UMPIRED IN more Test matches around the world than Yorkshireman Dickie Bird. A man of many nervous mannerisms and by his own admission a born worrier, he is generally regarded as the best umpire in Test cricket today.

His most famous feature, his white cap, somehow makes him appear almost bird-like, but his powers of concentration are immense and his attention to detail meticulous.

Harold Dennis Bird played his cricket for Yorkshire and

Leicestershire. He once made 181 not out opening for his native county against Glamorgan, but was then dropped for the next match.

If his achievements as a player were modest, then his record as an umpire has been unique.

His first Test as an umpire, in only his third season on the first-class list, was England v New Zealand at Headingley in July 1973. It was typical of the man that he arrived at the ground at a time when the players and his fellow umpire Charlie Elliott were still in bed!

Bird equalled Frank Chester's record of 48 Tests while standing in Zimbabwe's debut Test match against India in October 1992, and then became the world's senior Test umpire when Zimbabwe played New Zealand the following month.

That same winter he umpired in the West Indies with Steve Bucknor and the pair set a record by giving 17 lbw decisions in the first Test against Pakistan, an amazing statistic for a man regarded as a 'not outer'.

Still officiating in Tests despite passing the age of sixty, he has had a glittering career which has included umpiring in the first three World Cup finals at Lord's.

His less happy experiences include the day when he and David Constant were jostled on the pavilion steps at Lord's by irate MCC members for not resuming play after rain during the centenary Test against Australia in 1980.

His proudest moment, however, was to receive the OBE. Meetings with Royalty and senior public figures have always been cherished moments for him.

The affection in which he is held by the players has resulted in numerous practical jokes, many the work of Allan Lamb. The England batsman once handed Bird his mobile phone when walking in to bat.

Standing at square leg shortly afterwards, Bird was horrified to hear it ring. In what was a pre-arranged jape, Ian Botham was on the other end of the line. Lamb has also removed the wheels from Bird's car at Old Trafford, and once even

Hitting powerfully through the on-side in characteristic fashion, South Africa's Colin Bland.

locked him in a dressing-room.

Bird lives in Yorkshire, close to Geoffrey Boycott's home. A single man, he jokes that he is married to cricket. It will be a sad day for everyone when he eventually hangs up that white cap for the last time.

COLIN BLAND

South Africa

Born 1938

Rhodesia, Eastern Province and Orange Free State

HE WAS A STRONG AND purposeful batsman, but Colin Bland will probably be best remembered for his breathtaking fielding. His exploits during the 1965 South African tour to England made him a real crowd-puller, and it was the example of his ability in the covers that was partly responsible for the vast improvement in fielding standards throughout the world which followed over the next quarter of a century.

Bland made his Test debut against New Zealand in 1961/62 and toured Australasia and England. His strong hitting, and especially his partiality for lifting the ball between long-off and long-on, helped him to score three Test centuries, including 127 at the Oval in 1965 in what turned out to be the last Test between England and South Africa for nearly 30 years.

Crowds would gather to watch him practise. Nicknamed the Golden Eagle, he would regularly knock a single stump out of the ground when swooping in and throwing all in one movement.

He would save fifty runs or more in the field as well as being responsible for vital wickets. At Lord's in 1965 he changed the course of the game, and the series too, when he ran out Barrington and Parks.

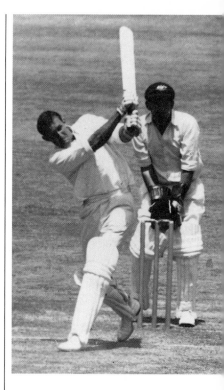

The career of a man who once said 'I live for cricket' came to a sad end. In the first Test against Australia in 1966 his left knee collapsed as he chased a ball to the boundary. He crashed into the boundary rails, badly injuring the leg.

First Class Career:
Runs – 7,208. Average 37.73 (13 centuries)

Test Match Career:
Tests – 21
Runs – 1,669. Average 49.08 (3 centuries)

BODYLINE

THE 'BODYLINE' SERIES when England regained the Ashes in Australia in 1932/33 was unquestionably one of the greatest crises the game of cricket has ever had to face.

So bitter were the emotions aroused that Australia came close to leaving the Commonwealth and the whole future of international cricket was thrown into jeopardy.

Wisden in 1934 records that: 'It is very doubtful if ever a team from England travelled through the Commonwealth and met with such openly expressed hostility as that visiting Australia in 1932/33.

'A method of bowling was evolved . . . which met with almost general condemnation among Australian cricketers and spectators and which, when something of the real truth was ultimately known in this

In the fourth Test at Brisbane in 1932/33, Australia's captain Bill Woodfull ducks under a rising ball from Harold Larwood, bowling to a leg-side field containing six men close to the wicket. On the far left is the England captain Douglas Jardine, whose so-called 'bodyline' tactics provoked such controversy.

country, caused people at home . . . to wonder if the winning of the rubber was, after all, worth this strife.'

Bodyline, or 'leg-theory' as the England captain Douglas Jardine always called it, was nothing new. It had been a tactic used before in England to stop batsmen scoring. But on Australia's faster, bouncier wickets, it became an altogether more potent – and dangerous – weapon.

Bodyline was introduced with one purpose in mind: to stop Don Bradman making runs. The Australian maestro, whose average after nine Tests against England was more than 100, was seen as the one man who could ensure that Australia retained the Ashes.

The plan was to bowl short at the batsman's rib cage. The resultant defensive back-stroke would then be caught by any one of up to six

fielders positioned in an arc close to the wicket on the leg side. If it was a largely negative tactic, it was to prove a highly successful one.

The MCC team arrived in Australia to find Bradman in dispute with the Australian authorities over articles he was writing in the Press. He was also unwell and missed the first Test at Sydney, which England won by ten wickets.

The hostile bowling of Larwood and Voce was largely responsible for the victory, although McCabe, in making 187 not out, played one of the finest innings ever by an Australian.

Bradman returned for the second Test at Melbourne, where the pitch was very much slower and looked likely to blunt the effectiveness of the English fast bowlers. Yet Bradman fell first ball to Bowes, trying to hook a bouncer and dragging it onto his stumps.

But Bradman's undefeated century in the second innings, a courageous effort and the last to be made against England in this series, set up an Australian victory by 111 runs.

It was in the third Test, on a lively Adelaide wicket, that the whole series boiled over in what *Wisden* said would go down in history 'as probably the most unpleasant ever played'. The whole atmosphere in which it took place, the almanac records, was a disgrace to cricket.

In reply to England's first innings 341, Australia had only just begun their reply when their captain Woodfull was struck above the heart by Larwood, then bowling to a conventional field.

Woodfull took some minutes to recover and before he faced another ball, Jardine moved his fielders to the leg side. What had been a noisy crowd now became an angry mob. Worse was to follow later when Bert Oldfield was struck on the head by a ball from Larwood and took no further part in the match.

It would be no exaggeration to say that the events in Adelaide came close to causing a riot, and Woodfull was heard to remark to the England manager Pelham Warner that two teams were out there, but only one of them was playing cricket.

At this stage, telegrams began to be exchanged between the Australian Board of Control and the MCC in London. In the first, on 18th January 1933, the Board said Bodyline was a menace to the game and was causing intensely bitter feelings.

They went on: 'In our opinion it is unsportsmanlike. Unless stopped at once it is likely to upset the friendly relations existing between Australia and England.'

The MCC replied, deploring the cable, and expressing the fullest confidence in their captain, team and managers.

The reply continued: 'We hope the situation is not now as serious as your cable would seem to indicate, but if it is such as to jeopardise the good relations between English and Australian cricketers and you consider it desirable to cancel remainder of programme we would consent, but with great reluctance.'

The series did in fact continue, amidst continuing exchanges of cables and the eventual retraction by the Australian Board of the word 'unsportsmanlike'. England went on to win by four Tests to one.

The tactics of stopping Bradman had worked. He totalled 396 runs and passed fifty four times, but that was a meagre return compared to his past achievements.

Larwood took 33 wickets in five Tests and was well supported by Voce and Bowes. Gubby Allen, who steadfastly refused to adopt the same tactics, took 21 wickets. The four fast bowlers took 71 wickets of the 99 that fell.

On their return to England, the two managers, Warner and R.C.N. Palairet, the captain Jardine, and Larwood and Voce were called to Lord's to explain matters. Surprisingly Allen and the vice-captain Bob Wyatt, the two leading players who had opposed the Bodyline tactics, were not called.

The full implications of all that had happened were now becoming apparent and the MCC later ruled that 'any form of bowling which is obviously a direct attack by the bowler upon the batsman would be an offence against the spirit of the game'.

Larwood always maintained that he never intended to injure a batsman during that tour.

Douglas Jardine always stood by his tactics and in his book *In Quest of the Ashes* he wrote: 'I venture the opinion that upon good wickets, if a good batsman is hit when playing leg-theory he has no one to blame but himself.' He was also critical of Australian crowds.

But Allen, Jardine's biggest critic, in correspondence to his father that was only released sixty years after the event, wrote: 'Douglas Jardine is loathed. He is a perfect swine and I can think of no words fit for Mum to see when I describe him.'

Of Larwood and Voce, he was merely of the opinion that they were just 'swollen-headed, gutless,

The Wankhede Stadium in Bombay. Home to some of the most passionate cricket supporters in the world, it generates a tremendous atmosphere when full.

uneducated miners'.

Perhaps the whole shameful episode was best summed up by the then editor of *Wisden*, Sydney Southerton, in 1934.

He wrote: 'I hope that we shall never see fast leg-theory bowling, as used during the last tour of Australia, exploited in this country. I think that (1) it is definitely dangerous; (2) it creates ill-feeling between the rival teams; (3) it invites reprisals; (4) it has a bad influence on our great game of cricket; and (5) it eliminates practically all the best strokes in batting.'

ALLAN BORDER

Australia

Born 1955
New South Wales,
Gloucestershire, Queensland
and Essex

A GRITTY LEFT-HAND batsman, Allan Border is the highest run-scorer in Test cricket. On 26th February 1993, playing in his 139th Test match for Australia, he overtook Sunil Gavaskar's record of 10,122 runs when he reached 50 in the first Test against New Zealand.

It is perhaps typical of the man that he referred to the achievement as a millstone rather than a milestone, having managed only one run in his three previous Test innings, including the first 'pair' of his life.

Border was a major part of Australian cricket for more than fifteen years. First as a middle-order batsman and latterly as captain too, he was a true 'Aussie' – as hard an opponent as you could imagine.

Sir Don Bradman said after his achievement: 'Australians look upon Border as a typical Aussie battler, who has served his country well.'

After his debut against England in 1978/79, Border missed only one Test. He captained his country more times than any other player.

Very much in the style of his earliest mentor Ian Chappell, he often had his disagreements with authority. He was fined for abusing umpires, and once threatened not to play following the omission of his vice-captain Geoff Marsh. He reported late for the match.

For all that, Border was the bedrock of the Australian team, providing solidity in a sometimes fragile batting line-up. During 'Botham's Summer' of 1981, he made two centuries when his side were on the rack.

He had many setbacks as captain of Australia, but also achieved much. He led them to World Cup success in 1987, successive series wins of 4–0 and 3–0 over England,

BOMBAY

BOMBAY TRADITIONALLY has been the capital of Indian cricket, and Test cricket has been played on three grounds in the city.

India played the first home Test at the Bombay Gymkhana, an attractive ground featuring a fine pavilion with mock-tudor facade.

When Test cricket began again after the Second World War the venue was switched to the more modern Brabourne Stadium, named after the Governor of Bombay.

It was looked upon as the real jewel of Indian cricket grounds. Unfortunately the wickets were a problem. They generally had little pace, and the lifeless pitches invariably produced dull cricket.

The third venue in Bombay, the Wankhede stadium, came into being after a row over ticket receipts at the Brabourne between the Bombay Cricket Association and the Cricket Club of India, India's equivalent of the MCC. The club took most of the profits while the association, which staged Test cricket and had to deal with rising costs, received very little.

The association therefore decided to build its own ground, and although it is able to accommodate the vast numbers that watch cricket in India, many feel that the Wankhede does not have the charm of the Brabourne. However, facilities for spectators are excellent.

The Wankhede staged its inaugural Test in 1974/75 when Clive Lloyd's West Indies were the visitors.

and then trounced the old enemy again 4–1 in England in 1993.

He announced his retirement at the end of the tour to South Africa in February 1994, after a typically gritty innings of 42 not out in the final Test at Durban had helped his side secure a hard-fought draw.

First Class Career:
Runs – 25,551. Average 51.30 (68 centuries)
Catches – 345

Test Match Career:
Tests – 156
Runs – 11,174. Average 50.56 (27 centuries)
Catches –156

IAN BOTHAM
England

Born 1955
Somerset, Worcestershire, Durham and Queensland

COLOURFUL AND controversial, Ian Botham can

Australian captain Allan Border led his country through some difficult years early on but reaped the rewards with a vengeance. His Test career statistics for matches, runs and catches are all records.

truly say of his magnificent career, 'I Did It My Way'.

He was quite simply the greatest all-rounder to play for England. Most critics would probably say Sobers was a better player, but there has surely never been a greater match-winner in the history of the game than Botham.

His batting was of awesome power. Coming in at number five or six, he could quickly transform a game. His bowling was at his peak often fast, and nearly always hostile.

Above all, Botham was a player who made things happen. He rose to the occasion and could score runs with outrageous shots and take wickets with bad balls.

Botham was on the MCC groundstaff before he made his Championship debut for Somerset in 1974, but his first Championship

century did not come until two years later, when he was awarded his county cap. During his time at Taunton, Somerset won all three one-day competitions.

He was in the England squad – but did not play – for the one-day internationals against Australia in 1977, then was called up for the third Test to replace Chris Old. Botham made an explosive start: his first victim was Greg Chappell, and he went on to take 5 for 74 on the first day.

The following year against Pakistan at Lord's, he became the first player to score a century and take eight wickets in a Test, and in his 21st Test the next season he reached the double of 1,000 runs and 100 wickets, the shortest time ever taken to reach the milestone.

In 1980 he took over the England captaincy at home against the West Indies and then led the touring party to the Caribbean, when England were beaten 2–0.

There then followed the remarkable summer of 1981. Botham resigned the England captaincy after bagging a pair in the second Test against Australia at Lord's, with England one down in the series.

That they went on to win the series 3–1 was largely due to him. His 149 not out transformed the Headingley Test to give England the chance of victory after following on. His 118 at Old Trafford and 5 for 11 at Edgbaston were also match-winning performances.

The following year he hit 208 against India, his highest Test score, in just 272 minutes. Problems began to mount for him off the field, but his generosity was there for all to see in 1985 as he walked from John o'Groats to Land's End to raise money for leukaemia research.

Botham the Gladiator: helmetless on the West Indies tour of 1985/86, powerful hitting and locks flowing. Although statistically his performances dipped in the latter part of his Test career, his powers of show-stealing remained undiminished.

Three years later he followed Hannibal's footsteps and crossed the Alps with elephants to help the same cause.

In 1986 he was banned by the TCCB until the end of July for admitting he had smoked cannabis. In true Botham style, he returned for the final Test against New Zealand, took the wicket of Bruce Edgar with his first ball, and then overtook Dennis Lillee's record of 355 Test wickets.

At the end of that season, angered by Somerset's decision to release Joel Garner and Viv Richards, a close friend, he resigned in protest and moved to Worcestershire.

He spent the winter playing for Queensland in Australia, but it was an unhappy episode.

Having missed most of the 1988 season, when Worcestershire won the Championship, with back trouble, Botham returned to help them repeat the feat the following year.

He joined county newcomers Durham and returned to the England squad for the World Cup in Australia in 1992, when he was also awarded the OBE.

In 1993 he announced his retirement from the game, appropriately bowing out playing for Durham against the touring Australians. He said that his body had taken enough punishment over the years. It says much for his influence that England still have not found a replacement for him in the Test side.

He may have quit the game, but he is still well known as a star of BBC Television's 'A Question of Sport', and his autobiography sold over 200,000 copies in 1994.

The Botham name survives in county cricket through his son Liam, now starting a career with Hampshire.

Doubtless cricket has not heard the last of his father either.

First Class Career:
Runs – 19,399. Average 33.97 (38 centuries)
Wickets – 1,172. Average 27.22
Catches – 354

Test Match Career:
Tests – 102
Runs – 5,200. Average 33.54 (14 centuries)
Wickets – 383. Average 28.40
Catches – 120

Sweeping to leg with impeccable technique, watching the ball carefully all the way, Geoff Boycott provides an irresistible contrast to Botham as he builds another solid innings for England.

GEOFFREY BOYCOTT

England

Born 1940

Yorkshire and Northern Transvaal

I F, AS THE ROMANTICS would have us believe, great Test players are born, not made, then Geoffrey Boycott was surely an exception to the rule. Through sheer hard work, application, and no little ability, he became one of the greatest opening batsmen in Test history.

It is hard to think of another player in modern times who has been quite so single-minded in his pursuit of excellence. Boycott was certainly a perfectionist, but his critics, among them fellow players, would argue that he was too self-centred, playing more for himself than for the team as a whole.

His success owed much to an insatiable appetite for practice and yet more practice. Whereas players such as Botham could never take net sessions seriously, Boycott would be forever honing his game, ironing out his faults.

Whatever the merits of this complex man, who at times both loved and hated being in the spotlight, his record speaks for itself.

His total of 8,114 Test runs was for a time the highest in world cricket. He beat Sobers' tally of 8,032 while making a century against India at Delhi in 1981/82. It was later surpassed by India's Sunil Gavaskar. In the summer of 1992 it was overtaken by another Englishman when David Gower returned to the team against Pakistan at Old Trafford.

Boycott's total might have been considerably higher. For three years, from 1974 to 1977, he went into exile after playing for a rebel side on a tour of South Africa, missing a possible thirty Tests.

He joined his native Yorkshire in 1962 and was capped the following year. Looking studious in glasses, he was chosen for England in 1964,

making 48 on his debut against Australia at Trent Bridge. The first of 22 Test centuries came later in that series, 113 at the Oval.

From then on, until the time of his suspension, he was just about an automatic choice for England and went on to score centuries against every other Test-playing nation of the time.

But even high scores sometimes brought him trouble. In 1967 he was dropped after making 246 not out, his highest Test score, against India at Headingley. The selectors considered it had been made too slowly, with Boycott supposedly putting his own interests ahead of those of the team.

With a great sense of timing, Boycott reached another milestone, his 100th first-class hundred, playing for England against Australia in front of his own adoring Headingley crowd in 1977, the first man to record that achievement in a Test match.

After setting the Test runs record in 1981/82, he left the tour of India complaining of ill health – India was never his favourite country. However, a few weeks later he appeared in South Africa on another rebel tour and that signalled the end of his Test career, earning him a three-year international ban.

His Yorkshire career also contained great record-breaking achievements and was no less controversial. Twice, in 1971 and 1979, he averaged more than 100 in an English season. He captained the county from 1971 until 1978, when, disappointed by the lack of success, the committee sacked him from the post – a decision that sparked a bitter civil war within the county.

In 1981 Boycott was suspended by his manager and former England captain Ray Illingworth when he complained publicly about being omitted from Yorkshire's Sunday League team. Two years later Boycott and his large number of supporters overthrew the Yorkshire committee, and he became a powerful man in the county set-up.

His achievements will always be remembered but so will the

disappointments, the biggest being his failure to become captain of his country on a regular basis.

Boycott, though, remains a high-profile figure in the game today, as a typically forthright television commentator and newspaper columnist.

First Class Career:
Runs – 48,426. Average 56.83 (151 centuries)

Test Match Career:
Tests – 108
Runs – 8,114. Average 47.72 (22 centuries)

SIR DON BRADMAN

Australia

Born 1908

New South Wales and South Australia

D ON BRADMAN WAS unquestionably the most prolific run-scorer the game of cricket has ever known. His sheer consistency, born of considerable powers of concentration and self-discipline, has been quite unrivalled.

Throughout a first-class career that spanned 21 years, he scored centuries at a rate of better than one every three innings. Consistent he may have been, but he was never boring.

Although only five feet seven inches tall, he scored his runs with every shot imaginable, and was always able to tailor his innings to what was demanded by his side.

Born in New South Wales, the son of a carpenter and farmer, Bradman first showed an interest in the game by hitting a golf ball against a water tank and then playing back the rebound with a stump. He scored 118 on his debut for New South Wales against South Australia at Adelaide in 1927/28.

He made his Australian debut the following season but was dropped to twelfth man for the second Test, only to return next match and score 79 and 112. He was never omitted again.

He toured England four times, in 1930, 1934, 1938 and 1948, and on each occasion he scored more than 2,000 runs. On the first tour he set a record of 974 runs in Tests (average 139.14), including 334 at Headingley, 254 at Lord's and 232 at the Oval.

Back home in 1931/32 he scored 806 runs at an average of 201.50 against West Indies. No one at this time, it seemed, could dismiss him.

It was largely to counteract the Bradman threat that the MCC in Australia in 1932/33 used the infamous 'bodyline' tactics. It curbed him only a little, as he finished with a respectable average of 56.57 in his four Tests.

He became captain of Australia against England in 1936/37 and quickly showed himself to be a tough opponent, the extra responsibility taking nothing away from his ability with the bat.

He led his side in five series between 1936 and 1948, winning all five, four of them comprehensively. On his last tour of England, he led an unbeaten team and made centuries at Trent Bridge and Headingley.

But for a man who achieved so much, the end when it came was a terrible anti-climax. In his final Test innings at the Oval in 1948, needing to score just four runs to finish with a Test match average of 100, he was bowled by Eric Hollies second ball for 0.

On his retirement, Bradman became the first Australian cricketer to receive a knighthood. He has also been a leading administrator, chairing Australia's Board of Control and selectors.

Given the demands of modern-day cricket, it is unlikely we will see such a player again.

First Class Career:
Runs – 28,067. Average 95.14
(117 centuries)
Scored more than 200 on 37 occasions

Test Match Career:
Tests – 52
Runs – 6,996. Average 99.94
(29 centuries)

Bradman returns to England, the scene of some of his finest innings, in 1953 for the Ashes tour, as an observer this time. He is pictured here with his great rival Len Hutton, now captain of England, before the first Test at Trent Bridge.

MIKE BREARLEY

England

Born 1942
Cambridge University and Middlesex

IT WAS THE AUSTRALIAN fast bowler Rodney Hogg who best described why the scholarly Mike Brearley was such a successful England captain.

'He's got a degree in people,' he said – and he was right. Few have been able to motivate a group of individuals quite like the man who eventually left the game to become a psychotherapist.

The captain's rapport with his team-mates was all the more remarkable for the fact that he could rarely claim to justify his place in the team on ability. He was a steady right-hand opening bat, but there were a number of players in county cricket with more pressing claims to a Test place.

Brearley had a brilliant sporting and academic career at Cambridge. In four years (1961–64) he amassed 4,348 runs, a record for a university career. He captained the side twice, and was for a time a very competent wicket-keeper.

Awarded his Middlesex county cap in 1964, he was chosen for the tour of South Africa in 1964/65 but it was a disappointment for him. He never played in a Test and managed only 406 runs from 19 innings.

He left the game to pursue his academic interests in 1966 and 1967, and played only a little first-class cricket in the following three years.

He forced his way into the England team on merit and did well against the fearsome West Indies pace attack in 1976. He became vice-captain to Tony Greig and then took over as skipper when Greig signed up with World Series Cricket. Brearley was never tempted to follow.

He admitted to luck in inheriting a developing England team at a time when other countries had lost their best players to the Packer rebels. Under his leadership, England chalked up ten wins and five draws before he suffered his first defeat, against Australia at Melbourne in 1978/79. It was only a temporary setback as England won the series 5–1.

But it was in the summer of 1981 that he enjoyed his greatest series as England captain. Restored to the captaincy after Ian Botham's unhappy reign, Brearley turned a 1–0 deficit after two Tests into a 3–1 series win.

Two matches were turned around when it seemed Australia had victory in their grasp, including the memorable Headingley Test when after following on, England won by 18 runs.

Brearley's motivation of such players as Botham and Willis, combined with his astute field-placing, produced a memorable summer's Test cricket.

His figures as a Test player do not tell the full story. He might never have scored a century for his country, but his influence was always evident.

He was equally successful as a captain in domestic cricket, leading Middlesex to the County Championship title four times in eleven years, including 1982 when he finally retired from the game.

Brearley still keeps in touch with the cricket scene, the thought processes he brought to captaincy now being employed in newspaper columns.

First Class Career:
Runs – 25,185. Average 37.81 (45 centuries)

Test Match Career:
Tests – 39
Runs – 1,442. Average 22.88

BRISBANE

THE GABBA, HOME OF THE Queensland Cricket Association in Australia, may not be one of the world's prettiest grounds, but it has seen more than its fair share of incidents in international cricket.

The first Test to be played at Brisbane was at the Exhibition ground in November 1928, but subsequently matches were moved to the Gabba, a name shortened from the Aboriginal word Woolloongabba.

It is a small ground by Australian standards and has undergone many changes, with millions of dollars spent in recent years to help it shed its stark appearance and old image

Mike Brearley could almost be studying the wicket at close quarters as he ponders another of captaincy's tricky decisions. He led England in 31 Test matches, winning 18.

of being an unfriendly place to watch cricket.

Australia played their first Test at the Gabba against South Africa in 1931/32, but it was the following season during the 'Bodyline' series that the ground really came to prominence.

Temperatures were over 100 degrees on every day of an epic encounter, which England eventually won thanks to Eddie Paynter, who left his hospital bed where he was suffering from tonsillitis to bat for four hours to make 83 in England's first innings. Later he struck the six which won the match and regained the Ashes for England.

The Gabba was also the scene of the first tied Test when Australia took on West Indies in the first match of a remarkable series in 1960/61.

In a last, breathtaking over from Hall, Australia lost three wickets with last man Ian Meckiff run out by a throw from Joe Solomon off the seventh ball. It was an amazing climax to a match often regarded as the greatest ever played.

It is one of the oldest Test grounds in the world, but has undergone modernisation that has turned it into a massive concrete bowl that can take as many as 70,000 spectators.

Calcutta has never produced the players of quality that have come out of Bombay. The city seems to be a bigger centre for spectators than players.

The ground was the venue for the 1987 World Cup Final between England and Australia, and although India were beaten in the semi-finals, there was still a full house for the final itself.

The only things matches at Calcutta seem to lack are results, despite often producing conditions to suit the Indian spinners. Draws are the regular outcome at Eden Gardens.

A magnificent panorama of the Eden Gardens arena in Calcutta, which hosted the World Cup final in 1987.

CALCUTTA

EDEN GARDENS IN Calcutta, on the banks of the Hooghly River, is now regarded as the most famous ground in India and with due cause.

CAMBRIDGE UNIVERSITY

THE STUDENTS OF Cambridge University may only just be clinging onto their first-class status nowadays, but there can be no doubting the impact the university has had on the development of some great players.

Counties generally no longer field their strongest sides on trips to Fenner's, but Cambridge's continued involvement in senior cricket gives the game much of its charm, even if batting or bowling records achieved against the students are not as highly valued as they were.

Formed around 1820, the Cambridge University side played their first match against Oxford University at Lord's in 1827, a game badly affected by the weather.

Their home ground of Fenner's was established in 1846 when

Cricket at the Newlands ground in Cape Town, South Africa, is played against the stunning backdrop of Table Mountain.

P.F. Fenner leased some land from Gonville and Caius College and two years later sub-let it to the club. The building of a pavilion followed in 1856. It was later replaced thanks to the hard work of the Rev. Arthur Ward who almost single-handedly raised the necessary funding.

With entrance to the university much harder than it was and with the increased importance for undergraduates of examinations, Cambridge have generally been unable in recent years to produce players to match their greatest post-war figures, such as the four England captains, Peter May, Ted Dexter, Mike Brearley and Mike Atherton.

Among a number of fine overseas players to represent the University were Majid Khan, who scored 200 in the 1970 Varsity match, captained the side in 1971 and 1972, and later went on to lead Pakistan, and Deryck Murray, captain in the 1966 Varsity match, who kept wicket for West Indies in 62 Tests (1963–80).

CAPE TOWN

THERE CAN SURELY BE NO more picturesque ground staging Test cricket than Newlands in Cape Town, South Africa. With oak trees on one side and the spectacular Table Mountain on another, it is a delight for spectators and players alike.

The ground has been in existence since 1887 and has changed very little except for the introduction of floodlight pylons for day/night cricket, now so popular in South Africa as well as Australia.

Newlands was the first venue for a Test match played on a turf pitch in South Africa. Until that occasion in 1931, matting had always been used.

The ground has seen many historic moments, but very few of them happy ones for South Africa. In 1957/58 Australian leg-spinner Lindsay Kline finished off an Australian victory with a hat-trick. They were the only wickets he took in the second innings, to secure Australia's innings victory.

It was not until 1969/70 that the home side finally won a Test there, the only other successes coming against MCC sides in 1905/06 and 1909/10.

That win over Australia by 170 runs came just before South Africa were thrown out of the Test-playing fraternity.

The ground held happy memories for New Zealanders – they won their first ever Test abroad there in 1961/62 as an entertaining series was shared 2–2.

However, in January 1995 South Africa made history at Cape Town by becoming the first side this century to come from behind to win a three-Test series, as new captain Hansie Cronje guided them to victory over New Zealand.

GREG CHAPPELL

Australia

Born 1948
*South Australia, Queensland
and Somerset*

THERE WAS PROBABLY NO finer batsman in the world for much of the 1970s than Greg Chappell. Brother of Ian and grandson of Victor Richardson, a top Australian batsman between the wars, Greg was a stylish player – upright, and like all the top players, with plenty of time to play his shots.

Like his brother, Greg became a tough competitor on the field, after

Greg Chappell succeeded his brother Ian as captain of Australia and led his country to victory in 21 of his 48 Tests in charge. An elegant strokemaker, he is pictured here on his way to another Test century against England at Adelaide in 1982/83.

gaining some useful experience of English conditions early in his career. His two seasons at Somerset saw him master the art of dealing with swing bowling on English pitches.

He made his Test debut in 1970/71 and immediately gave warning of how he was to become a thorn in English flesh. Coming to the crease with his side at 107 for 5, he scored 108.

From then on Chappell made his mark in the record books. Against New Zealand in 1973/74 he scored 247 not out and 133 in a match in which his brother Ian also scored two centuries.

Against England in 1974/75 Greg scored 608 runs at an average of 55.27, in a series in which he also took many magnificent slip catches.

He took over the captaincy of Australia in 1975/76, two years after he began learning the art with his move from South Australia to Queensland. He led from the front in the series against West Indies, scoring 123 and 109 and steering Australia to a 5–1 win in the rubber.

Chappell secured his financial future by joining World Series Cricket, but returned to the Test arena in 1979 and captained Australia in a further sixteen Tests.

He was a generally courteous captain, his only major blemish coming in 1981 when, with New Zealand needing a six to win off the last ball of a one-day international, he instructed his brother Trevor to roll the ball underarm along the ground, making the Kiwis' task impossible. It led to some indignant protests.

In 1982/83 Chappell achieved his greatest ambition when he led Australia to an Ashes win. It was no coincidence that Australia's two Test victories in the series came in matches where he scored centuries.

In 1983/84 his Test career ended as it had begun, with a century, and also with a highly prized record. His 182 against Pakistan took him past Sir Don Bradman's total of 6,996 Test runs. Taking three catches, he established another record as his 122 Test catches passed Sir Colin Cowdrey's total.

His figures bear testimony to an impressive career – figures that could have been better still but for his two years away from the Test scene in World Series Cricket.

First Class Career:
Runs – 24,535. Average 52.20
(74 centuries)

Test Match Career:
Tests – 87
Runs – 7,110. Average 53.86
(24 centuries)
Catches – 122

IAN CHAPPELL

Australia

Born 1943
South Australia

THE OLDEST OF THREE brothers to play Test cricket, Ian Chappell was an abrasive cricketer who was never afraid to take on the cricket establishment.

He became one of the leading lights in Kerry Packer's World Series Cricket, and while this guaranteed him unpopularity in many quarters, there could be no denying his success as an Australian captain.

From the moment he made his first-class debut, Chappell established himself as a gritty right-hand batsman. He was particularly strong at the pull and hook shots, but was also a delicate cutter. In the field, he was a magnificent first slip.

He made his Test debut for Australia against Pakistan in 1964/65 and toured England in 1968. He was a major success, scoring 348 runs in the series and establishing himself as a regular member of the side.

He took over the captaincy from Bill Lawry in the final Test of the 1970/71 Ashes series, a decision he himself criticised. Australia lost the series and failed to recapture the Ashes in England in 1972.

But thereafter, Chappell's record as captain was a fine one. In all he captained Australia in 30 Tests, winning 15 of them and suffering only five defeats – two of them coming in his first two matches in charge.

It could be said that he was lucky to have such wonderful resources to call upon; batsmen of the calibre of his brother Greg, fast bowlers Dennis Lillee and Jeff Thomson, and an inspirational wicket-keeper in Rodney Marsh.

Chappell's character seemed to rub off on his players too. There was an arrogance about the team and a fondness for the unattractive practice of 'sledging' – verbal abuse of opponents.

His brushes with officialdom became more frequent as he challenged the Australian Board of Control over pay and conditions for players, and went on to become a major advocate for World Series Cricket.

He returned to Test cricket after WSC folded, but the trouble continued. Chappell was suspended after swearing at an umpire in a Sheffield Shield match – and was also suspended for swearing on air when he later moved on to the television commentary box! He retired at the end of the 1979/80 season, when he seemed to lose his appetite for the game.

Despite his sometimes petulant outbursts and poor behaviour, however, Ian Chappell's captaincy and batting will long be remembered as being of the highest class.

First Class Career:
Runs – 19,680. Average 48.35 (59 centuries)

Test Match Career:
Tests – 75
Runs – 5,345. Average 42.42 (14 centuries)
Catches – 105

A stalwart of Kerry Packer's World Series Cricket after a highly successful Test career, Ian Chappell plays the pyjama game for Australia against the West Indies in 1979/80. Deryck Murray is the wicket-keeper.

CHRISTCHURCH

LANCASTER PARK IN Christchurch was the scene of New Zealand's entry into Test cricket in 1929/30 when England won by eight wickets.

It has been a multi-purpose ground over the years, with cricket and rugby being the main sports played there. However, it has hosted almost everything, including pop concerts, prayer meetings and Royal visits.

The ground is noted for its vast grandstands on the east side. These have been provided mostly for the benefit of rugby spectators. The western side now has a large expanse of concrete terracing.

Perhaps the most famous event on the Lancaster Park ground occurred in 1973/74 when New Zealand, for the first time in their history, beat the old enemy Australia by five wickets. It was a win set up splendidly by their opening batsman Glenn Turner, who scored a century in each innings.

Many fine players have graced the Lancaster Park ground. Regular spectators, though, will have particularly fond memories of their local hero Sir Richard Hadlee, one of the greatest bowlers in Test history, who took many wickets on his hometown pitch.

Above: Lancaster Park in Christchurch, New Zealand, with its huge east grandstand to the left of the picture.

Right: A recent study of Brian Close taken at the Headingley Test in 1994. A fine captain of Yorkshire, Somerset and England, he became famous for his determined efforts to withstand even the most hostile fast bowling; his autobiography was entitled I Don't Bruise Easily.

BRIAN CLOSE
England
Born 1931
Yorkshire and Somerset

STUBBORN AND BRAVE are just two ways of describing Brian Close. He made history as the youngest man to play for England, but his career was often affected by controversy both at Test and County level.

A left-hand batsman and right-arm medium pace or off-spin bowler, he did the double in his first season for Yorkshire, 1949, and was picked for England against New Zealand, aged 18 years and 149 days.

However, he never fully realised his potential and played for his country only another 21 times.

His bravery knew no bounds, whether fielding close at short-leg or when batting. His body was covered with bruises after facing the West Indies pace attack of Hall and Griffith at Lord's in 1963, and he faced another torrid time when,

aged 45, he was brought back to face the West Indies again. But even then, he never flinched.

In 1967 he lost the England captaincy after using delaying tactics for Yorkshire in a match against Warwickshire. He captained the county from 1963 to 1970, leading them to four Championships and one Gillette Cup win. In 1971 he moved to Somerset and captained them from 1972 to 1977, helping to nurture young talent such as Ian Botham.

He became a Test selector in 1979 and later returned to Yorkshire first as manager and then as cricket chairman. Here too, there was no escape from controversy as he became embroiled in the arguments that have dogged Yorkshire in recent times.

First Class Career:
Runs – 34,968. Average 33.30
(52 centuries)
Wickets – 1170. Average 26.38

Test Match Career:
Tests – 22
Runs – 887. Average 25.34
Wickets – 18. Average 29.55

CLUB CRICKET CONFERENCE

THE CLUB CRICKET Conference was founded in 1915 to work for the interests of club cricket and the amateur cricketers who play the game for fun and recreation every weekend in the summer.

About 2,300 clubs make up the membership, from counties mainly from the Midlands southwards. In all, about 250,000 players are affiliated. The Conference, with a full-time secretary, works closely with the MCC and the National Cricket Association.

For clubs, the Conference helps arrange fixtures and has an emergency fixture bureau to help clubs fill last-minute gaps. It also, in conjunction with the Association of Cricket Umpires, maintains a register of 120 umpires of proven ability.

For cricketers themselves, the Club Cricket Conference helps encourage clubs to run junior sections, an important function with cricket no longer as popular in secondary schools as it was.

The Conference runs a sponsored Inter-League competition involving almost fifty leagues in its area, with the final usually played on a top ground.

It also arranges representative matches, and has in the past organised tours to Australia, the West Indies, New Zealand, Sri Lanka and Kenya.

DENIS COMPTON
England
Born 1918
Middlesex

DENIS COMPTON possessed immense natural talent and proved to be one of the greatest artists and characters cricket has ever known. He became

a post-war hero, his appearance graced many advertising hoardings, and he had the ability to pack any ground.

Compton made his county debut for Middlesex in 1936 as a slow left-arm bowler, batting at number eleven. He quickly established himself as a batsman, making nearly 40,000 runs in his career, including more than 100 centuries.

He made 65 on his Test debut against New Zealand at the Oval in 1937 and followed that with a century in his next Test against Australia in 1938. However, it was after the war that he truly flourished.

In the summer of 1947 he rewrote the record books. He scored 753 runs against South Africa in five Tests, and made 3,816 runs in all first-class games for an average of 90.85. That included 18 centuries, beating Sir Jack Hobbs' record of 16 in the 1925 season.

Compton continued to be a regular member of the England team, and at the Oval in 1953 he made the winning hit to take back the Ashes after twenty years.

Being a cavalier cricketer, his major failing was running between the wickets. Trevor Bailey once remarked that a call from Denis was merely the basis for negotiation!

Away from cricket, his good looks made him a highly marketable figure in those post-war years and he became the original 'Brylcreem' boy. He was probably the first sports star to use an agent.

Compton was also a fine footballer. He won League and Cup winners' medals with Arsenal and earned 14 wartime England soccer caps. His brother Leslie also played cricket for Middlesex and football for Arsenal and England.

After retiring from the game Denis became a BBC commentator and cricket correspondent for the Sunday Express.

First Class Career:
Runs – 38,942. Average 51.85
(123 centuries)

Test Match Career:
Tests – 78
Runs – 5,807. Average 50.06
(17 centuries)

one of them coming in under an hour, and took 5 for 75.

After the war he became a writer and broadcaster, was called to the Bar, and became Minister of Works in the Trinidadian Government. He was knighted and later created a Life Peer.

First Class Career:
*Runs – 4,451. Average 24.32
(5 centuries)
Wickets – 424. Average 20.61*

Test Match Career:
*Tests – 18
Runs – 635. Average 19.24
Wickets – 58. Average 30.10*

COUNTY CHAMPIONSHIP

WHILE THE ONE-DAY competitions attract the biggest crowds in domestic cricket, it is the County Championship that is the bedrock of the game in England and is still the most sought-after title.

The structure of the Championship has seen many changes in more than a century, none more significant than those introduced for 1993, with each county now playing 17 four-day matches.

Yorkshire currently lead the list of successful counties, having won the title 30 times. However, Surrey hold

Opposite: A typically unorthodox piece of strokeplay from Learie Constantine, playing for the West Indian tourists against Surrey at the Oval in 1939 on his fourth and last tour of England.

SIR LEARIE CONSTANTINE
West Indies
*Born 1920. Died 1971
Trinidad and Barbados*

SIR LEARIE CONSTANTINE was something of an icon of West Indies cricket. His enthusiastic personality, and the wholehearted enjoyment he derived from the game of cricket, was infectious.

He was a gifted all-rounder, although his figures in Test cricket do not do him justice. He could be inconsistent with both bat and ball, but was never dull to watch. His general form on tours was invariably better than in Tests alone.

His batting was a mixture of shots, but invariably played with enormous power. His bowling was, in the early part of his career, genuinely fast, although later he became more of a medium pacer. In the field, he could rate with the very best, rivalling such men as Colin Bland and Clive Lloyd at their peak.

Constantine recorded many memorable achievements. On the 1928 tour of England he scored 1,381 runs and took 107 wickets. His 9 for 122 was crucial when the West Indies beat England for the first time at Georgetown in 1929/30.

His best all-round Test performance came in his very last appearance for West Indies at the Oval in 1939. He scored 79, all but the record for the most consecutive wins, seven from 1952 to 1958.

Although counties had played against each other for many years previously, it was not until 16th December 1889 that the secretaries of eight major counties gathered at Lord's to consider for the first time the method of deciding the order of merit. They came to the conclusion that the following season there should be one point awarded for a win and one point deducted for a defeat.

Until then, the decision each season as to who should be considered the champion county had rested largely with the press.

Although the historical evidence is inconclusive, many historians think Sussex may have been the first unofficial county champions in 1826, and again a year later.

Kent, Middlesex, Surrey and Sussex were playing regularly by the middle of the 19th century, occasionally having matches against counties further north such as Lancashire, Yorkshire and Nottinghamshire.

From 1864 several notable judges 'chose' their champion counties, often following the simple criterion of who had suffered the fewest defeats.

However, the counties themselves finally took matters into their own hands at that Lord's meeting, and the first official Championship match was played between Gloucestershire and Yorkshire at Bristol on 12–14 May 1890. The White Rose county won comfortably.

Surrey became the first champions under the new set-up with six points, ahead of the other seven clubs which made up the first-class counties: Lancashire, Kent, Yorkshire, Nottinghamshire, Gloucestershire, Middlesex and Sussex.

Somerset joined their ranks the following year, with Derbyshire, Essex, Hampshire, Leicestershire and Warwickshire coming in in 1895. Their inclusion meant that each county now had to play a minimum of sixteen games.

In 1910 the title was decided by the percentage of wins to matches played, a method which was to have a number of derivations over the years, including a system based on the average number of points won per match.

It was not until 1929 that each county played the same number of games (28) and the winners were the county with most points. But percentages returned in 1933 as counties had to play a minimum of 24 games and a maximum of 32.

Much tinkering with the points system has gone on over the years, then, but it was in 1957 that bonus points were first introduced for fast scoring.

Among the changes discarded after just one season have been the decision to reduce the championship from three-day to two-day matches (1919), and that the first innings in nearly half the matches played be restricted to just 65 overs (1966).

One change that was to have a fundamental effect on English cricket occurred in 1968 when for the first time, each county was allowed to register, without qualification, one overseas player.

This decision attracted much controversy. Spectators wanted to watch the best, but as a number of counties added other overseas stars in the years that followed, many examples were cited of young English talent being unable to break through and mature in county sides as a result.

In 1969 the championship was reduced to 24 matches with the introduction of the Sunday League, and then again to 20 in 1972 as the Benson and Hedges Cup was born.

Prize money was introduced for the first time in 1973, with champions Hampshire winning £3,000. It was therefore only a matter of time before the Championship, which had long since failed to be financially viable, considered a sponsor.

Cadbury Schweppes put in £260,000 in 1977 as part of a three-year deal, and the following year the competition became the 'Schweppes Championship'. In 1984 the current sponsors, Britannic Assurance, took over.

Each county played six four-day matches in 1988, as an experiment

COUNTY CHAMPIONSHIP

	Winners	Runners-up		Winners	Runners-up
1890	Surrey	Lancashire	1947	Middlesex	Gloucestershire
1891	Surrey	Lancashire	1948	Glamorgan	Surrey
1892	Surrey	Nottinghamshire	1949	Middlesex/Yorkshire	3rd: Worcestershire
1893	Yorkshire	Lancashire	1950	Lancashire/Surrey	3rd: Yorkshire
1894	Surrey	Yorkshire	1951	Warwickshire	Yorkshire
1895	Surrey	Lancashire	1952	Surrey	Yorkshire
1896	Yorkshire	Lancashire	1953	Surrey	Sussex
1897	Lancashire	Surrey	1954	Surrey	Yorkshire
1898	Yorkshire	Middlesex	1955	Surrey	Yorkshire
1899	Surrey	Middlesex	1956	Surrey	Lancashire
1900	Yorkshire	Lancashire	1957	Surrey	Northamptonshire
1901	Yorkshire	Middlesex	1958	Surrey	Hampshire
1902	Yorkshire	Sussex	1959	Yorkshire	Gloucestershire
1903	Middlesex	Sussex	1960	Yorkshire	Lancashire
1904	Lancashire	Yorkshire	1961	Hampshire	Yorkshire
1905	Yorkshire	Lancashire	1962	Yorkshire	Worcestershire
1906	Kent	Yorkshire	1963	Yorkshire	Glamorgan
1907	Nottinghamshire	Worcestershire/Yorkshire	1964	Worcestershire	Warwickshire
1908	Yorkshire	Kent	1965	Worcestershire	Northamptonshire
1909	Kent	Lancashire	1966	Yorkshire	Worcestershire
1910	Kent	Surrey	1967	Yorkshire	Kent
1911	Warwickshire	Kent	1968	Yorkshire	Kent
1912	Yorkshire	Northamptonshire	1969	Glamorgan	Gloucestershire
1913	Kent	Yorkshire	1970	Kent	Glamorgan
1914	Surrey	Middlesex	1971	Surrey	Warwickshire
1915–18	No Championship		1972	Warwickshire	Kent
1919	Yorkshire	Kent	1973	Hampshire	Surrey
1920	Middlesex	Lancashire	1974	Worcestershire	Hampshire
1921	Middlesex	Surrey	1975	Leicestershire	Yorkshire
1922	Yorkshire	Nottinghamshire	1976	Middlesex	Northamptonshire
1923	Yorkshire	Nottinghamshire	1977	Middlesex/Kent	3rd: Gloucestershire
1924	Yorkshire	Middlesex	1978	Kent	Essex
1925	Yorkshire	Surrey	1979	Essex	Worcestershire
1926	Lancashire	Yorkshire	1980	Middlesex	Surrey
1927	Lancashire	Nottinghamshire	1981	Nottinghamshire	Sussex
1928	Lancashire	Kent	1982	Middlesex	Leicestershire
1929	Nottinghamshire	Lancashire	1983	Essex	Middlesex
1930	Lancashire	Gloucestershire	1984	Essex	Nottinghamshire
1931	Yorkshire	Gloucestershire	1985	Middlesex	Hampshire
1932	Yorkshire	Sussex	1986	Essex	Gloucestershire
1933	Yorkshire	Sussex	1987	Nottinghamshire	Lancashire
1934	Lancashire	Sussex	1988	Worcestershire	Kent
1935	Yorkshire	Derbyshire	1989	Worcestershire	Essex
1936	Derbyshire	Middlesex	1990	Middlesex	Kent
1937	Yorkshire	Middlesex	1991	Essex	Warwickshire
1938	Yorkshire	Middlesex	1992	Essex	Kent
1939	Yorkshire	Middlesex	1993	Middlesex	Worcestershire
1940–45	No championship		1994	Warwickshire	Nottinghamshire
1946	Yorkshire	Middlesex			

Some spectacular evasive action is called for as Tim Robinson (Nottinghamshire) square-drives for four during Gloucestershire's annual Cheltenham Festival. Keeper Jack Russell looks on.

to see if better wickets and the chance to play longer innings would help produce quality Test players. The one-day competitions, many argued, didn't allow young players to develop the necessary skills.

The experiment was interesting. A higher proportion of the longer games produced a definite result. In contrast, too many three-day games were being decided by contrived finishes agreed between the captains, which often resulted in 'joke' bowlers being used and meaningless 'fastest centuries' recorded.

Over the next five years the debate about four-day cricket raged. In May 1992 the counties decided broadly to accept the Murray report and introduce four-day matches from 1993 for three seasons, as well as making changes to the Sunday League and Benson and Hedges Cup.

The players were generally in favour, and with matches running from Thursday to Monday – with a Sunday League fixture sandwiched in the middle – there was a greater symmetry to the fixture list.

However, county treasurers worried that a reduction in the number of days played and matches finishing early would lead to a drop in revenue, while many others feared that four-day cricket would mean slower, duller cricket, with no subsequent benefits to the Test team.

SIR COLIN COWDREY
England
Born 1932
Oxford University and Kent

ENGLAND HAVE HAD FEW more elegant or effective batsmen than Colin Cowdrey. Yet his contribution to the game has been more than just that of a player. Since his retirement, he has been one of the game's leading administrators and is a man respected worldwide.

It was not by chance that his cricket-mad father gave him the initials MCC, Michael Colin Cowdrey. The young Colin showed talent from a very early age and at 13 was the youngest player to represent the Public Schools at Lord's.

He made almost 3,000 runs in his five years at Tonbridge School, and the runs continued at Oxford University.

His technique as a batsman was sound and his strokemaking appeared effortless. While he was not perhaps the most athletic of men, his natural eye for the ball made him the safest of slip fielders.

Of his 22 Test centuries, five came against Australia. He toured there six times, although never as captain, from 1954/55. That tour saw him make his first Test century, 102 at Melbourne.

His last visit was in 1974/75, when at the age of 42 he was called up as an emergency replacement to face the fire of Lillee and Thomson, and showed great courage.

Cowdrey scored six centuries against the West Indies, the best and most memorable being his 154 at Edgbaston in 1957, when he put on 411 for the fourth wicket with Peter May in eight hours and twenty minutes. Cowdrey also captained England to one of their rare series wins in the Caribbean when in 1967/68 they won one Test and drew the other four.

He captained Kent from 1957 until 1971, leading them to the County Championship title in 1970. The name Cowdrey continues in Kent, his two sons Christopher and Graham both having played for the county.

Since retiring from playing, Cowdrey has been president of the MCC and also served as chairman of the ICC. He has sat on many committees at Lord's and has written a number of books. He was awarded the CBE and later knighted for his services to the game.

First Class Career:
Runs – 42,719. Average 42.89
        (107 centuries)
Catches – 638

Test Match Career:
Tests – 114
Runs – 7,624. Average 44.06
        (22 centuries)
Catches – 120

Left: Cowdrey in action for England against India in the fourth Test at Old Trafford in 1959. It was his first match as captain and he made a winning start as the Indians were defeated by 171 runs.

Opposite: A hugely talented batsman with a fine range of shots and an exceptional eye for the ball, New Zealand's Martin Crowe shows off his powerful hitting during a one-day international against England at Old Trafford.

THE CRICKET COUNCIL

THE CRICKET COUNCIL was established in 1968 and is the governing body of the game in the United Kingdom. Under it are the Test and County Cricket Board, the National Cricket Association, and Marylebone Cricket Club.

The formation of the Council at last gave the game a clearly defined constitution, and with the TCCB looking after the interests of the first-class game and the NCA attending to the needs of ordinary amateur players, cricket at last had a sense of direction. The MCC was included for its ownership of Lord's, its role as guardian of the laws, and as general 'friend' of the game.

The Cricket Council was largely born of necessity, with the game's finances being in poor condition. In the early days, the MCC held a dominating influence on the Council. The MCC president was its chairman, the MCC treasurer his deputy, and the MCC secretary also assumed the same role for the Council.

However, the Council is now made up of eight representatives from the Test and County Cricket Board, five from the National Cricket Association and three from the MCC.

The Minor Counties Cricket Association and the Irish and Scottish Cricket Unions also have non-voting representatives, although the Irish resigned in 1992 with a view to joining the International Cricket Council.

The first serious examination of the Cricket Council came in 1970 when the Labour Government summoned members and asked them to cancel the 1970 tour by

Eddie Barlow (left) and Graeme Pollock, team-mates in Currie Cup cricket for Eastern Province. Pollock holds the record for the most runs scored in the competition.

South Africa, following the D'Oliveira affair of 1968. Then the Council was particularly critical of incidents of dissent over umpiring decisions during the MCC tour of Australia in 1970/71.

However, in 1977 the Packer affair, which threatened the future of international cricket, saw the council take a back seat – the resultant legal action being fought by the International Cricket Conference and the TCCB.

The following year, proposals by a working party to dissolve the Council and replace it with a United Kingdom Board of Control, based largely on the first-class counties and the National Cricket Association, were rejected.

However, since the Council was re-constituted in 1983, the professional game, through the Test and County Cricket Board, now provides fifty per cent of the voting representatives.

MARTIN CROWE
New Zealand
Born 1962
Auckland, Central Districts, Somerset and Wellington

MARTIN CROWE WAS spotted at a young age as a player of great potential. The son of a first-class cricketer, and with a brother Jeff who also played for New Zealand, Martin became one of the top batsmen in the world and is

his country's leading run scorer.

As well as being an elegant strokemaker, he is a player with a sound technique who hits the ball with great power.

Crowe made his Test debut at the tender age of 19 in 1981/82 and although he did not fare particularly well, he quickly became a regular fixture in the New Zealand team. He decided to broaden his experience by playing in England, a decision that paid rich dividends.

In 1982 he played in Yorkshire League cricket and the following year he made important contributions for his country in the World Cup.

His first Test century helped New Zealand save a match against England in 1983/84. In England in 1984 he first appeared for Somerset as deputy for Viv Richards and after a shaky start went on to make 1,870 runs, including six centuries. In 1985/86 his 309 runs at an average of 77.25 helped New Zealand to their first series win over Australia.

After another successful summer with New Zealand in England in 1986 when he averaged 68 in Tests, Somerset took the controversial decision to offer him a contract and dispose of the services of Richards and Joel Garner.

Crowe repaid their faith by topping the English averages in 1987, scoring 1,627 runs at 67.79. The previous winter he had set a New Zealand record of 1,676 runs, including eight centuries, for an average of 93.11.

Crowe led New Zealand in series against England, Pakistan, Sri Lanka, and Zimbabwe. He has made more than 5,000 Test runs, his highest score being 299 against Sri Lanka at Wellington in 1990/91, and in December 1994 in the second Test against South Africa he passed John Wright's record of 5,334 runs for New Zealand.

First Class Career:
*Runs – 18,710. Average 55.85
(67 centuries)*

Test Match Career:
*Tests – 70
Runs – 5,364. Average 47.98
(17 centuries)*

CASTLE CUP/ CURRIE CUP

THE CASTLE CUP, formerly the Currie Cup, is South Africa's principal domestic first-class competition. It has traditionally produced some of the finest cricket in the world outside of Test matches.

Eight teams now compete for it each year: Orange Free State, Transvaal, Natal, Eastern Province, Western Province, Border, Northern Transvaal, and Boland.

Transvaal were traditionally the strongest side in the early years of the competition. However, since the Second World War, Natal have challenged them hard for supremacy.

During South Africa's exile from international cricket, the Currie Cup was, for those players who chose not to play county cricket in England, the only means of playing the game at top level.

Many, however, plied their trade both in England and back home in the South African summer. Players such as Richards, Procter, Rice, Wessels and Barlow became familiar faces in both countries, while never having the opportunity of playing many Tests.

As so little first-class cricket is played in South Africa compared to England, crowds are generally healthy.

CURRIE CUP/CASTLE CUP WINNERS

The Currie Cup was replaced by the Castle Cup in the 1991/92 season.

Season	Winner	Season	Winner
1889/90	Transvaal	1960/61	Natal
1890/91	Kimberley	1962/63	Natal
1892/93	Western Province	1963/64	Natal
1893/94	Western Province	1965/66	Natal/Transvaal (*tied*)
1894/95	Transvaal	1966/67	Natal
1896/97	Western Province	1967/68	Natal
1897/98	Western Province	1968/69	Transvaal
1902/03	Transvaal	1969/70	Transvaal/Western Province (*tied*)
1903/04	Transvaal		
1904/05	Transvaal	1970/71	Transvaal
1906/07	Transvaal	1971/72	Transvaal
1908/09	Western Province	1972/73	Transvaal
1910/11	Natal	1973/74	Natal
1912/13	Natal	1974/75	Western Province
1920/21	Western Province	1975/76	Natal
1921/22	Transvaal/Natal/ Western Province (*tied*)	1976/77	Natal
		1977/78	Western Province
1923/24	Transvaal	1978/79	Transvaal
1925/26	Transvaal	1979/80	Transvaal
1926/27	Transvaal	1980/81	Natal
1929/30	Transvaal	1981/82	Western Province
1931/32	Western Province	1982/83	Transvaal
1933/34	Natal	1983/84	Transvaal
1934/35	Transvaal	1984/85	Transvaal
1936/37	Natal	1985/86	Western Province
1937/38	Natal/Transvaal (*tied*)	1986/87	Transvaal
1946/47	Natal	1987/88	Transvaal
1947/48	Natal	1988/89	Eastern Province
1950/51	Transvaal	1989/90	Eastern Province/ Western Province (*tied*)
1951/52	Natal		
1952/53	Western Province	1990/91	Western Province
1954/55	Natal	1991/92	Eastern Province
1955/56	Western Province	1992/93	Orange Free State
1958/59	Transvaal	1993/94	Orange Free State
1959/60	Natal		

MIKE DENNESS

England

Born 1940
Scotland, Kent and Essex

A QUIETLY SPOKEN SCOT, Mike Denness had the unenviable job of taking over the England captaincy from Ray Illingworth and had to face an onslaught from an Australian side containing fearsome fast bowlers in Lillee and Thomson. That exposed his limitations, but he was nonetheless a player of quality.

After an outstanding career in schoolboy cricket at Ayr Academy, he joined Kent, forming a successful opening partnership with Brian Luckhurst. Denness went on to captain the county and led them to much success in the one-day competitions, winning the John Player League three times, the Benson and Hedges Cup twice and the Gillette Cup once.

He captained England in 19 of his 28 Tests, batting more often in the middle order. He was comfortable against spin bowling in India, Pakistan and Sri Lanka, but in the Ashes series in Australia in 1974/75, after a run of low scores, he dropped himself for the fourth Test at Sydney, when the home side regained the Ashes. He showed his fighting qualities by coming back for the fifth Test, and in the sixth Test of the series he scored a brilliant 188.

He moved to Essex in 1977 and played an important part in their County Championship and Benson and Hedges double winning side in 1979.

First Class Career:
Runs – 25,886. Average 33.48
(33 centuries)

Test Match Career:
Tests – 28
Runs – 1,669. Average 39.69
(4 centuries)

DERBYSHIRE

Founded: 1870

Entered Official
Championship: 1895
Honours:
County Champions – 1936
NatWest Trophy – 1981
Benson and Hedges Cup – 1993
Refuge Assurance League – 1990

F OR DERBYSHIRE, ONE OF the smaller and less prosperous counties, success has never come easily. They have won the Championship just once, in 1936, but in recent years have taken three one-day titles.

Although the first match to be played at the County Ground in Derby took place in 1863, it was not until seven years later that a county club was formed.

Before the official Championship began, Derbyshire were considered by one judge, the Reverend R.S. Holmes, to be unofficial champions in 1874. With three victories and a draw, Derbyshire took the title at a time when the team losing fewest matches were considered champions. It was therefore something of an advantage to play just a handful of games!

Derbyshire lost their first-class status as results deteriorated in the following years, but regained it in 1894 and the following year they were admitted to the official County Championship, finishing fifth.

But in the years leading up to the First World War, Derbyshire had a shortage of good bowlers and

regularly finished bottom of the table. Things failed to improve and in 1920 the club created a miserable record in losing seventeen out of eighteen matches played. Even the other match was abandoned without a ball being bowled.

But from that low point, the county's fortunes improved under the astute captaincy of G.R. Jackson. His talents earned him an invitation to lead the MCC to South Africa in 1927, but he was unable to accept.

A.W. Richardson took over the captaincy as Derbyshire enjoyed their finest seasons in the 1930s. After coming third in 1934 and second in 1935, they went one better to take the title in 1936.

arm straightening before delivery.

Three times in four seasons from 1971, Derbyshire finished bottom of the table, but nevertheless the discovery of fast bowling talent continued in the form of Alan Ward and Mike Hendrick, who went on to represent England.

While Hendrick became a steady member of the England attack, Ward was a controversial character whose career suffered from injury. In 1973 his county captain Brian Bolus sent him from the field after he refused to bowl against Yorkshire.

Ward later apologised and retired, but in 1976 he moved to Leicestershire, playing just two seasons there.

After Bolus the captaincy passed to Bob Taylor, a most popular character and a well-respected wicket-keeper of the highest class. His 57 Test appearances would have been many more but for the brilliance of his rival Alan Knott. However, Taylor, Hendrick and Geoff Miller, an all-rounder, brought credit to the county by becoming the first three Derbyshire players to appear simultaneously for England.

But it was the inspirational leadership of an overseas player, South African Eddie Barlow, that was to bring the most significant improvement in Derbyshire fortunes in the late 1970s. He was joined by John Wright from New Zealand and Peter Kirsten from South Africa, and with home-grown players also coming through, there was a greater spirit about the county's cricket.

They were beaten finalists in the Benson and Hedges Cup in 1978, but went on to take the NatWest Trophy in 1981 under the captaincy of the former Lancashire and England opening batsman Barry Wood. A second-wicket stand of 123 between Wright and Kirsten

With counties having to play a minimum of 24 and a maximum of 32 matches, Derbyshire topped the table with a percentage record of 56.90, winning thirteen of their 28 games. Their bowling was particularly strong, with W.H. Copson, a hostile quick, taking 140 wickets, and A.V. Pope 94.

Derbyshire have always had a reputation for producing formidable fast bowlers, most coming from a coal-mining background. Perhaps their best was Les Jackson, the county's leading wicket-taker, who from 1947 to 1963 took 1,578 wickets at an average of 17.20. He played just twice for England and would surely have had more caps had he represented a more fashionable county.

For most of that period the team was led by Donald Carr, an Oxford blue who in 1959 became the only Derbyshire batsman to score more than 2,000 runs in a season. He later went on to become a leading cricket administrator.

If the 1930s were Derbyshire's greatest years, then the 1960s and 1970s were to contain some of their poorest.

Controversy surrounded fast bowler Harold Rhodes, who played twice for England. He was called for throwing in a match for the county against the South Africans. The row over his action raged for years before he was eventually cleared, the authorities deciding that he had a 'hyper-extension' of his elbow which gave an optical illusion of his guided them to a narrow victory over Northamptonshire, Derbyshire having lost fewer wickets with the scores tied.

Kim Barnett, who went on to be the county's longest-serving captain, led them to the Refuge Assurance League title in 1990, as once again Derbyshire provided a fast bowler for England, this time the fast but erratic Devon Malcolm.

County Championship performances also improved under Barnett, Derbyshire finishing third in 1991 and fifth in 1992, and the following year they took the Benson and Hedges Cup in something of a needle match against Lancashire. An unbeaten 92 by Dominic Cork laid the foundation for their win by just six runs.

TED DEXTER

England

Born 1935
Cambridge University and Sussex

TED DEXTER WAS A handsome, dashing figure on the cricket field. An exciting, attacking right-hand bat and useful medium-pace bowler, he captained England but retired from the game while still at his peak to concentrate on a wide variety of outside interests.

Like a number of England captains, Dexter was born abroad, in Milan, Italy. He was a batsman who always rose to the occasion, with many of his finest innings coming against the best of attacks.

He was often seen as somewhat aloof and earned the nickname 'Lord Edward'. But there was no doubting that he was a player of great charisma who could fill any ground.

It was as a bowler that he first attracted attention, taking eight wickets in the Gentlemen v Players match at Lord's in 1957.

A Cambridge blue who went on to captain Sussex to victory in the first Gillette Cup final, Dexter led England against Australia, West Indies, New

Zealand, Pakistan and India during his ten-year Test career.

He first established himself in the England side in the Caribbean in 1959/60 when he topped the averages. He went on to make some big scores for England, among them 180 and 174 against Australia and

Looking every inch the young Corinthian, Dexter poses for the photographers at Fenner's, at the start of the 1958 season in which he skippered Cambridge University. Within a few years he had gone on to captain both Sussex and England.

● THE GUINNESS

his highest, 205, against Pakistan in Karachi when he shared a record fourth-wicket partnership of 188 with Peter Parfitt. He captained England in 30 of his 62 Tests.

After his retirement he became noted for his love of adventure, flying planes and riding motorcycles, as well as playing amateur golf to a very high standard. He also stood as a Conservative candidate at the 1964 General Election, losing to James Callaghan in Cardiff. Dexter runs his own public relations company and has been a writer and broadcaster.

He became the first paid chairman of the England Test selectors – on a contract of £30,000 a year – in 1989, but announced his resignation in 1993 at the end of another disastrous Ashes series. He had previously told the TCCB he would not be seeking re-election when his contract ended in March 1994.

His decision did not come as a surprise. Under his guidance England played 44 Tests, winning only nine, losing 21 and drawing 14. Like all men to take on the job he was heavily criticised over selection policy.

First Class Career:
Runs – 21,150. Average 40.75
(51 centuries)
Wickets – 419. Average 29.92

Test Match Career:
Tests – 62
Runs – 4,502. Average 47.89
(9 centuries)
Wickets – 66. Average 34.93

BASIL D'OLIVEIRA
England
Born 1931
Worcestershire

BASIL D'OLIVEIRA WAS one of the most popular cricketers to play for England. As a South African coloured, he broke new ground in the game and through no fault of his own became one of its most controversial characters. Yet through it all he displayed great charm and dignity.

As early as 1956, D'Oliveira wrote to England asking how he could learn to become a coach, so that he could teach the game to the poverty-stricken coloured community in Cape Town.

After attracting the attention of English professionals in a match in South Africa in 1959/60, D'Oliveira joined Middleton in the Lancashire League. As a 29-year-old he could hardly have imagined that a glittering international career was about to begin.

Three years later his ability as a right-handed batsman and medium-pace bowler was spotted by Tom Graveney and D'Oliveira joined Worcestershire, making a century for the county against the Australians while qualifying.

In 1965 he became a regular county player, scoring five centuries, and then a year later, at the age of 35, he was chosen for England, his adopted country. On his debut against the West Indies at Lord's, he was unluckily run out for 27.

However, he went on to establish himself in the side and for the next six years was a regular. But in 1968 he found himself the innocent victim at the centre of an international storm.

In the final Test at the Oval that summer, D'Oliveira scored 158, his highest score and an innings that set England up for victory. But the following day when the tour party for South Africa that winter was

In the final Test of the 1968 Ashes series, D'Oliveira drives his way to a fine century which he must have thought would earn him selection for the winter tour of South Africa. It did . . . eventually, but too late to calm the passions inflamed by his original omission.

announced, D'Oliveira's name was not included.

There was outrage at the decision. MPs protested, some MCC members resigned, and a special meeting was called to demand D'Oliveira's inclusion. Fate, however, took a hand. Tom Cartwright declared himself unfit to make the trip and D'Oliveira was invited to replace him.

South Africa refused to admit him, claiming that his selection was a political decision, and the tour was cancelled. It was the first step towards South Africa's eventual isolation from the rest of the cricket world.

D'Oliveira's final series for England was in 1972 against Australia. He continued to play for Worcestershire, becoming full-time coach when age and injury finally caught up with him, in 1979. His son Damian followed in his footsteps

and became a regular in the Worcestershire team.

First Class Career:
*Runs – 18,919. Average 39.57
(43 centuries)
Wickets – 548. Average 27.41*

Test Match Career:
*Tests – 44
Runs – 2,484. Average 40.06
(5 centuries)
Wickets – 47. Average 39.55*

DUCKS

NOTHING RUINS A batsman's day quite like making 0. Somehow, being out for one you can live with, but making a duck is the lowest of low points, especially if it is a golden duck – out

The unkindest duck of all: in his last Test, Don Bradman is bowled second ball by a googly from Eric Hollies. Bradman always denied being overcome by the emotion of the occasion, but some were not convinced.

first ball. Yet no batsman that ever lived has avoided it.

The phrase 'making a duck's egg' first came into use in about 1860 and was quickly shortened to 'duck'. In recent years the figure 0 on a scoreboard has even been replaced by the likeness of a duck. On television, especially in Australia, the duck is often animated and as the batsman departs for the pavilion, the duck trudges off wiping away tears.

There have been many notable ducks down the years. Some of the world's top batsmen began their first-class careers by 'failing to trouble the scorers', among them W.G. Grace, Ted Dexter, Tom Graveney and Sir Learie Constantine.

One of England's greatest ever batsmen, Sir Len Hutton, almost made it an art form. He may have made 167 centuries, but he made a duck on his debut for Yorkshire 2nd XI, a duck on his debut for the full county side against Cambridge University at Fenner's, and a duck in his first innings for England against New Zealand.

If there is one thing worse than being out for a duck, it is making a 'pair' – a duck in each innings. Taken from the phrase 'a pair of spectacles', there are again some notable names in this section.

Perhaps the most famous pair in Test cricket was recorded by a young Essex batsman making his England debut against Australia at Edgbaston in 1975. He lasted just three balls in the first innings and seven in the second. However, it did him little harm in the long run. Graham Gooch went on to become the third highest run scorer in Test cricket.

It is tail-end batsmen, though, who can claim the long-distance records. B.J. Griffiths of Northamptonshire made 10 noughts on the trot during a run of 17 from 19 innings, although some of these were not out. In 1929, A.S. Clark of Somerset played nine first-class innings in his career – and failed to score a run.

There have, over the years, been some highly valuable ducks. In 1946 J.A. Young helped R.W.V. Robins put on 75 for the last wicket for MCC against Yorkshire without actually scoring any runs himself.

Cricket is, of course, a team game, and the fortunes of fate are quite happy to go along with that as far as ducks are concerned. In August 1855 the Second Royal Surrey Militia played Shillinglee in Sussex. The Militia's first innings scorecard read:

Private Dudley	b	Challen junior	0
Private Plumridge	b	Heather	0
E. Hartnell	b	Heather	0
A. Marshall	b	Challen junior	0
Private Ayling	b	Challen junior	0
Lieut Pontifex	b	Heather	0
Corp Heyes		run out	0
Lieut Ball	b	Heather	0
Major Ridley		not out	0
Sgt Ayling		run out	0
Private Newberry	b	Heather	0
Extras			0
TOTAL			0

It was a wonderful achievement, all but spoilt by number ten Sgt Ayling. He went for a quick single to cover point, but was sent back by Major Ridley. Never one to disobey an order, Ayling turned, fell over and was run out by more than half the length of the pitch.

Making a duck, however, has its good side. As listeners to BBC Radio's Test Match Special commentaries will know, anyone who has ever been out first ball can send a cheque to join the Primary Club. In receiving a tie, members know they are helping to support cricket for blind children.

DURBAN

THE KINGSMEAD GROUND at Durban will always have a place in history as the venue for the one and only 'Timeless Test' between South Africa and England in 1939. Despite progressing for ten days, the game still ended in a draw as the tourists had to catch their boat home.

The ground was built after the First World War and staged its first Test match in 1922/23. Before that, Test cricket in Durban was played at the 'Lord's' ground, presumably named after the headquarters of the game.

A tradition at Kingsmead was for players who had made a particularly great achievement there to plant a tree. Among the planters were Jack Fingleton, Wally Hammond and Hedley Verity.

Kingsmead used to host two Tests every series, but after the Second World War, the introduction of Test cricket at Port Elizabeth reduced this to one.

Two of the finest Tests on the ground were against Australia – the final two before South Africa was cast into the cricket wilderness.

In 1966/67 South Africa won by eight wickets thanks to some brilliant batting by Denis Lindsay. The game also saw the Test debut of Mike Procter.

In 1969/70 the crowd saw an electrifying display of batting by Barry Richards and Graeme Pollock. Richards came close to scoring a century before lunch, and Pollock went on to make 274, South Africa's highest score.

DURHAM
Founded: 1882

Entered Official Championship: 1992

ON 1992 DURHAM FINALLY achieved their long-held ambition and became a first-class county. The first county to be admitted to the County Championship since Glamorgan in 1921, they brought the total number of counties to eighteen.

Their record in Minor Counties cricket was unsurpassed. They took the title nine times, a joint record, and achieved a number of notable successes against first-class opposition in one-day competitions.

A Durham county side is first recorded in 1874, but today's Durham County Cricket Club was founded on 23rd May 1882. Life was not easy in the early days with fixtures being difficult to arrange, and twice before the turn of the century they were forced to pull out of the Second-Class Counties Competition and play friendly matches.

Their first success in the Minor Counties competition was in 1895, its inaugural year, when they shared the title with Norfolk and Worcestershire.

Further championship titles followed in 1900 and 1901, but Durham then had to wait until 1926 before bringing the title back to an

The Kingsmead ground at Durban, which saw the return of Test cricket to South Africa in 1992/93, here plays host to the Australians in the drawn series of 1993/94.

area severely hit by economic depression. Another title followed in 1930, as the county built formidable teams around professionals from the leagues.

There then followed 46 years without success, but when it eventually returned it did so with a vengeance.

The first sign of an upturn came in 1973 when Durham made history by becoming the first Minor county to beat first-class opposition in the Gillette Cup. At Harrogate they dismissed mighty Yorkshire for just 135 in 58.4 overs, then knocked off the runs to win by five wickets with more than eight overs to spare.

They were then defeated by Essex in the second round.

From 1976 Durham became the dominant force in Minor Counties cricket. They took the title that year and repeated the achievement in 1980, 1981 and 1984. They were runners-up in 1977, 1978 and 1979. During that period, they set a record run of 65 championship matches without defeat.

In 1985 they created another record, becoming the first Minor county to defeat first-class opposition twice when they beat Derbyshire in the NatWest Trophy. Another 'first' came in 1991 when, despite going down to Glamorgan, they became the first junior side to score more than 300 runs in an innings in the competition.

Having declared their intentions over a number of years, Durham formally applied to the Test and County Cricket Board for first-class

status in November 1990. Their excellent presentation was warmly received and they were granted admission for the 1992 season. The decision meant the dissolution of the club and the establishment of a limited company.

Admission to the ranks of the first-class counties may have taken 110 years, but during that time Durham was the birthplace of many fine players who went on to make their mark in the professional game. Among those who played for England were Colin Milburn, Bob Willis and Peter Willey. Wasim Raja of Pakistan and Mohinder Amarnath of India also represented the county as professionals.

The eighteen months that led up to Durham's first County Championship game was a busy period indeed. The club went about recruiting experienced cricketers from other counties to supplement

THE GUINNESS

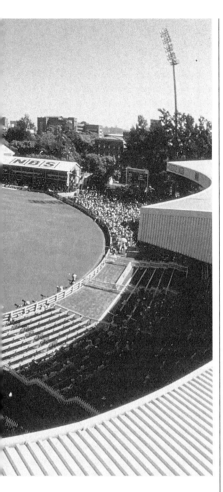

little disappointing.

After drawing their first match in 1992 against Oxford University at the Parks, opener John Glendenen hitting a century on his first-class debut, Durham began brightly, winning two Championship matches by early June. At that stage they were third in the table. But they lost eight of their remaining matches and finished bottom, 36 points adrift of Worcestershire in seventeenth place.

In the one-day competitions they were knocked out of the Benson and Hedges Cup in the zonal matches, finished a respectable ninth in the Sunday League, and reached the quarter-finals of the NatWest Trophy before being beaten by Leicestershire, the eventual beaten finalists.

It was Durham's lack of depth in bowling that was their undoing, with left-arm opener Simon Brown shouldering much of the work. He finished the season with 58 wickets. Dean Jones' early departure for the Australian tour of Sri Lanka was also a factor.

The club learned much from that first season but still finished bottom of the County Championship table in 1993, where four-day cricket exposed every weakness. There was an improvement of two places in 1994, but it seemed it would take them a good while to reach their ambition of fielding a side of largely home-grown players.

Encouragingly, however, it seems that Durham will not be content with mere consolidation as a first-class county. A brand new stadium at Chester-le-Street's Riverside Park will be their new home, with the aim of bringing it up to Test match standard in due course. The club have ambitions to make their mark in first-class cricket as firmly as they did in more than a century in the Minor Counties.

David Graveney, nephew of Tom and like his uncle a former Gloucestershire captain, guided Durham through their first seasons in county cricket. He is now an England selector.

their talented younger players.

Led on the field by David Graveney, formerly of Gloucestershire, and off it by Geoff Cook, once of Northants, their biggest catch was the mighty Ian Botham, who joined them from Worcestershire. He became the first Durham representative in an England team when he played against Pakistan in Tests and one-day internationals.

Other players of experience who signed for the county were Wayne Larkins of Northants, Paul Parker of Sussex, Phil Bainbridge of Gloucestershire and Simon Hughes of Middlesex. Their overseas signing was also guaranteed to be a crowd-pleaser – he was Dean Jones, the exciting Australian batsman.

Despite such an impressive line-up, Durham's first seasons in the County Championship have been a

EDGBASTON

EDGBASTON, HOME OF Warwickshire County Cricket Club, is very much the junior member among England's 'team' of six Test venues.

Having hosted its first Test in 1902, it then staged only another three before 1929. It was then left out of consideration for 28 years, but was chosen again in 1957 and has been a regular Test ground since.

Now boasting facilities as good as any in the world, Edgbaston is unquestionably the ground where England have enjoyed most success.

It was William Ansell, founding father of Warwickshire, who persuaded the authorities to hold the first Test of 1902 at Edgbaston, rather than at Trent Bridge.

It proved to be an historic debut as a Test arena. Batting first, England made 376 for 9, before dismissing Australia in less than ninety minutes for just 36, their lowest total in Test cricket.

A downpour left the ground underwater thereafter, and gatemen and police were sent away with little prospect of further play. But play there was, later in the day, with Australia finishing at 46 for 2 and the match ending in a draw.

Warwickshire received just £750 from receipts distribution at the end of the series, leaving them with severe financial problems.

In 1909 England celebrated a second Edgbaston Test with a ten-wicket win over Australia, and then in 1924 a Test against South Africa followed a similar pattern to that first encounter with Australia.

England made 438 before Gilligan and Tate dismissed the visitors for just 30 in less than an hour. The two bowlers did the trick again when South Africa followed on, giving England victory by an innings.

Edgbaston's period of Test exile was the result of Trent Bridge boasting better facilities and larger crowds. However, after the Second World War a big rebuilding programme began, with about

half a million pounds being spent.

Concrete terracing, comfortable seats and the purchase of more land helped turn the ground into a fine stadium.

The return of Test cricket in 1957 was greeted by big crowds to watch the West Indies, with a capacity 32,000 in the ground on the Saturday. It turned out to be another memorable Edgbaston Test.

With England 288 behind on first innings and still well adrift at 113 for 3 in their second, Peter May (285 not out) and Colin Cowdrey (154) then batted for a day and a half to add 411, the highest ever England

The City End at Edgbaston before redevelopment, with the familiar scoreboard and stand behind the sightscreen. The Birmingham public have been blessed with some exciting Test matches over the years.

stand. At the end, West Indies just held on for a draw at 72 for 7.

As a regular on the Test circuit, Edgbaston continued to see various milestones, such as Colin Cowdrey's century in his 100th Test match against Australia in 1968.

England's first Test defeat at Edgbaston came in 1975 when Mike Denness paid dearly for inserting Australia. The tourists made 359 before a thunderstorm changed the nature of the wicket and England were beaten by an innings and 85 runs.

Edgbaston continued its reputation for drama in 1981, Ian Botham's remarkable summer. Australia were set a modest 151 to win and needed just 46 more with six wickets in hand. But then Botham struck, taking five wickets for one run in an amazing 28-ball spell, and England won by 29 runs.

Ground improvement work has continued at Edgbaston, with another new stand at the city end. Meanwhile on the field, the ground became famous for the 'Brumbrella', which covered the whole playing surface and often allowed play to resume quickly when a whole day might have been lost at other grounds.

JOHN EDRICH
England
Born 1937
Surrey

A SHORT, CHUNKY AND very strong man, John Edrich was a wonderfully consistent left-handed opening bat. He came from a famous Norfolk family, his cousin Bill being a regular member of the England team in the post-war years.

John was a player who knew his strengths and played to them. He had a sound technique and was particularly strong off his legs, but could also strike the ball hard through the off side. In his nineteen-year first-class career, he became only the third left-hander to pass the 100 hundreds landmark.

A happy John Edrich in 1968 after hearing of his selection for the abortive South African tour. His consistent scoring saw him pass 1000 runs each season from 1959 to 1977, and his England career spanned 13 years.

In his 77 Test matches, Edrich was renowned for his courage, never flinching against even the most hostile bowling.

One particular example of his bravery came at Old Trafford in 1976 when, together with Brian Close, he took an awful battering from the West Indies bowlers in the final ninety minutes of play on the Saturday evening.

Edrich was a key member of three MCC touring teams to Australia in the sixties and seventies, scoring centuries on four different grounds. He captained England in the fourth Test of 1974/75 after Mike Denness had dropped himself, and played an innings of great courage after sustaining broken ribs from his first ball from Dennis Lillee.

A familiar face behind the stumps for Lancashire and India in the 1970s, Farokh Engineer was on the winning side in one-day finals at Lord's on four occasions.

His highest Test score came in 1965 when he reached 310 not out against New Zealand at Headingley. His five sixes and 52 fours amounted to the most runs scored in boundaries in a Test innings.

A loyal Surrey stalwart, he captained the county from 1973 to 1977, leading them to Benson and Hedges Cup success in 1974.

In 1981 he became a Test selector, but gave it up after a season to concentrate on his business interests.

First Class Career:
*Runs – 39,790. Average 45.47
(103 centuries)*

Test Match Career:
*Tests – 77
Runs – 5,138. Average 43.54
(12 centuries)*

FAROKH ENGINEER
India
*Born 1938
Bombay and Lancashire*

AS GOOD A WICKET-keeper as India has ever produced, Farokh Engineer was a popular cricketer who became an integral part of the successful Lancashire one-day sides of the 1970s.

He was an acrobatic and enthusiastic wicket-keeper and also a fine batsman, either as an opener or in the middle order. He delighted in an unorthodox style, often forcing the ball through the leg side.

He made his first Test appearance in 1961/62 but did not become a permanent fixture in the side until 1965, when as an ever-present against New Zealand he established himself as a batsman. His two Test centuries came against West Indies (109) in 1966/67 and England (121) at Bombay in 1972/73.

First Class Career:
*Runs – 13,436. Average 29.52
(13 centuries)
Catches – 703. Stumpings – 121*

Test Match Career:
*Tests – 46
Runs – 2,611. Average 31.08
(2 centuries)
Catches – 66. Stumpings – 16*

ENGLAND
V
AUSTRALIA

THERE ARE FEW SPORTING contests to rival a Test series between England and Australia. Clashes for the Ashes, whether in England or 'down under', have an atmosphere all of their own and have produced many of the finest moments in the history of sport.

There are highlights a-plenty: the Bodyline series of 1932/33,

Bradman's all-conquering team of 1948, England's recapture of the Ashes in 1953, Botham's extraordinary summer of 1981. The list is endless.

Test cricket began in 1876/77 when two matches were played in Australia, the home side winning by 45 runs in the first match at Melbourne, England by four wickets in the second. The English side, however, couldn't truly claim to represent the best the country could offer.

The first Test in England came at the Oval in September 1880 when W.G. Grace made 152 as England won by five wickets. But it was defeat on the same ground two years later that led to the famous mock-obituary notice written about English cricket (see The Ashes).

The Ashes series began in Australia in 1882/83 but it wasn't until 1891/92 that Australia first took them, beating England, led by W.G. Grace, by three matches to one.

The pattern of playing five-match series became established just before the end of the century. The 1890s had been the start of England's golden age, with the development of many fine players.

One of the most dramatic series was in 1911/12 when England had a strong all-round team. They lost the first Test at Sydney, but then an opening bowling partnership of Barnes and Foster was established and they proved the trump card that saw England to a 4–1 win.

The ramifications of the Bodyline series of 1932/33 constituted the biggest crisis since Test cricket began (see Bodyline). It was sparked off by the determination of the English captain, Douglas Jardine, to blunt the effectiveness of Don Bradman, the finest batsman the game has seen.

Bradman was to dominate Tests between cricket's oldest rivals for twenty years, leading his country to four successive series wins between 1936/37 and 1948.

Touring England in 1938, Bradman captained Australia to a 2–1 win, a series that featured Stan McCabe's magnificent 232 at a time when Australia were in deep trouble

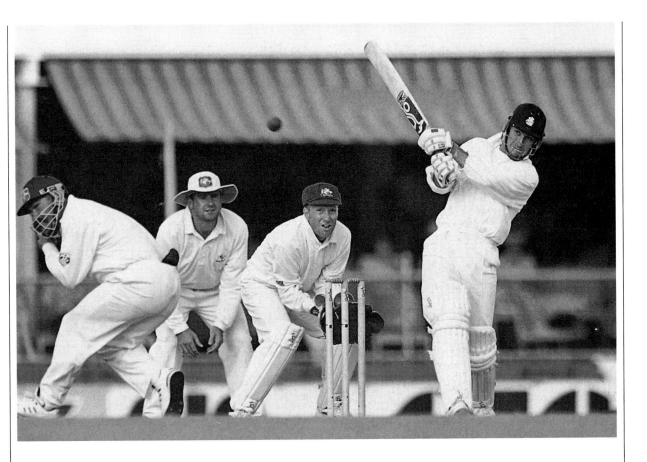

at Trent Bridge, and Len Hutton's 364 as England won the final Test at the Oval.

Ten years later Bradman said farewell to Test cricket by making a duck in his final innings at the Oval. It was an anti-climax, tempered by the memory of Australia's total superiority in the series as they won four of the five matches.

Lindsay Hassett's side continued the convincing winning sequence in Australia in 1950/51, but England at last regained the Ashes for the first time since that Bodyline series in 1953, in memorable fashion.

Four Tests had been drawn as Hutton led England into the final match at the Oval. Amid great celebrations in Coronation Year, England won by eight wickets, appropriately enough with cricketing hero Denis Compton hitting the winning runs.

It heralded a period of English success, first under Hutton and then under Peter May. The 1956 series will always be remembered for Jim Laker's 19 wickets at Old Trafford as England won 2–1.

Richie Benaud's arrival as captain of Australia signalled a new era of supremacy for them as they retook the Ashes 4–0 in 1958/59 and held onto them until Ray Illingworth's party regained them in Australia in 1970/71.

England had come close in 1968 when drawing a home series 1–1. Their victory came after a downpour flooded the Oval and the spectators had to help prepare the ground for a resumption of play. A deadly display of spin bowling by Derek Underwood removed the final Australian batsman with just five minutes left.

Australia regained the initiative in the early 1970s but in 1978/79, when racked by internal divisions over Kerry Packer's World Series Cricket, they were trounced 5–1 by England.

One of the most memorable series of all time came in what has become known as Botham's

One of the few English batsmen to emerge from the 1994/95 Ashes tour with his reputation enhanced, Graham Thorpe hits out during his innings of 67 in the first Test at Brisbane. He topped the England averages for the series.

Summer, 1981. England had returned from a winter tour of the West Indies a well-beaten side, and after losing the first Ashes Test and drawing the second, Ian Botham resigned as England captain, pre-empting his inevitable sacking. It was to change the course of the series.

With Mike Brearley back as captain, the third Test at Leeds made history – the first time this century that a team had won a Test having being made to follow on. With Ladbroke's offering 500 to 1 on an England win, Botham, with 149 not out, gave England a glimmer of hope as they set Australia 130 to win.

Season	Ven	Tests	Winner	Res	Season	Ven	Tests	Winner	Res
1876/77*	Aus	2	—	1-1	1936/37	Aus	5	Australia	3-2
1878/79*	Aus	1	Australia	1-0	1938	Eng	4	—	1-1
1880*	Eng	1	England	1-0	1946/47	Aus	5	Australia	3-0
1881/82*	Aus	4	Australia	2-0	1948	Eng	5	Australia	4-0
1882*	Eng	1	Australia	1-0	1950/51	Aus	5	Australia	4-1
1882/83	Aus	4†	—	2-2	1953	Eng	5	England	1-0
1884	Eng	3	England	1-0	1954/55	Aus	5	England	3-1
1884/85	Aus	5	England	3-2	1956	Eng	5	England	2-1
1886	Eng	3	England	3-0	1958/59	Aus	5	Australia	4-0
1886/87	Aus	2	England	2-0	1961	Eng	5	Australia	2-1
1887/88	Aus	1	England	1-0	1962/63	Aus	5	—	1-1
1888	Eng	3	England	2-1	1964	Eng	5	Australia	1-0
1890	Eng	2	England	2-0	1965/66	Aus	5	—	1-1
1891/92	Aus	3	Australia	2-1	1968	Eng	5	—	1-1
1893	Eng	3	England	1-0	1970/71	Aus	6	England	2-0
1894/95	Aus	5	England	3-2	1972	Eng	5	—	2-2
1896	Eng	3	England	2-1	1974/75	Aus	6	Australia	4-1
1897/98	Aus	5	Australia	4-1	1975	Eng	4	Australia	1-0
1899	Eng	5	Australia	1-0	1976/77*	Aus	1	Australia	1-0
1901/02	Aus	5	Australia	4-1	1977	Eng	5	England	3-0
1902	Eng	5	Australia	2-1	1978/79	Aus	6	England	5-1
1903/04	Aus	5	England	3-2	1979/80*	Aus	3	Australia	3-0
1905	Eng	5	England	2-0	1980*	Eng	1	—	0-0
1907/08	Aus	5	Australia	4-1	1981	Eng	6	England	3-1
1909	Eng	5	Australia	2-1	1982/83	Aus	5	Australia	2-1
1911/12	Aus	5	England	4-1	1985	Eng	6	England	3-1
1912	Eng	3	England	1-0	1986/87	Aus	5	England	2-1
1920/21	Aus	5	Australia	5-0	1987/88*	Aus	1	—	0-0
1921	Eng	5	Australia	3-0	1989	Eng	6	Australia	4-0
1924/25	Aus	5	Australia	4-1	1990/91	Aus	5	Australia	3-0
1926	Eng	5	England	1-0	1993	Eng	6	Australia	4-1
1928/29	Aus	5	England	4-1	1994/95	Aus	5	Australia	3-1
1930	Eng	5	Australia	2-1					
1932/33	Aus	5	England	4-1					
1934	Eng	5	Australia	2-1					

* Ashes not at stake

† England won the Ashes 2-1 in a series of three matches

ENGLAND
v
INDIA

UNTIL FAIRLY RECENTLY, India had recorded only a handful of victories against England, mainly at home and against weakened sides. But in the winter of 1992/93 they inflicted one of England's most humiliating series defeats by three Tests to nil.

It took almost twenty years of playing Test cricket for India to achieve their first win against England, during a drawn series in 1951/52. England were without established players such as May, Bedser and Hutton, and went down to a heavy defeat at Madras by an innings and eight runs.

Until that series England had invariably proved too strong, especially on home soil. In 1936, for instance, India won only four of their

It seemed an easy task for Australia, but after Botham took the first wicket Bob Willis then took over, returning figures of 8 for 43 in a devastating spell of fast bowling that brought England victory by 18 runs.

In the next Test at Edgbaston Australia again began needing a modest 151 to win. But on an extraordinary Sunday afternoon, Botham took five wickets for one run in 28 balls to secure a win.

A century and five wickets from Botham meant England retained the Ashes with a victory in the next Test at Old Trafford. It had been a remarkable turnaround.

Since then, however, Australia have once again reasserted their superiority. They regained the Ashes in 1989 and have dominated all subsequent series. In 1993,

inspired by leg-spinner Shane Warne, they took the series 4-1, their only defeat coming against a rejuvenated England side under Michael Atherton at the Oval.

Any hopes England had of running the Australians closer in 1994/5 disappeared with heavy defeats in the first two Tests at Brisbane and Melbourne, where they were humiliatingly bowled out for 92. Although England came back to win the fourth Test at Adelaide, Australia's 3-1 win was thoroughly deserved.

Phil Edmonds claims the wicket of Mohammed Azharuddin as England head for victory in the fourth Test at Madras in 1984/85.

THE GUINNESS

28 first-class matches on the tour.

England won a four-match series 3–0 in 1952 when India were bowled out twice in a day for 58 and 82 at Old Trafford, the first time it had happened in a Test for half a century.

Then in 1959, led at first by Peter May and for the last two Tests by Colin Cowdrey, England achieved a 5–0 whitewash. In fine weather and on good pitches, India could never contain a strong England batting line-up in which Ken Barrington, M.J.K. Smith, and Geoff Pullar scored heavily.

But India won their first series in 1961/62 thanks to victory in the last two Tests after the first three had been drawn. England's batting became poorer as the tour went on, and without major strike bowlers Trueman and Statham they always had trouble with a strong Indian middle order.

India suffered a 3-0 whitewash in 1967, with English batsmen helping themselves to runs against a poor

attack. But four years later came a complete change and a slightly unexpected first series win for India in England.

They achieved it by winning the final Test at the Oval. England made 355 in their first innings but collapsed to just 101 in the second, their lowest total against India, as the fine spin-bowler Chandrasekar took 6 for 38. Indian supporters celebrated their win long afterwards as the team, led by Ajit Wadekar, acknowledged their support from the Oval balcony.

With the exception of narrow defeats on tour in 1972/73 and 1981/82, England continued to win fairly comfortably until the summer of 1986, when they lost both home series against India and New Zealand.

England played poorly as India, the 1983 World Cup winners, recorded their first ever victory at Lord's and then took the second Test at Headingley. England's batting was dismal, with only

Gatting averaging over 30.

England returned to winning ways in the 1990 series, but the tour of India in 1992/93 was to prove the lowest point in England's record.

England were totally outplayed in the first Test at Calcutta, going down by eight wickets as the Indian spin trio of Kumble, Venkatapathy and Chauhan twice dismissed them for under 300.

Defeats by an innings then followed in the remaining Tests at Madras and Bombay, as the England party capitulated and India's batsmen compiled big scores.

Season	Ven	Tests	Winners	Res
1932	Eng	1	England	1–0
1933/34	Ind	3	England	2–0
1936	Eng	3	England	2–0
1946	Eng	3	England	1–0
1951/52	Ind	5	—	1–1
1952	Eng	4	England	3–0
1959	Eng	5	England	5–0
1961/62	Ind	5	India	2–0
1963/64	Ind	5	—	0–0
1967	Eng	3	England	3–0
1971	Eng	3	India	1–0
1972/73	Ind	5	India	2–1
1974	Eng	3	England	3–0
1976/77	Ind	5	England	3–1
1979	Eng	4	England	1–0
1979/80	Ind	1	England	1–0
1981/82	Ind	6	India	1–0
1982	Eng	3	England	1–0
1984/85	Ind	5	England	2–1
1986	Eng	3	India	2–0
1990	Eng	3	England	1–0
1992/93	Ind	3	India	3–0

ENGLAND
v
NEW ZEALAND

ENGLAND'S RECORD against New Zealand has been one of almost total domination in the 65 years that the two countries have played Test cricket against each other. New Zealand have recorded just four Test wins during that time, all of them coming in a short seven-year period.

An England party first played Test

Season	Ven	Tests	Winners	Res
1929/30	NZ	4	England	1–0
1931	Eng	3	England	1–0
1932/33	NZ	2	—	0–0
1937	Eng	3	England	1–0
1946/47	NZ	1	—	0–0
1949	Eng	4	—	0–0
1950/51	NZ	2	England	1–0
1954/55	NZ	2	England	2–0
1958	Eng	5	England	4–0
1958/59	NZ	2	England	1–0
1962/63	NZ	3	England	3–0
1965	Eng	3	England	3–0
1965/66	NZ	3	—	0–0
1969	Eng	3	England	2–0
1970/71	NZ	2	England	1–0
1973	Eng	3	England	2–0
1974/75	NZ	2	England	1–0
1977/78	NZ	3	—	1–1
1978	Eng	3	England	3–0
1983	Eng	4	England	3–1
1983/84	NZ	3	N. Zealand	1–0
1986	Eng	3	N. Zealand	1–0
1987/88	NZ	3	—	0–0
1990	Eng	3	England	1–0
1991/92	NZ	3	England	2–0
1994	Eng	3	England	1–0

cricket in New Zealand in 1929/30, winning the series 1–0 thanks to victory by eight wickets in the first Test at Christchurch. Maurice Allom, the English fast bowler, made history in the match, taking four wickets in five balls, including a hat-trick.

New Zealand were welcomed to England in 1931 where C.S. Dempster proved himself a fine batsman, averaging 111.8 in his first 11 innings.

A more than creditable draw for New Zealand at Lord's led to two more Tests being arranged. England won by an innings at the Oval and the third at Old Trafford was ruined by rain.

There were three drawn series out of four between 1932/33 and 1949, before England took a very firm grip for the best part of a quarter of a century.

Len Hutton's side had two easy wins in 1954/55 and the first five-Test series between the two in 1958 resulted in a comfortable 4–0 win for England. Peter May's batting and the spin bowling of Lock and Laker were too much for a young and inexperienced New Zealand side.

Ted Dexter led England to a 3–0 whitewash in New Zealand in 1962/63 and M.J.K. Smith handed out the same treatment in England in 1965. Series after series went England's way until 1977/78.

Then England, led by Geoffrey Boycott, deputising for the injured Mike Brearley, suffered their first defeat by a New Zealand team which had also finally beaten Australia four years earlier.

On a difficult pitch at the Basin Reserve, Wellington, England were left needing only 137 for victory. But the left-arm opening bowler Richard Collinge quickly took three wickets, and with Richard Hadlee also bowling well, England were 53 for 8 going into the final day.

Although rain delayed the start, Hadlee soon took the remaining wickets to give the home side victory by 72 runs as England recorded their lowest score against New Zealand, just 64. Hadlee took six wickets in the innings, ten in the match.

The next England tour in 1983/84 saw Geoff Howarth lead New Zealand to their first series win against an England side led, ironically, by the man who had befriended him when he arrived in England to join Surrey, Bob Willis.

It was an unhappy winter for England. They lost in Pakistan, and in New Zealand the single victory that clinched the series, at Christchurch, saw them humiliated by an innings and 132 runs. Abysmal bowling – described by Willis as the worst he had seen in eighty Tests – was followed by batting of similar standard as England were dismissed for 82 and 93, the first time this century they had been bowled out for under 100 in both innings. Again Hadlee had a major part to play, scoring 99 and taking eight wickets.

New Zealand followed up that success with a first series win in England in 1986 when Jeremy Coney's side played with great spirit and confidence throughout the tour. The deciding match was their eight-wicket win at Trent Bridge. Even at the age of 35, Hadlee again proved the main difference between the two sides.

Since then, however, England have regained the ascendancy. Their tour in 1991/92 saw them win 2–0 with comfortable victories at Christchurch and Auckland, and in 1994 they always held the upper hand in a three-Test series which was won 1–0.

ENGLAND
V
PAKISTAN

FOR THE FIRST THIRTY years of Tests between the two countries, England held the upper hand. But since the mid-1980s Pakistan have been in command, with England winning just one of their last 16 meetings.

Pakistan made a bright start to Test cricket when they first toured England in 1954. One down after losing the second Test at Trent Bridge, they won the fourth and final match at the Oval. In a low-scoring, rain-affected match, they squeezed home by 24 runs. It was to be their last win for 28 years.

England won a three-Test tour, which was split by five Tests in India, in 1961/62, and that summer in England – another wet one – the home side recorded a convincing series win by four Tests to nil. Two of the Tests were won by an innings, the others by nine wickets and ten wickets, as England's batsmen dominated a poor Pakistan attack.

England won the next series in 1967 by two matches to nil, despite the emergence for Pakistan of an impressive batsman in Majid Khan and in Wasim Bari a fine wicket-keeper. For England, Ken Barrington scored three centuries in succession, including 109 not out in seven hours on a difficult pitch at Trent Bridge.

England won the 1971 series thanks to an exciting win by 25 runs at Headingley when, after Boycott had scored a century, Peter Lever of Lancashire finished things off with

THE GUINNESS

three wickets in four balls.

Three tours of Pakistan ended without either side gaining a positive result. The slow wickets which favoured batsmen made them poor contests. Crowd disturbances marred the tour of 1968/69, which was abandoned when a riot disrupted play on the third day of the Karachi Test.

England's first series defeat, and Pakistan's first home Test win against them, came in 1983/84. It was brilliant leg-spin bowling from Abdul Qadir, who took eight wickets, that secured the crucial victory in the first Test at Karachi.

Sadly, the last three series between the two countries have been marred by bad feeling and rows that have caused nightmares for administrators. One incident proved to be almost on a par with the Bodyline episode more than fifty years before.

The trouble began when England lost a home series to Pakistan for the first time in 1987. There were arguments over a number of issues, the most notable being Pakistan's objections to the English umpiring.

But England's tour of Pakistan the following winter turned out to be even more explosive, as England players, in turn and not for the first time, felt *they* were being given a raw deal by Pakistani umpires.

In the first Test at Lahore the English were incensed at the decisions of umpire Shakeel Khan. In the second innings, Chris Broad at first refused to leave the pitch after being given out caught behind.

Then at Faisalabad came the flashpoint. Umpire Shakoor Rana halted play after he considered the England captain Mike Gatting was moving a fielder without the batsman's knowledge. Accusations of cheating were hurled by both men, and pictures of the two arguing were front-page news.

The row held up the Test for a day at a time when England were in a strong position. Demands were made for apologies, the England tour management dug in their heels, and the Test and County Cricket Board sent chairman Raman Subba Row and chief executive Alan Smith to mediate.

Play eventually resumed and the match was drawn, but at the end of the series England's players each received an extra 'hardship' bonus payment of £1,000. It was at best a misguided gesture, appearing as it did to condone bad behaviour.

In 1992 England did at least win a

Asif Mujtaba catches Graham Gooch off Mushtaq Ahmed in the fourth Test at Headingley in 1992. Pakistan eventually won an exciting five-Test series which was sadly marred by ill-feeling between the two sides.

Test for the first time in ten years in a hard-fought, exciting series which Pakistan won 2–1. But again the cricket was marred by off-the-field claims of cheating.

England players, officials, journalists and spectators were suspicious of the movement achieved with the 'old' ball by the two main Pakistani pace bowlers, Wasim Akram and Waqar Younis.

Allegations of ball-tampering were rife and at the end of the series one England player, Allan Lamb, was fined for going into print in a national newspaper to accuse the Pakistanis of cheating. Otherwise there was a deafening silence from the game's administrators and the whole sorry episode ended up being brushed under the carpet.

One can only hope that the next series between the two, so far not scheduled, is played in a very much better spirit.

Season	Ven	Tests	Winners	Res
1954	Eng	4	—	1–1
1961/62	Pak	3	England	1–0
1962	Eng	5	England	4–0
1967	Eng	3	England	2–0
1968/69	Pak	3	—	0–0
1971	Eng	3	England	1–0
1972/73	Pak	3	—	0–0
1974	Eng	3	—	0–0
1977/78	Pak	3	—	0–0
1978	Eng	3	England	2–0
1982	Eng	3	England	2–1
1983/84	Pak	3	Pakistan	1–0
1987	Eng	5	Pakistan	1–0
1987/88	Pak	3	Pakistan	1–0
1992	Eng	5	Pakistan	2–1

ENGLAND
v
REST OF THE WORLD

WHEN THE TOUR BY SOUTH Africa to England was cancelled at the eleventh hour in 1970, a series of five matches between England and the Rest of the World was arranged.

The England players were given caps and the matches had all the trappings of Test fixtures, but they are not now recognised by statisticians as full Tests.

The Rest of the World side was captained by Gary Sobers and managed by the former England player Freddie Brown. Ironically, it featured five South Africans – Mike Procter, Eddie Barlow, Barry Richards and Graeme and Peter Pollock lined up alongside five from the West Indies, with Clive Lloyd, Rohan Kanhai, Lance Gibbs and Deryck Murray joining the captain.

Against a background of a General Election, the football World Cup in Mexico and the Commonwealth Games in Edinburgh, attendances at the games were poor, although some very good cricket was played.

The Rest of the World won by four matches to one, England's only victory coming in the second match at Trent Bridge. However, the results of two matches were in doubt until late on the final day.

Sobers proved his class, being the highest run-scorer (588, average 73.50) and leading wicket-taker (21, average 21.52) on either side. Eddie Barlow with 20 wickets and 353 runs as an opener showed what a good all-rounder he was.

For England, John Snow was the most successful bowler with 19 wickets and Geoffrey Boycott topped the batting averages at 65. Surprisingly, Raymond Illingworth was England's leading run-scorer with 476 at an average of 52.88.

For one England player, however, the series brought disappointment. The Glamorgan opener Alan Jones had for many seasons been a consistent run-scorer in county cricket, but despite having his supporters in Wales and outside, had always been overlooked for England.

Having finally been given his chance in the first match at Lord's, he scored just 5 and 0, and was left out for evermore. He may have represented England in an unofficial Test, but he finished his career never having played a full Test for England.

ENGLAND
v
SOUTH AFRICA

THE TEST SERIES IN THE summer of 1994 brought a happy end to a period of almost thirty years when cricketing relations between England and South Africa were severed.

After the D'Oliveira Affair in 1968 and the subsequent cancellation of the 1970 tour, it was another 24 years before official links were resumed.

Although the two countries have met 105 times in Tests, most of the matches in South Africa never saw a fully representative England team until just before the Second World War. Of South Africa's 19 victories,

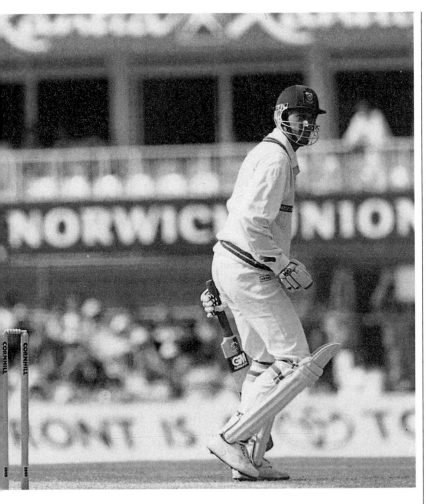

Season	Ven	Tests	Winners	Res
1888/89	SA	2	England	2–0
1891/92	SA	1	England	1–0
1895/96	SA	3	England	3–0
1898/99	SA	2	England	2–0
1905/06	SA	5	S. Africa	4–1
1907	Eng	3	England	1–0
1909/10	SA	5	S. Africa	3–2
1912	Eng	3	England	3–0
1913/14	SA	5	England	4–0
1922/23	SA	5	England	2–1
1924	Eng	5	England	3–0
1927/28	SA	5	—	2–2
1929	Eng	5	England	2–0
1930/31	SA	5	S. Africa	1–0
1935	Eng	5	S. Africa	1–0
1938/39	SA	5	England	1–0
1947	Eng	5	England	3–0
1948/49	SA	5	England	2–0
1951	Eng	5	England	3–1
1955	g	5	England	3–2
1956/57	SA	5	—	2–2
1960	Eng	5	England	3–0
1964/65	SA	5	England	1–0
1965	Eng	3	S. Africa	1–0
1994	Eng	3	—	1–1

11 came at home in the pre-war period.

The first Test between the two was played on a matting wicket in March 1889 and was comfortably won by England by eight wickets. They then took the second match, in Cape Town, by an innings.

Pelham Warner led the first official MCC team to South Africa in 1905/06. The home side had a strong array of talent, and there was much excitement when they won their first Test at Johannesburg by just one wicket.

They went on to win the series 4–1 thanks largely to the strength of their batting. The same eleven South African players were used in all five matches.

The first series in England took place in 1907 and the South African batsmen found it difficult adapting from matting to grass wickets. At

Devon Malcolm is elated as he claims another victim during his nine-wicket haul at the Oval in 1994. This time the unfortunate South African batsman is Craig Matthews, caught behind for 0.

Headingley they bowled England out for their lowest score, 76, yet still lost the match by 53 runs, being dismissed themselves for just 75 in the second innings. The weather saved them from defeat at Lord's.

South Africa were invited to play in the triangular tournament with England and Australia in 1912. However, the poor weather and South Africa's dismal form – they lost all three Tests against England by wide margins – meant it was not a success.

As South Africa's decline

continued, England were rarely troubled in series until 1930/31, when the home side achieved victory at Johannesburg. This tour saw the first Test in South Africa on a grass wicket, at Cape Town. Matting wickets were never used for Test matches in South Africa thereafter.

South Africa then achieved their first series win in England in 1935, thanks to victory at Lord's by 157 runs, and for the first time England sent their strongest team to South Africa in 1938/39, when a piece of cricketing history, the timeless Test, was played at Durban.

England needed 696 for victory and had reached 654 for 5 when the tenth day was washed out by rain, leaving the match a draw as England had to catch the boat home. In all, about 50 records were set during the match, including the largest number of runs scored in a Test – 1,981.

After the war England were very much in control of meetings between the two, but South Africa's visit in 1955 provided some exciting cricket. England won the first two Tests and South Africa the third and fourth before, in a thrilling climax at the Oval, the spin bowling of Lock and Laker, who took sixteen wickets between them, gave England victory by 92 runs.

England had a comfortable 3–0 series win at home in 1960, but five years later a fine South African side led by Peter van der Merwe won 1–0, thanks to the efforts of the brothers Peter and Graeme Pollock at Trent Bridge. Batsman Graeme made a brilliant 125 in the first innings, and fast bowler Peter took ten wickets in the match.

South Africa's refusal to accept Basil D'Oliveira as a member of the England party led to the cancellation of the 1968/69 tour, and it was no surprise when South Africa's tour to England suffered a similar fate in 1970.

The 1994 Lord's Test, when Kepler Wessels led his side to an historic, emphatic victory, finally confirmed South Africa's return to the international fold. They enjoyed an impressive tour, sharing the series after England fought back well at the Oval.

ENGLAND
V
SRI LANKA

ENGLAND HAD MAINLY enjoyed the better of their contests with the young Test-playing nation until the winter of 1992/93. Then, after a depressing tour of India, and with their captain returning home, England were defeated in Colombo as Sri Lanka achieved their first Test victory over them.

Ironically the tour manager Keith Fletcher had led England in the first Test in the former Ceylon in 1981/82, when the spin bowling of Emburey and Underwood set up a win by seven wickets.

Sri Lanka had the better of a draw in their first Test at Lord's in 1984, but England, under the captaincy of Graham Gooch, won the other two

Tests between them on the same ground in 1988 and 1991.

Gooch travelled home before England moved on from India to Sri Lanka in 1992/93 and Alec Stewart took over the captaincy, but the miserable performances seen in India continued. England lost by five wickets, with the off-spinners Warnaweera and Muralitharan largely responsible.

It brought England their fifth Test defeat in succession. For Sri Lanka, it was their fourth victory in 43 Tests, all of them at home.

Season	Ven	Tests	Winners	Res
1981/82	SL	1	England	1–0
1984	Eng	1	—	0–0
1988	Eng	1	England	1–0
1991	Eng	1	England	1–0
1992/93	SL	1	Sri Lanka	1–0

ENGLAND
V
WEST INDIES

IT IS MORE THAN TWENTY years since England last beat the West Indies in a Test series either at home or in the Caribbean – a mark of the superiority the West Indies have enjoyed not just against England but over all other countries in recent times.

Their dominance over the past two decades is shown in the bare facts: between 1973 and 1993, England won just four Tests to West Indies' 27, with 13 drawn.

Few people could have envisaged such a situation when England won the first series between the two in 1928. Indeed, they won all three Tests by an innings. The visitors made an impression only with their athletic fielding and fast bowling.

The 1929/30 series was shared, but West Indies achieved their first series win, 2–1, when England returned to the Caribbean in 1934/35. It was an under-strength England party which, after winning the first Test, eventually lost the fourth by an innings and 161 runs at Kingston.

The West Indies achieved another series win at home before arriving in England in 1950 to win by three Tests to one, in a summer when their cricket captured the imagination of the British people.

The batting was led by the 'Three W's', Walcott, Weekes and Worrell, while the spinners, the unknown 19-year-olds Ramadhin and Valentine, tormented the best English batsmen.

England won the first Test at Old Trafford, but the second Test at Lord's saw the West Indies' first ever win in England by the impressive margin of 326 runs. Ramadhin had match figures of 11 for 152, Valentine 7 for 127.

West Indies followed up that triumph with further comprehensive wins, by ten wickets at Trent Bridge and by an innings and 56 runs at the Oval, despite a fine 202 by Hutton.

The 1953/54 series was a stormy affair, with England's players having little confidence in the local umpires and often refusing to fraternise with the opposition. On a brighter note, the final Test at Kingston saw the first appearance of 17-year-old

A depressingly familiar sight for English supporters: four slips, a gully and a silly mid-off as the West Indies press home their advantage at Old Trafford in 1988.

Garfield Sobers, who made 40 runs and took four wickets.

In England in 1957 the magic that had brought the West Indies victory seven years previously had disappeared, as England recorded a comfortable win. But when the West Indians next returned in 1963, Worrell as captain got the best from his side while England badly missed the influential Peter May.

The tourists had a wonderfully varied bowling attack, featuring the speed of Hall and Griffith, the guile of off-spinner Lance Gibbs, and the many talents of Sobers.

The series will forever be remembered for the Lord's Test, where with one over remaining any one of four results was possible. England needed eight to win with two wickets left, but when Shackleton was run out off the fourth ball, Colin Cowdrey, who had suffered a broken arm earlier in the match, had to come to the wicket.

He stayed at the bowler's end as David Allen blocked the final two deliveries. It was one of the finest Test matches the game had seen.

The real period of West Indies domination began in 1973 when Rohan Kanhai led his side to a 2–0 series win, with their victory in the first Test at the Oval being their first against England in nine Tests

By 1976 Clive Lloyd had taken over as captain and he ensured that his England counterpart Tony Greig would regret his pre-series statement, 'We'll make them grovel'. After two drawn matches, Lloyd's team won the last three Tests for a conclusive 3–0 success.

This marked the start of West Indies' reliance on a battery of fast bowlers. In Roberts, Holding and Daniel they had an attack that was to give the English batsmen no respite and which was capable of bowling very short and very fast.

Meanwhile, the batting of Viv Richards brought back memories of Bradman. He averaged 118 in 4 Tests, scoring 291 at the Oval and 232 at Trent Bridge.

England's dismal run continued through the 1980s as the West Indies completed two 5–0 'blackwashes'. The first came in 1984 as England, led by David Gower, had no answer to the pace of Marshall, Garner and Holding.

Then in the Caribbean in 1985/86, with Richards taking over the captaincy from Lloyd, a fourth quick bowler, Patterson, was added and England were made to look quite hapless during an unhappy tour.

In 1988 England turned to four different captains, Mike Gatting, Chris Cowdrey, Graham Gooch and John Emburey. But the results were no better, a 4–0 defeat with one draw being salvaged.

However, there was just a suspicion that the West Indies superiority was beginning to diminish when England pulled off a shock win in the first Test in 1989/90 and were a little unlucky to lose the series. This seemed to be confirmed when England managed to share the 1991 series 2–2, thanks to a memorable victory in the last Test at the Oval.

England visited the Caribbean for a five-match series in 1993/94 on the back of a dismal Ashes contest and promptly lost the first three Tests. Fears of another blackwash sparked a fightback of sorts, however, as they won in Barbados and then drew in Antigua after Brian Lara had made his Test record 375.

Season	Ven	Tests	Winners	Res
1928	Eng	3	England	3–0
1929/30	WI	4	—	1–1
1933	Eng	3	England	2–0
1934/35	WI	4	W. Indies	2–1
1939	Eng	3	England	1–0
1947/48	WI	4	W. Indies	2–0
1950	Eng	4	W. Indies	3–0
1953/54	WI	5	—	2–2
1957	Eng	5	England	3–0
1959/60	WI	5	England	1–0
1963	Eng	5	W. Indies	3–1
1966	Eng	5	W. Indies	3–1
1967/68	WI	5	England	1–0
1969	Eng	3	England	2–0
1973	Eng	3	W. Indies	2–0
1973/74	WI	5	—	1–1
1976	Eng	5	W. Indies	3–0
1980	Eng	5	W. Indies	1–0
1980/81	WI	4	W. Indies	2–0
1984	Eng	5	W. Indies	5–0
1985/86	WI	5	W. Indies	5–0
1988	Eng	5	W. Indies	4–0
1989/90	WI	4	W. Indies	2–1
1991	Eng	5	—	2–2
1993/94	WI	5	W. Indies	3–1

From 1963: for The Wisden Trophy

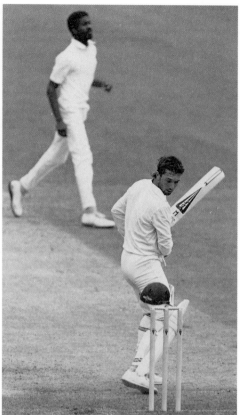

The cricketer's equipment has been known to prove his undoing in the strangest of ways. Here Matthew Maynard of Glamorgan loses his helmet, it dislodges a bail and he is out hit-wicket to Michael Holding, who can't believe his luck. An important wicket, too: it happened in the semi-final of the Benson & Hedges Cup at Swansea in 1988; Derbyshire went on to win.

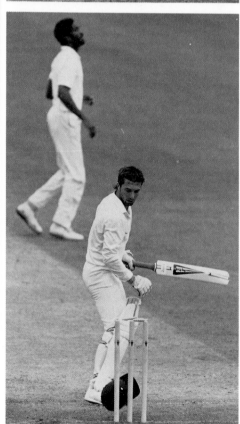
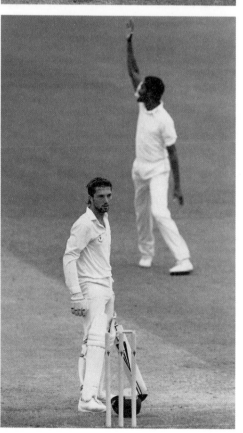

THE GUINNESS

EQUIPMENT

THE LOOK OF THE MODERN-day cricketer has evolved over the hundreds of years the game has been played. But never has it changed faster than in the past decade.

Advances in technology have generally meant lighter and more effective equipment, but batsmen at the wicket now wear more protection than ever. That modern phenomenon, the batting helmet, is now a standard part of every professional's kit.

The development of the cricket bat has now almost gone full circle. In the early part of the 19th century, bats would weigh about four pounds, but by the middle of the 1970s they typically weighed about two and a quarter pounds, a lighter weight that allowed batsmen to play a full range of shots with ease.

However, one of the game's leading bat manufacturers, Gray-Nicolls, then developed what became known as the scoop bat. Instead of having a ridge at the back, the bat was scooped out, with the weight pushed towards the edges. This effectively produced a bigger centre or 'sweet spot'.

Demand for the bat was enormous and other manufacturers responded by developing models without the scoop but which achieved the same effect.

It meant bats became heavier, much to the chagrin of some coaches who began to find schoolboys unable to wield the heavy pieces of timber. But players such as Clive Lloyd and Ian Botham, powerfully-built men, used the heavier bat to great effect.

Its advocates argue that if a heavy bat is picked up straight, it is less likely to stray off-line when coming down to play the ball. Against that, though, wristy shots are not as common in the game as they were.

Batting gloves, which once consisted of just rubber spikes covering the fingers, have improved greatly. Cotton waste was used in the new generation of 'sausage fingered' gloves, but now PVC foam is more commonly used, being lighter, more flexible and offering greater shock absorbency.

Pads have also become lighter and yet more protective. Wicket-keepers now have their own pads, cut down to the knee, giving them greater flexibility of movement.

Players nowadays also regularly use chest protectors and arm guards in addition to the traditional thigh-pad.

No piece of cricket equipment, though, has caused greater controversy in recent times than the helmet. Modern county and Test players put on a helmet before going out to bat as routinely as putting on pads and gloves. Helmets are also becoming more common in club cricket.

Retired players, however, often argue that batsmen are hit on the head more frequently nowadays because the weight of the helmet slows down head movement. The extra protection is also encouraging players to attempt hook shots they might have ducked away from in the past.

ESSEX

Founded: 1876

Entered Official Championship: 1895

Honours

County Champions – 1979, 1983, 1984, 1986, 1991, 1992

NatWest Trophy – 1985

Benson and Hedges Cup – 1979

John Player League – 1981, 1984, 1985

IT TOOK ESSEX MORE THAN a hundred years to win a trophy. But when at last they achieved the breakthrough, it proved to be no flash in the pan. The club went on to establish themselves as England's most consistent side.

Their 1979 double success of County Championship and Benson and Hedges Cup was warmly received by cricket followers. Over their 103-year history, they had gained a reputation for playing attractive cricket and had produced some good players for England. At last they had achieved the consistency needed to win prizes.

The county's supporters had long been used to seeing their team beat the best and then lose to the humblest. The change in their fortunes can probably be put down to first-rate organisation off the field, with a settled base at Chelmsford, together with the sound development of mainly home-grown talent.

Essex achieved first-class status in 1894 and joined the County Championship the following year, finishing a respectable eighth, with five victories. In each of the next four years they finished inside the top six, and so immediately established themselves as a force to be reckoned with.

In the early days all their matches were played in the London suburb of Leyton. But as a result of poor attendances and the financial problems this created, Essex then took their cricket around the county and in the early part of this century regularly used grounds at Southend, Westcliff, Ilford, Brentwood, Colchester, Romford, Clacton and Chelmsford.

This inevitably had an unsettling effect on the team – it seemed as if they were almost permanently 'on tour', never truly having the advantage of playing at home. The travelling entourage of stands, seats, boundary boards and marquees passed into cricket folklore, and later came the famous double-decker buses – one being the scoreboard, the other the ladies' lavatory.

Life was always a struggle, never more so than between the wars. In 1924 the county launched a public appeal for £1,000 to ensure survival. There were other problems too. In 1928 John Douglas, who had been captain since 1911, was sacked after refusing to resign the post when his form deserted him.

In that year there were major problems with team selection, with

The all-conquering Essex side which did the first ever County Championship and Sunday League double in 1984. Keith Fletcher, holding the trophies, skippered the side, ably assisted by his right-hand man and successor, Graham Gooch.

38 different players called upon, 26 of them bowlers. But in the 1930s matters improved and Essex were among the top sides again, thanks largely to an impressive array of fast bowlers.

Sadly, the war was to cost the club a number of fine players, among them Kenneth Farnes, Claude Ashton and Laurie Eastman. But the post-war years saw the emergence of Trevor Bailey, an all-rounder, and Doug Insole, a batsman. Both went on to play major roles in the development of the county both on and off the field.

Bailey, now a well-known radio commentator, held the positions of both secretary and captain at the same time before finding the combination too onerous. Insole was at times both captain and chairman, and at national level went on to become chairman of the Test and County Cricket Board and England tour manager.

For Essex, the sixties provided more financial crises, culminating in a reduction of the playing staff to just twelve in 1967. But under the astute captaincy of Brian Taylor, four young players who were to play an important part in the club's eventual success, John Lever, Keith Boyce, Ray East and David Acfield, were introduced.

England batsman Keith Fletcher took over the captaincy in 1974, and with the emerging talent of Graham Gooch, the county were never far from the honours. In their centenary year, 1976, that first trophy almost arrived as they finished second in the John Player League.

Second place in the Championship and defeat in the semi-finals of the Gillette Cup provided another near miss in 1978, and then at last came the break-through in 1979. They dominated the County Championship, eventually winning by 77 points.

Fletcher's shrewd captaincy was supported by the batting experience of Mike Denness, the former England captain who had joined from Kent, together with the power of Gooch and McEwan. The bowling, too, was consistent, led by

John Lever who took 99 wickets at an average of 14.74.

The Benson and Hedges Cup was won by 35 runs in a high-scoring final against Surrey at Lord's. Gooch was man of the match, his 120 being the first century in a B&H final.

Further championship victories followed in 1983 and 1984, when Essex also took the John Player League, the first time that particular double had been achieved. They made it three Championships in four years with a further success in 1986.

Their 1991 triumph was perhaps the most dramatic. In early August they were 51 points behind the leaders, Warwickshire, but six wins in their last seven matches saw Essex storm home to take the title by 13 points.

A year later there was a more emphatic success as they made sure of the Championship on 3rd September, with two matches still to play.

With Gooch then leading both his county and England, and Fletcher's intelligent management rewarded with his promotion to succeed Mickey Stewart as England manager, Essex men were given a commanding voice in the running of English cricket.

The county's failure to take the title again since the introduction of the four-day Championship has, given their previous superiority, been something of a surprise.

GODFREY EVANS
England
Born 1920
Kent

GODFREY EVANS, A wonderful extrovert, in many ways broke the mould that was used to make wicket-keepers.

While the best were always considered to be those who went about their business unnoticed, Evans was quite the opposite. A showman to his fingertips, he was also an excellent wicket-keeper, and until his fellow Kent player Alan Knott surpassed him, he held the record for the most Test dismissals.

Evans was England's regular wicket-keeper from right after the Second World War until 1958/59. He was also a very capable lower-order batsman who came to his country's rescue on more than one occasion.

He unquestionably took the art of wicket-keeping to a new level. Evans was spectacular in diving to take catches and was blessed with a good eye and speed of movement. He would stand up to bowlers as much as possible – a fact demonstrated by the high number of stumpings in his career record, amounting to almost a quarter of all his dismissals.

He twice scored centuries for England, the first coming against West Indies at Old Trafford in 1950, the second against India at Lord's in 1952, when he only just failed to reach the three figures in the pre-lunch session. But his defensive qualities were well to the fore when he batted for 95 minutes without scoring against Australia at Adelaide in 1946/47.

Evans is still a regular fixture around English Test match grounds. Easily recognisable with his mutton-chop sideburns, he is now involved in delivering the betting odds on the eventual outcome.

First Class Career:
Runs – 14,882. Average 21.22
(7 centuries)
Catches – 811. Stumpings – 249

Test Match Career:
Tests – 91
Runs – 2,439. Average 20.49
(2 centuries)
Catches – 173. Stumpings – 46

An automatic choice behind the stumps for England for twelve years after the Second World War, Evans is pictured here testing his fitness before the final Test of the 1956 series against Australia.

FAZAL MAHMOOD

Pakistan

Born 1927

Northern India, Punjab and Lahore

FAZAL MAHMOOD WAS the mainstay of the Pakistan bowling attack during his country's early years in Test cricket. His strength was his accuracy of line and length, and his style was often compared to that of England's Alec Bedser. He was also a forceful, hard-hitting batsman in the lower middle-order.

He began his career with Northern India and seemed certain to tour Australia, but stood down when Partition was announced. As Pakistan prepared for full Test status, Fazal was consistently their best bowler. He took twenty wickets in two matches against Ceylon in 1950 and played a decisive part in ensuring victory over the MCC in 1951/52.

With the arrival of official Tests, he faced all the other countries with the exception of South Africa. On the first tour of India he took twenty Test wickets, his best performance coming at Lucknow where he took 12 for 94.

Pakistan's first tour of England saw him take half his side's Test wickets (20), and in all he took 77 wickets in sixteen first-class fixtures. The highlight of the tour was Pakistan's memorable Test win at the Oval, when he took 12 for 99.

His bowling was also responsible for Pakistan's first win over Australia. He returned match figures of 13 for 114 in 75 overs, a clear demonstration of his stamina and accuracy.

Between 1958/59 and 1960/61 he captained Pakistan in ten Tests with mixed success, and eventually lost the job after five successive draws against India.

His last appearance in Test cricket came on the 1962 tour of England when he was flown in to cover for injuries. However, by this time he was past his best and made little impression.

First Class Career:
*Runs – 2,602. Average 23.02
(1 century)
Wickets – 460. Average 19.18*

Test Match Career:
*Tests – 34
Runs – 620. Average 14.09
Wickets – 139. Average 24.70*

KEITH FLETCHER

England

Born 1944

Essex

KEITH FLETCHER WAS A batsman of great ability and a particularly shrewd captain, enjoying much success with his native Essex. He continued to nurture talent at Essex after his playing days were over, and in 1992 took over as England team manager from Mickey Stewart. However, county success never followed him to the England job.

His somewhat shy nature – he was nicknamed 'The Gnome' – sometimes held him back at Test level, where he would let bowlers dominate him too often.

That characteristic also affected him as a manager. He was unable to galvanise an England side where individuals sometimes appeared wanting technically and lacking in motivation.

Fletcher enjoyed an international playing career that spanned 59

In his 50th Test, Fletcher takes a fine catch to dismiss Sandeep Patil at Calcutta in 1981/82.

Tests and featured some fine innings. His highest Test score, 216, came against New Zealand at Auckland in 1974/75.

Many of his innings for England were back-to-the-wall efforts. He was chosen for eight overseas tours for the MCC, but appeared to lose some of his appetite for international cricket after a traumatic time against Lillee and Thomson in Australia.

However, he was recalled as captain of England for the 1981/82 tour of India and Sri Lanka. England lost 1–0 in India but went on to win the first Test ever played against Sri Lanka. On his arrival home Fletcher was discarded, harshly in the opinion of many observers.

He captained Essex from 1974 to 1985, bringing them County Championship titles in 1979, 1983 and 1984, and was vice-captain when they won the title again in 1986. He also led them to their NatWest Trophy win in 1985, as well as Benson and Hedges and Sunday League titles.

He continued to have a major influence in the Essex success story off the field after his retirement, and it was no surprise when he took over the management of the England team after the series against Pakistan in the summer of 1992.

However, his first tour in charge was little short of disastrous. With his long-time friend and colleague Graham Gooch as captain, Fletcher saw England suffer their first-ever whitewash by a relatively modest Indian side, three Tests to nil.

Ensuing tours of West Indies and Australia, both of which resulted in 3–1 defeats, did nothing to improve Fletcher's standing with his critics. In March 1995 he was dismissed.

First Class Career:
*Runs – 37,665. Average 37.77
(63 centuries).*

Test Match Career:
*Tests – 59.
Runs – 3,272. Average 39.90
(7 centuries)*

THE GUINNESS

JOEL GARNER

West Indies

Born 1952
*Barbados, Somerset and South
Australia*

GIVEN THE NICKNAME 'Big Bird', Joel Garner was a formidable fast bowler delivering the ball from a mighty height and regularly making it lift. At six feet eight inches tall, there have been few taller players than him in Test cricket.

Garner, though, was more than just a giant. He could make the ball move off the pitch in either direction and had an almost unplayable yorker. He was an integral part of the West Indies pace attack during a period where no other country could seriously challenge them.

He made an impressive start to Test cricket, taking 25 wickets in a series against Pakistan in the Caribbean in 1976/77. The following year against Australia he took 13 wickets in two Tests, but then joined Kerry Packer's World Series Cricket.

He returned to the official fold to help the West Indies win the World Cup in 1979, taking 5 for 38 against

A classic action shot of the aptly named 'Big Bird'. Delivering the ball from such a great height, Garner made it well-nigh impossible for batsmen to dominate him.

England in the final.

This was the year he joined Somerset full-time, having played for them on a part-time basis the previous two years. He was to enjoy a long and happy county career in the West Country until the end of the 1986 season, when he and Viv Richards were sacked and Ian Botham left with them.

His figures for the remainder of his Test career were impressive. He took 31 wickets in the home series against Australia in 1983/84, and 29 in five Tests the following summer in England. That winter in Australia he took another 19 to complete a memorable 12 months in which the West Indies achieved 11 consecutive Test victories.

A cheerful character, Garner finished his Test career as the third highest wicket-taker for the West Indies.

In 1985 he was awarded the MBE, and he has continued playing the game past the age of 40, for a club side in Somerset.

First Class Career:
Wickets – 881. Average 18.53

Test Match Career:
Tests – 58
Wickets – 259. Average 20.97

MIKE GATTING
England
Born 1957
Middlesex

A PUGNACIOUS AND determined cricketer, Mike Gatting took a long time to establish himself as an England player. Having done so he went on to captain his country, only to run into a storm of controversy. He finally announced his international retirement during the last Test of an unhappy Australian tour in 1994/95.

Throughout his career in county cricket Gatting has been a heavy run-scorer, and, taking over the Middlesex captaincy from Mike Brearley, has continued to bring many honours to the London county.

A natural sportsman whose brother became a professional footballer, Gatting won his Middlesex cap in 1977 and was selected for the England touring party to Pakistan and New Zealand that winter.

He struggled for a number of years to make a place his own, being in and out of the England side. After 30 Tests his top score was still only 81, but he at last came good in India in 1984/85, making his first Test century at Bombay in his 54th innings.

He then made 200 at Madras and the following summer recorded two more centuries against Australia. In a period of 11 Tests he scored 1,102 at an average of 91.83.

He suffered a major setback in

Captain of his country with a triumphant Ashes tour behind him, Gatting's expression gives no hint of the trouble that that was to dog him thereafter.

the West Indies in 1985/86, having to return home after his nose was badly broken by a ball from Malcolm Marshall. Back in the Caribbean after a month, he promptly broke his thumb! But he recovered and took over the England captaincy from David Gower after the defeat by India in the first Test of 1986.

After a triumphant Ashes tour in 1986/87 and a successful World Cup which saw England make the final, Gatting's period in charge ran into controversy first in Pakistan when he had a row on the field with umpire Shakoor Rana.

Then back in England in 1988, newspapers reported, the day after the first Test against West Indies at Trent Bridge, that Gatting had entertained a barmaid in his room during the course of an evening. Gatting denied any impropriety but was relieved of the captaincy.

Coupled with a dispute with the TCCB over chapters in a book outlining his row with Shakoor Rana, it was an unhappy period in his life. But ultimately his record had been poor, with just two Test victories out of his 23 matches in charge.

In 1990 it was announced that a rebel England party was to tour South Africa, with Gatting as captain. He fully realised the consequences of his actions, but, upset at his treatment from England officials, was prepared to accept the five-year Test ban which resulted.

With South Africa's return to international cricket, that ban was rescinded, and in 1992/93 Gatting returned to the England side for the tour of India and Sri Lanka. He was then dropped after the first two Tests against Australia in 1993 and omitted from the touring party to the West Indies the following winter.

Despite another England setback, he once again led Middlesex to the County Championship title as the side was beaten just once, in the final game of the season at Worcester.

Surprisingly, he was recalled to the England party that toured Australia in 1994/95, but despite a century at Adelaide his form was poor. He finished the series with an average of just 20 and his decision to retire from the Test arena came as no surprise.

First Class Career:
Runs – 32,317. Average 50.57 (84 centuries).

Test Match Career:
Tests – 79.
Runs – 4,409. Average 35.55 (10 centuries)

SUNIL GAVASKAR
India
Born 1949
Bombay and Somerset

SMALL IN STATURE BUT A giant of an opening batsman, Sunil Gavaskar made cricket history by becoming the first man to score more than 10,000 Test runs. His record aggregate of 10,122 from 125 Tests stood as the highest number of Test runs until Australia's Allan Border overtook him in February 1993.

During a Test career that spanned seventeen years, Gavaskar proved himself the most consistent opening

Gavaskar ended his playing career with a glorious innings of 188 for the Rest of the World in the MCC bicentenary match at Lord's in 1988.

Princes ⚔ Ground

GENTLEMEN OF SOUTH v PLAYERS OF NORTH

JULY 19th, 20th, & 21st, 1875.

Players.	First Innings.		Second Innings.
Lockwood	c Thornton. b Gilbert	69	
J. Selby	b W. G. Grace	15	
Greenwood	c H. Ross, b Gilbert	31	
W. Oscroft	c sub, b Gilbert	22	
Ulyett	c Talbot, b Gilbert	11	
M. McIntyre	c H. Ross, b Gilbert	7	
Emmett	c Talbot, b W. G. Grace	29	
A. Shaw	st H. Ross, b W. G. Grace	8	
Hill	c Gilbert, b W. G. Grace	12	
Pinder	st H. Ross, b Gilbert	0	
F. Morley	not out	0	
	b 5, l-b 1	6	

Total 205

Gentlemen.	First Innings.		Second Innings.	
W. G. Grace, Esq.	c Emmett, b Shaw	9	c Selby, b Shaw	0
G. N. Wyatt, Esq.	c Selby, b Morley	9	c Greenwood. b Morley	13
W. R. Gilbert, Esq.	l-w, b Shaw	8	c Greenwood, b Morley	8
J. M. Cotterell, Esq.	st Pinder, b Shaw	11	c Greenwood b Morley	0
G. F. Grace, Esq.	c Shaw, b Morley	18	c Ulyett, b Morley	18
H. Renny-Tailyour, Esq.	c Greenwood, b Morley	1	b Morley	10
Hon. M. G. Talbot	b Morley	1	c Lockwood, b Morley	0
H. Ross, Esq.	b Shaw	2	b Shaw	0
C. I. Thornton, Esq.	b Shaw	0	st Pinder, b Morley	7
C. H. A. Ross, Esq.	c Hill, b Morley	0	not out	0
C. J. Brune, Esq.	not out	0	c Oscroft, b Morley	2
	Leg Byes	2	Byes	2

Total 56   Total 55

Umpires, Willsher and Shoesmith.   Scorers, T. Box, Jun. and Luff.

---

bat in world cricket. He set many records along the way from the moment he entered the Test arena with 65 against the West Indies at Port of Spain in March 1971.

At just over five feet four inches tall, he was never a great hooker against fast bowling, but more than made up for this by being a splendid cutter and driver.

He was also a player of great concentration and patience – a quality India had need of on the many occasions when he held the innings together.

Gavaskar was already a prolific scorer for Bombay when that first series against West Indies showed just what a talent India had uncovered. He made four centuries in four Tests, finishing the series with 124 and 220 at Port of Spain as his country recorded their first series win against the West Indies.

His tour of England the following summer was a disappointment, with 57 at Old Trafford being his highest score. However, that was only a temporary setback to a career which saw Gavaskar score more than 1,000 Test runs in a calendar year three times, in 1976, 1978, and 1983.

It says much for his courage and ability that of his 34 Test centuries – still a record – 13 came against the mighty West Indies, including his highest score of 236 not out. He made eight hundreds against Australia and four against England.

Gavaskar is perhaps best remembered in England for a remarkable innings of 221 in more than eight hours at the Oval in 1979, when India needed 438 to win and just failed to reach the total, the match ending with them on 429 for 8.

Among other noteworthy feats, he was on the field for all but four

minutes of the Bangalore Test against England in 1981/82, when he made 172.

He became the world's highest Test run-scorer when he overtook Geoffrey Boycott's total of 8,114 in 1983/84, and in that season he also surpassed Bradman's tally of 29 Test centuries.

Gavaskar played just one season in English county cricket, scoring 664 runs for Somerset in 1980. Happily, he is now an honorary member of the MCC, having at first declined the honour after a row with a gateman at Lord's.

First Class Career:
Runs – 25,834. Average 51.46 (81 centuries)

Test Match Career:
Tests – 125
Runs – 10,122. Average 51.12 (34 centuries)

GENTLEMEN
V
PLAYERS

ON TODAY'S SUPPOSEDLY 'classless' society, it is perhaps hard to understand how a fixture between the best of the first-class amateurs and professionals in England lasted for more than 150 years.

The annual match at Lord's came to an end in 1962, by which time the genuine amateur in English county cricket was hard to find. The game's overtones of elitism had by then become an anachronism in the egalitarian, swinging sixties.

However, many matches, especially in the period after the Second World War, produced a high standard of cricket and the fixture was often closely observed by Test selectors.

The first match, in 1806, was played at Thomas Lord's ground in Dorset Square, when the Gentlemen were given two professionals to bolster their team. Indeed it was largely thanks to their efforts that the Gentlemen won!

From the mid-1860s almost until the end of the century the game was considered the top event of the English season, with W.G. Grace dominating proceedings for the Gentlemen. He twice made a double hundred and recorded fifteen centuries in all, in his tally of 6,008 runs in the fixture.

The Players generally had the upper hand after the First World War, with the Gentlemen winning only three matches at Lord's after 1919. Despite that, big crowds would often be in attendance for games that were always keenly contested.

In the final match at Lord's in 1962 the sides were captained by Mr. E.R. Dexter and F.S. Trueman, as the Lord's scorecard traditionally referred to the two sets of players. The match was drawn, leaving the final tally of the 137 games played at Lord's standing at Gentlemen 41, Players 68, with 28 draws.

Seventy-two games were played at the Oval, with the Gentlemen winning 16, the Players 34, 21 drawn, and the match in 1883 tied. There were also 39 matches at Scarborough. The Gentlemen won 4, the Players 15, 20 were drawn.

In November 1962, amateur status in first-class cricket was abolished by the Advisory County Cricket Committee, only four years after the MCC had concluded that 'the distinctive status of the amateur cricketer was not obsolete, was of great value to the game, and should be preserved'.

The move was not wholeheartedly welcomed. The editor of *Wisden*, Norman Preston, wrote: 'By doing away with the amateur, cricket is in danger of losing the spirit of freedom and gaiety which the best amateur players brought to the game.'

Sir Jack Hobbs, one of the game's greatest professionals, expressed his sadness at the passing of the amateur, which marked the end of an era in cricket. But he added: 'Now times are different, I can understand the position of the amateur who has to make his living. You cannot expect him to refuse good offers outside cricket.'

In his last Test match in 1976, Lance Gibbs set a new record for Test wickets, passing Fred Trueman's total of 307. A cousin of Clive Lloyd, Gibbs was also a fine gully fielder.

LANCE GIBBS
West Indies

Born 1934
Guyana, South Australia and Warwickshire

LANCE GIBBS WAS A skilful spin bowler who for a number of years held the record for the highest number of Test wickets, 309.

With a rhythmic, if rather chest-on action, Gibbs could extract considerable turn from the pitch with the aid of long lean fingers. He was a master of deception, regularly

fooling batsmen with changes of pace and flight.

He made an immediate impression on the international scene when in his first Test series against Pakistan in 1957/58 he topped the bowling averages with seventeen wickets at 23.05 from four Tests.

He performed the hat-trick against Australia at Adelaide in 1960/61, having already taken three wickets in four balls in the previous Test at Sydney! But his best Test performance came against India in Barbados in 1961/62, when he took 8 for 38. It clinched the series.

Later in his career, when fast bowling was looked upon as the best means of winning Test matches, Gibbs continued to hold his place in the West Indies team, often coming into his own as the wicket became more helpful to spin on the latter days of a match. He took five or more wickets in a Test on 18 occasions.

In the County Championship, Gibbs had six years with Warwickshire. His most successful season was 1971, when he took 131 wickets at an average of 18.89.

First Class Career:
Wickets – 1,024. Average 27.22

Test Match Career:
Tests – 79
Wickets – 309. Average 29.09

GLAMORGAN
Founded: 1888

Entered Official Championship: 1921

Honours:
County Champions – 1948, 1969.
Axa/Equity and Law League –
1993

UNTIL THE ENTRY OF Durham in 1992, Glamorgan were the last county to join the first-class ranks, having been admitted to the County Championship in 1921. Considered an unfashionable yet friendly club, they have twice been champions, although their record in one-day competitions

Viv Richards (left) and club captain Hugh Morris show off the Axa/ Equity & Law League trophy won by Glamorgan in a dramatic finale to the 1993 season at Canterbury. An undefeated innings from Richards saw them home.

before 1993 was poor.

Glamorgan, a county currently split into three administrative areas, are seen very much as the standard bearers of Welsh cricket. They take matches to other Welsh counties, regularly playing at Abergavenny in Gwent, Aberystwyth in Dyfed, and Colwyn Bay in Clwyd.

However, the aspirations of some to have the side consist totally of Welshmen have never been achieved, and indeed there has been criticism in recent years of the club's decision to engage players released by other counties – players often past their prime.

After their formation Glamorgan enjoyed a memorable win against Surrey at the Oval in 1889 and as a result their fixture list improved, with two-day friendlies against neighbouring English counties and an annual tour to London.

They joined the Minor Counties Championship in 1897, finished second in their first year and became joint champions with Durham in 1900. With industry and commerce moving into South Wales, Glamorgan's playing resources were improved by people who had played the game at public school and top-class club level in England.

There were high hopes of joining the County Championship in 1913, when plans were advanced to bring in the more successful minor counties. Much activity ensued in the county, with fund-raising games and fixtures against touring sides arranged, but the outbreak of war put paid to their dreams.

After a great deal of canvassing, Glamorgan were eventually admitted to the first-class ranks in 1921. Sadly though, many of their players were by now past their best and *Wisden* recorded that the club's entry to the Championship was not justified by results.

Despite beating Sussex in their first match at Cardiff Arms Park, Glamorgan finished bottom of the table in that debut season, and were only one place better in the following two years.

Although life continued to be a struggle, Glamorgan did make an impact on the Championship. In 1927 they beat Nottinghamshire by an innings in the final game of the season, robbing them of the title, Lancashire taking it by a mere decimal point.

Maurice Turnbull became the first Glamorgan player to be capped by England when he went on the 1929/30 tour of New Zealand. Turnbull, who did so much to ensure the club's survival in those early years, was a fine all-round sportsman who captained Cambridge and Glamorgan, was also the county's secretary, and played rugby and hockey for Wales.

He died on active service in Normandy in 1944 and news of his death came as the county were playing a fund-raising match at Cardiff Arms Park to help the war effort. The pavilion bell was sounded as players and spectators paid their respects.

Glamorgan regrouped after the war and in 1948 came an unexpected first County Championship title. Wilf Wooller, who would become such a dominating and often controversial figure, led the side. They got off to a great start, but their lead was whittled away and they knew that victory was needed in their final match against Hampshire at Bournemouth.

Johnnie Clay, Wooller's mentor, had been recalled to the team at the age of fifty, and his spin bowling produced figures of 6 for 48 in the second innings to clinch the title.

Glamorgan continued to hold their own, usually in mid-table, through the fifties, although there was acrimony off the field with Wooller often at odds with the committee.

They came close to taking a second title in 1962, when, under the captaincy of Ossie Wheatley, they finished second to Yorkshire.

In 1965 Glamorgan finished third, a feat they repeated three years later, by which time their home ground in Cardiff had become Sophia Gardens.

By now, a more than useful team had been built up under the leadership of Tony Lewis. The batting was spearheaded by the brilliant Majid Khan from Pakistan, but the strength of the side was probably its all-rounders, Walker, Nash, Cordle and Shepherd.

In 1969 Glamorgan took their second title, being undefeated in 24 games. Victories over Essex and Worcestershire sealed their success with one match still to play. They followed up that achievement with second place behind Kent the following year, but the last two decades have been largely ones of disappointment.

Some of their signings from other counties in recent years have been unsuccessful, beginning with the decision to engage Robin Hobbs, the former Essex and England leg-spinner, as captain in 1979. He had retired from the game three years earlier, and found the task of bringing success back to the Welsh county too tough.

There has been better luck, though, with overseas players. Majid Khan and Javed Miandad flourished, but the real prize was the capture of Viv Richards in 1989. Illness and injury prevented him from playing that season, but his influence on the younger players between 1990 and 1993 was considerable.

Only twice since 1970 had Glamorgan finished inside the top ten in the Championship, and their record in one-day competitions was poor. But the 1993 season changed all that.

They finished third in the County Championship table, and then in a dramatic climax to the season beat Kent at Canterbury to take the Axa/Equity and Law Sunday League title in what proved to be a 'winner takes all' contest. Fittingly, it was an undefeated innings of 46 by Richards that saw them home.

It was Glamorgan's first one-day title and their first trophy for 24 years. Having reached the semi-final stage of the NatWest Trophy as well, Hugh Morris's young side appeared to be on the threshold of becoming a much stronger force in English cricket. But 1994 proved a terrible disappointment as the club finished last in the Championship.

GLOUCESTERSHIRE
Founded: 1871

Entered Official Championship: 1890

Honours:
Gillette Cup – 1973
Benson and Hedges Cup – 1977

THE CLUB WAS THERE AT the beginning of the official County Championship, but Gloucestershire supporters have had to endure the disappointment of never seeing their side win the title. Their most successful seasons were in the two decades before the Championship proper was formed.

Two one-day cup victories are all the record books show, yet

Gloucestershire's impact on English cricket has been enormous.

The county has produced many fine cricketers, among them two of the greatest batsmen the game has ever seen, W.G. Grace and Walter Hammond.

For many years, the Grace brothers *were* Gloucestershire cricket. The current club is believed to have been founded in 1871, although a Gloucestershire team containing three Graces, W.G., E.M. and G.F., played the previous year.

Organised county cricket began in 1873. Gloucestershire shared the title that year with Nottinghamshire and went on to take it in their own right in 1874, 1876 and 1877, when they were unbeaten.

The three Graces, together with Frank Townsend, dominated the national batting averages. In all, W.G. is believed to have played 618 innings for the county, and it was his leadership and ability that enabled what was an amateur team to overcome professional sides such as Surrey and Yorkshire.

Although Gloucestershire's fortunes declined in the 1890s, W.G. Grace's influence continued. He had perhaps his greatest year in 1895, when at the age of 47 he made 1,000 runs in May and the county finished fourth in the table.

In 1899 Grace left Gloucestershire, severing all connections with the club, and went to live in the London area. The county's fortunes slumped dramatically as they finished one from bottom in 1901 and 1902.

In the seasons after the First World War, Gloucestershire finished mainly in the bottom half of the table. But some fine cricketers came to the fore, including Walter Hammond.

His presence in the Gloucestershire side from the mid-1920s to 1946 made them generally feared opposition. In his first-class career he scored 167 centuries while amassing more than 50,000 runs. He was also a useful fast-medium bowler.

The county's most famous match between the wars came in 1930 when they played the Australian tourists at Bristol. No county had beaten the Aussies since 1912 and it seemed Gloucestershire had little chance of breaking that sequence when they were dismissed for 72 in their first innings. But with Hammond scoring 89 they made 202 in the second innings, setting the visitors 118 to win. The Australians seemed to be well on their way at 59 for no wicket, but then collapsed as C.W.L. Parker took 7 for 54. Amid high excitement, the match ended in a tie.

Gloucestershire were runners-up in 1947, and the fifties saw the emergence of Tom Graveney, one of England's most stylish batsmen, who sadly for the county's long-suffering supporters left to join Worcestershire when C.T.M. Pugh was given the captaincy after the 1960 season.

Other players who came to the fore then and went on to play for England were Arthur Milton, who also played football for his country, and two off-spinners, David Allen and John Mortimore.

In 1969 Tony Brown, an all-rounder, took over as captain and the county went on to enjoy their most successful decade since the

The pride of Gloucestershire, Mr W.G. Grace. Known simply as 'The Champion', he represented the county from its very first season until 1899.

days of Grace. They were runners-up in the Championship that year and finished third in 1972.

Then in 1973, with the batting talents of Pakistan's Zaheer Abbas and Sadiq Mohammed, and the all-round ability of South African Mike Procter, Brown led his side to victory in the Gillette Cup final. Procter made 94 and Brown 77 not out as Gloucestershire defeated Sussex by 40 runs, and Brown's triumph was complete when Alec Bedser named him man of the match.

Four years later, with Brown now succeeded as captain by Procter, Gloucestershire triumphed in the Benson and Hedges Cup, beating Kent in the final by 64 runs. Their triumph was marred by pitch invasions in the closing stages.

The eighties brought little further success for the county, apart from third place in 1985 and the runners-up spot the following year. They were also years of some acrimony, with rows over relieving David Graveney of the captaincy splitting the county.

Recently the club have possessed a potent fast bowling attack, featuring Courtney Walsh from the West Indies and David Lawrence, whose promising England career was so cruelly curtailed by a broken knee-cap on the tour of New Zealand in 1991/92. The injury occurred again before the 1993 season and effectively ended his career.

The fielding has been led by the effervescent Jack Russell, generally regarded as England's best wicket-keeper of recent times. Alas, the batsmen have never scored consistently enough in recent seasons for Gloucestershire to mount a serious challenge for the County Championship.

Bat raised as always, Graham Gooch faces up to another delivery. His 333 and 123 in a memorable Test against India at Lord's in 1990 is a Test record match aggregate, and he set another record that year by reaching 1000 Test runs in an English summer.

GRAHAM GOOCH
England
Born 1953
Essex and Western Province

GRAHAM GOOCH'S retirement from international cricket after the final Test of the Ashes series in 1994/95 brought to an end a significant chapter in English cricket history.

He was England's most consistent batsman and is the country's highest Test run-scorer. As captain, a post he relinquished after four Tests against Australia in 1993, he led from the front, placing a high importance on the work ethic.

His period at the helm placed a heavy burden on him, his record as captain reading Won 10, Drawn 12, Lost 12. Many of those defeats came during a miserable final twelve months when England lost series against Pakistan, India and Australia.

After making himself unavailable for the tour to the West Indies in 1993/94, he returned to the side against New Zealand and South Africa and was then picked for the Ashes tour.

Many feared it might be a tour too many, and so it proved. The spirit was still willing but dismissals when appearing well set, and dropped catches in the field, suggested that at 41, time had caught up with Gooch.

He made his county debut in 1973 and his first appearance for England followed two years later. It was not a happy one: he made a pair against Australia at Edgbaston.

However, his consistent scoring in county cricket earned him another chance and his first Test century (123) came against the West Indies at Lord's in 1980.

With Gooch now having established himself as an England player, it was a shock when he captained a party of England players on a rebel tour of South Africa in 1982, a move that is thought to have earned him about £50,000 but also brought a three-

year ban from Test cricket. His suspension served, he returned to the England fold as the country's top opening batsman.

He was first installed as captain of England in the disastrous summer of 1988 when he deputised for the injured Chris Cowdrey. He led England in two Tests that season, against West Indies and Sri Lanka, and was given the job permanently in 1990.

Series against New Zealand and India were won, with Gooch making a memorable 333 against India at Lord's, the highest score of his career and the highest score by a Test captain.

But as problems piled up for a poor England side, Gooch, although he certainly led by example, was unable to improve their fortunes. A man who drove himself to extremes in pursuit of a high level of physical fitness, his captaincy was often criticised for a lack of imagination in the field and in the selection room.

After giving up the captaincy, in the final Test against Australia at the Oval in 1993 he passed David Gower's record of 8,231 runs to become England's highest scorer.

Gooch had already reached 100 hundreds – not, as was first thought, at Cuttack in India in January 1993, but against Cambridge University the following May.

In between, the ICC ruled that a Gooch century scored on the rebel tour of South Africa should be struck from the records as not first-class.

A loyal Essex man, Gooch has led the county to many successes in the County Championship and one-day competitions, and helped make them a leading force in English cricket.

His final Test innings at Perth was an emotional affair, with spectators applauding him to the wicket. Sadly, after being dropped twice, he was dismissed for just four.

First Class Career:
Runs – 40,859. Average 48.93
(113 centuries)

Test Match Career:
Tests – 118
Runs – 8,900. Average 42.58
(20 centuries)

DAVID GOWER
England
Born 1957
Leicestershire and Hampshire

DAVID GOWER WAS England's most gifted batsman of recent years. Yet his apparently carefree approach to cricket and life in general contrasted sharply with the style of the England management in the early nineties, and his omission from the Test side provoked much controversy.

The announcement of Gower's retirement on 14th November 1993 at the age of 36 brought dismay to his many disciples, who still felt he was worth a place in the England side. Gower himself, having been omitted from the party to tour the West Indies in 1993/94, saw no way back, and felt he could no longer motivate himself for the more humdrum existence of county cricket with Hampshire.

Coming just months after a similar decision from another former England captain, Ian Botham, it seemed to mark the end of an era.

As a left-handed batsman, Gower always made the game appear easy when in full flow. But a lack of concentration and his susceptibility to edging the ball outside off-stump often turned watching such a gifted player into a frustrating experience.

For all that, he was England's most capped player with 117 Tests until Graham Gooch overtook him in his final Test in 1994/5. Gooch had also passed Gower as England's top run-scorer.

An outstanding schoolboy cricketer, Gower joined Leicestershire and in 1978 made his England debut against Pakistan, scoring 58 at Edgbaston. That same summer he made his first Test century against New Zealand at the Oval.

Having made a sparkling 200 not out against India in 1979, he then went through a lean spell and was left out against the West Indies in 1980. But he fought back and by 1982 was vice-captain of England.

He went on to lead his country against Pakistan that year, standing in for Bob Willis who was injured.

Gower's captaincy record in 32 Tests for England was a chequered one. A memorable 3–1 win over Australia in 1985 regained the Ashes, but he lost them in a 4–0 drubbing four years later.

He captained England in two series against rampant West Indies sides who inflicted 5–0 defeats, being perhaps unfortunate to lead a side that was no match for the finest team in the world.

However, his batting record speaks for itself. Apart from his Test

The young smoothie: Gower as Golden Boy of English cricket.

appearances, he also played in 114 one-day internationals, scoring 3,170 runs at an average of 30.77.

Having achieved, he felt, all he could at Leicestershire, Gower moved on to Hampshire in 1990, but his performances for his second county were for the most part modest.

As he reached the twilight of his career, it seemed that the more laid-back side of his character came to the fore. He got into trouble on the

1990/91 tour of Australia for an ill-advised plane trip with Derbyshire's John Morris, buzzing the field while his team-mates were struggling.

That action left him out in the cold, but he worked his way back into the Test side against Pakistan in 1992, when he passed Geoffrey Boycott's total as top England run-scorer with a typical flowing cover drive at Old Trafford. It was then that Gower was surprisingly left out of the party to tour India and Sri Lanka that winter.

His omission caused a storm of protest in the Press and among some MCC members, who forced the club to call an extraordinary meeting to express their displeasure.

There were more calls for his return to the Test team as England faced Australia in 1993, but to no avail. His non-selection for the West Indies tour the following winter was therefore not a surprise, but it sealed his decision to retire.

A great talent was therefore lost on the field, but his media interests ensure that David Gower will not be lost to cricket. He now enjoys a career in commentary and press boxes around the world.

First Class Career:
Runs – 26,339. Average 40.08
(53 centuries)
Catches – 280, 1 stumping

Test Match Career:
Tests – 117
Runs – 8,231. Average 44.25
(18 centuries)
Catches – 74

DR W.G. GRACE
England
Born 1848. Died 1915
Gloucestershire and London County

WITHOUT QUESTION, DR William Gilbert Grace is the most famous cricketer of all time. With that burly figure and thick beard, he was instantly recognisable.

It has been said that no one would ever stand ahead of W.G.

Grace in modern cricket because he was the man who created it. He was certainly far superior to his playing contemporaries, playing with enormous strength, albeit not always within the laws. But if he occasionally bent the rules, it was always with a chuckle.

Born in Gloucestershire, Grace was the fourth of five brothers who were all devoted to the game. He was just fifteen when he made his first major appearance, scoring 170 for South Wales against the Gentlemen of Sussex.

On his 56th birthday he scored his last century, the 126th of his career, making 166 for London County against the MCC.

W.G. set all kinds of records at a time when cricket was played on some particularly rough and dangerous wickets.

He had the longest continuous career in first-class cricket, 43 seasons. He became the first cricketer to do the 'double' (in 1873), to score 100 hundreds, to reach 50,000 runs and take 2,500 wickets. Twelve times he took ten or more wickets and scored a century in the same match.

He captained Gloucestershire for 25 years, leading them to the County Championship title on two occasions.

There was not a great deal of Test cricket played during Grace's career, and he was 32 before he first represented his country in the first Test to be played in England, scoring 152 at the Oval. His highest Test score came in 1886, 170 against Australia at the Oval.

Stories of his at times outrageous behaviour abound, and most are considered true. Opponents could be overawed by him. Once, when bowled in a minor match, he is said to have replaced the bails and carried on batting, contending that the crowd had come to see him bat, not see the bowler bowl.

He once declared for no apparent reason when just seven short of a century, explaining later that 93 was the one score between 0 and 100 he had never recorded.

His stature as a man and within the game can never be doubted. A

poster advertising a match once demanded an admission price of three pence, but added that this would be doubled to six pence if Grace was playing.

Grace died of a heart attack during an air raid in 1915. The gates erected in his memory at Lord's sum him up quite simply: 'W.G. Grace, the Great Cricketer 1848–1915.'

First Class Career:
Runs – 54,986. Average 39.45
(126 centuries)
Wickets – 2,876. Average 17.99

Test Match Career:
Tests – 22
Runs – 1,098. Average 32.29
(2 centuries)
Wickets – 9. Average 26.22

TOM GRAVENEY
England
Born 1927
Gloucestershire, Worcestershire and Queensland

FEW PLAYERS BROUGHT more style to the art of batting than Tom Graveney. A tall, right-handed middle-order batsman, he had a full array of shots, with his cover drive being right out of the textbook.

He was a prolific run-scorer, being the first exclusively post-war batsman to reach 100 centuries, and totalling more than 10,000 runs for two different counties.

Although he played 79 Tests for England, he was often left on the sidelines while apparently less able players were chosen. Selectors would sometimes see his easy style as reflecting a rather casual approach to the game.

Graveney was at his most successful against West Indies, both at home and abroad. In 1957 he scored 258 against them at Trent Bridge with England in trouble. In 1966 he was recalled to face West Indies again, scoring 459 in four Tests at an average of 76.50.

was spotted as an outstanding talent and the former England captain Ray Illingworth was keen to have him chosen for England.

Gordon chose instead to play for the West Indies and went on to play in 108 Tests at a time when the men from the Caribbean totally dominated international cricket.

Having represented Hampshire since 1970, Greenidge made his Test debut against India at Bangalore in 1974/75, making 93 and 107. He made 909 runs on the tour, and in England in 1976 made 592 runs in the Tests for an average of 65.77.

That series featured perhaps the best batting of his career. On a difficult wicket at Old Trafford he made a century in each innings, scoring 134 (out of a total of 211) and 101. In the next Test at Headingley he added another century.

He joined World Series Cricket but when he returned to the Test scene, although his batting was usually effective, he was often restricted by a growing number of injuries, mostly to his knees.

He could still compile big scores, however, as was evident on the 1984 tour of England when he made 214 not out off 242 balls to win the Lord's Test for West Indies. He also scored a patient 223 in ten hours when his side were in trouble at Old Trafford.

In all he scored 7,558 Test runs, the third highest in West Indies history behind Viv Richards and Gary Sobers. He shared record opening partnerships for West Indies with Haynes against England, Australia, New Zealand and India, and with Roy Fredericks against Pakistan. Greenidge was also formidable in one-day internationals, scoring 11 centuries.

He never enjoyed the same success against Australia, finding their bouncy pitches unsuited to his front-foot style of play. But he did make a fine century there, 111 in just two hours at Sydney in 1954.

Domestically, he captained Gloucestershire in 1959 and 1960, but an internal disagreement led to him joining Worcestershire where he led the side from 1968 to 1970.

Towards the end of his career he played and coached in Queensland, Australia, but later returned home where he became well known to cricket followers as an articulate broadcaster.

First Class Career:
*Runs – 47,793. Average 44.91
    (122 centuries)
Catches – 547. Stumping – 1*

Test Match Career:
*Tests – 79.
Runs – 4,882. Average 44.38
    (11 centuries)*

GORDON GREENIDGE
West Indies
*Born 1951
Barbados and Hampshire*

GORDON GREENIDGE, who might so easily have played for England, became one of the great post-war opening batsmen and with Desmond Haynes formed the most successful opening pair in Test cricket during the 1970s and 80s. Greenidge had all the natural flair and excitement of a West Indian batsman, and his many seasons with Hampshire ensured he also developed a sound technique which brought him thousands of runs in county cricket.

Greenidge came to England from Barbados with his family at the age of 12. Brought up in Reading, he

For Hampshire he formed what was at the time the best opening partnership in county cricket, with Barry Richards of South Africa. Greenidge was particularly effective in the Sunday League, scoring more than 6,000 runs including 11 hundreds.

He topped the national averages in England in 1986, scoring 2,035 runs at 67.85, including four successive hundreds.

First Class Career:
Runs – 37,354. Average 45.88
(92 centuries)

Test Match Career:
Tests – 108
Runs – 7,558. Average 44.72
(19 centuries)

TONY GREIG
England
Born 1946
Border, Eastern Province and Sussex

A GIANT OF A MAN AT SIX feet seven inches tall, Tony Greig was a fiercely combative cricketer and a very controversial one too.

Many in the establishment will never forgive him for the part he played in setting up World Series Cricket, which for a time took many of the world's most gifted players out of Test cricket. But he was a gifted player who brought a great sense of purpose to the job of England captain.

A handsome all-rounder, Greig was the son of a Scottish father and South African mother, and only came to live in England at the age of 20. In his first county appearance he saved Sussex from collapse, scoring 156 against Lancashire.

His career statistics illustrate perfectly his love of the big occasion, his Test batting average being better than his first-class one. Furthermore, many of his best innings were played away from England, in India, the West Indies and Australia.

He enjoyed an especially fine tour of the Caribbean in 1974, scoring two Test centuries and being the leading wicket-taker with 24 victims. But he also showed the ultra-competitive side of his nature when he ran out Alvin Kallicharran as the batsman walked off after the final ball of the day! Greig later apologised and Kallicharran was happily reinstated the following morning.

Greig could inspire a team both with deeds and words, although some of these came back to haunt

An attacking opening batsman of the highest class for Hampshire and West Indies, Gordon Greenidge played a fluent and exciting game when settled.

Greig leads England on a triumphant lap of honour after beating India at Madras in 1976/77. Just months later, he would face the full fury of the cricket establishment when his role in the setting-up of Kerry Packer's breakaway 'circus' was revealed.

him. Before the home series against the West Indies in 1976 he said England would make them grovel. The visitors took the series by three Tests to nil.

He had captained England fourteen times when in 1977 it was revealed that he had signed up as Kerry Packer's right-hand man in establishing World Series Cricket.

Greig had secretly travelled the world recruiting players, his own English colleagues among them. He knew the consequences: when the full extent of his involvement in the

'rebel circus' became apparent he was dismissed as captain of both England and Sussex.

He continued to play for England for a time under Mike Brearley's leadership, and in all played 58 times for his adopted country.

A wealthy man, Greig quit England in the late 1970s to live in Australia, where he built up an insurance company and became a television commentator.

First Class Career:
Runs – 16,660. Average 31.19 (26 centuries)
Wickets – 856. Average 28.85
Catches – 345

Test Match Career:
Tests – 58
Runs – 3,599. Average 40.43 (8 centuries)
Wickets – 141. Average 32.20
Catches – 87

CHARLIE GRIFFITH
West Indies
Born 1938
Barbados

CHARLIE GRIFFITH WAS, in his prime, just about the fiercest and fastest bowler in world cricket. He also had a reputation as a bad boy of the game.

Whatever headlines he made, one thing was inescapable: Griffith's partnership with Wesley Hall gave the West Indies a fearsome opening attack, and one which paved the way for the outstanding fast bowlers that have followed in their footsteps.

Surprisingly for such a big man, Griffith first came into the game as an off-spinner. Then he was asked to fill in as a fast bowler by his club side, took seven wickets for just one run, and a new West Indian legend was born.

Much controversy surrounded his action. Many judges considered he threw his faster ball, usually a yorker. He was called for throwing in a match in 1961/62 when India's captain, Nari Contractor, ducked into a bouncer and suffered a fractured skull.

Griffith was called on one other occasion in his career – by Arthur Fagg in a match against Lancashire at Old Trafford in 1966.

On his first tour of England in 1963 Griffith was often unplayable, taking 32 wickets in the Tests and 119 on the tour overall. He took eight wickets at Lord's in the exciting drawn second Test, and nine wickets at both Headingley and the Oval.

He was never as effective on his second tour of England in 1966, nor in subsequent series.

First Class Career:
Wickets – 332. Average 21.60

Test Match Career:
Tests – 28
Wickets – 94. Average 28.54

GUYANA

THE BOURDA GROUND AT Georgetown, Guyana, is home of Georgetown Cricket Club, the oldest in the Caribbean.

It is in many ways an extraordinary ground, being situated below sea level and surrounded by canals which provide much needed drainage. A big sea-wall does its best to keep the elements at bay.

The Guyana climate of heavy rainfall has had a big influence on matches at the ground over the years. In 1987 the outfield was raised six inches, with many tons of soil brought in, in an attempt to solve the problem.

However, the natural soil at the Bourda is ideally suited for preparing fine batting wickets and many good players have prospered there over the years.

Crowds in Guyana have always been vociferous and at times highly volatile. Play between the West Indies and England was halted for a time amid a barrage of bottles in 1954 when local wicket-keeper Cliff McWatt was given run out.

The greatest flare-up came in 1979, when Kerry Packer's World Series Cricket visited the ground for a 'Supertest'. The players' reluctance to perform on a wet outfield inflamed the crowd. Seats were hurled, fences were pulled down, and the pavilion invaded!

For all the good batting conditions, the West Indies record in Georgetown is not particularly impressive. The ground has a reputation for producing drawn Test matches.

The Bourda lived up to its reputation for rain in 1990 when the second Test of England's tour was washed out without a ball bowled. It followed the cancellation in 1980/81 of the previous Georgetown Test scheduled between the two countries, when England's Robin Jackman was refused entry to Guyana because of his South African connections.

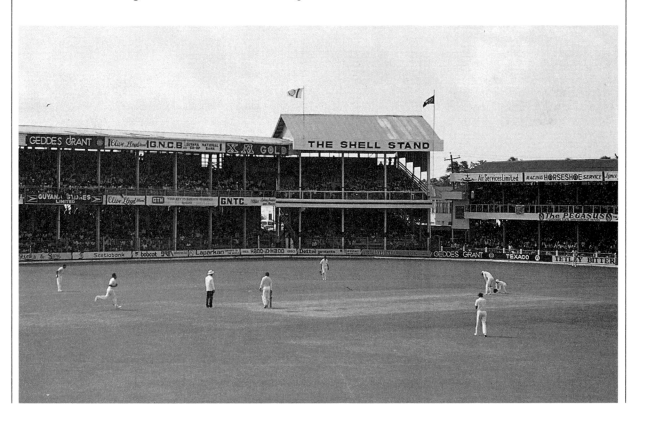

SIR RICHARD HADLEE

New Zealand

Born 1951
Canterbury, Nottinghamshire and Tasmania

SIR RICHARD HADLEE, knighted in the 1990 Birthday Honours, was the greatest player ever to represent New Zealand, one of the finest bowlers the game has seen, and until being overtaken by Kapil Dev of India, the highest wicket-taker in Test cricket.

He was noted for his economy of effort – a simple run to the wicket and a smooth, flowing action. Above all he was an intelligent bowler, who would study a batsman's weakness and invariably exploit it with his ability to move the ball through the air and off the seam.

As his Test career (1973–90) progressed, he also developed into a fine all-rounder, with his left-handed batting often coming to the aid of his side.

Only Botham, Kapil Dev and Imran Khan have matched his Test 'double' of scoring more than 3,000 runs and taking 300 wickets. No opponents could consider they were through the New Zealand batting until Hadlee had been removed.

Few would have anticipated his place in the record books when he first played for his country against Pakistan in February 1973. One of five sons of the New Zealand batsman Walter Hadlee, Richard was initially noted more for speed and inconsistency than accuracy.

He played just one Test on the 1973 tour of England, but by the time he next faced England at home in 1977/78 he was acknowledged as New Zealand's top bowler and one of the best in the world. In that series he took 15 wickets and his match figures of 10 for 100 were a telling factor in his country's first ever victory over England.

Other notable achievements during this period of his career were his 19 wickets in the victorious series against the West Indies in 1979/80. In the match that ultimately decided the series, Hadlee took 11 for 102 and scored 51 runs in the first innings. He scored his maiden Test century in the next match.

He shortened his run-up to the wicket in 1980 and his effectiveness throughout the decade increased as he continued to bowl fast and make the ball move.

In English domestic cricket he had joined Nottinghamshire in 1978 and was a regular wicket-taker. In 1981 Hadlee, with 105 wickets, helped bring the County Championship to Notts, admittedly on some very helpful Trent Bridge wickets.

In 1984, a year after he had suffered from exhaustion that came close to causing a nervous breakdown, he became the first man to do the double in England since 1967. He took 117 wickets at 14.05 and made 1,179 runs, including 210 not out against Middlesex, when he reached his

On New Zealand's tour of India in 1988/89, Hadlee (below) became the leading wicket-taker in Test cricket as he passed Ian Botham's total of 373.

century off 93 balls.

His Test career ended on 10th July 1990 at Edgbaston, after he had taken five wickets in an innings for the 36th time. His best innings analysis was 9 for 52 against Australia at Brisbane in 1985/86, his highest score 151 not out against Sri Lanka in 1986/87.

He was also effective in one-day cricket, taking 158 wickets in 115 international matches.

After his retirement, his growing health problems led to him needing open-heart surgery, after a serious attack. He has now recovered and is a well-respected guest at cricket grounds all over the world.

First Class Career:
Runs – 12,052. Average 31.71
(14 centuries)
Wickets – 1,490. Average 18.11

Test Match Career:
Tests – 86
Runs – 3,124. Average 27.16
(2 centuries)
Wickets – 431. Average 22.29

WESLEY HALL
West Indies
Born 1937
*Barbados, Trinidad and
Queensland*

A SUPERB ATHLETE, Wesley Hall was generally considered to be the fastest bowler in the world for a time in the 1960s. With Charlie Griffith at the other end, the pair provided a hostile and menacing opening attack that was exciting to watch – albeit not if you were the batsman.

At six foot two inches tall, Hall had a classical action. He was always hostile and wanted to take a wicket with every ball he bowled. But whereas Griffith had an image as the bad boy of the team, Hall was a popular man, always courteous.

Perhaps it was his friendly nature that led Ted Dexter to write that being hit by a ball from Wes Hall was never as painful as when it was delivered by some other bowlers.

Early in his career Hall was a wicket-keeper and batsman. He turned to fast bowling, but did not at first achieve great success. His breakthrough came on the tour of India and Pakistan in 1958/59 when he took 46 wickets from eight Tests.

He played a crucial part in the famous tied Test at Brisbane in 1960/61. With an over to go, Australia needed six to win with three wickets left. Hall took one wicket and there were two run-outs. Earlier in the game he had made a valuable fifty.

In 1963 at Lord's one of his deliveries broke Colin Cowdrey's arm in a match that could have had one of four results going into the final over and eventually ended as a draw. Hall bowled for three hours and twenty minutes unchanged to bring his side back into a game England looked like winning.

The popular West Indian played several seasons in the Lancashire League and also represented Queensland in the Sheffield Shield. Since his retirement, he has managed West Indies sides abroad, and was for a number of years a senator in the Barbados Parliament.

First Class Career:
Wickets – 546. Average 26.14

Test Match Career:
Tests – 48
Wickets – 192 wickets. Average 26.38

Hall's popularity and friendly nature belied the fact that he was a menacingly quick bowler. He is pictured here on tour in England in 1963.

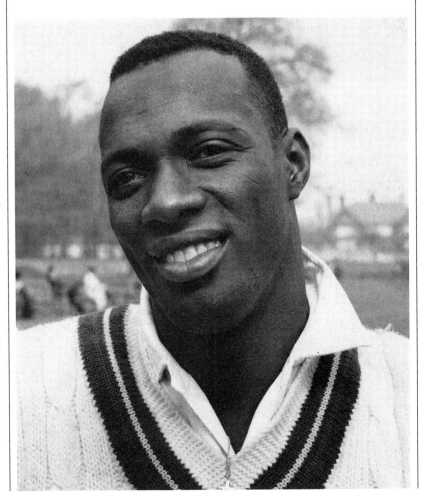

WALTER HAMMOND

England

Born 1903. Died 1965
Gloucestershire

WALLY HAMMOND WAS simply one of the finest batsmen ever to play for England, scoring more than 7,000 runs for his country at an average of 58.45 in his 85 Tests.

He was a forceful right-hand batsman, always keen to dominate a bowling attack. His career for both county and country featured many

Every schoolboy's hero,
Hammond goes out to bat for
England against Australia in the
first Test at Trent Bridge in 1930.

wonderful innings, but he was also a fast-medium bowler, taking 732 wickets in his first-class career.

In 1927 he reached 1,000 runs before the end of May, the first man to achieve that feat in the 20th century. Establishing himself in the England team, he enjoyed a particularly good tour of Australia in 1928/29 when he made more than 900 runs in the Tests for an average of 113.12.

In 1932/33 he made 336 not out against New Zealand at Auckland, which was the highest score in Tests until Len Hutton passed it in 1938. Hammond also scored six double centuries.

His form in home Tests was never quite so good, although his 240 against Australia at Lord's in 1938 was one of the best innings seen on the famous ground. He captained England in that series and also led

his country against South Africa, West Indies, New Zealand and India.

He retired from regular first-class cricket after leading England in Australia in 1946/47, where his form in the Tests never matched his record in other matches as England lost the series 3–0.

After finally retiring from cricket in 1951, Hammond went to live in South Africa where he died at the age of 62.

First Class Career:
Runs – 50,551. Average 56.10
   (167 centuries)
Wickets – 732. Average 30.58
Catches – 819. Stumpings – 3

Test Match Career:
Tests – 85
Runs – 7,249. Average 58.45
   (22 centuries)
Wickets – 83. Average 37.80
Catches – 110

HAMPSHIRE

Founded: 1863

Entered Official
Championship: 1895

Honours:
County Champions – 1961, 1973
NatWest Trophy – 1991
Benson and Hedges Cup – 1988,
   1992
John Player League – 1975, 1978,
   1986

OF HAMPSHIRE HAVE ONLY enjoyed modest success in the County Championship – just two titles in almost 100 years – they have at least had better fortune in one-day cricket, taking all three of the major trophies in the past ten years.

The county had enjoyed a reputation, until recent seasons, of having a side of talented players that should perhaps have won more. But at least their cricket has rarely been anything but entertaining.

The present county club was formed in 1863, and it was Clement Booth, as captain and secretary from 1875, who really laid the

foundations by improving the fixture list. He also created the conditions for first-class status that followed in 1894, when Hampshire played matches against Derbyshire, Essex, Leicestershire and Warwickshire.

The club joined the Championship a year later, winning their first match against Somerset and finishing a respectable tenth with a total of six wins.

The first few years of the 20th century saw Hampshire rooted to the bottom of the table. But things improved as one batsman in particular, Philip Mead, established himself in the side. Over thirty years from 1906 to 1936, Mead set records galore.

His 46,268 runs were the most ever made in county cricket. He was a steady accumulator rather than a flamboyant stroke-maker, his 132 centuries mostly being the result of great concentration and patience.

Mead's greatest seasons came after the First World War, when over a period of ten years he seven times averaged over 60 for the county.

Twice, in 1921 and 1928, he made more than 3,000 runs.

At this time Hampshire had fine bowlers in Jack Newman and Alec Kennedy, and the side was ably led by the Honourable Lionel (later Lord) Tennyson.

In 1922 Hampshire took part in one of the most remarkable games ever played. Replying to Warwickshire's first innings total of 223, they were bowled out for just 15. Following on 208 behind, they proceeded to make 521, with George Brown, a highly popular player, scoring 172, and wicket-keeper Walter Livsey, batting at number ten, 110 not out.

Needing 304 for victory, Warwickshire were then dismissed for 158, giving Hampshire an unlikely win by 155 runs.

Through the 1930s Hampshire were again one of the weaker sides, but after the Second World War Derek Shackleton came onto the scene. He was to become one of the leading English bowlers of the modern era.

Skipper Mark Nicholas shows how it feels after 25 years as Hampshire, in their first ever Lord's final, celebrate victory in the 1988 Benson & Hedges Cup.

Between 1948 and 1969 he took more than 2,500 wickets for the county at an average of just 18.12. Consistency was his greatest quality, some fine judges claiming he only bowled half a dozen bad balls a season. Certainly he would often tie the very best batsmen in knots, and it still seems hard to understand why he only won seven England caps over a period of twelve years.

In 1953 Roy Marshall, a West Indian, became registered. He was to become the second highest run-scorer in the county's history, with more than 27,000 to his name.

Five years later the flamboyant Colin Ingleby-MacKenzie took over as captain, and it was his ability to bring out the best in Shackleton, Marshall and others that brought

Hampshire their first County Championship title in 1961.

It proved to be a three-way contest, with Yorkshire and Middlesex also strongly in contention. Hampshire took over the lead on 1st August and exactly one month later they clinched the title. In all they won 19 of their 32 matches, five of them on the trot during those final few weeks.

Ingleby-MacKenzie had proved himself to be an astute captain. An experimental law abolishing the follow-on put a greater emphasis on the importance of well-timed declarations on the final day. Ten of Hampshire's victories came that way, conclusive proof of the captain's fine judgement.

Hampshire were unable to follow that with more success, although having thwarted Yorkshire's hopes of a hat-trick of title wins they did further add to the White Rose county's embarrassment in 1965, when they dismissed them for just 23, their lowest total ever.

The team was very different by the time Hampshire took their second title in 1973. Led by Richard Gilliat, a fine left-handed batsman, they were blessed with the talents of Barry Richards and Gordon Greenidge, a South African and a West Indian, as their opening pair. They could, when the mood took them, dominate any pace attack in the country.

Hampshire also had one of the world's fastest bowlers, Andy Roberts, from Antigua. Like Richards and Greenidge, he served the county well for many years.

Despite having such talented players, Hampshire were considered outsiders for the title, with the rest of the bowling attack rated no more than modest. But six wins in seven matches late in the season saw them home by 31 points from Surrey.

Their attempts to make it a double the following year were thwarted by the weather, as they lost five days' play in their last three matches and Worcestershire, enjoying better luck with the elements, pipped them by two points – frustration indeed.

Greater success in recent years has come in the one-day competitions. Hampshire took the John Player League in 1975 and again in 1978, this time without the services of Richards and Roberts, and made it a third triumph in 1986.

They finally put to rest their record of never having appeared in a Lord's one-day final when in 1988 Mark Nicholas, a captain in the Ingleby-MacKenzie/Gilliat mould, led them to victory over Derbyshire in the Benson and Hedges Cup.

Nicholas was to miss the triumph of their first NatWest Trophy win through injury in 1991. Instead, David Gower, the former England captain who had joined the county from Leicestershire, held the trophy aloft after a four-wickets win over Surrey.

But Nicholas was back the following year for further Benson and Hedges success as Hampshire overcame Kent to make it three successful Lord's finals in five years.

Hampshire's Championship form has remained disappointing, despite the talents of such players as Robin Smith and Shaun Udal.

HANIF MOHAMMAD
Pakistan
Born 1934
Bahawalpur and Pakistan International Airlines

HANIF WAS THE ELDEST and the most gifted of four cricket-playing brothers. A small right-hand batsman, he became a legend in his country, earning himself the nickname 'The Little Master' for his many run-scoring achievements.

Hanif was a talented stroke-maker, but many of his great innings came when Pakistan had their backs to the wall and needed him to drop anchor. Few were more successful at that task.

Two of his records stand out. In 1958/59, playing for Karachi, he made 499, the highest first-class score until Brian Lara made 501 for Warwickshire in 1994.

The previous year Hanif had recorded the longest time at the wicket, taking 16 hours and 10 minutes to score 337 in a Pakistan total of 657, after they had been forced to follow on by the West Indies.

Hanif made his Test debut as a seventeen-year-old and went on to play 55 times for his country, captaining them on 11 occasions. His final appearance against New Zealand in Karachi in 1969/70 saw him open the batting with his brother Sadiq, while a third brother, Mushtaq, was at number four. It was only the third time three brothers had played in the same Test.

After his retirement Hanif went on to become head of the Pakistan selectors.

First Class Career:
Runs – 17,059. Average 52.32 (55 centuries)

Test Match Career:
Tests – 55
Runs – 3,915. Average 43.98 (12 centuries)

Neil Harvey on tour in England in 1956. On his retirement, he was second only to Bradman in Test runs for Australia.

NEIL HARVEY

Australia

Born 1928

Victoria and New South Wales

THERE HAVE BEEN FEW better left-handed bats in the history of the game than Robert Neil Harvey. A small, neat player, he hit the ball with great power. He also displayed nimble footwork, a tactic he employed regularly when playing spin bowlers.

For the sixteen years after he made his Test debut against India in 1947, Harvey played in more Tests than any of his fellow countrymen, and only Bradman scored more runs.

Each time he stepped up a grade of cricket, he made spectacular progress. Centuries in his first club game and his first state game were followed by another in only his second Test match, against India.

The youngest member of the 1948 Australians in England, he scored a century in his first Test at Headingley. His best score against England was 167 at Melbourne in 1958/59. In all he faced England 37 times, scoring 2,416 runs at an average of 38.34.

In 1952/53 when South Africa toured Australia, Harvey beat a Bradman record by scoring 834 runs in the series, making four centuries including his highest Test score, 205 at Melbourne.

His highest first-class score was 231 not out for New South Wales against South Australia in 1962/63. His reputation for deep concentration and stamina are clear from his record of scoring seven double centuries in his career.

His Sheffield Shield record bears comparison with anyone. In 75 matches he made 5,853 runs at an average of 50.46. After his

retirement, he stayed involved with the game and was a Test selector.

First Class Career:
Runs – 21,699. Average 50.93
(67 centuries)

Test Match Career:
Tests – 79
Runs – 6,149. Average 48.42
(21 centuries)

DESMOND HAYNES

West Indies

Born 1956

Barbados and Middlesex

DESMOND HAYNES, A lively character with a cheerful smile, has been a stalwart of West Indies teams for more than fifteen years. With Gordon Greenidge, he formed a most formidable opening partnership that generally ensured the West Indies a sound start at a time when they dominated world cricket.

Less aggressive than Greenidge, Haynes nonetheless showed a solid technique early in his career and adapted easily to Test cricket when he succeeded Roy Fredericks in the West Indies team in 1977.

His Test career had only just begun when he joined World Series Cricket. But he returned to the fold and has been an indispensable part of the team, the rock on which many West Indies innings have been based.

From December 1979 until June 1988 Haynes played 72 consecutive Tests, and during that period he set record opening partnerships for the West Indies with Greenidge against

Desmond Haynes, a mainstay of the West Indies batting for more than a decade, in action in the final Test at the Oval in 1988 as England dance to his tune.

England, Australia, New Zealand and India. He also holds the record against South Africa with Phil Simmons, who succeeded Greenidge.

In more than 100 Tests Haynes has scored 7,000 runs, his highest score being 184 against England at Lord's in 1980. He has twice carried his bat through a West Indies innings, making 88 not out against Pakistan at Karachi in 1986/87 and 75 not out against England at the Oval in 1991.

He captained the West Indies, in the absence of Viv Richards, on the 1990/91 tour of Pakistan, when the three-Test series was shared.

He has played 25 World Cup matches, a West Indies record, and helped the side to victory over England at Lord's in 1979. He has appeared in more than 200 one-day internationals.

Haynes came into English county cricket comparatively late, joining Middlesex in 1989. He scored more than 2,000 runs in 1990, hitting eight hundreds including unbeaten double centuries against Essex and Sussex.

First Class Career:
Runs – 23,246. Average 46.30
(54 centuries)

Test Match Career:
Tests – 116
Runs – 7,487. Average 42.29
(18 centuries)

HEADINGLEY

TEST MATCHES IN Yorkshire have always been played at Headingley with just one exception – the 1902 Test between England and Australia which was played in Sheffield at Bramall Lane, which is now a football ground only.

The Headingley ground in Leeds, headquarters of the Yorkshire County Cricket Club, is owned by the Leeds Cricket, Football and Athletic Club, taking in the famous rugby league ground next door.

The main stand, which faces two

ways for cricket and rugby, is the centrepiece, with the rest of the ground giving a very open feel. The former players' pavilion, square of the wicket, is a modern building but with little character. It is now a hospitality area.

Headingley staged its first Test match in 1899, when for the first time a five-match series was played against Australia. With two Yorkshiremen in the side, Jackson and Browne – but no Rhodes – the match ended in a draw.

The Test wicket nowadays has the reputation of being a medium-pacer's delight, slow and low, that generally produces a finish within five days. It wasn't always like that, especially in Bradman's heyday, but the first example of a low-scoring encounter was as early as 1907.

Then, with scores of England 76 and 162, South Africa 110 and 75, victory was England's by 53 runs. Spin bowling was largely responsible on a sticky wicket. Despite the wet conditions for much of the game, there was much criticism of the pitch.

Botham's Test in 1981: Headingley witnessed a charmed innings in which he hit whatever Australia could throw at him – including this beamer from Geoff Lawson – and turned what seemed a certain innings defeat into the unlikeliest of wins for England.

Australia's comfortable victory in 1921 was a dramatic match, with a new England captain at the helm. Tennyson led a side showing seven changes, but split his hand stopping a hard hit. England also lost Hobbs, who went down with appendicitis on the first day.

The Test with Australia in 1930 will always be remembered for the arrival of Don Bradman at a ground he always found to his liking, making 936 runs at an average of 192.60 in six Test innings there.

Bradman, then just 21 years old, made a century before lunch, going on to make 309 in the day. He scored 304 in 1934, 103 and 16 in 1938, and 33 and 173 not out on his final appearance in 1948 when

Australia made 404 to win in 344 minutes, losing just three wickets in the process.

In 1951 Peter May made a century on his Test debut and the following year against India there was plenty to delight the home crowd.

Yorkshire's Hutton was appointed England's first regular professional captain, and Fred Trueman announced himself as a true international fast bowler by taking seven wickets in the match, including three in eight balls at the start of India's second innings which saw them reduced to 0 for 4.

After a previous ten fruitless attempts on the ground, England finally beat Australia in 1956, with Laker and Lock sharing eighteen wickets on a pitch that took spin after the first day.

The match also saw the return of Cyril Washbrook, a selector who had not played international cricket for five years. He was out just two short of his century.

There was more high scoring on the ground in 1965 when John Edrich made 310 not out against New Zealand, England's first triple century since Hutton in 1938. It also contained a record number of boundaries in a Test, 5 sixes and 52 fours.

In 1967 there was a furore as Geoffrey Boycott on his home ground took nine and a half hours to score 246 not out against India. His slowness cost him his place in the next Test.

But it was on the same ground in 1977 that Boycott delighted the locals with a great sense of timing to score his 100th first-class hundred in the Test against Australia.

The greatest Test match ever seen at Headingley, and arguably the greatest of all time, came in 1981. Following on 227 runs behind, England were quoted at 500 to 1 to beat Australia. No team in the 20th century had ever won a Test following on.

Ian Botham's innings of 149 not out, after England had been reduced to 135 for 7 in their second innings, gave them just the slightest chance, but it was still odds-on Australia, who needed a mere 130 for victory.

At 56 for 1 it seemed a formality, but then Bob Willis took charge. His 8 for 43 was a magnificent spell of bowling and England won an extraordinary game by eighteen runs.

GEORGE HEADLEY
West Indies
Born 1909. Died 1983
Jamaica

GEORGE HEADLEY WAS A fine right-handed batsman who quickly established a reputation as a player of the highest class. He had a wide variety of shots and his personality made him popular wherever he played. It was not for nothing that he earned the title 'The Black Bradman'.

He was simply the dominant player in West Indies cricket from the time he made his first-class debut for Jamaica. He had the option to study to become a dentist in the United States, but chose instead to play cricket.

He played his first Test for West Indies against England in 1929/30, immediately made his mark and dominated the series. He began with innings of 21 and 176 at Bridgetown, Barbados, then made centuries in both innings of the third Test as his side won for the first time. In the fourth Test he scored

Not the most elegant of strokes, perhaps, but four more runs for Headley on the West Indies' 1939 tour of England, on which he made 1745 runs at an average of 72.20. Cambridge University are the opponents.

223 in six hours when his team had been set 836 to win. He totalled 703 runs in the series at an average of 87.87.

He earned the 'Black Bradman' tag in Australia in 1930/31 when he made more than 1,000 runs on the tour, including two Test centuries.

The 1933 tour of England was another triumph for Headley, with seven centuries out of a total of 2,320 first-class runs.

His highest first-class score came in 1931/32 for Jamaica against Lord Tennyson's side as he made 344 not out. His highest Test score of 270 not out came against England at Kingston, Jamaica in 1934/35. His record breaking continued in Tests; one particular highlight was a century in each innings at Lord's in 1939.

He became the first black cricketer to captain the West Indies after the Second World War. Sadly, injuries were to plague his career thereafter, although he played his final Test against England in 1953/54 at almost 45 years of age, the oldest West Indian Test player.

His son Ron played for West Indies in two Tests, but was better known as a stalwart at Worcestershire for 16 years.

First Class Career:
Runs – 9,921. Average 69.86
(33 centuries)

Test Match Career:
Tests – 22
Runs – 2,190. Average 60.83
(10 centuries)

OMAR HENRY
South Africa

Born 1952

Western Province, Boland, Orange Free State and Scotland

OMAR HENRY MADE cricket history on 13th November 1992 when, as South Africa played their first Test match in the Republic for 22 years, he became his country's first non-white

Test cricketer. He also became South Africa's oldest Test debutant at 40.

Cricketing life in South Africa has not been easy for Henry. He turned his back on other coloured cricketers in 1976 and played alongside white men, suffering fifteen years of contempt from people of his own race.

As a fourteen-year-old he impressed the watching Basil D'Oliveira, and in his youth played his cricket under the Indian-dominated South African Cricket Board. But he fell out with the Board when he stopped at a whites sports ground to watch a match played by members of the South African Cricket Union.

That was against the Board's rules, and when he refused to

Henry: an historic selection.

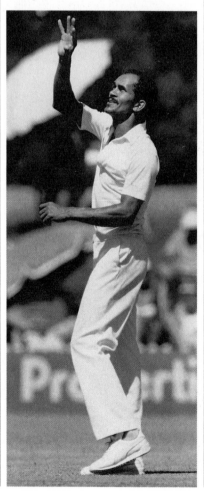

apologise he was prevented from playing with people of his own race. Forced to play with whites, he sometimes was not allowed to drink in the same bar as his team-mates, but nonetheless his ability was evident and he went on to play first-class cricket for Western Province.

He dropped down a grade to Boland, but then returned to the first-class game with Orange Free State in 1991. Away from South Africa, he spent ten years as a professional in Scottish League cricket, captaining Scotland in the NatWest Trophy and Benson & Hedges Cup.

In South Africa's rain-affected home return to Test cricket, Henry took 2 for 56 and made 3 runs. He was omitted in the next Test to make way for an extra batsman.

First Class Career:
Runs – 4,441. Average 28.65
(5 centuries)
Wickets – 434. Average 24.97

GRAEME HICK
England

Born 1966

Worcestershire

IT IS SOMETHING OF A mystery why a player as naturally gifted as Graeme Hick should have taken so long to come to terms with Test match cricket. However, after being given more chances than many, it seems he is at last establishing himself.

In addition to his batting, he is a brilliant slip fielder and a more than useful off-spinner who, to the frustration of the England selectors, does not get enough opportunity to bowl for his county.

Born in Harare, Zimbabwe, Hick made his first century at the age of seven in junior school. He went on to become a prolific run scorer in schools cricket and at the age of 17 he was selected for the Zimbabwe World Cup party in 1983.

The following year he went to Worcestershire on a cricket

scholarship and by the end of the season had already made his county debut, scoring 82. In 1985, playing for both his county and the

Hick's tribulations at Test level have tended to overshadow some remarkable performances in county cricket for Worcestershire, the highlight of which was his 405 against Somerset in 1988.

touring Zimbabweans, he scored 1,265 runs at an average of 52.70.

Back in Zimbabwe he set a remarkable record against the Irish touring team. He scored 155 not out in a one-day game, and then made 309 in less than seven hours in a three-day game.

By the end of 1986 Hick had decided to concentrate on qualifying to play Test cricket for England. During his five-year wait

he produced some wonderful performances with the bat, and it was assumed that he would step straight into the England side when his qualification was complete in 1991.

His most remarkable innings came in 1988 when he made 405 not out against Somerset at Taunton – the first man to make 400 in England this century. Twice, in 1987 and 1988, he was the leading run scorer in an English season.

But his Test career got off to a rocky start. Flaws in his game became exposed, particularly his discomfort in the face of short-pitched bowling. It seemed, after a torrid time against Australia, Pakistan and West Indies, that Hick might not make the grade at the highest level.

However, he began to improve on the otherwise unhappy 1992/93 tour of India, scoring his maiden Test century. He added a second against South Africa in the summer of 1994.

Against Australia in 1994/95, despite some lapses, he was enjoying a good tour until he succumbed to the injury jinx affecting the England team. A back injury forced him to return home early, ahead of the last two Tests.

First Class Career:
*Runs – 24,001. Average 57.42
(80 centuries)*

Test Match Career:
*Tests – 32
Runs – 1,933. Average 35.80
(2 centuries)
Wickets – 19. Average 51.21*

HISTORY

TRYING TO DEFINE JUST when the game of cricket began has proved a fruitless task for historians down the years.

Some say there are references to the Prince of Wales playing 'creag' during the time of Edward I. No one knows for sure, but people have probably been hitting a ball with

A modern reconstruction of 18th-century cricket, staged in period costume and using the old two-stumped wicket and wide-bottomed bat. The importance of a good eye for the ball, however, remains unchanged.

pieces of wood for centuries. Cricket almost certainly just evolved.

What is known is that from about the middle of the 16th century cricket was played at the Royal Free School of Guildford, in Surrey.

Not much information is available on the game in the 17th century but its popularity grew in the late 1600s, with the first eleven-a-side game documented as taking place in Sussex in 1697.

It appears that the Weald – Kent and Sussex – saw the development of the first cricket grounds, with the game spreading throughout England from there. The earliest known Laws were drawn up in 1744, although these are a revision of others long since lost.

Wherever the game may have begun, the village of Hambledon, in Hampshire, has always been considered the 'cradle' of cricket. The club on Broadhalfpenny Down was formed around 1750.

It seems extraordinary that in a time of poor transport, a small village, miles from anywhere, should have attracted the best cricketers in the land in the latter part of the 18th century.

Yet for about thirty years Hambledon was the centre of the cricket world, and it was there that the game was refined. The men of Hambledon regularly took on and beat the Rest of England.

In London, the Marylebone Cricket Club was formed in 1787 when Thomas Lord, a Yorkshireman, bought his first ground at Dorset Square. Almost at once the MCC took on the role of lawmakers and controllers of the game.

Lord's moved to North Bank in 1808, although the first ground was not vacated until two years later. The third ground to bear Lord's name, the present one at St John's Wood, was opened in 1814.

In the early 19th century three matches dominated the cricket season – Eton v Harrow, the Gentlemen v the Players, and the University fixture between Oxford and Cambridge. Those fixtures began to lose their glamour when touring began, leading to the start of Test match cricket.

Before that, however, the game had continued to move northwards through England and soon matches were being arranged between the counties. In 1846 William Clarke, creator of Trent Bridge, formed an All-England XI, composed of the best cricketers of the day.

At around this time came the formation of an annual county championship, at first on unofficial lines, before the official County Championship, as we know it today, began in 1890. Surrey were the first winners, although Yorkshire have won the title the most times.

The first overseas tour had taken place in September 1859 when George Parr led 12 players from England on a short visit to Canada and the United States. Australia, however, were keen to join in, and in 1861/62 the first English team toured 'down under'.

England have always been the initial trailblazers for cricket, making the first tours to South Africa, the West Indies, New Zealand, and many more countries.

The first Test match took place in March 1877, with Australia beating England by 45 runs at Melbourne. (By an amazing coincidence, the centenary Test between these oldest of rivals 100 years later produced exactly the same result.)

The administration of the world game remained with the MCC until 1909 when the first Imperial Cricket Conference met at Lord's, featuring the MCC, the Australian Board of Control, and the South African Cricket Association.

The West Indies, New Zealand and India joined in 1926, and in 1947 the ICC laid down the classification for first-class matches. Pakistan joined in 1952, Sri Lanka in 1981 and Zimbabwe in 1992. They are all full members of what is now the International Cricket Council.

Domestically, the MCC lost its power most obviously in 1968, with the formation of the Cricket Council. Under its umbrella, the Test and County Cricket Board was formed to administer first-class and minor counties cricket, and the National Cricket Association to look after the welfare of the game below that. The MCC is still the custodian of the laws.

Cricket is now an international game which has adapted to the modern age and the demands of the watching public and media. But every summer weekend, on village greens all over England, the spirit of Hambledon lives on.

SIR JACK HOBBS
England

Born 1882. Died 1963
Cambridgeshire and Surrey

THERE ARE MANY FINE judges who consider Hobbs, known to his contemporaries as 'The Master', to have been the greatest batsman that ever lived. He was also a delightful character, displaying charm, honesty and great dignity.

His batting seemed almost effortless, the cover drive being a particular favourite of his. He was also an occasional medium-pace bowler and brilliant cover-point fieldsman.

He enjoyed outstanding success, scoring more runs than anyone else (61,237), more centuries (197), and more seasonal totals of 2,000 runs or more (17). Yet for all that, he was no creature of statistics. He simply took each game and each innings as he found it.

The son of a groundsman at Fenners, Hobbs was recommended to Surrey by his boyhood idol Tom Hayward. In his first two matches for Surrey in 1905 he scored 88 and 105, and was immediately awarded his county cap.

From that time, his career fell into two sections. Before the First World War, he was a wonderfully attacking batsman, quick of foot, with the ability to pick up the line and length of the ball early. Even the finest bowlers found it hard to contain him.

After the war, at 36, by now a mature player, he tended to play

more off the back foot. His speed of thought, though, was still there, and it is interesting to note that 98 of his 197 centuries were scored after he had passed the age of forty.

He set records with a number of his partners. In Tests he shared 23 opening partnerships of over 100, eight with Wilfred Rhodes and fifteen with Herbert Sutcliffe. For Surrey, he shared 63 opening partnerships in three figures with Andrew Sandham.

Hobbs' modesty and good humour were never better

The Master at the wicket before the start of the 1930 season, his last as a Test player for England. The previous year he had become the first batsman to pass 5000 Test runs.

demonstrated than when he made his final first-class century, playing in a benefit match at the age of 51. He explained he had done it to keep warm on a bitterly cold day.

He was unfailingly courteous, posting handwritten replies to the

hundreds of letters he would receive from well-wishers and hero-worshipping schoolboys.

He enjoyed three benefit seasons with Surrey and used the proceeds to set up a well-known sports shop business in London. In 1953 he was knighted for his services to cricket, the first professional to be so honoured.

He died in 1963 just a few months after his wife Ada, whom he had nursed through the difficult last few years of her life. A man who inspired great affection, Sir Jack Hobbs will be remembered quite simply as one of the great legends of the game.

First Class Career:
Runs – 61,237. Average 50.65 (197 centuries)

Test Match Career:
*Tests – 61
Runs – 5,410. Average 56.94 (15 centuries)*

MICHAEL HOLDING

West Indies

Born 1954

Jamaica, Lancashire, Derbyshire, Tasmania and Canterbury

MICHAEL HOLDING WAS a man who made fast bowling look easy. One of the quickest bowlers of his generation, he had an effortless approach to the wicket, so light-footed and quiet that he was given the sobriquet 'Whispering Death'.

A natural athlete – he was a fine 400 metres runner – Holding operated in a quartet of fearsome West Indies 'quicks' which at

If anyone can be said to have made fast bowling look effortless, it was surely Holding, his beautifully smooth action generating fantastic pace. Geoff Boycott considered an over from Holding in the Caribbean to be the fastest piece of bowling he ever encountered.

various times during his Test career also included Andy Roberts, Joel Garner, Vanburn Holder, Wayne Daniel and Malcolm Marshall. Few batting line-ups could cope with such a non-stop barrage of pace.

Yet Holding made an inauspicious start to his Test career on the tour of Australia in 1975/76, taking no wickets in his first Test and only ten in the series at an average of 61.40.

In England in 1976, however, he took 55 wickets on the tour, 28 of them in Tests, when he averaged 12.71. He proved he could bowl in all conditions, taking 5 for 17 as England were dismissed for 71 on a difficult pitch at Old Trafford, and 14 for 149 on a hard, fast wicket at the Oval.

Throughout his career he always bowled at a distinctly lively pace, although he concentrated more on accuracy in his later years, coming in off a shorter run-up, often as first change.

He was generally a quiet man both on the field and off it, although he once showed unusual temper, kicking the stumps down when angered by the decisions of New Zealand umpires.

First Class Career:
Wickets – 778. Average 23.43

Test Match Career:
*Tests – 60
Wickets – 249. Average 23.68*

GEOFFREY HOWARTH

New Zealand

Born 1951

Northern Districts, Auckland and Surrey

THE YOUNGER OF TWO cricketing brothers, Geoff Howarth was a quality Test batsman who went on to become a successful New Zealand captain.

A right-handed middle-order bat, he would often open in one-day cricket. He was particularly strong driving through the covers.

After representing the New

Howarth defies England in the final Test at Lord's in 1978; he made a century in both innings.

Zealand Under-23 side, Howarth joined Surrey in 1969. He was a consistent run-scorer in the 1970s and went on to become county captain in 1984.

He first represented his country in 1974/75 in a series against England. But it was not until 1978 against the same opponents that he truly came of age, scoring 122 and 102 to save his side and becoming only the second New Zealander to score two centuries in a Test.

From then on he flourished. He captained his country against the West Indies in 1980, a series New Zealand won, and that same year he led Northern Districts to a Shell Trophy/Shell Cup double.

Howarth also captained New Zealand on such memorable occasions as their win over Australia in 1981/82 and first victory in England in 1983.

His career ended on a sad note in 1985. Although still captain of Surrey, he was not selected for any Championship matches; nor did he ever lead his country again. He went on to become the New Zealand team manager, relinquishing the position in 1994/95.

First Class Career:
Runs – 17,294. Average 31.90
(32 centuries)

Test Match Career:
Tests – 47
Runs – 2,531. Average 32.44
(6 centuries)

KIM HUGHES
Australia
Born 1954
Western Australia

KIM HUGHES WAS A stylish right-handed batsman who had the distinction of captaining his country at just 25 years of age, after only eleven Tests. He had the misfortune to be at the helm during several difficult overseas tours, but nevertheless generally acquitted himself well with the bat.

Hughes first appeared for Western Australia in 1975/76, but despite being chosen for two tours, it wasn't until the 1978/79 Ashes series that he established himself in the Australian side. He scored a century at Brisbane to bring a degree of respectability to a poor Australian performance.

Hughes took over the captaincy from Graham Yallop at the end of the season. He led his country in the 1979 World Cup in England and on the tour of India later that year. Although Australia lost that series, Hughes had shown himself to be a man who could lead by example, scoring 594 Test runs including a century at Madras.

Greg Chappell took over the captaincy on his return from World Series Cricket, but Hughes continued to record big scores, making 117 and 84 in the Centenary Test at Lord's in 1980 and 213 against India at Adelaide.

Hughes resumed the captaincy when Chappell decided not to tour England in 1981. Despite a win for Australia in the first Test, Hughes had wretched luck as Ian Botham enjoyed an inspired summer to take England to victory by three matches to one.

From then on Hughes seemed to alternate captaincy duties with Chappell. He was at the helm during a dreadful tour of the West Indies when Australia were whitewashed 3–0, and after losing the first two Tests against them at home in 1984/85 Hughes tearfully resigned the captaincy.

As his form with the bat disappeared he was dropped from the team, and he chose to lead an unofficial team to South Africa in 1985/86.

First Class Career:
Runs – 10,810. Average 38.19
(24 centuries)

Test Match Career:
Tests – 70
Runs – 4,415. Average 37.41
(9 centuries)

'I had no idea you were a religious man, skipper.'
'I'm not, but with Botham in this mood . . .'
Hughes (left) and Mike Whitney look for some inspiration during the Ashes tour in 1981.

SIR LEN HUTTON
England
Born 1916. Died 1990
Yorkshire

SIR LEN HUTTON'S career as a batsman and captain of England was one of almost non-stop success. Once over the disappointment of making 0 and 1 on his Test debut, he went from strength to strength and became a major British sporting hero of the post-war years.

He will best be remembered for two particular achievements. At the Oval in 1938 he made 364, then a Test record and still a record score for England v Australia matches. Then as the first professional to be

● THE GUINNESS

Hutton looks back to his best form as he goes for a big hit in the final Test against Australia at the Oval in 1948. He made a brave recovery from a wartime injury and went on to become the first professional to lead England.

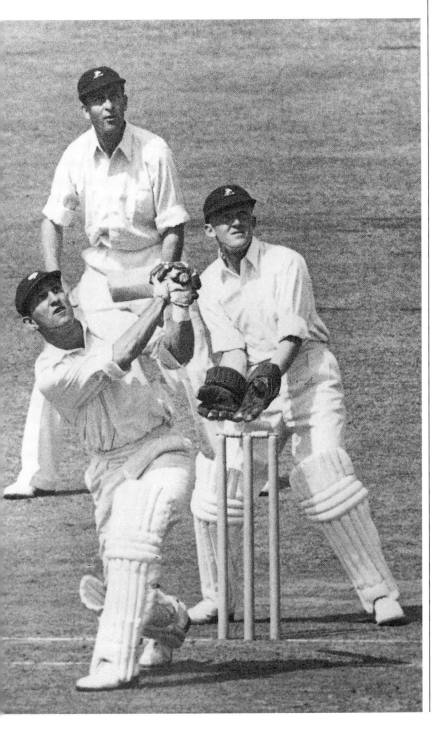

regularly appointed captain of England, he won back the Ashes after twenty years in Coronation Year, 1953.

Sir Len displayed true Yorkshire characteristics in his play. Concentration and a stylish range of shots marked his game. He was never one to take risks, but could play defensively or give full rein to his strokes as the occasion demanded.

After that poor start in the Test arena against New Zealand in 1937, he made a century in the next match. Then in 1938 he averaged 118.25 against the Australians, and 96.00 against West Indies the following year.

A wartime injury and subsequent operation resulted in his left arm being shorter than his right. But after taking some time to adjust, he continued to flourish. He and Denis Compton became the mainstays of the England batting, their success sometimes masking a fragile line-up.

In Australia in 1950/51 Hutton was far and away the best batsman on either side, averaging 88.83, a full 50 more than the next English batsman.

In 1953 he captained England to that Ashes success. It was a memorable season, and Hutton led the side unobtrusively and yet with great skill both on and off the field, at a time when there was still considerable snobbery in England at having a professional at the helm.

He retained the Ashes in Australia in the 1954/55 series despite the setback of a heavy defeat in the first Test.

He captained his country in 23 Tests in all, winning 11 of them and losing only four. He never lost a rubber.

In domestic cricket, he holds the record for the highest number of runs scored in a single month: 1,294 in June 1949, a figure that included three successive ducks!

After his retirement he became a successful businessman and was, for a time, a selector. His son Richard, a fast-medium bowler and right-hand bat, played five times for England.

First Class Career:
Runs – 40,140. Average 55.15
(129 centuries)

Test Match Career:
Tests – 79
Runs – 6,971. Average 56.67
(19 centuries)

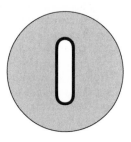

RAYMOND ILLINGWORTH

England

Born 1932
Yorkshire and Leicestershire

RAYMOND ILLINGWORTH has joined the few who, after being captain of England, have gone on to become chairman of selectors. Typical of the Yorkshireman that he is, his thoughts on the state of the team he chooses are never less than forthright. Now, as team manager too, he is unquestionably the most powerful figure in English cricket.

He became captain of England at a time of life when most players would have thought about retiring. But after a distinguished career as an all-rounder in county cricket, he surprised many people by improving as a player under the burden of leading his country – a rare achievement indeed.

He was never an outstanding player, but was an accurate off-spinner, steady lower middle-order batsman and sound fielder.

He spent 18 years with his native Yorkshire, playing occasionally for England, before moving to Leicestershire and taking up the captaincy in 1969, a year that was to be the start of virtually a second career.

It was in that same year that he took over the England leadership from the injured Colin Cowdrey, originally just as a stop-gap. So shrewd and successful was Illingworth, however, that he went on

to captain his country in 31 Tests, as well as five matches against the Rest of the World when the series against South Africa was cancelled in 1970.

His greatest achievement was to regain the Ashes in Australia in 1970/71 by two matches to nil and then retain them in a shared series in England in 1972.

His best batting for England came in 1969 when he made 113 against the West Indies at Lord's. His best bowling figures were 6 for 29 against India two years earlier.

His success as a captain continued in county cricket, as he led Leicestershire to the Championship in 1975 as well as four other major trophies.

On his retirement from the game he became manager of Yorkshire in 1979, but became sucked into the internal squabbling that bedevilled the county. In 1982, at the age of fifty, he returned to action as captain.

Although under his leadership Yorkshire finished bottom of the Championship table the following

year, they did manage to record their first triumph for 14 years, winning the Sunday League.

In 1986 Illingworth was offered the job of England team manager but turned it down. He became a BBC television commentator, but eight years on he took over from Ted Dexter as chairman of selectors. In March 1995 he added the manager's role after Keith Fletcher was dismissed.

First Class Career:
Runs – 24,134. Average 28.06
(22 centuries)
Wickets – 2,072. Average 20.28

Test Match Career:
Tests – 61
Runs – 1,836. Average 23.24
(2 centuries)
Wickets – 122. Average 31.20

A canny tactician and a great motivator of his players, Illingworth enjoyed a fine record as captain of England.

IMRAN KHAN

Pakistan

Born 1952
Lahore, Pakistan International Airways, Oxford University, Worcestershire, Sussex and New South Wales

IMRAN KHAN WAS THE inspirational all-rounder who led Pakistan to their greatest moment in international cricket, victory in the 1992 World Cup in Australia.

Considered to be one of the world's most eligible bachelors, Imran was always more than just one of the greatest all-rounders the game has seen. He was also a widely respected captain and a unifying force in a country where internal divisions have become a part of cricket.

Imran was best known for his bowling. He was genuinely fast and able to maintain that pace in long spells. His batting, usually at number five or six, was invariably aggressive, and he was always keen to dominate a bowling attack.

He won blues at Oxford University between 1973 and 1975, having first played county cricket for Worcestershire in 1971. He was

made a record 28 World Cup appearances, he and Javed Miandad being the only men to play in all of the first five tournaments.

The World Cup victory in Melbourne on 25th March 1992 was, according to Imran, his finest hour. His innings of 72 was the top score in the final against England, and it was his canny leadership that had steered Pakistan through some erratic early performances to ultimate success.

First Class Career:
Runs – 17,771. Average 36.79 (30 centuries)
Wickets – 1,287. Average 22.32

Test Match Career:
Tests – 88
Runs – 3,807. Average 37.69 (6 centuries)
Wickets – 362. Average 22.81

INDIA

THERE IS A DEPTH AND intensity to the passion for cricket in India that is quite unique. In the major cities such as Bombay, Madras and Calcutta, Test matches and one-day internationals attract huge, noisy crowds.

Broadcasts of those matches on television and radio are heard by millions all over the country, and throughout India the leading players are nothing less than national heroes. Cricket offers them the chance of rising to a degree of status and wealth most can only dream of.

Little wonder then that there is such a ready supply of youngsters keen to make their way in the game. They dream of glory at cricket in the same way as do the youth of South America of success on the football field.

capped in 1976 but moved to Sussex the following season and helped his second county to Gillette and NatWest trophies.

He first played for Pakistan in 1971 and toured England, Australia, New Zealand and the West Indies before joining World Series Cricket.

In 1982/83 he took 40 wickets in a six-Test series against India. The previous year he had returned his best Test match analysis of 14 for 116 against Sri Lanka at Lahore.

However, a stress fracture to his left leg stopped him from bowling in Tests for three years in the mid-1980s – otherwise his total of 362 Test wickets, at an average of

22.81, would have been much higher.

The doubts over his fitness led to trouble within Pakistan, as Zaheer Abbas was chosen to lead the touring party to Australia in 1983/84. The president of the Pakistan Board overturned the decision, the selectors were sacked and Imran was reinstated.

It was a gamble that failed. Imran did not play until the fourth Test, when he returned to score 83 and 72 not out.

In all he captained Pakistan in 48 Tests, a record only surpassed by Allan Border of Australia and Clive Lloyd of West Indies. Imran also

The Indian team celebrate a landmark victory over England at Bombay in 1992/93; it completed a clean sweep of three wins in the series.

Cricketing links between England and India run deep, with a number of England captains having been born there, among them Douglas Jardine and Colin Cowdrey.

The game began to be played in India as early as the late 18th century, taken there by the British. The Calcutta Cricket Club was formed as early as 1792 on the site of Eden Gardens.

But at this time the game was played almost exclusively by the English, the local population showing little interest.

The game was transported to Bombay a few years later, and it was here that the native Indians began to take up the game. In 1848 the first Indian club, the Orient, was formed, and with equipment in short supply they were forced to use old gear supplied by their colonial masters.

India joined the ranks of the Test-playing nations in May 1926, at the same time as the West Indies and New Zealand. Before then, some notable players from India had represented England.

Ranjitsinhji was selected for England to face Australia at Old Trafford in 1896 and made a superb 154 not out. He became a prince in Nawanagar and, coupled with the loss of an eye in a shooting accident, was thus prevented from playing as much as he might have done in later years.

But Ranji had created enormous interest in the game and had set a path that was to be followed by two other Indian princes, his nephew Duleepsinhji and the Nawab of Pataudi.

Coaches were recruited from England to take the game to a population which was by now becoming engrossed. Teams were generally formed on religious lines. The Parsees had led the way, and Hindus joined the Europeans to make a triangular tournament in 1907. The Mohammedans followed five years later. Even Jews and

Christians joined forces to field a side known as the Rest.

It was not until six years after their election to the Imperial Cricket Conference, as it then was, that India played their first Test match. The delay was partly due to the time taken to form the Indian Board of Control.

At Lord's in 1932 India lost that initial Test, but only after causing England some embarrassment for a time.

It was after that first Test that a national competition was formed in India, not surprisingly along similar lines to the County Championship.

While Indian standards took time to improve, England held the upper hand in Tests between the two countries, India having to wait until the drawn series of 1951/52 to register their historic first Test victory. It may have been a long wait, but when that win came, it came in emphatic style.

It was in the fifth Test at Madras that India enjoyed that historic moment, beating England by an innings and eight runs, thanks to centuries from Roy and Umrigar, and twelve wickets in the match by Vinoo Mankad.

Their first series win came against the England tourists a decade later. The visiting side, led by Ted Dexter, was not as strong as it might have been, with many fast bowlers unavailable.

The younger Nawab of Pataudi then took over as captain of the side throughout most of the 1960s, and although hampered by being almost blind in one eye as the result of a car accident, he still managed to play several notable innings.

When Ajit Wadekar succeeded him, it also heralded the start of the career of Sunil Gavaskar, an opening batsman who was to become the leading run-scorer in Test cricket until Australia's Allan Border passed his total in 1993.

It was Wadekar's leadership and Gavaskar's heavy scoring that paved the way for India's first series win in England with victory at the Oval in 1971. The Indians also won the next series between the two at home in 1972/73.

India have won just one series against Australia, in 1979/80, and two against the West Indies, in 1970/71 and 1978/79.

Perhaps their finest hour in international cricket came in 1983, when their young all-rounder Kapil Dev led them to victory over the West Indies in the World Cup final. The men from the Caribbean were firm favourites, especially after India could only manage 183 batting first.

But the team quoted at 66 to 1 before the start of the tournament pulled off a great shock, dismissing the West Indies for 140 to claim victory by 43 runs.

Kapil Dev became a national hero, and by the time he announced his retirement from the game in November 1994 he had become the leading wicket-taker in Test cricket, his 434 wickets beating Sir Richard Hadlee's record.

Not surprisingly, in a country of great traditions, India's major domestic competition is named after one of their greatest players, albeit representing another country – the Ranji Trophy. The other senior competition is the Duleep Trophy.

INDIA
V
PAKISTAN

CLOSE NEIGHBOURS THEY may be, but cricketing relations between India and Pakistan have inevitably been affected by wars and regular bouts of tension between the two countries.

Given the generally slow wickets in both countries, it is perhaps not surprising that the most notable feature of matches between them has been the number of draws – 33 out of 44 Tests played.

Pakistan made their first Test appearance against India in New Delhi in 1952/53. The game marked the debut, at the age of 17 years and 300 days, of the man who was to dominate Pakistani batting in the country's formative years, Hanif Mohammad. He was his country's top scorer with just 51 as India won easily by an innings and 70 runs.

Somewhat surprisingly, Pakistan hit straight back in the next Test at Lucknow. Fazal Mahmood, for years Pakistan's leading fast bowler, took twelve wickets in the match as India were twice dismissed for under 200, giving the visitors a win by an innings and 43 runs.

India won the third Test in Bombay to take the series, with the final two Tests being drawn.

The first series in Pakistan in 1954/55 ended in a dull stalemate, with all five Tests being drawn, the first time that had happened in Test cricket. Neither side seemed willing to chance their arm to force a result.

A similar outcome followed in India in 1960/61, with the same defensive attitudes being displayed. Pakistan batted first in four of the five Tests and their slow scoring was never likely to set up a result. It meant the countries had played out 12 consecutive draws.

Two wars and continuing bad feeling meant that no cricket was then played between the two for seventeen years. Test cricket restarted in 1978/79 when India made a three-Test tour, only to find

Pakistan a class above them.

A high-scoring draw at Faisalabad was followed by two eight-wicket wins for Pakistan at Lahore and Karachi. Pakistan's success owed much to the batting of Zaheer Abbas and Javed Miandad, who both averaged over 100, and the fast bowling of Sarfraz Nawaz and Imran Khan.

India replied with a 2–0 win at home in 1979/80. Four of the six matches were drawn, but it was the Indian batsmen Gavaskar and Vengsarkar who laid the platform for victory. The series was most notable, however, for the all-round contribution of Kapil Dev, who took 32 wickets at an average of 17.68 and scored 278 runs at 30.88.

Back on their own wickets in 1982/83, Pakistan assumed dominance again with a 3–0 win in another six-Test series.

Three of their batsmen, Zaheer, Mudassar Nazar and Javed, averaged more than 100, but it was again the bowling of Sarfraz and Imran that turned the series. Imran in particular was outstanding, taking 40 wickets at an average of 13.95.

Since that series, however, drawn matches have again dominated proceedings.

After three draws in India in 1983/84, there followed two more in Pakistan the following season. India made much of what they saw as bad umpiring decisions being given against them, and a number of players showed dissent when given out.

After four dull draws in the series in India in 1986/87 the sequence ended with an exciting fifth Test, when, in a low scoring game in which only Gavaskar truly mastered

Season	Ven	Tests	Winners	Res
1952/53	Ind	5	India	2–1
1954/55	Pak	5	–	0–0
1960/61	Ind	5	–	0–0
1978/79	Pak	3	Pakistan	2–0
1979/80	Ind	6	India	2–0
1982/83	Pak	6	Pakistan	3–0
1983/84	Ind	3	–	0–0
1984/85	Pak	2	–	0–0
1986/87	Ind	5	Pakistan	1–0
1989/90	Pak	4	–	0–0

Indian skipper Azharuddin welcomes his Zimbabwean counterpart David Houghton to Test cricket in 1992/93.

INDIA
V
ZIMBABWE

ZIMBABWE MADE THEIR entrance into the Test arena with a single Test against India at Harare Sports Club on 18th October 1992.

They proved themselves able to handle the big occasion, having the better of a draw which saw their captain David Houghton score his country's first Test century. The wily bowling of John Traicos, who had played three Tests for South Africa in 1969/70, accounted for five Indian wickets.

Their next meeting at Delhi was a different story, with India winning by an innings and 13 runs thanks to a formidable first innings total of 536 for 7, with Kambli making 227, his second successive Test double hundred.

Zimbabwe looked to have safely negotiated a draw but then lost seven wickets for 75 runs as they crashed to defeat. Kumble took eight wickets in the match to give him 53 in ten Tests, the fastest any Indian bowler has reached the 50-wicket mark.

Season	Ven	Tests	Winners	Res
1992/93	Zim	1	–	0–0
1992/93	Ind	1	India	1–0

INTERNATIONAL
CRICKET COUNCIL

AS THE GOVERNING BODY of world cricket, the International Cricket Council (ICC) has had to face many difficult decisions in recent years amid mounting criticism of its actions.

The ICC's origins derive from a meeting at Lord's in July 1909, when representatives from England, Australia and South Africa formed the Imperial Cricket Conference. They agreed a principle of

the conditions, Pakistan scraped home by 16 runs to win their first series in India.

Their next meeting in Pakistan in 1989/90 continued the pattern, with all four matches being drawn.

INDIA
V
SRI LANKA

INDIA HAVE FOR THE MOST part held the upper hand over their close neighbours, but Sri Lanka have at least recorded one memorable series win.

The first Test in 1982/83 was an evenly poised draw. India, needing 175 to win, finished on 135 for 7.

The first three-match series, in Sri Lanka in 1985/86, produced the home side's first ever victory in a Test rubber. The deciding win came at Colombo where the bowling of Ratnayake, who took nine wickets, was the telling factor. Sri Lanka's first Test victory had come in their fourteenth Test, less than five years after they had been granted full Test status.

The following season in India, however, saw a different story. Rain caused the first Test to be drawn, but the home side then went on to win the remaining two by an innings. India's varied bowling attack and the powerful batting of Kapil Dev and Vengsarkar proved too strong for the Sri Lankans.

India have continued to dominate meetings between the two ever since; in the most recent series, in 1994 on home soil, they won all three matches by an innings. The final Test of that rubber saw Kapil Dev, in his 130th match, pass Sir Richard Hadlee's record for most Test wickets.

Season	Ven	Tests	Winners	Res
1982/83	Ind	1	–	0–0
1985/86	SL	3	Sri Lanka	1–0
1986/87	Ind	3	India	2–0
1990/91	Ind	1	India	1–0
1993/94	SL	3	India	1–0
1993/94	Ind	3	India	3–0

'triangular' Tests, as well as details concerning the appointment of umpires, the hours of play and the rules for playing qualification.

Three years later, the triangular Tests idea was opposed by Australia and it was agreed that visiting teams should receive half of the gate receipts.

India, New Zealand and the West Indies were elected to the Conference in 1926, Pakistan in 1952, Sri Lanka in 1981 and Zimbabwe in 1992. South Africa ceased to be a member on leaving the British Commonwealth in 1961, but was elected a full member again in 1991.

In 1965 the word Imperial was changed to International, with new rules adopted to permit the admission of countries outside the British Commonwealth. This led to a new category of Associate Members being established, each having one vote. The Conference was later renamed the International Cricket Council in 1989.

Now there are four categories of membership. Australia and the United Kingdom are the senior figures as Foundation Members and the other Test-playing countries are Full Members. Countries where cricket is firmly established as a sport, from Denmark to West Africa, Argentina to Bangladesh, are classified as Associate Members. Countries where the game is simply played in accordance with the laws are recognised as Affiliate Members but have no voting rights.

Between 1959 and 1963, two of the most difficult issues which had to be dealt with were the no-balling problem of bowlers 'dragging' their feet, and the explosive issue of throwing, while the problem of South Africa and its eventual isolation from the Test match scene frequently dominated meetings in the 1960s and 1970s .

Perhaps the ICC's biggest crisis, however, was over World Series Cricket, the Packer Affair, when Australian media tycoon Kerry Packer signed up the top players around the world to take part in his 'circus'.

The ICC's attempts to impose its authority and ban Packer players were thrown out of court on the grounds of restraint of trade. This cost the ICC a great deal, both financially and morally, but later links were made with the Packer organisation and peace eventually returned as World Series Cricket folded.

More recently the ICC has failed to reach agreement on a number of major problems, with countries unwilling to put aside vested interests for the good of the game overall. It faces an uphill task to re-establish its credibility with administrators and cricket followers around the world.

INTIKHAB ALAM
Pakistan
Born 1941
Karachi, Pakistan International Airlines and Surrey

INTIKHAB ALAM, 'INTI' TO everyone in the game, was a crowd pleaser in all senses. A high class leg-spin and googly bowler, he was also a remarkably hard-hitting batsman, often going in at number 7 or 8.

He was playing first-class cricket for Karachi before his seventeenth birthday and enjoyed a long career, spanning 24 years.

His Test career began in encouraging fashion in 1959 when he took the wicket of Australia's Colin McDonald with his first ball. He struggled to establish himself in the Pakistan side, however, and it wasn't until 1964/65, when he took 7 for 92 against New Zealand at Karachi, that he really proved his worth.

Fielders could expect sore hands when Intikhab held a bat, but he could defend too, and his 51 in a stand of 190 with Asif Iqbal against England at the Oval in 1967 became the highest ninth-wicket stand in Test cricket.

Intikhab captained his country to their first overseas series win against New Zealand in 1972/73,

and in March 1973 he made his highest Test score and only century, 138 against England at Hyderabad. He also took seven wickets in the match.

In England he was a popular member of the Surrey team from 1969 to 1981, helping the county to Championship success in 1971.

A year after leaving Surrey he became the manager of Pakistan, and with Imran Khan as captain the Pakistanis achieved great success.

Intikhab was also in charge of the 1992 side in England, a difficult and bad-tempered tour that tried his easy-going manner to the full.

First Class Career:
Runs – 14,331. Average 22.14
(9 centuries)
Wickets – 1,571. Average 27.67

Test Match Career:
Tests – 47
Runs – 1,493. Average 22.28
(1 century)
Wickets – 125. Average 35.95

A familiar face in Pakistani cricket both as player and administrator, Intikhab's diplomatic skills have been called upon on more than one occasion.

JAMAICA

SABINA PARK IN Kingston, Jamaica, will forever be remembered as the ground on which Sir Garfield Sobers beat Sir Len Hutton's individual Test record in scoring 365 not out against Pakistan.

The home of Kingston Cricket Club, Sabina Park is a small ground with particularly short straight boundaries. It is a venue that generates plenty of noise and atmosphere and tests a player's nerves to the utmost.

The outstanding feature of the ground is the enormous grandstand at the southern end, named after the island's greatest player and best loved son, the great George Headley.

Sabina Park used to have the reputation of being the fastest and truest of all wickets in the West Indies. The pitch was relaid in 1968, however, and now it is slower and of much more uneven bounce. Nonetheless, West Indies teams still manage to amass big totals there.

Apart from Sobers, who scored five of his 26 Test centuries there, the only other man to score a triple century on the ground has been the Surrey and England batsman Andrew Sandham. His marathon

A fine study of Test cricket at Sabina Park, taken on England's 1990 tour.

THE GUINNESS

effort of 325 was part of England's 849 in the inaugural Test at Sabina Park in 1930.

There have been some memorable bowling achievements too: Trevor Bailey's 7 for 34 destroyed the West Indies batting in 1954, John Snow returned memorable figures of 7 for 49 in 1968, and Patrick Patterson took seven wickets on his debut for West Indies against England in 1986.

But it was Wesley Hall who extracted most from the pitch. His five Tests on the ground netted him 35 wickets at an average of 15.25.

JAVED MIANDAD
Pakistan
Born 1957
Karachi, Sind, Sussex, BHL and Glamorgan

THERE ARE FEW BETTER, more aggressive or more controversial batsmen in world cricket than Javed Miandad. He is currently the fourth highest run-scorer in Test cricket behind Allan Border, Sunil Gavaskar and Graham

Gooch, and may yet go on to overtake them all.

There are few finer sights on a cricket field than Javed at the wicket in full flow. In common with other top Pakistani batsmen, he is a wristy player and fine square cutter.

His volatile temperament has often landed him in trouble. He has rowed with the authorities in Pakistan, and has resigned the captaincy more than once. He has also been involved in a number of flare-ups on the pitch, most notably with Dennis Lillee in Australia in 1981/82, and Mike Gatting after being given out lbw during a World Cup match.

For all that, there is no denying his wonderful ability. He made his first-class debut at the age of sixteen and a half, and his Test debut in

Previous page: Javed shows his colleagues the way on the successful 1987 tour of England. He made a fine double century in the last Test at the Oval.

1976/77 at nineteen, scoring 163 against New Zealand. In his third Test he made 206 to become the youngest man ever to score a double century in international cricket.

His highest first-class score is 311 for Karachi Whites against National Bank when he was just 17.

His first period as Pakistan captain, between 1979 and 1982, ended when his own players revolted against him. During this time he recorded his highest Test score, 280 not out against India in Hyderabad in 1981/82.

He eventually returned to the captaincy of his country, leading them to a victory in New Zealand in January 1993, but then Wasim Akram took over for the subsequent tour of the West Indies.

Javed has now scored more than 8,500 runs for his country, including more than 20 centuries.

In England he qualified for Sussex, but his opportunities there were limited and he moved to Glamorgan in 1980. The following

year he scored eight centuries and more than 2,000 runs, and in 1982 he took over the captaincy during the second half of the season.

His career with Glamorgan ended when the Welsh county signed Winston Davies as their overseas player to boost a rather weak bowling attack.

First Class Career:
Runs – 28,647. Average 53.44 (80 centuries)

Test Match Career:
Tests – 124
Runs – 8,832. Average 52.57 (23 centuries)

JOHANNESBURG

THE WANDERERS CLUB OF Johannesburg is famous around the world, and Test cricket in this South African city has seen many fine moments.

The birth of the Wanderers club came at the time of the first overseas tour to South Africa in 1888/89. The ground was known as a venue for fast run-scoring, thanks to an outfield with very little grass.

Perhaps the most famous game at the Old Wanderers ground came in 1906 when South Africa beat England by one wicket, thanks to the last-wicket pair of Nourse and Sherwell putting on 45.

After the Second World War, Test cricket in Johannesburg moved to Ellis Park, the Wanderers having outgrown the facilities at their old ground. Six Tests were played at Ellis Park between 1948/49 and 1953/54.

Meanwhile preparations for a new Wanderers stadium at Kent Park went ahead and the first Test there was played in 1956/57. Perhaps the most memorable moment came in a match between Transvaal and the 1966 Australians. Ali Bacher, now the leading figure in the new South African cricket set-up, made a double century, took a magnificent catch, and led his side to a win that saw the Australians lose for the first time on South African soil.

The Test match that followed saw South Africa win by 233 runs thanks to a score of 620 in their second innings, Denis Lindsay making 182, and Graeme Pollock 90.

BRIAN JOHNSTON

Born 1912; Died 1994

THE DEATH OF BRIAN Johnston on 5th January 1994 marked the end of an era in cricket broadcasting.

He was an integral part of the BBC Radio Test Match Special team – unquestionably the star performer – and Prime Minister John Major perhaps best summed it up when he said: 'Summers will never be the same.'

Johnston was the consummate professional. He made an often difficult job appear easy and was the master of the ad lib.

But he was perhaps best known for his double entendres and his love of chocolate cake sent in by devoted listeners.

With an upbringing that included Eton, Oxford and the Grenadier Guards, Johnston moved into broadcasting after the Second World War when an old friend suggested he should audition for the BBC. He became a household name in the great age of radio for his work on 'In Town Tonight' and 'On the Job'.

His cricket commentaries began on television in 1946 and carried on until 1970 when he was sacked without any real explanation. He was thought to be sometimes too flippant, it was said, as television looked to appoint ex-players as commentators.

It turned out to be a blessing in disguise both for 'Johnners', as he was known to colleagues, and the great British listening public. On radio the overgrown schoolboy-type approach, which never masked his sheer love of the game, was given full rein.

His gaffes when commentating were legendary. Among the more famous: 'Neil Harvey, standing at slip, legs wide apart waiting for a tickle.' He made broadcasting history in 1991 when he collapsed in fits of giggles after his co-commentator Jonathan Agnew described Ian Botham's hit-wicket dismissal thus: 'He just didn't quite get his leg over.'

However, the humour should never detract from the simple fact that he was a superb broadcaster. His happy-go-lucky attitude to life made him a personal friend to the many millions of cricket lovers who had never met him. His death was like losing a member of the family.

The late Brian Johnston in the commentary box at the Oval for the fifth Test between England and West Indies in 1991. Behind him is Bill Frindall, scorer and statistician for the Test Match Special team, and like the rest of his colleagues, now almost better known by the customary nickname ('The Bearded Wonder') bestowed on him by 'Johnners'.

ALVIN KALLICHARRAN

West Indies

Born 1949

Guyana, Warwickshire, Queensland, Transvaal and Orange Free State

ALTHOUGH AT JUST FIVE feet four inches he was one of the smallest players ever to play Test cricket, Alvin Kallicharran was one of the most successful batsmen of recent times to play for the West Indies.

Hailing from the east coast of Guyana, the same area that produced Basil Butcher and Rohan Kanhai, Kallicharran was always a most fluent left-hand bat. A friendly, smiling character, his excellent temperament combined with great natural timing led him to be a crowd pleaser wherever he played around the world, either in domestic cricket or for his country.

At seventeen he became the youngest cricketer to play for Guyana in 1966/67. He went on to make his Test debut against New Zealand in 1971/72, scoring

Kallicharran in action for Warwickshire, with whom he enjoyed a long and successful county career. He twice exceeded 2000 runs in a season, and also shared an English record fourth-wicket stand of 470 with Geoff Humpage in 1982.

centuries in his first two innings.

Although he enjoyed much personal success with Warwickshire in the County Championship, his best Test performances came on hard wickets, either in the Caribbean or elsewhere overseas.

Kallicharran's career also had its fair share of controversy. In the first Test of 1973/74 against England at Port of Spain, he had made 142 when he walked off the pitch at close of play, without grounding his bat. Tony Greig threw down the

stumps and umpire Douglas Sang Hue gave him run out.

However, the next day the umpire diplomatically allowed his decision to be overruled and Kallicharran went on to make 158.

He signed for Kerry Packer's World Series Cricket but then had to pull out after realising it contravened a contract he had with a radio station in Queensland. Soon after, in 1977/78, he took over the captaincy of the West Indies side from Clive Lloyd.

THE GUINNESS

He effectively ended his own Test career when, after being dropped following an unsuccessful series against Pakistan, he agreed a £20,000 deal to play for Transvaal in 1981/82 and went on to join two West Indies 'rebel' touring parties in South Africa.

First Class Career:
Runs – 32,650. Average 43.64
(87 centuries)

Test Match Career:
Tests – 66
Runs – 4,399. Average 44.43
(12 centuries)

ROHAN KANHAI

West Indies

Born 1935

Guyana, Trinidad, Warwickshire, Western Australia and Tasmania

ROHAN KANHAI WAS FOR many years the linchpin of the West Indies batting line-up. He had all the shots in the textbook – and quite a few more besides – but above all, he had great concentration and a determination never to throw his wicket away.

Many will remember this right-handed batsman for the improvisation he would show, in particular his pull-shot to leg when he would hit a full-length ball with such a lunge that it would lift him off his feet. The ball invariably finished up over the boundary rope.

Kanhai first represented the West Indies in 1957 and immediately established himself in the side. From the tour of England that year he went on to play 61 Tests without a break, the sequence ending when he had to return to England from the Caribbean for a cartilage operation.

His first Test century came in 1958/59 and it turned out to be his highest score. In just six and a half hours against India in Calcutta he scored 256, including 42 fours. He made 538 runs in the series at an average of 67.25.

That winter he made another double century, scoring 217 when the West Indies moved on to Lahore. It was an innings that helped inflict Pakistan's first home defeat.

He eventually succeeded Gary Sobers as West Indies captain in Australia in 1972/73. It was not a successful tour, Australia winning the series. The following summer, however, Kanhai led the West Indies to victory in England, winning two of the three Tests played.

For Warwickshire he gave admirable service over a period of ten years, scoring 1,000 runs in a season ten times. In 1972 he equalled a county record with eight

In the latter part of his career, as well as joining Kallicharran, his fellow Guyanan, at Edgbaston, Kanhai led the West Indies on a successful tour of England in 1973, scoring a century (below) in the third Test at Lord's.

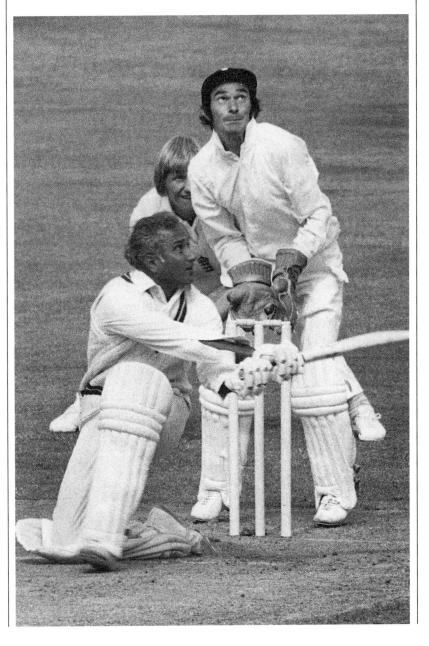

centuries, and in 1974 he shared a world record second-wicket stand of 465 with John Jameson against Gloucestershire at Edgbaston, Kanhai making 213 not out.

First Class Career:
Runs – 28,774. Average 49.01
(83 centuries)

Test Match Career:
Tests – 79
Runs – 6,227. Average 47.53
(15 centuries)

KAPIL DEV

India

Born 1959
Haryana, Northamptonshire
and Worcestershire

AT THE TIME OF HIS retirement in November 1994, Kapil Dev was the world's leading all-rounder. He could be classified among the greats of the modern game alongside Ian Botham, Sir Richard Hadlee and Imran Khan.

Kapil was India's best fast-medium bowler for more than a decade, always proving a lively proposition even on the most benign of pitches. His batting in the middle order was invariably aggressive, his aim always to impose himself on the bowling attack.

The highlight of his career came on 8 February 1994 when, in his 130th Test, he dismissed his 432nd victim, Tillekeratne of Sri Lanka, and became the leading wicket-taker in Test cricket, overhauling Sir Richard Hadlee.

Kapil took just two more Test wickets before deciding to start a new career as a television commentator.

He made his first-class debut in the Ranji Trophy in 1975/76, taking 6 for 39 for Haryana against Punjab. He continued to take wickets regularly at home and won his first Test cap in Pakistan in 1978/79.

That winter he took 17 wickets in six Tests against the West Indies and scored 329 runs at an average of 65.80.

He showed a liking for English conditions on his first tour in 1979, taking 16 wickets in the series, twice as many as the next successful bowler, although his batting was disappointing.

At only 21 years of age and in

One of the 'big four' all-rounders who dominated international cricket in the 1980s, Kapil Dev outlasted his rivals and finished his career as the leading wicket-taker in Test cricket, having claimed 434 victims.

only his 25th Test, Kapil became the youngest man ever to achieve the Test double of 1,000 runs and 100 wickets.

He became a national hero in 1983 when he led India to an unlikely World Cup win at Lord's against West Indies, the overwhelming favourites. His outstanding performance in that tournament was his 175 not out against Zimbabwe, after arriving at the wicket with his side in trouble at 10 for 4.

Three years later at Lord's, having returned to the captaincy, he led India to their first win over England at cricket's headquarters, and victory at Headingley too brought India a series win.

His career strike rate of a wicket every 63.81 balls does not match that of Botham, Hadlee or Imran Khan, and certainly his potency was much diminished in later years.

But it is important to remember that he played most of his Test cricket on benign Indian wickets and without a penetrative new-ball

bowler to help him at the other end. He also felt that the vast amount of one-day cricket he played – more than 200 one-day internationals in all – took its toll on him.

His best bowling figures in an innings were 9 for 83 against West Indies at Ahmedabad in 1983/84.

His batting could often be commanding, some of his best innings setting up victories. His top score was 163 against Sri Lanka at Kanpur in 1986/87.

In India's conclusive 3–0 series win over England in 1992/93, Kapil averaged 50.50, having previously topped the batting averages on India's tour of South Africa a few months previously.

First Class Career:
Runs – 11,356. Average 32.91
(18 centuries)
Wickets – 835. Average 27.09

Test Match Career:
Tests – 131
Runs – 5,248. Average 31.05
(8 centuries)
Wickets – 434. Average 29.62

KARACHI

KARACHI WAS THE CITY which saw the great Hanif Mohammad score his world best 499, a record that stood until Brian Lara beat it while playing for Warwickshire in the summer of 1994.

Hanif's innings in 1959 took place on matting at the Karachi Parsi ground. He only failed to reach 500 by being run out attempting the second run that would have produced that great landmark.

All Test matches in Karachi have, however, been played at the National Stadium, about ten miles from the city centre. At first, Tests were played on matting, as watering a ground so close to the desert was always going to be a problem.

But with grass wickets now standard throughout the country, the problem at Karachi, as at other grounds in Pakistan, is in producing a definite result.

KENT

Founded: 1870

Entered Official Championship: 1890

Honours:

County Champions – 1906, 1909, 1910, 1913, 1970, 1977 (joint), 1978

Gillette Cup – 1967, 1974

Benson and Hedges Cup – 1973, 1976, 1978

John Player League – 1972, 1973, 1976

OF ESSEX WERE THE TEAM of the 1980s and early nineties, then Kent were unquestionably the team of the seventies. Their record of three Championship titles, three John Player League and four one-day competitions was testament not just to their talented individuals but to their tremendous strength in depth.

The first official Kent county club was created in 1842, but after it had run into financial trouble another was founded at Maidstone in 1859. The two merged in 1870.

After taking an unofficial County Championship in 1847, Kent had relatively little success until the official championship began. Lord Harris had been appointed captain in 1875 and he guided the county through the rest of the century. Perhaps his greatest success was leading Kent to five victories over the touring Australians between 1884 and 1899.

The creation of the Tonbridge nursery in 1897 was to provide Kent with a seemingly limitless supply of good professional players. It led directly to their first Championship title in 1906. This was a fine all-round side – amateurs making up most of the batting, professionals

the bowling. They were also first-rate in the field.

That year saw the emergence of Frank Woolley, a batsman who went on to make more than 43,000 runs for the county before his retirement in 1938. Batting always looked easy for Woolley as he compiled 112 centuries, his highest score being 270 against Middlesex at Canterbury in 1923. He was also a skilful slow left-arm bowler, taking over 1,500 wickets in his Kent career.

Further Championship success followed for the county in 1909, 1910, and 1913. By then only three amateurs remained as regular members of the side. After the First World War Kent were not as strong, with the bowling losing much of its venom. However, they were still good enough to finish runners-up to Yorkshire in 1919.

The bowling in the inter-war years depended mainly on 'Tich' Freeman. In seventeen seasons between 1920 and 1936, this leg-spin and googly bowler took 3,776 wickets, most of them for Kent. His best year was 1928 when he took 304, a record that is unlikely ever to be beaten.

The batting at this time was led by Leslie Ames, a brave player of fast bowling who was also particularly quick on his feet against the spinners. His contribution as wicket-keeper was enormous too. He created a new double in 1928 and 1929 – 1,000 runs and 100 dismissals. No other wicket-keeper has achieved it.

Ames had a worthy successor as wicket-keeper in Godfrey Evans. An exuberant, outgoing character, he played 91 Tests for England and altogether took more than 1,000 dismissals in his first-class career.

Although they never achieved any success in this period, Kent were invariably in the top half of the table until the 1950s when something of a slump set in.

But it was then that one of the greatest of English batsmen came to the fore. Colin Cowdrey's style was right out of the textbook. An upright player, he had all the shots and, that essential ingredient, time to play them. His record of 21,000

runs for Kent would have been greater but for his many England appearances.

Kent's revival began in 1957, when Cowdrey was appointed captain and Ames manager (he later became secretary as well). A new era was beginning, with Alan Knott taking on the mantle of wicket-keeper/batsman, Derek Underwood emerging as a slow-medium left-armer, and Mike Denness and Brian Luckhurst forming an impressive opening partnership.

These home-grown players were supported by two all-rounder 'imports' who were to have a major bearing on the county's fortunes – John Shepherd from Barbados and Asif Iqbal from Pakistan.

In 1967 came victory in the Gillette Cup, as well as second place behind Yorkshire in the County Championship. The placings were repeated the following year. Many considered that the absence of Cowdrey, Knott and Underwood on England duty had made the vital difference.

In 1970, the club's centenary year, came their first Championship title for 57 years. Bottom of the table at the beginning of July, the side were pulled around by Cowdrey, and when he was absent, by his able number two Denness. Three players, Johnson, Woolmer and Ealham, were awarded county caps – they were all to play an important part in the glory years to come.

With the addition of another foreigner, West Indian Bernard Julien, in 1971, the team was just about complete and barely a year went by without the addition of some silverware.

Denness took over the captaincy in 1972 as one-day success followed over the next few years. Asif Iqbal was at the helm in 1977, providing much flair, when Kent shared the County Championship title with Middlesex.

But the county's almost total domination of English cricket was severely threatened by the Packer affair. Originally the committee decided to part company with the Packer players, Knott, Underwood, Asif, Julien and Woolmer. That decision was eventually overturned by a new committee and Alan Ealham had the unenviable job of leading a side affected by political overtones in 1978.

He led it magnificently, to achieve a notable double of County Championship and Benson and Hedges Cup. Ealham was unquestionably helped by the fact that for the first time since 1909, Kent did not have to provide a single member of the England team.

Since then, Kent have failed to win a trophy. In 1992 they finished runners-up in the County Championship and were beaten finalists in the Benson and Hedges Cup, and the following year they were just pipped for the Sunday League title by Glamorgan in the decisive final match of the season against the Welshmen.

ALAN KNOTT
England
Born 1946
Kent

ALAN KNOTT WAS A bright, perky, genius of a wicket-keeper who broke records galore during his Test career. He was a fine batsman too, with a style all of his own – and how England were grateful for it.

His obsession with health and fitness was legendary. Between each ball, whether keeping wicket or batting, he would be seen performing stretching exercises. Off the field, he took meticulous care in his diet for fear of losing his renowned agility.

His keeping was always quick and lively and often unorthodox – he preferred, for example, to stand back to medium pacers to be sure of taking more catches. He also kept well against spin bowling, and his almost telepathic understanding with Derek Underwood brought many wickets for both England and Kent.

As a batsman Knott was a fine player of fast bowling and his

eccentric approach would often leave opposition bowlers furious. He was a hard man to bowl to when he was in the mood to cut over the slips or cart the ball to leg from outside off-stump.

A family man first, he decided to

Kent's wicket-keeping tradition was in safe hands when Alan Knott took up the gloves and succeeded Godfrey Evans – as was England's. In his 78th Test, Knott passed Evans' record total of 220 dismissals, and by the time of his retirement had set a new record of 250.

opt for security when he joined Kerry Packer's World Series Cricket. Since his retirement after the 1985 season he has kept involved with cricket, and has been one of England's team of coaches.

First Class Career:
Runs – 18,105. Average 29.63 (17 centuries)
Catches – 1,211
Stumpings – 133

Test Match Career:
Tests – 95
Runs – 4,389. Average 32.75 (5 centuries)
Catches – 250. Stumpings – 19

LAHORE

TEST MATCH CRICKET IN Lahore is now played at the giant Gaddafi Stadium, which boasts one of the largest playing areas in the world.

The ground is a vast concrete bowl where as many as 50,000 spectators can be accommodated. In the off-season it is used for hockey matches.

As at so many grounds in Pakistan, slow wickets at Lahore mean drawn matches. In an effort to redress the situation, Len Flack, groundsman at Edgbaston, was flown over to offer advice, but little change in the pitches has resulted.

Before the Gaddafi Stadium became the leading venue in Lahore, Test cricket was played at Lawrence Gardens, a much more picturesque ground.

It was the venue for the first first-class match to be played in Pakistan, which took place in February 1948 between the Punjab Governor's XI and Punjab University.

Sadly, after just three Tests at Lawrence Gardens, administrators decided they needed a bigger ground and Test cricket has now been played at the Gaddafi Stadium for more than thirty years.

The Gaddafi Stadium in Lahore, packed to capacity for a one-day international against England in 1984.

JIM LAKER
England
Born 1922. Died 1986
Surrey and Essex

JIM LAKER'S PLACE IN cricket history is assured thanks to his nineteen wickets in the Old Trafford Test against Australia in 1956. He was the finest off-spin bowler of his generation, perhaps the greatest of all-time.

An exiled Yorkshireman, he played most of his county cricket for Surrey. His 66 wickets for the county in 1947 earned him a place on the tour to the West Indies that winter, where he was leading wicket-taker. But unfortunately for Laker the 1948 Australians found him to their liking, and it wasn't until 1956 that he established a regular place in the England side.

The omens looked bad for Australia when Laker took ten wickets against them for Surrey that year. One month later at Manchester

A fine action study of Jim Laker, taken in 1958 towards the end of the great Surrey decade. In partnership with Tony Lock, Laker contributed massively to the club's domination of the County Championship: in the 1950s he took 957 wickets in the competition at an average of 16.61, exceeding 100 for the season in 1950 with 142, his best year, and in 1954 with 112.

he took 9 for 37 in the first innings and 10 for 53 in the second to become the only man to take nineteen wickets in a Test. He took 46 wickets in the series – another record.

For Surrey, he was a major contributor in the county's most successful period, as they won the Championship seven years in succession in the 1950s. Laker enjoyed some great days at the Oval with slow left-arm bowler Tony Lock operating at the other end. Lock, incidentally, was the man who took the 'other' wicket in that famous Old Trafford Test.

Laker left Surrey in 1959 but made a comeback with Essex three years later, eventually retiring in 1964.

An outspoken autobiography *Over to Me* brought trouble for Laker at both the Oval and Lord's. But he later returned to the fold, serving on the Surrey Cricket Committee.

He was generally a man of few words, so it was something of a surprise that he became a renowned cricket commentator for BBC Television, where his laconic style only served to emphasise an astute mind which brought the subtle tactical battles of Test cricket home to the viewer.

First Class Career:
*Runs – 7,304. Average 16.60
(2 centuries)
Wickets – 1,944. Average 18.40*

Test Match Career:
*Tests – 46
Runs – 676. Average 14.08
Wickets – 193. Average 21.24*

LANCASHIRE
Founded: 1864
*Entered Official
Championship: 1890*
Honours:
County Champions – 1897, 1904, 1926, 1927, 1928, 1930, 1934, 1950 (joint)

Gillette Cup – 1970, 1971, 1972, 1975

NatWest Trophy – 1990

Benson and Hedges Cup – 1984, 1990

John Player League – 1969, 1970

Refuge Assurance League – 1989

IT HAS BEEN MORE THAN forty years since Lancashire last won the County Championship, an undistinguished record for a county blessed with some highly talented players.

But if that has disappointed the purists among the county's supporters, there can be no doubt that Lancashire's contribution to English cricket in recent years has been considerable.

In the early days of the one-day competitions, Lancashire reigned supreme. Four times in six years they won the Gillette Cup, including a hat-trick of victories.

Successive John Player League titles in 1969 and 1970 proved that their one-day success was not just a case of coming good on the day.

More recently, the one-day magic has returned, with another Sunday title in 1989 and a NatWest/Benson & Hedges double in 1990, while a Lancashire player, Michael Atherton, has captained England.

Formed in 1864, the Lancashire club's teams consisted mostly of amateur players in the early days. In 1881, they took the unofficial championship title outright under the captaincy of A.N. Hornby, who later became president for 23 years.

Another important figure in those early years was S.H. Swire. Honorary secretary until 1905, he was largely responsible for the purchase of Old Trafford and the building of the pavilion in 1895.

Lancashire were a powerful force

in the early years of the official championship, finishing second five times in seven seasons before eventually taking the title in 1897.

Johnnie Tyldesley was a leading batsman at the time and he went on to score almost 32,000 runs for the county between 1895 and 1923, winning 31 England caps.

Another heavy scorer was A.C. MacLaren, who made a century on his debut, and his 424 against Somerset in 1895, the highest individual score for Lancashire, was made at a rate of 54 runs an hour.

MacLaren went on to captain England, and although never successful in an Ashes series against Australia, he did lead Lancashire to a famous victory over the tourists in 1921.

Only one more Championship was won prior to the First World War, in 1904 when Lancashire went through the season unbeaten.

Lancashire played an important part in the development of cricket after the war, proposing two-day championship matches in 1919 – an experiment which was abandoned after one season. The club were also at the forefront of drying out grounds artificially.

The county dominated the championship in the latter half of the 1920s, winning it in 1926, 1927 and 1928. They were then runners-up to Nottinghamshire in 1929 before taking the title again in 1930.

Under the captaincy of Leonard Green, their success was based on wonderful bowlers in the form of E.A. McDonald and Richard Tyldesley.

McDonald, an Australian who had already established himself as a Test player, was a genuinely quick bowler. He did not join the club until he was 32, but took more than 1,000 wickets between 1924 and 1931.

Tyldesley provided the contrast, using the subtleties of flight to take 303 wickets with his leg-spin in those three successive championship years.

Among the batsmen, Ernest Tyldesley, younger brother of John, dominated, playing in a total of five championship winning teams, including Lancashire's next success

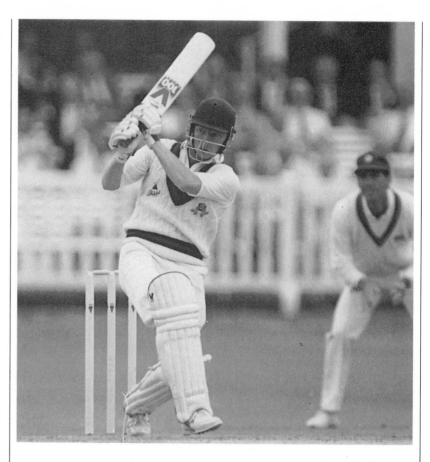

in 1934. He went on to become the county's leading run-scorer, making almost 32,000 between 1909 and 1936. He was a model professional, always going about his business in a calm, authoritative way.

Lancashire's fortunes declined in the late thirties. Then after the Second World War, Cyril Washbrook became the club's leading player, representing his country in 37 Tests and becoming the county's third highest run-scorer of all-time.

In 1950 Lancashire shared the title with Surrey but came in for heavy criticism over the state of the Old Trafford pitch. In their defence, restrictions had been introduced on watering and rolling and a cold wet summer complicated matters.

Whatever the complaints, the pitch undeniably gave great help to the spinners in general and Roy Tattersall in particular. He took 163 wickets – a dramatic increase on a mere 32 the previous season!

Although Lancashire's performances through the fifties

Lancashire have traditionally been strong contenders in all limited-overs competitions; in 1990 they completed the Lord's 'double' by defeating Northants in the NatWest Trophy final, with Neil Fairbrother, perhaps the best one-day cricketer in England, top-scoring (above) with a fine 81 off 68 balls.

were erratic, players continued to win England honours, none more so than Brian Statham.

Over a period of eighteen years from 1950 Statham took 1,683 wickets for his county, a remarkable achievement as he was always considered an unlucky bowler, often missing the stumps or having batsmen playing and missing. For England he formed one of the best opening attacks ever with Yorkshire's Fred Trueman.

If Lancashire supporters tired of lacklustre performances from their heroes in the Championship, the introduction of one-day cricket

THE GUINNESS

reawakened their interest with a vengeance.

Led by Jack Bond, the club's successful one-day side of the early seventies contained a fine balance – hostile fast bowlers such as Peter Lever and Ken Shuttleworth, consistent spinners in Jack Simmons and David Hughes, a steady opening pair in David Lloyd and Barry Wood. In addition there was the flamboyant batting talent of Clive Lloyd, from the West Indies, and Farokh Engineer, from India, who also gave such a lift to the fielding from behind the stumps.

Another successful one-day side was formed in the late eighties under the leadership of the now veteran Hughes and featuring the hugely talented Neil Fairbrother.

A notable one-day double was achieved in 1990 when in two Lord's finals, Lancashire first won the Benson and Hedges Cup, beating Worcestershire by 69 runs, and then followed that with victory over Northamptonshire by seven wickets for the NatWest Trophy.

After that, however, Lancashire returned to the doldrums. In 1992 coach Alan Ormrod was sacked and former England players Graeme Fowler and Paul Allott released, as the committee moved to try to stem rumbling discontent both on and off the field.

BRIAN LARA
West Indies
Born 1969
Trinidad and Tobago and Warwickshire

BRIAN LARA IS WITHOUT question the greatest batsman playing cricket today. His ability has been clear for all to see since he began playing first-class cricket. But his achievements during 1994 put

Lara plays a straight bat for West Indies during the second Test of the 1992/93 home series against Pakistan at Bridgetown.

him on a different level from everyone else.

This talented young left-hander was at a very young age earmarked by reliable judges in the West Indies as a future star.

His introduction into the West Indies Test team promised much, and eventually he delivered with a superlative innings of 277 against Australia at Sydney in 1992/93.

It was a clear demonstration that here was an exceptional player. But little were cricket fans around the world to know what was to come.

He was the leading West Indies batsman during the home series against England in 1993/94, scoring one century and two half centuries in the first four Tests.

But it was in the fifth Test in Antigua that he made history by beating Sir Garfield Sobers' record Test score of 365 not out.

Lara's 375 was the thirteenth triple century in Tests, the third by a West Indian, and when he passed Sir Donald Bradman's 334 he set the highest individual score made against England.

He came to the wicket with the West Indies in some trouble at 12 for 2, and was last man out with the total at 593 for 5 declared. He dominated partnerships of 179 with Arthurton, 183 with Adams and 219 with Chanderpaul.

His innings had been watched by Sir Garfield, and he – and many hundreds more – came onto the pitch to congratulate the young master when he passed the landmark.

That achievement, however, was only the start of a remarkable 50 days. At the end of the series Lara flew into Britain to begin his county career with Warwickshire. In his first innings he scored 147 against Glamorgan at Edgbaston.

He followed that with two centuries in the match against Leicestershire and then scored 136 off just 94 balls against Somerset at Taunton. His five successive centuries equalled Everton Weekes' West Indies record. But his hopes of going one better were dashed when he was dismissed for 26 against Middlesex at Lord's.

It was merely a temporary hiccup. In the second innings he made 140, and then he started the fourth day of Warwickshire's next game against Durham at Edgbaston on 111 not out. He made 175 before lunch and then the records began to tumble.

He passed 305 not out, the highest individual score for the county; 322, the highest score by a West Indian in England; and when he reached 325 it brought up his 1,000 runs for the English season in his seventh innings, equalling Bradman's record from 1938.

Lara beat his own highest ever total of 375 and then became the second man to score 400 in England this century after Graeme Hick. He passed 424 to claim the individual record for all English cricket and Hanif Mohammad's world record 499 loomed.

His 72nd boundary brought up the magic 500 and the game finished as a draw with Lara 501 not out. It came from 427 balls, 390 of his runs coming in one day.

Lara helped Warwickshire to a remarkable domestic treble, and finished the season with 2,066 runs to his credit for an average of 89.82. He scored 9 centuries and 3 fifties.

The one sour note of 1994 for Lara came on the West Indies tour of India in the autumn. He became only the second player to be suspended under the ICC's Code of Conduct when he challenged an umpiring decision in a one-day game against New Zealand.

Given out stumped for 32, he showed dissent when the umpire refused to consult the third official. He was also fined fifty per cent of his match fee.

It was a sad end to a calendar year of quite monumental proportions. But provided Lara keeps his appetite for the game, there must surely be many more records ahead.

First Class Career:
Runs – 7,320. Average 58.10
(22 centuries)

Test Match Career:
Tests – 16
Runs – 1,628. Average 62.61
(3 centuries)

HAROLD LARWOOD
England
Born 1904
Nottinghamshire

HAROLD LARWOOD WAS A supremely fast bowler. He was a mild, quiet-spoken man. Yet he will forever be associated with one of the most turbulent and unsavoury episodes in the history of the game.

The name of Larwood will always be linked with Bodyline, the intimidatory practice of bowling short and packing the leg side with fielders to take the inevitable catches offered. It was Larwood's speed and accuracy that made the tactic, dictated by the captain Douglas Jardine, work.

Larwood was selected for England against Australia in his first full season, 1926, and was also chosen to tour down under in 1928/29, but didn't reach his peak until that eventful tour of 1932/33.

The 'leg theory' method, as it was called, was largely devised to deal with the batting genius of Don Bradman and to an extent it worked: Bradman averaged only 56.57 in four Tests, which was modest by his standards. Larwood took 33 wickets in the series at an average of 19.51.

The hard work he put in that winter cost him dear. The strain on his left foot, as a result of the hard Australian wickets, meant he never played for England again after that tour.

However, in 1936 he was particularly effective in domestic cricket, taking 119 wickets. In eight full seasons he took more than 100 wickets each year.

He was also a useful batsman. He hit an impressive 98 in his final Test match.

Looking back on that infamous series in Australia, he wrote a book in 1933 entitled *Bodyline*. In it he remained fiercely loyal to Douglas Jardine and maintained that 'leg-theory' bowling had to be accurate to be effective.

'I have no excuses to make for bowling which I shall always hold needs no excuse,' he wrote. 'My conscience is absolutely clear that I have never bowled at any batsman, and I know that I never shall.' Few Australians at that time would have agreed with him.

In view of the rumpus, it was ironic that in 1950, on the initiative of his former Australian opponent Jack Fingleton, Larwood emigrated to Sydney with his wife and five daughters.

However, he settled there happily and a further twist in his story came in June 1993 when at the age of 88, he was awarded the MBE in the Queen's Birthday Honours, sixty years after the Bodyline series.

It was an honour warmly received in the cricket world, and bore the stamp of a Prime Minister, John Major, whose office is said to be adorned by a picture of Harold Larwood.

First Class Career:
Runs – 7,290. Average 19.91
(3 centuries)
Wickets – 1,427. Average 17.51

Test Match Career:
Tests – 21
Runs – 485. Average 19.40
Wickets – 78. Average 28.35

BILL LAWRY
Australia
Born 1937
Victoria

BILL LAWRY WAS THE kind of opening batsman most captains would love to have in their side. Tall and lanky, he was a left-hander capable of immense feats of concentration, able to make big scores and occupy the crease for long periods.

He certainly had a 'no-frills' style and hence was often dour and unattractive to watch. He had very little back-lift and was fearless against fast bowling, happy to hook the quickest of them. He was always strong on the leg side, but as his career progressed he added steadily to his repertoire of shots.

When Lawry arrived in England with the 1961 Australians, very little was known of him. English bowlers knew a lot more by the end of a series that had seen him score 420 runs at an average of 52.50, including two centuries at Lord's and Old Trafford. He was the top run-scorer on the tour, scoring nine centuries that summer.

On his return home Lawry was made captain of his state side, a position he held for ten years, and continued to be the hardest man to dismiss in the Australian side.

His highest Test score was 210 against the West Indies at Bridgetown in 1964/65, as he and Bobby Simpson put on 382 for the first wicket – the first time an opening pair had scored double centuries in the same innings of a Test.

Lawry went on to captain his country in two series against England, and against West Indies, India and South Africa. In 1968 he shared the series in England as Australia retained the Ashes, but at home in 1970/71 his side lost to Ray Illingworth's tourists and he was replaced as captain by Ian Chappell in the final Test.

Since retiring he has become a regular television commentator in Australia.

First Class Career:
Runs – 18,734. Average 50.90
(50 centuries)

Test Match Career:
Tests – 67
Runs – 5,234. Average 47.15
(13 centuries)

Lawry steals a single in the final Test against England in 1968, which saw Australia, under his leadership, share the series and retain the Ashes.

LAWS

COMPARED TO A NUMBER of other sports, the laws of the game of cricket have changed very little for more than two hundred years, having stood the test of time very well.

It is generally considered that the first serious set of laws was drawn up in 1774, when a committee of Noblemen and Gentlemen met at the Star and Garter, Pall Mall, and produced 'New Articles of the Game of Cricket'.

They produced a comprehensive set of rules, dealing with such things as the ball, the bat, the stumps, and the methods in which the batsman could be out. Many of their decisions survive today.

The last full revision, only the fourth since 1744, came in 1980, with the MCC invited by the International Cricket Conference to re-codify the laws. Taking opinions from all over the cricket world, the MCC, guided by their former secretary S.C. Griffith, produced a final draft that was accepted at a special meeting.

Probably the most contentious law has always been that concerning the leg before wicket (lbw) decision. There have been a number of changes to it over the years, mainly to discourage negative play by batsmen.

At present, Law 36 states that a batsman shall be given out if he first intercepts a ball that would have hit the wicket, provided it has pitched between wicket and wicket or on the off-side, or was intercepted full pitch. He can also be given out if hit outside the line of the off-stump if the umpire considers he was offering no stroke and the ball would have hit the stumps.

Another law to provoke much discussion over the years has concerned no-balls, with the position of the bowler's front foot rather than the back now being the determining factor. This move eliminated the practice of 'dragging' which allowed some bowlers to deliver the ball from no more than about nineteen yards.

It had led to some inconsistency of interpretation by umpires, and although batsmen now complain they have less time to make the most of a no-ball, it is generally considered an improvement.

Perhaps the most contentious issue in recent times has concerned intimidatory bowling. Many have felt that umpires, especially those officiating in Tests involving the West Indies pace attack, have not invoked Law 42, which deals with unfair play, strictly enough.

The umpires' judgement is tested to the full when tail-end batsmen find themselves facing what they are more used to dishing out! Here Craig McDermott (Australia) gets a short-pitched delivery from the West Indies' Curtly Ambrose.

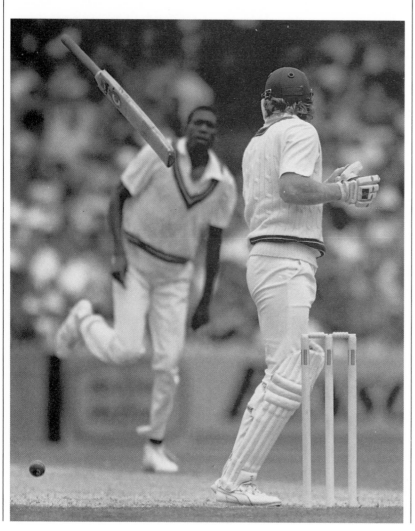

LEAGUE CRICKET

OUTSIDE THE FIRST-class counties and the Minor Counties, the highest standard of cricket in England is generally to be found in the leagues.

Professionalism has long been established in the Lancashire and Yorkshire Leagues and many great players from all over the world have been introduced to English conditions through the leagues.

Now, almost every county in England has at least one league, but traditionally it has been those in the north of England that have produced the highest standards.

The League Cricket Conference, the parent body of 62 member leagues all over the country, has in recent times had to take firm action in dealing with the problems that have arisen from the growth in the number of overseas professionals now playing.

The Conference had to ask its members to support bans on overseas players breaking their contracts and returning home before the end of a season.

Matters were brought to head when the Indian Cricket Board ordered four of its players home during the 1992 season. Retribution was swift, with the Bolton League banning all players under Indian jurisdiction and demanding £2,500 in compensation.

Finding the money to support a quality overseas professional has never been easy for most clubs, but as in the first-class game, sponsorship has grown in the leagues to the benefit of the game in general and many clubs in particular.

LEICESTERSHIRE
Founded: 1879
Entered Official Championship: 1895
Honours:
County Champions – 1975
Benson and Hedges Cup – 1972, 1975, 1985
John Player League – 1974, 1977

SUCCESS HAS NEVER come easily for Leicestershire in almost a century of trying in the official Championship. The county's best years came in the 1970s when they were the side which came closest to challenging Kent's domination of domestic cricket.

Although the club as it is known today was formed in 1879, records of cricket in Leicestershire date

back much further. The Wharf Street ground, opened in 1825, was the venue for many of the most important matches in England over the following three decades. It was after its closure in 1860 that cricket in the county declined, being played mostly on private grounds.

However, despite this setback, the Leicestershire Cricket Association was created in 1873 and a ground at Grace Road, now the county's permanent home, was opened five years later.

In the years immediately prior to joining the official Championship, probably the highlight for Leicestershire was victory over the Australians in 1888, as the club finished top of the second-class counties.

Their early years in the Championship saw Leicestershire regularly occupy places near the bottom of the table. Fortunes did improve briefly in 1904 and 1905, after the move to Aylestone Road, as they finished seventh and fifth. The following year at Worcester, Leicestershire scored their highest total, a massive 701 for 4 declared.

It was at this time that an effective and consistent opening batsmen, Cecil Wood, came to prominence. He made 225 in that record total and seventeen times he carried his bat through an innings. It was a feat he managed twice in a match against Yorkshire in 1911, scoring 107 and 117.

Two men dominated Leicestershire cricket in a period beginning just before the First World War and continuing right through to the start of the Second.

William Astill, who played for England against South Africa and West Indies, scored more than 22,000 runs and took over 2,000 wickets with his subtle off-spin, completing the double nine times in ten seasons.

George Geary, whose leg-cutter surprised even the great Don Bradman, was a medium-fast bowler of great accuracy and clever changes of pace. A member of two Ashes-winning sides, he went on to become coach at Charterhouse school, encouraging many young

players, among them Peter May.

It was Astill, the first professional captain of the county, who took Leicestershire to a fine sixth place in the table in 1935, with a record eleven matches won.

After the war the club returned to Grace Road, and in 1950 Charles Palmer joined the county from Worcestershire. As captain and secretary, he set about rebuilding the team and achieved some early success, the county finishing third in 1953 after topping the table for a time in August.

However, little success followed as Leicester, for all the efforts of such players as Maurice Hallam, a big-scoring opener, still failed to mount a realistic title challenge.

The tide turned, though, with the arrival at the club in 1965 of Tony Lock, the former Surrey and England spinner. The following year he was made captain as Leicestershire finally bought their Grace Road ground and brought the amenities up to true first-class standard.

In 1967 Lock's infectious enthusiasm led them to joint second in the table, the highest position in their history. Sadly, he decided not to return from Western Australia the following year, but the impetus he had created was maintained by the signing of Ray Illingworth from Yorkshire in 1969.

Although often absent on England duty, Illingworth provided the know-how for players such as Roger Tolchard, Chris Balderstone, the Rhodesian Brian Davison and above all the talented young David Gower to prosper.

In 1972 Leicestershire finally broke their duck by winning the Benson and Hedges Cup in its first year. In the final at Lord's they defeated Yorkshire by five wickets, thanks largely to some fine bowling by two of their most experienced players, the Australian Graham McKenzie and the former Lancashire stalwart Ken Higgs.

Further success followed two years later when Leicester took the John Player League and were also beaten finalists in the Benson and Hedges Cup. Illingworth was an

The Leicestershire side which won the Benson & Hedges Cup in 1985.

ever-present that year, the first time he had been fully available, and his experience told.

But if 1974 had been a good season then 1975 was to be Leicestershire's vintage year. At last the County Championship was theirs, coupled with victory again in the Benson and Hedges Cup. Just for good measure, they also beat the touring Australians, for the first time since 1888.

The Championship was a nail-biting affair, with the title secured in the last match of the season at Chelmsford. The batting had been consistent all season, and in McKenzie, Higgs, Birkenshaw, Steele and McVicker there was no shortage of bowling talent.

With more luck, further success could have followed in 1976, but in 1977 the county again took the John Player League.

Although a third Benson and Hedges Cup triumph arrived in 1985, more recently there has been little to cheer the county's followers. David Gower left to try greener pastures at Hampshire, and another England Test player, Chris Lewis, moved to Nottinghamshire.

The experiment of appointing the Australian manager Bobby Simpson as cricket supremo failed to bring about an improvement in fortunes.

Membership slipped and at the end of the 1992 season the club had a deficit of almost £70,000.

In September 1993 Mike Turner, for 33 years the club's driving force off the field, dramatically resigned as chief executive.

The departure of Turner came at the end of another largely undistinguished season, despite a semi-final appearance in the Benson and Hedges Cup. However, 1994 saw the county produce much better performances, as they eventually finished Championship runners-up behind Warwickshire.

TONY LEWIS
England
Born 1938
Cambridge University and Glamorgan

TONY LEWIS BECAME A Test player and captain of England all at once, when he took over from the unavailable Ray Illingworth for the tour of India and Pakistan in 1972/73.

He was a fine all-round sportsman, winning blues at Cambridge for rugby and cricket. He captained the university at Lord's in 1962. An elegant batsman with a wide range of strokes, it was only a lack of consistency that prevented him from representing England earlier in his career.

In his debut Test he recovered from a first innings duck to make 70 not out in the second innings, and then went on to make his only Test

DENNIS LILLEE
Australia
Born 1949
Western Australia

FAST BOWLERS HAVE never come much better or quicker than Dennis Keith Lillee. In a Test career that spanned 13 years, he took 355 wickets, retiring in 1984 as the world's leading wicket-taker at that time.

Lillee had a classical action that allowed him to bowl at great speed, and yet with an economy of movement that meant he could sustain long spells and keep fit. He was always determined, sometimes to the point of near hatred of opposition batsmen – especially English ones.

Mean and with a fiery temperament, Lillee often made headlines for the wrong reasons. He once lost his temper in a Test match against Pakistan at Perth, aiming a kick at Javed Miandad.

Lillee also introduced to cricket the aluminium bat, and took exception when, against England at Perth, the umpires made him change to a wooden one. The game

Lillee leaves the umpire in no doubt about the decision he's looking for as he appeals for lbw at Headingley in 1981. He took 39 wickets in the six Tests that summer, maintaining a fine record in Ashes series.

century (125) at Kanpur.

He continued in the side for the first Test against New Zealand in 1973, but lost his place through injury and never played for England again.

Lewis had a successful career with Glamorgan, captaining them from 1967 to 1972 and leading them to only their second County Championship success in 1969.

Since his retirement he has shown himself to be a man of many talents. He has been chairman of Glamorgan, and is now best known as a writer and broadcaster on the game. In 1992 he added another significant string to his bow when he was appointed chairman of the Wales Tourist Board.

First Class Career:
Runs – 20,495. Average 32.42
        (30 centuries)

Test Match Career:
Tests – 9
Runs – 457. Average 32.64
        (1 century)

was held up for ten minutes, the incident ending with Lillee hurling his bat some twenty yards.

All of this, though, could never disguise the fact that Lillee was a truly great fast bowler. On the 1972 tour of England he took 31 wickets in five Tests, including match figures of 10 for 81 at the Oval. Later he broke down in the West Indies with stress fractures to his back, but he returned to full fitness to join Jeff Thomson in destroying the English batting in Australia in 1974/75.

He played a major role in the formation of World Series Cricket, but after its demise he returned to the Test scene, helping Australia to three victories over England in 1979/80 and going on to pass Richie Benaud's tally of 248 Test wickets in his 48th match, against India at Melbourne in 1980/81.

He broke the all-time record number of Test wickets in his 58th match, against West Indies, beating Lance Gibbs' tally of 309 by removing Larry Gomes.

Lillee eventually bowed out of Test cricket after the 1983/84 tour of

Pakistan. He took almost half his wickets, 167, against England.

He has continued to make his mark on the game as a writer with forthright views. He has also given a lot back to cricket. Among a number of ventures he has helped encourage the development of fast bowlers in India by regularly giving coaching sessions.

But perhaps most importantly, he has also encouraged youngsters at Australia's Institute of Sport Cricket Academy in Adelaide. Lillee is one of a team of coaches led by Rodney Marsh, and their success in producing top-class youngsters is now the envy of the world.

First Class Career:
Wickets – 845. Average 22.86

Test Match Career:
Tests – 70
Wickets – 355. Average 23.92

RAY LINDWALL
Australia
Born 1921
New South Wales and Queensland

IN THE DECADE AFTER THE Second World War Ray Lindwall was the dominant Australian fast bowler, and he is rightly considered to be one of the best his country has ever produced. He formed a partnership with Keith Miller that proved much too good for many batsmen.

Lindwall was genuinely fast, his main weapon being a late out-swinger. He also laid claim to being an all-rounder, and if that was a slight exaggeration, he did score more than 1,500 runs in Test cricket, including two centuries.

He seemed to reserve his best performances for Tests against England, taking 114 wickets, exactly half his total, against the old enemy. On the 1948 tour he took 27 wickets, including a remarkable 6 for 20 at the Oval as England were dismissed for just 52.

Lindwall was a consistent wicket-

taker throughout his career. His first 100 Test wickets came after just 26 matches, his second hundred after 52.

He captained his country against India in 1956/57 and was later awarded the MBE for his services to cricket.

First Class Career:
Runs – 5,042. Average 21.82
*   (5 centuries)*
Wickets – 794. Average 21.35

Test Match Career:
Test 61
Runs – 1,502. Average 21.15
*   (2 centuries)*
Wickets – 228. Average 23.03

CLIVE LLOYD
West Indies
Born 1944
Guyana and Lancashire

CLIVE LLOYD WAS A player to bring an extra buzz of excitement to any cricket ground. In his prime he was the world's best cover fieldsman, and the power of his batting was awesome.

But most of all he will go down in history as captain of the phenomenally successful West Indies sides of the 1970s and early eighties. In 1984 he led the team to a record eleven straight wins, including a 5–0 'blackwash' in England.

It was as a fieldsman that he first caught the eye in the 1960s. Although six feet five inches tall and wearing thick spectacles, he was wonderfully supple and acrobatic, often swooping in to run out unsuspecting batsmen. Later in his career he suffered from knee injuries, but that did not stop him displaying a safe pair of hands in the slips.

A left-hander who usually batted in the lower middle-order, he would hit the ball with incredible power. He was one of the first modern cricketers to use the heavier 3lb bat, but unlike some who have followed that lead, Lloyd had the strength

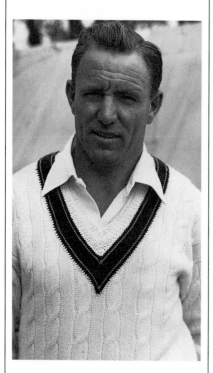

Ray Lindwall at 34, pictured at the start of his third tour of England in 1956.

and timing to make full use of it.

He was a skilful captain who had the benefit of leading a talented team of attractive, quick-scoring batsmen and tremendously hostile fast bowlers. His man-management brought the best out of every player, but he would still lead from the front, 14 of his 19 Test centuries coming as captain, and often on the few occasions when his side was in trouble.

Lloyd, a cousin of Lance Gibbs, began his first-class career with British Guiana in 1963/64 and was

An imperious back-foot drive from Lloyd, a magnificent attacking batsman and the most successful West Indies captain.

unlucky not to be chosen for the England tour of 1966. He subsequently toured England five times, three as captain.

His first Test series was in India in 1966/67, and he made 82 and 78 not out in his first appearance at Bombay. His most prolific series was his first as captain, also in India in 1974/75 when he scored 636 runs at an average of 79.50. It included his highest Test score, 242 not out in the fifth Test at Bombay.

His attacking abilities really came to the fore in one-day internationals. He led his side to victory in the first two World Cups, held in England in 1975 and 1979. In the first he scored a magnificent 102, a match-winning innings.

Records never meant much to

him, but he created some notable ones. He played the most Test innings before recording his first duck – 58, from December 1966 until February 1974. He equalled the record for the fastest double century when, playing for the West Indies against Glamorgan in 1976, he took eighty minutes for the first hundred and a further forty for the second.

He captained the West Indies in 74 Tests, winning 36 and losing just 12. Of the eighteen rubbers in that time, he lost just two – against Australia in 1975/76 and, perhaps most unlikely of all, against New Zealand in 1979/80.

In English county cricket he was a stalwart for Lancashire, scoring 1,000 runs in a season ten times. He joined the county in 1968 and became captain in 1981. He helped them to several one-day successes, most notably in the Gillette Cup.

First Class Career:
Runs – 31,232. Average 49.26
(79 centuries)

Test Match Career:
Tests – 110
Runs – 7,515. Average 46.67
(19 centuries)

LORD'S

L ORD'S IS QUITE SIMPLY the most famous cricket ground in the world and is rightly regarded as the headquarters of the game.

Set in the London district of St John's Wood, the ground has many features instantly recognised by cricket lovers everywhere. There are the various stands such as the Mound, the Warner, the Compton and the Edrich; the pavilion; the Tavern; and the Father Time weathervane above the Grandstand.

Little wonder that it should be the arena at which everyone who has ever picked up a bat or ball would love to play. There is nothing quite like the atmosphere generated by a Test match at Lord's.

Lord's is owned by the MCC, a private club of 18,000 members,

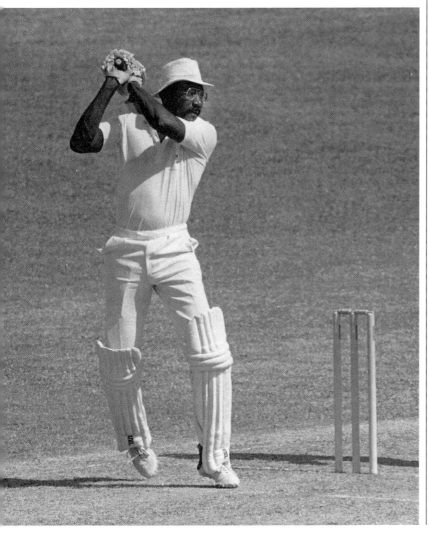

and their histories are inextricably linked. The MCC's role as the governing body of English cricket has now passed on to the Cricket Council, with the Test and County Cricket Board now in charge of the professional game. They have their offices at the ground.

Middlesex County Cricket Club, as tenants of the MCC, play most of their home matches at Lord's. The ground also traditionally stages the second Test of five- or six-match series, one-day knock-out finals, and traditional fixtures such as Oxford v Cambridge and Eton v Harrow.

It is a heavy burden on a not particularly large playing area that slopes six and a half feet from the Grandstand down to the Tavern. The ground holds 28,000 spectators, and the early days of Test matches, one-day internationals and domestic finals are nearly always sold out months in advance.

Away from the playing area itself, Lord's has practice facilities outside at the Nursery end and inside too, with the opening in 1977 of the MCC's indoor cricket school. There is also a Memorial Gallery, home of the Ashes, and a library. At the entrance to the ground are the famous Grace Gates, in memory of the great W.G.

The ground takes its name from its founder, Thomas Lord, a Yorkshireman. It is the third ground to bear his name. The first opened in 1787 about a mile away at Dorset Fields. Twenty-one years later, when a rise in rent was demanded, another ground was used nearby; then the present site was established in 1814.

In 1825 William Ward, a formidable cricketer, eventually bought out the lease from Lord after the founder had prepared plans to build seven pairs of houses on part of the ground. But Ward was immediately faced with a catastrophe.

The original pavilion was destroyed by fire in that year and with it went all the club records. However, a replacement was quickly built, ready for the following season, and a year later Lord's staged its first Oxford v Cambridge university match.

The MCC eventually acquired the freehold of the ground in 1866 for £18,000 – they could have had it six years previously for less than half that figure but did not bid for it.

The first Test at the ground came in 1884 when England beat Australia by an innings and five runs. Lord's became recognised as a Test ground, and every touring team since then has played there.

The present pavilion was built in 1889/90 and completed in a matter of eight months at a cost of £21,000. Inside, there have been a number of changes over the years, but externally it is still very much as it was originally.

There have been many famous moments on the ground, although because it usually hosts the second Test of a series, they do not quite compare with the dramatic climaxes witnessed at the Oval.

After South Africa played a first Test match on the ground in 1907, the West Indies, New Zealand and India made their debuts there

between the wars.

However, Australia were still the real 'foe', and Tests in the thirties provided some thrilling cricket. In 1930 Bradman, on his first tour of England, made a fluent 254, often regarded as one of his best innings.

In 1934 the spin of Hedley Verity – fourteen wickets in a day, and fifteen in the match – saw England achieve their first success against Australia at Lord's since 1896. Sadly, their last to date!

Although Lord's escaped relatively lightly from German bombing during the Second World War, there were a number of incidents at the ground.

Andrew Ducat of Surrey and England died of a heart attack while batting in 1942, and during the match between the Army and the RAF in 1944 the players had to throw themselves to the ground as a 'flying bomb' passed overhead, eventually to land in nearby Regent's Park.

In the immediate post-war years, the Middlesex batsmen Denis Compton and Bill Edrich attracted huge crowds to the ground, scoring thirty centuries between them in the glorious summer of 1947.

In 1950 there were wild celebrations as the West Indies achieved their first Test victory in England at Lord's. It was the year of the three W's, Worrell, Weekes and Walcott, and the spin twins Ramadhin and Valentine.

The Lord's Test between England and the West Indies in 1963 will go down as one of the greatest of all time. With one over remaining, any one of four results – a win for either side, a draw or a tie – was still possible.

With two balls left, Colin Cowdrey, his left arm in plaster following the break inflicted by Wesley Hall earlier in the match, came to the wicket with England needing six to win with one wicket standing. BBC Television abandoned a news bulletin to stay with the drama, as David Allen blocked those final deliveries to earn England a draw.

That summer was an important one, Lord's staged its first one-day final as Sussex beat Worcestershire to take the Gillette Cup.

The Benson and Hedges Cup final followed in 1972, with international one-day cricket spawning the first World Cup final at Lord's in 1975.

Other notable achievements on the ground in recent years have included the sixteen wickets taken by Bob Massie for Australia on his Test debut in 1972, and the first three Australian batsmen scoring centuries against England in 1993. It was one run away from being a Test record when their number four, Mark Waugh, fell for 99.

With facilities at the ground constantly being updated and improved, and with such a wealth of history behind it, Lord's will unquestionably continue to be the true home of the game of cricket.

The new Mound Stand at Lord's, with its tented roof. The corporate hospitality areas in the upper tiers are some of the most sought-after in English sport.

MAJID KHAN

Pakistan

Born 1946

Lahore, Pakistan International Airlines, Punjab, Cambridge University, Glamorgan and Queensland

IT IS HARD TO IMAGINE that Majid Khan could have been anything but a top-class cricketer. With an Indian fast bowler for a father, a brother who was also a Cambridge blue, and two cousins, Imran Khan and Javed Burki, as fellow captains of Pakistan, Majid had all the right credentials.

An intelligent, but at the same time laid-back character, Majid was a gifted all-rounder – an attractive attacking batsman, useful medium-pace or off-spin bowler, and fine close-to-the-wicket fielder.

He made 111 not out and took 6 for 67 on his first-class debut for Lahore at fifteen years of age. Soon afterwards, playing for Punjab University, he scored an undefeated 286 to win a match after his side had been reduced to 5 for 4.

Test cricket followed by the time he was eighteen. He made a duck on his debut against Australia, but took three wickets. There were

Majid pictured at Lord's in 1982, towards the end of a Test career which lasted almost twenty years after he made his Pakistan debut aged just 18.

doubts about his bowling action and he altered it, but decided to concentrate mainly on his batting.

It turned out to be a sound decision. Although his first tour of England in 1963 saw him score few runs in Tests, he had one extraordinary innings when he made 147 not out in 89 minutes against Glamorgan at Swansea, hitting off-spinner Roger Davis for five sixes in one over.

Glamorgan were impressed and soon signed him. It proved a successful move, Majid helping them to the County Championship title in 1969.

He also went to Cambridge, scoring a double century in the 1970 Varsity match and captaining the side in 1971 and 1972, when they recorded their first win over Oxford for fourteen years.

He captained Glamorgan from 1976 until his resignation in 1979, when he moved to Queensland, for whom he made two centuries.

Majid remains one of the few players to have a scored a century before lunch on the first day of a Test, against New Zealand at Karachi in 1976.

Intelligent character that he was,

Majid surprisingly captained his country on only three occasions, the series against England in 1972/73 when all three Tests were drawn.

A pleasant character and an attractive batsman to watch, it may be that he never quite realised his full potential at Test level.

First Class Career:
Runs – 27,444. Average 43.01 (73 centuries)

Test Match Career:
Tests – 63
Runs – 3,931. Average 38.92 (8 centuries)

MANAGERS

THAT CRICKET IS beginning to mirror other major sports such as football has never been more clearly demonstrated than in the emergence of the cricket 'manager' – and with it has come football's love of hiring and firing.

At Test level, Micky Stewart became England's first tracksuited off-the-field general, a permanent

figure while the captains would come and go. His successor as England manager, Keith Fletcher, continued on the same lines, stressing the importance of the partnership between manager and captain.

The humble county coach of past years is now being replaced by the manager. While in most cases the captain still retains control of the major decisions, such as team selection, the influence of the manager is growing.

In truth the appointment of a manager has often been a simple step up from the title of county coach, but some counties have adopted a bolder approach. Leicestershire, for example, went overseas and hired the Australian manager and former Test captain Bobby Simpson. However, he was unable significantly to improve the county's fortunes.

What every tracksuit manager likes to see . . . Australian players are put through their paces before the start of play in a one-day international against England at Old Trafford.

The end of the 1993 domestic season saw a growing trend of counties, feeling their sides had under-achieved, sacking their managers. David Hughes of Lancashire was the first to lose his job, followed by Surrey's Geoff Arnold, who was also one of Keith Fletcher's right-hand men in the England set-up. Some weeks later Mike Hendrick of Nottinghamshire suffered a similar fate.

Before long it could be that cricket writers will, like their football colleagues, be drawing conclusions when a county chairman gives his manager a vote of confidence.

RODNEY MARSH

Australia

Born 1947
Western Australia

AUSTRALIAN CRICKETERS have always been combative, but few more so than Rodney Marsh. He was a belligerent batsman, usually coming in at number seven, and an athletic

wicket-keeper, despite a burly frame.

He became an integral member of the successful Australian side under Ian Chappell, keeping wicket against the pace of Lillee and Thomson, and providing quick runs and powerful hitting in the lower middle-order. Yet the omens were far from rosy when he started his Test career.

In his first Test series in 1970/71, he was soon labelled 'Irongloves' for the number of times he would drop the ball. However, he steadily improved as a wicket-keeper and made the position secure.

He frequently played a major role with his batting, scoring three Test centuries. Although most noted for his aggression, he could also defend when necessary.

He joined the Packer rebels but returned to Test cricket, where his batting lacked some of its previous effectiveness. He was appointed vice-captain of the party that toured England in 1981.

It was in the famous Headingley Test of that summer that Marsh made almost as many headlines as Ian Botham and Bob Willis. He overtook Alan Knott's record of Test

dismissals, his 264th victim being Ian Botham, appropriately enough, caught off Dennis Lillee.

Then the Press discovered that with England seemingly destined for defeat, Marsh and Lillee had placed a bet on England winning at 500 to 1. No one could have tried harder for an Australian victory, but in the end the two Australians had to be content with the money as England pulled off their amazing win.

Marsh went on to other records, his 28 catches in the 1982/83 Ashes series being the highest number of dismissals in a series.

Marsh's contribution to Australian cricket has continued since his retirement from playing. He is now head coach at the Institute of Sport Cricket Academy in Adelaide, from where great talents such as Michael Slater and Shane Warne have emerged.

First Class Career:
*Runs – 11,067. Average 31.17
(12 centuries)
Catches – 804. Stumpings – 65*

Test Match Career:
*Tests – 96
Runs – 3,633. Average 26.51
(3 centuries)
Catches – 343. Stumpings – 12*

MALCOLM MARSHALL
West Indies
*Born 1958
Barbados and Hampshire*

SMALLER IN STATURE than the normal Caribbean fast bowler, Malcolm Marshall is the leading West Indies Test wicket-taker. With a whippy action, he has nevertheless been one of their quickest and most hostile bowlers for more than fifteen years.

He has had a long and distinguished career, making his Test debut in 1978/79 in India after just one first-class game in which he took 6 for 77 for Barbados against Jamaica in the Shell Shield.

He followed Andy Roberts to Hampshire in English county cricket and showed himself to be a worthy successor with the ball as well as a more than useful batsman.

He had to wait a few years to establish himself in the West Indies side, with the selectors at first using him as first reserve to Roberts, Holding, Croft and Garner.

However, in 1982 he took 134 wickets for Hampshire, the highest number of wickets taken by a player in a 22-match championship, to make him easily the most successful bowler in county cricket.

From then on he enjoyed enormous success for the West Indies. In India in 1983/84 he took 33 wickets in the series, but his best tally came in 1988 when he took 35 wickets in England for an average of 12.65, as the West Indies took the series 4–0.

It took him 49 Tests to reach the double of 1,000 runs and 100 wickets, and he has now taken almost 400 wickets.

First Class Career:
Wickets – 1,599. Average 19.08

Test Match Career:
Wickets – 376. Average 20.94

MARYLEBONE CRICKET CLUB

THE MCC, FOR SO LONG the ruling body in world cricket, may no longer have the power it once did, but it still retains considerable influence in the game.

The MCC's role in cricket was once described by Sir Pelham Warner as being a 'private club with a public function'. He is also believed to have said that the MCC reigns but does not rule.

The MCC controlled the organisation of cricket from its formation in 1787 until 1968, when the Cricket Council was formed and the Test and County Cricket Board and the National Cricket Association were established as autonomous bodies.

The club, with its famous orange and yellow colours, remains the maker and overseer of the laws of the game. But its ability to dictate matters has diminished, a fact clearly demonstrated by the attempt by some members to have the club condemn the England selectors for their choice of the party to tour India in 1992/93.

England touring sides are no longer known as the MCC in matches other than Tests, although they still wear the club's colours. Membership of the MCC is highly prized, 18,000 strong and with the waiting list extending for decades ahead.

The club still plays many fixtures, although not at first-class level. Matches now are usually against club sides and schools.

The histories of the MCC and Lord's cricket ground, its headquarters, are inextricably linked. The club was formed when Thomas Lord opened his first ground in Dorset Fields in 1747, eventually moving to its third and present site in 1814.

Benjamin Aislabie became the first secretary, and his death in office in 1842 led to a general decline in the club's affairs. But that was turned around by Bob Fitzgerald, a popular character.

Other important figures in the development of the MCC include Sir Spencer Ponsonby-Fane, who served as treasurer for 36 years and began the now distinguished art collection, and Francis Lacey, who became the first paid secretary from 1898 to 1926.

Lacey was the first man to be knighted for his services to cricket, and he formed a highly successful partnership with Lord Harris, who served as treasurer.

The Bodyline controversy of 1932/33 tested the MCC as never before. The club stood by the captain, Douglas Jardine, and took a hard line against the incoming Australian cables that condemned his tactics. But the matter was investigated at greater length when the side returned home, and

The action is all his own, the problems are all the batsman's: Malcolm Marshall's 'whippy' delivery makes him very difficult for batsman to read, any variation in pace and length almost impossible to anticipate.

Managing to look for all the world like Our Man in Trinidad waiting for Commander Bond to make himself known, this MCC member wears his colours at the Queen's Park Oval in 1980.

eventually the law on unfair play was altered.

Other crises followed such as the D'Oliveira affair, and with it the eventual exclusion of South Africa from Test cricket, and Kerry Packer's World Series Cricket.

The changes to the administrative structure of the game in England came about in 1968 when the Labour Government agreed to make public grants available to sports and games, but could not be seen to be making them to private institutions, however public their function.

Hence the MCC voluntarily relinquished much of its control for the general good of the game. However, as owners of Lord's and arbiters of the laws, the MCC's function is still a vital one.

PETER MAY
England

Born 1929. Died 1994
Cambridge University and
Surrey

ENGLAND HAVE produced few finer batsmen than Peter May. Six feet tall, he had a sound defence and was a fine driver of the ball. He invariably made batting look easy.

Although an amateur who combined his cricket with a busy life in the insurance business, he possessed a ruthless streak as a captain which seemed at odds with his otherwise gentle, self-effacing manner.

After a glittering schoolboy and University career, May made his first

May, another great hero of the post-war generation, batting for England against India in 1952.

Test appearance at the age of 21, against South Africa at Headingley in 1951, scoring a century.

In 1953 he had problems against the Australians and the pace of Ray Lindwall in particular, but returned to the England side for the final Test at the Oval where the Ashes were regained.

His finest hour came at Edgbaston in 1957 when England were struggling against the spin of Sonny Ramadhin. Deciding to play him as an off-spinner, May and Colin Cowdrey made 411 together, England's highest ever partnership and the world record for the fourth wicket.

May's contribution was 285 not out, the highest score by an England Test captain in office.

May captained Surrey from 1957 until 1962, having been a part of the successful Championship winning sides of the 1950s under Stuart Surridge.

His business, family commitments and illness led him to retire early from the game in 1963. He captained England on 41 occasions, winning 20 matches and losing ten.

He continued to play a full part in cricket off the field. He was chairman of the Test and County Cricket Board's cricket committee, president of the MCC in 1980/81, and chairman of selectors from 1982 until Ted Dexter's appointment seven years later. He was created a CBE.

The cricket world was shocked by his death on 27 December 1994 at the age of 64. He was to have been president of Surrey in 1995, his club's 150th anniversary.

First Class Career:
Runs – 27,592. Average 51.00 (85 centuries)

Test Match Career:
Tests – 66.
Runs – 4,537. Average 46.77 (13 centuries)

Australia's Graham McKenzie shows his classic sideways-on action during nets.

GRAHAM McKENZIE
Australia
Born 1941
Western Australia and Leicestershire

GRAHAM McKENZIE WAS one of the best fast bowlers to represent Australia. With a classical action and beautiful sideways-on delivery, he could mix in a deliberate change of pace that often claimed wickets.

A strong man, he was nicknamed 'Garth' after a cartoon character. He broke into the Test team on the 1961 tour of England, opening the bowling with Alan Davidson. By the time he was 23, he had become the youngest Australian to take 100 Test wickets, and in the least time – 3 years 165 days.

Despite being hostile on the pitch, McKenzie was always a gentle giant off it. Among his best performances was one at Lord's in 1961 when he took five wickets in each innings in Australia's win.

He was also more than useful with the bat. He made 76 against South Africa in 1963/64, and would often chip in with vital scores just when they were needed.

His haul of 246 Test wickets was second only to Richie Benaud at the time.

With the best of his Test career behind him, McKenzie joined Leicestershire. He gave admirable service over seven seasons from 1969, helping the county to a notable double in 1975 – their first ever Championship success and

victory in the Benson and Hedges Cup.

First Class Career:
Wickets – 1,219. Average 26.96

Test Match Career:
Tests – 60
Wickets – 246. Average 29.78

MELBOURNE

IT WAS AT THE MELBOURNE Cricket Ground, known as the MCG, that Test cricket was born when Australia beat England by 45 runs in March 1877.

It is now the largest cricket ground in the world, a vast bowl of a stadium that can hold 130,000 spectators, 110,000 of them seated. Apart from cricket, it hosts Australian Rules football's greatest occasions, and was the venue for the 1956 Olympic Games.

Not surprisingly, the MCG takes vast sums of money in gate receipts, especially for the one-day games the Australian public seems to relish. Figures in excess of A$2.5 million for a cricket season have been commonplace since the mid-1980s.

The home of the Melbourne Cricket Club, considered to be the top sporting body in Australia, the MCG was established at Yarra Park in 1853. Like the Marylebone Cricket Club in England, this MCC ran Australian cricket until the creation of the Australian Cricket Board.

The two highest totals in first-class cricket have been made at Melbourne. In 1922/23 Victoria made 1,059 against Tasmania, and then topped that with 1,107 against New South Wales in 1926/27.

The ground has seen controversy too. In 1954/55 the groundsman watered the wicket during the rest day of the third Test between Australia and England. The teams

The Melbourne Cricket Ground's huge stands are packed to capacity at the start of the 1992 World Cup final between England and Pakistan.

agreed to play on, but his mistake cost Australia the game.

Their last eight wickets fell for 36 runs in the final innings, Frank Tyson taking 6 for 16 with some of the most hostile fast bowling seen at the ground.

In 1977 Australia faced England again in a centenary Test to mark that first international fixture. Remarkably, Australia won again in a fine game of cricket by exactly the same score, 45 runs.

Bigger and better stands have been built at the MCG over the years, and floodlighting pylons now dominate the skyline.

The first night-time game staged there was the opening match of the World Championship of Cricket in

1985, and games under floodlights are now commonplace.

The ground has also become famous for the MCG roar, where the noise of the crowd echoes around the ground. It remains an awe-inspiring place to play cricket.

VIJAY MERCHANT
India

Born 1911. Died 1987
Bombay

VIJAY MERCHANT WAS the linchpin of the Indian batting when the country made its entrance into the Test arena. Although small in size, he was quick-footed and, like many short men, was a good cutter and puller. Merchant was his country's first really big star.

He played for India in the first series against England in 1933/34. But it was in England in 1936 that he made his mark as the top Indian batsman, scoring 1,745 in first-class matches. He averaged 47.00 in Tests, his best effort being 114 at Old Trafford.

Touring England again in 1946 he did even better, scoring 245 runs in Tests. His most notable achievements, though, were double centuries against Lancashire and Sussex.

His highest first-class score, 359 not out, was made for Bombay against Maharashtra in 1943/44. Throughout his career he was a prolific scorer in Indian domestic cricket.

In his final Test against England in Delhi in 1951/52, he scored 154. However, an old shoulder injury flared up again in the field and he retired from cricket to become an administrator.

First Class Career:
Runs – 13,228. Average 71.11
(44 centuries)

Test Match Career:
Tests – 10
Runs – 859. Average 47.72
(3 centuries)

MIDDLESEX
Founded: 1864

Entered Official
Championship: 1890

Honours:
County Champions – 1903, 1920, 1921, 1947, 1949 (joint), 1976, 1977 (joint), 1980, 1982, 1985, 1990, 1993
Gillette Cup – 1977, 1980
NatWest Trophy – 1984, 1988
Benson and Hedges Cup – 1983, 1986
Sunday League – 1992

MIDDLESEX HAVE unquestionably been one of the two most powerful sides in English cricket in recent times. Since 1980, they have won eleven major titles, including the County Championship five times.

Together with Essex, they have dominated the county scene thanks to a strong batting line-up, a more than useful fast bowling line-up, and the best spin attack in the domestic game.

The club was formed in 1864 at a meeting at the London Tavern in Bishopsgate. One of their most inglorious records still dates from that season, being dismissed for just 20 by the MCC at Lord's.

The club gave up their ground at Islington in 1868 and another ground in West Brompton proved unsuitable. Indeed the club came close to folding, with some members feeling that London could not support a third first-class club in addition to Surrey and the MCC.

In 1877 Middlesex eventually accepted an invitation from the MCC to make Lord's their home, having previously turned down a number of requests. At first they paid nothing for the privilege, but after they started to make regular donations to the MCC, a regular arrangement was formalised in 1899.

In 1890 Middlesex were one of eight counties to contest the inaugural official County Championship. With the side made up almost entirely of amateurs, there

were considerable problems keeping a settled team.

A.E. Stoddart and Sir Timothy O'Brien were important figures at that time, with Stoddart, arguably the greatest amateur batsmen to play for Middlesex, going on to captain England in Australia in 1894/95 and 1897/98.

By the time the 20th century began Middlesex were a major force in the game and they won their first title in 1903, one of the wettest English summers ever. It was to be their only success before the First World War, but under the captaincy of Pelham 'Plum' Warner, the club made steady progress.

Two players who were to become the county's highest scoring batsmen were coming to the fore. E. 'Patsy' Hendren made more than 37,000 runs for Middlesex in the Championship, in a career that stretched until 1937 and included 51 England appearances. J.W. Hearne, who played 24 times for England, was another fine strokemaker who scored more than 25,000 runs in Championship cricket.

These two were largely responsible for Middlesex's second Championship win in 1920, with Hendren averaging 69 and Hearne 54. It was Warner's last season as captain and a gloriously successful one, with the county winning their last nine games, and defeating London rivals Surrey in the final match, to take the title.

F.T. Mann took over the following year as Middlesex retained the Championship, when again the final match of the season against Surrey at Lord's proved decisive. There wasn't quite the same excitement this time, however, with Middlesex leading the table from the start.

That was to be the county's last success until after the Second World War, with inconsistent bowling and the lack of a settled side preventing further titles coming to Lord's. But they gave notice that better times were coming by finishing second four years in succession from 1936 to 1939.

Another second place in the wet summer of 1946 was followed by the

Dennis Compton (right) and Bill Edrich coming out to bat for Middlesex against The Rest in the last match of the 1947 season. They signed off in style, between them contributing 426 runs to the Middlesex total of 543–9: Compton 246, Edrich 180.

title itself in the glorious summer of 1947. Middle-order batsmen Denis Compton and Bill Edrich and opener J.D. Robertson each made more than 2,000 runs and, importantly, made them quickly, giving a bowling attack based on the spinners Sims and Young time to dismiss the opposition.

Middlesex won nineteen of their 26 matches that season, and were favourites to take the title again the following year. But England calls robbed them of Compton, Edrich and Young, and their lack of strong reserves allowed Glamorgan to surprise everyone to claim their first success.

In 1949 Middlesex shared the championship with Yorkshire thanks to a three-wicket win over Derbyshire in the final match at Lord's. With the home side needing 193 for victory on a difficult pitch, Compton's 97 not out proved the turning point after they had been reduced to 36 for 5.

Although no further titles were to follow in the fifties and sixties, the county produced many notable England players, the highlight coming when the 1964/65 tour to South Africa saw Middlesex provide five players: batsmen Peter Parfitt and a young Mike Brearley, bowlers John Price and Fred Titmus, and wicket-keeper John Murray.

Titmus, a canny off-spinner, had taken 158 wickets in 1955, and in seven seasons did the double. But in contrast to his achievements, the side generally played below its potential.

In 1971 Mike Brearley took over the captaincy and brought a greater sense of purpose to Middlesex cricket. Older players such as Mike Smith, Clive Radley and Titmus were joined by talented younger players like Mike Gatting, Graham Barlow and spinners Phil Edmonds and John Emburey.

In 1975 they were defeated in both one-day knock-out finals, but the Championship was won the following year in another particularly hot, dry summer. In 1977 Middlesex shared the Championship with Kent, after Gloucestershire had led the table at the start of the final day. They made it a double by taking the Gillette Cup on home territory at Lord's.

England calls did not help their pursuit of further success, with Brearley, Radley, Edmonds and Emburey regularly unavailable. But in 1980 they completed another Championship/Gillette Cup double, thanks largely to a powerful overseas bowling attack in Wayne Daniel from the West Indies and Vincent van der Bijl of South Africa.

They took the Championship again in 1982 as an emotional farewell to Brearley.

The success continued under the leadership of the pugnacious Mike Gatting. Two more championships, in 1985 and 1990, and four more one-day titles provided evidence of a steady supply of talent, helped by quality overseas 'imports' such as the West Indies opening bat Desmond Haynes.

In 1992 they achieved another first by winning the Sunday League, making Gatting only the second captain after Keith Fletcher of Essex to lead a team to success in all four major competitions.

The following year the new four-day, 17-match Championship title was secured in a season which saw Middlesex lose only one game in the competition, their final match at Worcester. Five batsmen averaged over 40, and Emburey and Tufnell were the leading wicket-takers, well supported by a fit-again Angus Fraser.

KEITH MILLER

Australia

Born 1919

Victoria, New South Wales and Nottinghamshire

KEITH MILLER WILL GO down as one of the greatest all-rounders the game of cricket has seen. For the decade after the Second World War he was probably the most exciting player in the world, becoming hugely popular with crowds wherever he played.

He was an extrovert, never letting the disciplines of cricket interfere with his determination to get the most out of life off the field.

He had a passion for an unusual combination of classical music and horse racing. Such was his interest, he once led his side off the field to listen to a commentary on the Melbourne Cup race.

As a right-handed batsman he was unpredictable, but with a powerful drive had the ability to take any attack apart. He could bowl faster than Lindwall when the mood

The power of Miller's batting is captured here in this shot from the 1956 tour of England.

took him, and as a pair they brought Australia much success.

Miller had served as a pilot in Britain during the Second World War, once crash-landing a Mosquito with an engine on fire. He first attracted the attention of English crowds by scoring 185 in 165 minutes for the Dominions at Lord's as part of the post-war celebrations.

He was a player who needed to be stretched. If things became too easy, he got bored. Such was the case in 1948 when the Australians scored more than 700 runs in a day against Essex. Miller deliberately removed his bat from the first ball he faced and was bowled for a duck.

He had already proved his ability by that time, having scored 79 and taken 7 for 60, his best bowling for Australia, against England at Brisbane in 1946/47. He went on to record his first Test century in that series, 141 not out at Adelaide.

Miller loved facing England. He played 29 Tests against them, scoring 1,511 runs at an average of 33.57, and took 87 wickets at 22.40.

Seven times in his career he made a double century, his highest score being 281 not out against Leicestershire in 1956.

He retired from international cricket at the end of the 1956/57 season, resenting, it is said, the appointment of Ian Johnson as captain of the 1956 touring party to England.

At the age of 40 he played for the MCC and Nottinghamshire, scoring an unbeaten century for the county against Cambridge University. He was awarded the MBE and went on to become a well-known journalist and commentator on the game.

First Class Career:
*Runs – 14,183. Average 48.90
    (41 centuries)
Wickets – 497. Average 22.30*

Test Match Career:
*Tests – 55
Runs – 2,958. Average 36.97
    (7 centuries)
Wickets – 170. Average 22.97*

MINOR COUNTIES

THE MINOR COUNTIES Cricket Association was formed in Birmingham in 1895 to provide competition for non-first-class counties and the 2nd XIs of first-class counties, although a separate competition for the latter was eventually created in 1959.

The Association has representatives on the two main governing bodies in English cricket, the Cricket Council and the Test and County Cricket Board.

Over the years, many minor counties have moved up to achieve full first-class status, the most recent being Durham in 1992.

MINOR COUNTIES CHAMPIONS			
1895	Norfolk, Durham and Worcestershire	1949	Lancashire II
1896	Worcestershire	1950	Surrey II
1897	Worcestershire	1951	Kent II
1898	Worcestershire	1952	Buckinghamshire
1899	Northamptonshire and Buckinghamshire	1953	Berkshire
1900	Glamorgan, Durham and Northamptonshire	1954	Surrey II
		1955	Surrey II
1901	Durham	1956	Kent II
1902	Wiltshire	1957	Yorkshire II
1903	Northamptonshire	1958	Yorkshire II
1904	Northamptonshire	1959	Warwickshire II
1905	Norfolk	1960	Lancashire II
1906	Staffordshire	1961	Somerset II
1907	Lancashire II	1962	Warwickshire II
1908	Staffordshire	1963	Cambridgeshire
1909	Wiltshire	1964	Lancashire II
1910	Norfolk	1965	Somerset II
1911	Staffordshire	1966	Lincolnshire
1912	*In abeyance*	1967	Cheshire
1913	Norfolk	1968	Yorkshire II
1914	Staffordshire	1969	Buckinghamshire
1920	Staffordshire	1970	Bedfordshire
1921	Staffordshire	1971	Yorkshire II
1922	Buckinghamshire	1972	Bedfordshire
1923	Buckinghamshire	1973	Shropshire
1924	Berkshire	1974	Oxfordshire
1925	Buckinghamshire	1975	Hertfordshire
1926	Durham	1976	Durham
1927	Staffordshire	1977	Suffolk
1928	Berkshire	1978	Devon
1929	Oxfordshire	1979	Suffolk
1930	Durham	1980	Durham
1931	Leicestershire II	1981	Durham
1932	Buckinghamshire	1982	Oxfordshire
1933	*Undecided*	1983	Hertfordshire
1934	Lancashire II	1984	Durham
1935	Middlesex II	1985	Cheshire
1936	Hertfordshire	1986	Cumberland
1937	Lancashire II	1987	Buckinghamshire
1938	Buckinghamshire	1988	Cheshire
1939	Surrey II	1989	Oxfordshire
1946	Suffolk	1990	Hertfordshire
1947	Yorkshire II	1991	Staffordshire
1948	Lancashire II	1992	Staffordshire
		1993	Staffordshire
		1994	Devon

Many Test players began their careers as youngsters at this level of cricket, and such is the quality of it now that 'alternative' might be a better description than 'minor'.

In all, nineteen English counties contest Minor Counties competitions, together with Minor Counties, Wales.

The introduction of one-day cricket has brought the Minor Counties more into the public eye, with the junior 'upstarts' springing the occasional surprise over first-class opposition.

Durham led the way, beating Yorkshire in the Gillette Cup in 1973. From 1964 to 1979, the previous season's top five Minor Counties were invited to enter the Gillette Cup, and they were joined by Ireland in 1980.

In 1983 the competition was expanded to embrace 13 Minor Counties, although the number dropped to twelve in 1992 when Durham joined the County Championship. Only Hertfordshire have gone as far as the quarter-finals, beating Berkshire and then Essex in 1976.

Sides representing various regions of the Minor Counties regularly appeared in the Benson and Hedges Cup when, before 1993, the early rounds were played as zonal leagues. The Minor Counties now has just one representative side in the competition.

The Minor Counties side have also achieved notable success against touring teams. They defeated the Australians at Sunderland in 1977 and the New Zealanders at Torquay the following year. In 1992 they beat the powerful Pakistan team in a thrilling one-wicket, last-ball victory at Marlow.

The Minor Counties Championship underwent a radical reorganisation in 1983 with the separation of the counties into two parallel divisions of ten, roughly split on an East and West basis.

Each team plays one two-day match against the other teams in its own group, with the title being decided, from 1994, by a two innings, two-day match between the two divisional winners (this replaced a one-day 55-overs game). In a rain-affected match, Devon beat Cambridgeshire.

In 1983 the Minor Counties also started their own knock-out competition and since 1989 the final has been played at Lord's. In 1993 Staffordshire completed the Minor Counties 'double', a feat repeated by Devon a year later.

Minor Counties tours have been undertaken and much work is done to develop youth cricket, with the majority of counties running teams at a variety of ages, including Under-19 and, increasingly, Under-25 levels.

A delighted Mushtaq holds the Gillette Cup after leading Northamptonshire to victory in the 1976 final at Lord's.

MUSHTAQ MOHAMMAD
Pakistan
Born 1943
Pakistan International Airlines, Karachi, Northamptonshire and Staffordshire

THE FOURTH OF THE FIVE cricketing Mohammad brothers, Mushtaq had the concentration of Hanif but was a more flamboyant strokemaker. He was also a leg-spin bowler of high quality who could be a match-winner in the right conditions.

Like his elder brother he was a record-setter, most notably by being a child prodigy. At 13 years 41 days he made his first-class debut, scoring 87 and taking 5 for 28 for Karachi Whites against Hyderabad.

In March 1959 Mushtaq made his Test debut against West Indies at the age of 15 years 124 days, the youngest player ever to be so honoured. Despite making only 14 and 4, he took to Test cricket at once and had scored centuries against India and England before his 19th birthday.

Mushtaq spent eleven years with Northamptonshire from 1966 to 1977. In 1976 he led the county to victory in the Gillette Cup, their first success in a major competition, and second place in the County Championship.

But the following year there was criticism of his leadership within the county and he left the club to play Minor Counties cricket with Staffordshire.

First Class Career:
Runs – 31,091. Average 42.07
(72 centuries)
Wickets – 936. Average 24.34

Test Match Career:
Tests – 57
Runs – 3,643. Average 39.17
(10 centuries)
Wickets – 79. Average 29.24

NATIONAL CLUB CHAMPIONSHIP

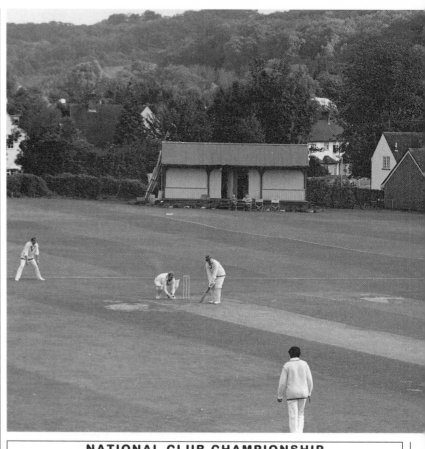

AFTER THE SUCCESS OF the Cricketer Cup, the one-day competition for school old boys' teams, a new national club cricket knock-out competition was launched in 1969 – the National Club Championship.

In that first season, 256 clubs took part in what was then the D.H. Robins Trophy, named after the competition's founder. They were first grouped into regions, with the winners then entering a non-geographical knock-out.

The first final brought success for Hampstead who beat Pocklington Pixies by 14 runs. It provided the Londoners with a unique treble, with their having won the Kemp's Cup for teams in the Club Cricket Conference the previous two years.

Scarborough are still the most successful side in the history of the competition, having won the trophy five times, in 1972, 1976, 1979, 1981 and 1982. In 1993 Old Hill recorded their fourth win in ten years by beating West Bromwich Dartmouth. It reversed the Birmingham League placings, where Dartmouth had finished as champions with Old Hill just four points behind.

Matches are of 45 overs per side, with no bowler allowed more than nine overs.

NATIONAL CLUB CHAMPIONSHIP

	Winners	Runners-up	
1969	Hampstead	Pocklington Pixies	14 runs
1970	Cheltenham	Stockport	3 wickets
1971	Blackheath	Ealing	8 wickets
1972	Scarborough	Brentham	6 wickets
1973	Wolverhampton	The Mote	5 wickets
1974	Sunbury	Tunbridge Wells	7 wickets
1975	York	Blackpool	6 wickets
1976	Scarborough	Dulwich	5 wickets
1977	Southgate	Bowdon	6 wickets
1978	Cheltenham	Bishop's Stortford	15 runs
1979	Scarborough	Reading	2 wickets
1980	Moseley	Gosport Borough	9 wickets
1981	Scarborough	Blackheath	57 runs
1982	Scarborough	Finchley	4 runs
1983	Shrewsbury	Hastings & St Leonards Priory	2 runs
1984	Old Hill	Bishop's Stortford	5 wickets
1985	Old Hill	Reading	9 wickets
1986	Stourbridge	Weston-super-Mare	4 wickets
1987	Old Hill	Teddington	5 wickets
1988	Enfield	Wolverhampton	9 wickets
1989	Teddington	Old Hill	11 runs
1990	Blackpool	Cheam	3 wickets
1991	Teddington	Walsall	11 runs
1992	Optimists	Kendal	7 wickets
1993	Old Hill	West Bromwich Dartmouth	7 wickets
1994	Chorley	Ealing	5 wickets

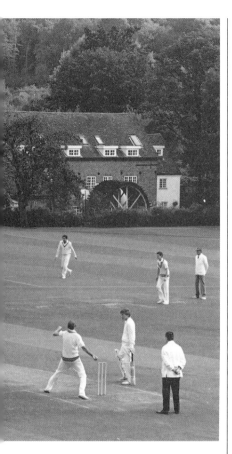

Perhaps the true spirit of English cricket is to be found not in the Long Room at Lord's but at the many hundreds of club grounds such as this one at High Wycombe. Never mind the weather: the game goes on.

NATIONAL CRICKET ASSOCIATION

THE NATIONAL CRICKET Association (NCA), which looks after the interests of the game below first-class level, was formed in 1968 as part of the administrative shake-up of English cricket that left the Cricket Council as head of the domestic game.

The NCA was first set up in 1965 as the MCC Cricket Association with the purpose of organising coaching on a national basis and to raise money by such means as applying for Government grants and attracting help from the business community.

It also administered national and local competitions, mainly through its affiliated counties, encouraged youth cricket and provided assistance to cricket clubs through the county associations.

Now 51 county associations and 18 national cricketing organisations are affiliated.

NATWEST TROPHY

ENGLISH CRICKET'S premier one-day competition, this event, sponsored by the National Westminster Bank, is to cricket what the FA Cup is to football. It ends with a glorious showpiece final each season, which invariably produces a carnival-like atmosphere at Lord's.

The competition, backed then by the sponsorship of Gillette, began in 1963 with the aim of improving the finances of the county clubs. Attendances for championship matches had dwindled, and the counties were desperately looking for new ways to increase their income.

The cricketing authorities were wary of sponsorship, however, and in its first season the competition was called 'The First-Class Counties Knock-Out Competition for the Gillette Cup', a dreadful mouthful which was generally shortened to the Knock-Out Cup and then became the Gillette Cup in 1964.

Gillette at first agreed to underwrite the competition for £6,500 – a tiny sum by today's standards. The money was divided up among the counties with each club taking a share for each match played.

To encourage individual players, a 'Man of the Match' award was introduced. This idea, too, had its critics, but has now become firmly established in one-day cricket throughout the world and in other sports as well.

In the first season of the competition, matches were 65 overs a side, with no bowler allowed to bowl more than 15. This was reduced to the current 60 overs in 1964, with bowlers now restricted to 12 each.

Wisden recorded two main criticisms of the competition in its first year, which saw Sussex beat Worcestershire in an exciting final by 14 runs.

First, there were fears that it could be the death of slow bowling, with most of the counties using medium pacers. Happily, the Man of the Match award in that first final went to the slow left-armer Norman Gifford, who took 4 for 33, and most teams now include at least one spinner, often to great effect.

Second, common tactics of placing fielders around the boundary to prevent rapid scoring were looked upon as negative. Restrictions on field-placing in one-day competitions generally have improved matters.

The success of the first year led to others wanting to enter the competition. In 1964 five Minor Counties took part, with no one ever expecting them to beat a first-class county. So it proved, until 1973 when Durham caused the biggest of upsets, beating Yorkshire at Harrogate by five wickets.

Under the Gillette sponsorship Sussex and Lancashire were the early kings of the one-day game, Sussex winning three of their six appearances in the final, Lancashire winning four from six.

There were many memorable moments. Geoffrey Boycott scored 146 for Yorkshire in the 1965 final against Surrey, an innings that left his supporters and critics dumbfounded, given his methodical play in Championship and Test matches.

One of the most famous matches was a semi-final at Old Trafford in 1971 when, at just before nine o'clock at night and in almost total darkness, Lancashire eventually beat Gloucestershire, thanks to David Hughes hitting 24 off one over from John Mortimore. An exciting match, watched by more than

23,000 people at the ground and many millions more on television – so successful had the competition become that Gillette eventually gave up their connection with it, partly because the name was becoming better known for cricket than their shaving products.

In 1981 the National Westminster Bank took over and the competition continued to flourish. Scotland, Wales and Ireland now compete in addition to the Minor Counties. Now called the NatWest Trophy, the competition still provides great enjoyment for spectators and much needed cash for the counties.

The 1993 final set new records, with Sussex, batting first, making a record 321. But amazingly Warwickshire were equal to the task and took the trophy for the first time in their history.

They just failed to repeat the achievement the following year when victory would have given them a unique clean sweep of the four domestic titles.

NEW ZEALAND

DESPITE BECOMING A Test playing nation in 1926, it is only in the past decade that New Zealand have enjoyed any appreciable success in international cricket. Their first fifty years of Test cricket produced few victories, and in truth were more notable for a number of heavy defeats.

For all the disappointments, New Zealand have produced players of true world class. Sadly though, there have generally never been enough of them at the same time to make them into a formidable Test playing unit. Workaday players have had to back up the odd true star.

However, the Kiwis have usually been recognised as trying to play entertaining cricket, even if that has cost them defeats on occasions.

New Zealand became a country in 1840, and organised cricket was played on the islands almost at once, thanks to the English influence. In 1894 the New Zealand Cricket Council was formed in Christchurch, coming almost at the same time as the creation of the New Zealand Rugby Union. The All

The scoreboard tells the story of an amazing NatWest final in 1993, won off the last ball (below) by Warwickshire.

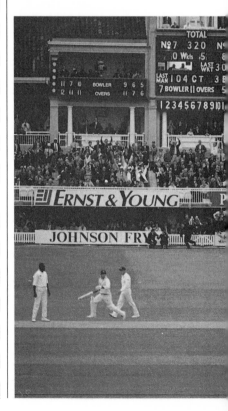

GILLETTE CUP

	Winners	Runners-up	
1963	Sussex	Worcestershire	14 runs
1964	Sussex	Warwickshire	8 wickets
1965	Yorkshire	Surrey	175 runs
1966	Warwickshire	Worcestershire	5 wickets
1967	Kent	Somerset	32 runs
1968	Warwickshire	Sussex	4 wickets
1969	Yorkshire	Derbyshire	69 runs
1970	Lancashire	Sussex	6 wickets
1971	Lancashire	Kent	24 runs
1972	Lancashire	Warwickshire	4 wickets
1973	Gloucestershire	Sussex	40 runs
1974	Kent	Lancashire	4 wickets
1975	Lancashire	Middlesex	7 wickets
1976	Northamptonshire	Lancashire	4 wickets
1977	Middlesex	Glamorgan	4 wickets
1978	Sussex	Somerset	5 wickets
1979	Somerset	Northamptonshire	45 runs
1980	Middlesex	Surrey	7 wickets

NAT WEST TROPHY

	Winners	Runners-up	
1981	Derbyshire	Northamptonshire	Lost fewer wickets
1982	Surrey	Warwickshire	9 wickets
1983	Somerset	Kent	24 runs
1984	Middlesex	Kent	4 wickets
1985	Essex	Nottinghamshire	1 run
1986	Sussex	Lancashire	7 wickets
1987	Nottinghamshire	Northamptonshire	3 wickets
1988	Middlesex	Worcestershire	3 wickets
1989	Warwickshire	Middlesex	4 wickets
1990	Lancashire	Northamptonshire	7 wickets
1991	Hampshire	Surrey	4 wickets
1992	Northamptonshire	Leicestershire	8 wickets
1993	Warwickshire	Sussex	5 wickets
1994	Worcestershire	Warwickshire	8 wickets

Blacks have certainly enjoyed more success than their cricketing compatriots.

By 1906/07 the game of cricket had become so well established that the Governor-General, Lord Plunkett, presented a shield as the prize for the major competition between the first-class provinces.

At the time, that was made up of teams from the major centres of population, Auckland, Wellington, Canterbury and Otago. In 1950/51 a fifth area, Central Districts, was formed, with a sixth, Northern Districts, following in 1956/57.

The Plunkett Shield was replaced by the Shell Trophy from 1975/76. No side has totally dominated the competition, although Auckland did take the honours four years in succession just before the war.

In the early days, New Zealand received regular tours from their nearest neighbours Australia. It was on one of those visits in 1914 that home supporters witnessed what was one of the most remarkable batting feats of all time.

The legendary Victor Trumper scored 293 against Canterbury in an innings that lasted just three hours. His first century came up in 73 minutes, his second in 131 minutes

Visits from MCC sides were regular occurrences too, with tours becoming more common after the First World War. A.H.H. Gilligan led England to a narrow 1-0 victory in the first Test series between the two in New Zealand in 1929/30.

Three years later Douglas Jardine's team drew two Tests in New Zealand following the Bodyline tour of Australia. The most notable feature of those games was an innings of 336 by Walter Hammond, who beat Bradman's then Test record, set at Headingley, by two runs.

The lack of a sufficiently high-quality domestic competition left New Zealand struggling to compete at international level, and they had to wait until a tour by the West Indies in 1955/56 to record their first Test victory. Having lost the first three matches in the series, the home side came back well in the final Test at Eden Park to win by 190 runs.

It was appropriate that the win came there, for it was on that Auckland ground in 1954/55 that New Zealand had suffered their greatest humiliation, being dismissed for just 26 against the side Sir Leonard Hutton had led to Ashes success. It is still the lowest score in Test cricket.

New Zealand were humbled by the superb bowling of Statham, Tyson and Appleyard and it was a disastrous result, with administrators fearing for the future of the game if such humiliations were to continue. The victory against the West Indies was therefore a blessed relief.

In 1974 the Kiwis recorded their first win over Australia, thanks largely to a century in each innings by Glenn Turner. Then, after 48 years of trying and in the 48th Test between the two countries, New Zealand eventually recorded their first win over England at Wellington in February 1978.

The fast bowling of Richard Hadlee and Richard Collinge was to prove England's undoing, with the opening pair skittling the tourists out for just 64 in their second innings when they needed a moderate 137 to win.

Hadlee, son of Walter the former New Zealand captain, was later knighted for his services to cricket. He was the world's leading wicket-taker in Tests with 431 until that total was overtaken by Kapil Dev of India. Hadlee was also a highly effective left-handed, late middle-order batsman.

New Zealand have generally been better known for their batsmen, in particular Turner, John Reid, Bert Sutcliffe, Geoff Howarth, John Wright, and their leading Test scorer, Martin Crowe.

Since 1979 success has been much more frequent for New Zealand than their previous history would have ever led them to expect. Perhaps their finest hour came in 1979/80 when they won one Test and drew the other two against Clive Lloyd's mighty West Indies in the Caribbean.

In 1983/84 and again in 1986, New Zealand achieved series wins over England. They also achieved two series wins over Australia in the 1985/86 season and won other series in the eighties against India, Pakistan and Sri Lanka.

However, they found life difficult again on their tour of England in 1994, losing one Test at Trent Bridge and only being saved by the weather in another at Old Trafford.

However, in recent years, New Zealand have taken well to one-day cricket and surprised a number of people by their success in reaching the semi-finals of three World Cups.

NEW ZEALAND
V
INDIA

NEW ZEALAND AND INDIA began playing Tests in 1955/56 with a five-match series in India that was marked by some high scoring. Three drawn Tests and two heavy defeats were all New Zealand had to show for their efforts.

India's two heroes from the series were Vinoo Mankad, who scored 526 runs and averaged 105.20, and 'Fergie' Gupte who took 34 wickets at 19.67.

It was almost ten years before the two met again, in India following New Zealand's tour of Pakistan. The first three Tests were drawn before India took the series through a seven-wicket win in the final match at New Delhi, the off-spin of Venkataraghavan dominating as he took 12 for 152.

In 1967/68 India recorded their first ever series win outside their

New Zealand skipper Ken Rutherford has to hurry to prevent a run-out by Paul Taylor (England) at Lord's in 1994. Rutherford took over as captain in 1993/94 and later that season passed 2000 Test runs.

homeland, winning a four-Test series in New Zealand 3–1. Once again, it was the Indian spin bowlers who dominated.

New Zealand looked as if they would gain their revenge in India in 1969/70. India took the first Test, New Zealand the second, and in the decider at Hyderabad, rain and rioting affected the outcome of a low-scoring game.

Set 268 to make on the final day, India struggled to 76 for 7 before rain stopped play.

A drawn series followed in New Zealand in 1975/76, before a familiar story, the dominance of India's spinners, resulted in a 2–0 win for the home side in India in 1976/77.

New Zealand at last won a series at home in 1980/81. Their sole victory came in the first Test at Wellington, when a century from their captain Geoff Howarth

established a strong base after his side had been put in to bat. India fell 62 runs short of the modest 253 they needed to win, thanks to the bowling of Richard Hadlee.

Since then, series wins have gone with home advantage. India won 2–1 at home in 1988/89, with New Zealand winning 1–0 in 1989/90. A one-off Test in New Zealand in March 1994 ended in the tamest of draws.

Season	Ven	Tests	Winners	Res
1955/56	Ind	5	India	2–0
1964/65	Ind	4	India	1–0
1967/68	NZ	4	India	3–1
1969/70	Ind	3	–	1–1
1975/76	NZ	3	–	1–1
1976/77	Ind	3	India	2–0
1980/81	NZ	3	N. Zealand	1–0
1988/89	Ind	3	India	2–1
1989/90	NZ	3	N. Zealand	1–0
1993/94	NZ	1	–	0–0

NEW ZEALAND
v
PAKISTAN

PAKISTAN HAVE ENJOYED almost total domination in series against New Zealand since Tests between them started in the 1950s. To date, New Zealand have recorded four wins, although they have managed two series victories.

Pakistan were far too strong for the Kiwis when they played three Tests in Pakistan in 1955/56. The home side won the first two matches and would have made it a clean sweep but for rain in the final Test at Dacca, when New Zealand still needed another 56 to make Pakistan bat again with only four second innings wickets left.

Three dull draws followed in New Zealand in 1964/65 before Pakistan clocked up another 2–0 win at home that same winter. In the one drawn match, Hanif Mohammad scored 203 not out, his highest Test score at home.

New Zealand recorded their first series win against any opposition, after forty years of trying, in Pakistan in 1969/70. The only victory came in the second Test at Lahore when Graham Dowling's side dismissed the hosts for 114 and 208. That left them needing only 82 to win, but still New Zealand wobbled before securing victory by five wickets.

Normal service was resumed in New Zealand in 1972/73, Pakistan winning 1–0. They followed that up by winning a high-scoring series 2–0 at home in 1976/77. Javed Miandad was the leading batsman with 504 runs from three Tests at an average of 126.00.

Further Pakistan series wins continued until 1984/85, when, only a month after losing 2–0 in Pakistan, New Zealand managed to reverse the scoreline at home.

On a green wicket at Auckland, Hadlee and Cairns twice dismissed Pakistan for under 200 to give New Zealand an innings win. An exciting two-wicket victory at Dunedin secured their best ever series result against Pakistan.

That was to be New Zealand's last success and Pakistan have continued to hold the upper hand since. Their most recent three-Test series in New Zealand in 1993/94 saw the fast bowling of Wasim Akram and Waqar Younis pave the way for a 2–1 win.

The home side had the consolation of recording only their fourth Test victory over Pakistan in the final Test at Christchurch, where maiden centuries from Young and Thomson helped them score their highest ever fourth innings total, 324, to win by five wickets.

Season	Ven	Tests	Winner	Res
1955/56	Pak	3	Pakistan	2–0
1964/65	NZ	3	–	0–0
1964/65	Pak	3	Pakistan	2–0
1969/70	Pak	3	N. Zealand	1–0
1972/73	NZ	3	Pakistan	1–0
1976/77	Pak	3	Pakistan	2–0
1978/79	NZ	3	Pakistan	1–0
1984/85	Pak	3	Pakistan	2–0
1984/85	NZ	3	N. Zealand	2–0
1988/89	NZ	2	–	0–0
1990/91	Pak	3	Pakistan	3–0
1992/93	NZ	1	Pakistan	1–0
1993/94	NZ	3	Pakistan	2–1

NEW ZEALAND
v
SRI LANKA

SINCE SRI LANKA'S arrival on the Test scene in 1981, they have played New Zealand in five series, winning just one Test of the eleven played.

The teams first met in New Zealand in 1982/83, the home side winning comfortably by 2–0. They took the first Test at Christchurch by an innings, Cairns taking eight wickets in the match, and Sri Lanka then recorded their lowest score against New Zealand, being dismissed for just 93 in the second innings at Wellington, to give the hosts victory by six wickets.

New Zealand's domination continued in Sri Lanka in 1983/84 when they won a three-Test series by the same 2–0 margin. Comfortable victories were gained in the first and third Tests, but Sri Lanka did at least have the better of the drawn second match.

Civil unrest wrecked New Zealand's next tour in 1986/87. After the sides played out a draw in the first Test, the authorities were forced to cancel the remaining Tests of the three-match series.

Three drawn matches followed in New Zealand in 1990/91 before Sri Lanka finally triumphed in 1992/93. New Zealand escaped with a draw in the first Test at Moratuwa but were totally outplayed in the second at Colombo. They were made to follow on after being dismissed for 102, and only a century by Martin Crowe made Sri Lanka bat again. They duly knocked off the runs to win by nine wickets.

Season	Ven	Tests	Winner	Res
1982/83	NZ	2	N. Zealand	2–0
1983/84	SL	3	N. Zealand	2–0
1986/87	SL	1	–	0–0
1990/91	NZ	3	–	0–0
1992/93	SL	2	Sri Lanka	1–0

NEW ZEALAND
v
ZIMBABWE

NEW ZEALAND AND Zimbabwe have played just one series, in November 1992.

The first match at Bulawayo was an uninspiring draw, thanks to ten hours of torrential rain which for once was greeted with cheers by the spectators – Zimbabwe's drought problems being of more concern than the country's cricketing fortunes.

The game was notable only for Greatbatch and Latham becoming the first New Zealand openers to share century partnerships in each innings of a Test.

The match was also a landmark for English umpire Dickie Bird. It was his 49th Test, a world record.

At Harare Sports Club, two days later, the second Test saw New

Ali Shah (Zimbabwe) is run out in the first Test against New Zealand at Bulawayo in 1992/93.

Zealand record a comfortable victory by 177 runs. The home side surprisingly collapsed to 137 all out on the final day, with Dipak Patel taking 6 for 50.

Season	Ven	Tests	Winner	Res
1992/93	Zim	2	N. Zealand	1–0

NORTHAMPTONSHIRE

Founded: 1878

Entered Official Championship: 1905

Honours:

Gillette Cup – 1976

NatWest Trophy – 1992

Benson and Hedges Cup – 1980

ONE-DAY CRICKET HAS provided Northamptonshire with their only trophies in senior cricket. Their limited resources have meant they have rarely been able to mount a serious challenge for the Championship, their best placing being second on four occasions.

As a small county, they have often had to rely on players from outside Northamptonshire and indeed from overseas. Nevertheless, they have generally made the most of the talent available, with teamwork invariably the main feature of their cricket.

In 1820 the Northamptonshire County Cricket Club evolved from the Northampton Town Club and in 1878, during the annual North v South Northants match, it was decided to put the county club on a proper footing.

The first match on their current ground – which until 1994 doubled as home for Northampton Town FC in the football season – was in May 1886 when Surrey Club and Ground won by six wickets.

In 1905 Northamptonshire achieved first-class status and entered the County Championship. Their elevation was credited to the ability of one player in particular, George Thompson. A fast-medium bowler and steady batsman, it was Thompson, according to *Wisden*, who 'rendered the promotion possible'.

Those early seasons saw Northamptonshire struggle to establish themselves. The bowling, led by Thompson and William East, was of a satisfactory standard, but the batting often let them down. Their lowest ever total, 12, came against Gloucestershire in 1907.

In the period leading up to the First World War, Northants created quite a surprise by finishing a close second to Yorkshire in 1912, winning ten of their eighteen matches.

Their captain G.A.T. Vials led a team that called upon the services of just twelve players. The collective will of the side produced results that would never have been expected of the individual talent.

Fourth place the following year showed that this was a more than useful side; and although ninth in 1914 was rather an anti-climax, the county was on a sound footing.

Sadly, Northants were unable to recreate that sense of purpose, and between the wars they were often an easy touch. The batting was generally weak with just A.H. Bakewell as their one shining light.

Between 1928 and 1936, when he was badly injured in a road accident which ended his career, Bakewell scored almost 13,000 runs.

No chance for Justin Benson (Leics) as Curtly Ambrose sends the stumps flying and Northants head for victory in the final of the 1992 NatWest Trophy.

In 1933, when Northants beat the West Indies by an innings, he became the first player to reach 2,000 runs in a season. That total included 246 against Nottinghamshire and 257 against Glamorgan. He played six times for England and would surely have made many more appearances but for the tragedy that struck him at just 27 years of age.

It was in 1949 that the county's fortunes really improved. Their most pressing need, a strong leader, was answered in the shape of the Surrey and England all-rounder F.R. Brown.

The appointment was good for Northamptonshire and good for Brown. He had all but given up the game, but now found a new sense of purpose. In his first season with the county, at 38 years of age and twelve years after his last Test appearance, he returned to the England fold as captain against New Zealand.

During Brown's reign as county captain, Northants never finished higher than eighth or lower than 13th – modest returns for many counties, but a considerable improvement to the Northants record of the previous thirty years.

Among the 'imports' to play under Brown were Frank Tyson, at the time the fastest bowler in the country, and a number of Australians. Tyson and wicket-keeper Keith Andrew made history when in 1954 they became the first Northants professionals to be chosen for an MCC tour of Australia.

Under the captaincy of Dennis Brookes, a Yorkshireman, the county finished seventh that season, their best placing since 1913. Three years later, in Brookes' final season as skipper, they were runners-up to Surrey, winning a record fifteen matches.

Raman Subba Row, now one of the most senior figures in the English game, took over, but it was under the leadership of Andrew in the early sixties that Northants once again looked strong, finishing as

high as third in 1964.

By now the county was on a sound financial footing, with the ground at Northampton turned into a modern stadium. Much of the credit went to club secretary Ken Turner. He was also responsible for recruiting many of the quality overseas players such as Mushtaq Mohammad, Bishen Bedi and Sarfraz Nawaz.

In the sixties the county had one of the most charismatic players to grace the game since the war. Colin Milburn was made for the word 'beefy'. He was an exciting batsman who had recorded the fastest centuries of the season in 1966 and 1967.

Sadly, this player who could tear the best international attacks apart was blinded in his left eye in a road accident in 1969, just a few hours after Northants had beaten the West Indies for the second consecutive tour.

Despite a vain attempt at a comeback, Milburn's career was over. However, he continued to be a larger-than-life figure, being particularly popular on the after-dinner speaking circuit. His untimely death at the age of 48 in 1990 was mourned throughout the international cricket world.

It was in 1976 that Northamptonshire enjoyed their finest season since entering the Championship. At Lord's they beat Lancashire in the Gillette Cup final, with Mushtaq, in his first season as captain, holding aloft the first trophy the county had ever won. It was a fitting end to a season in which they also took second place in the Championship behind Middlesex.

Four years later there was further success when they won the Benson and Hedges Cup, England's South African-born batsman Allan Lamb leading the way against Essex in the final with an innings of 72.

It was with Lamb as captain that Northants, in 1992, enjoyed their most successful season since 1976 as he led them to a comfortable eight-wickets victory over Leicestershire in the NatWest Trophy and third place in the Championship table.

NOTTINGHAMSHIRE
Founded: 1841
Entered Official Championship: 1890
Honours:
County Champions – 1907, 1929, 1981, 1987
NatWest Trophy – 1987
Benson and Hedges Cup – 1989
Refuge Assurance League – 1991

NOTTINGHAMSHIRE WERE one of the original eight counties to play in the first official County Championship in 1890. Yet by far their most successful period came in the 1980s, with two championship titles and two one-day prizes won.

Much of that success could be put down to the influence of Richard Hadlee from New Zealand and Clive Rice from South Africa.

The first records of a match being played in the county date back to 1771, when the Nottingham club played Sheffield. A proper county club was set up at a meeting in 1841.

However, it nearly died before it was properly established. William Clarke, who in 1838 had moved to the Trent Bridge Inn and laid out a pitch in the meadow alongside, formed the All England XI in 1846, taking the best Notts players with him.

There followed a gap of four seasons when no matches were played, but by 1852 the club had been re-formed. In 1865 Nottinghamshire were judged to be county champions and over the next twenty years were generally considered to be the best side in the country.

They had a particularly strong batting line-up including Arthur Shrewsbury, second only to W.G. Grace at the time, and William Gunn, the first member of that famous family to play for the county.

Yet when the official championship began in 1890, Nottinghamshire went into the doldrums, never seriously mounting a challenge for the title. By 1901 the editor of *Wisden* was moved to write: 'The outlook for Notts in the future is not hopeful and the committee must use every possible effort to discover fresh talent.'

In 1907 Notts did become champions, thanks largely to the bowling exploits of Tom Wass, a rough diamond of a man who on his day was the best in England. With his fast leg-breaks he went on to become the county's leading wicket-taker with more than 1,500 victims.

He was ably supported by A.W. Hallam, an off-spinner, who proved to be the perfect foil. Between them they took 298 Championship wickets in 19 matches.

The batting at this time was led by George Gunn, nephew of William. George first played in 1901 and is still the county's top run-scorer with more than 30,000 to his name – all of them compiled in a stylish manner.

His brother John was a fine all-rounder, taking more than 1,000 wickets and scoring 21,000 runs in almost thirty years from 1895.

Nottinghamshire's second Championship title came in 1929 when they had the best new-ball attack in England, made up of Harold Larwood and Bill Voce. Larwood was fast with a rhythmical approach, Voce a tall left-armer who could make the ball swing dramatically in the air. It was perhaps surprising that with such bowlers to call upon, Notts did not win the title more than once during this period.

Although the batting was still sound, a decline in the bowling led to a gradual waning of Nottinghamshire's fortunes. Perhaps it was due to an improvement in working conditions at the county's mines; certainly the desire to escape the grime and play cricket in the open air did not seem as strong as it had been. The days of whistling down a pit to find a fast bowler were over.

After the Second World War things got no better. In 1950 Reg Simpson, an elegant batsman and superb fielder who played 27 times for England, became club captain,

THE GUINNESS

Nottinghamshire's favourite son, Harold Larwood. He served the county for 14 years.

but could do nothing to stop Nottinghamshire slipping into their worst ever period. They finished bottom in 1951 and only one place higher the following year.

The committee decided to turn to an overseas player and engaged Bruce Dooland from Australia. The leg-spinner helped them improve to eighth in 1953 and then fifth the following year, when he created a Nottinghamshire record of 179 championship wickets. Sadly for Notts, he then decided to return to his native country in 1957.

His departure led to the county finishing bottom three times in five years and the 1960s, too, generally saw Notts in the lower positions. But a dramatic change was to occur in 1968 when Nottinghamshire scooped all other counties by signing the great Garfield Sobers.

With 1,500 runs and 83 wickets, the West Indian captain raised spirits as well as the team's position, as they spectacularly rose to fourth. But it was something of a false dawn. Sobers missed much of the following season and then captained the Rest of the World in 1970. By the time he left in 1974, his bowling had lost much of its effectiveness and Notts were again struggling to win matches.

An unknown all-rounder from the Transvaal, Clive Rice, replaced Sobers, and he was chosen to captain the county in 1978. However, the Packer Affair then broke and Rice was sacked, only to be reinstated as a player but not, at that stage, as captain.

Another addition to the ranks was the New Zealand fast bowler Richard Hadlee, and it was his new-ball partnership with Rice that took Notts to the title in 1981. Nine wins in the final eleven games secured their first such success for 52 years, with the Hadlee/Rice partnership making the most of some very grassy Trent Bridge pitches. Their strength with the new ball also shielded a slightly suspect batting line-up, although Derek Randall, Tim Robinson and Basharat Hassan all had good moments.

Six years later it was Rice and Hadlee to the fore again as Nottinghamshire carried off a notable Championship/ NatWest Trophy double and only just failed to make it a treble, having to settle for the runners-up spot in the Sunday League.

A quirk of the fixture list meant Notts played seven of their last nine matches at home, and they won five of them. There were rumblings again about the green Trent Bridge wickets, but no one could deny that Hadlee in particular was more than a match for most batsmen on any type of wicket.

Their 1987 NatWest final was hit by rain and the game went into a second day. The team beat Northamptonshire by three wickets with three balls to spare.

In 1989 they proved they could manage without both Rice and Hadlee when they won the Benson and Hedges Cup, with Tim Robinson, Derek Randall and Chris Broad spearheading the batting. In an exciting final against the favourites, Essex, they won with a four off the last ball of the match.

When the Refuge Assurance League title followed in 1991, it meant that all four domestic titles had been won in just five years – the kind of success the county had waited a long time to see.

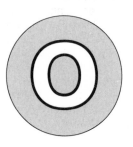

OLD TRAFFORD

MANCHESTER'S TEST match ground rightly claims a place as one of the famous cricket stadiums in the world. Old Trafford is second only to the Oval in terms of seniority as a Test venue in England, its first match against Australia having been staged in 1884.

For all the vintage moments on the pitch, Old Trafford has unfortunately become just as well known for the rain that comes out of the clouds above it. The first day of that first Test was rained off, and the Tests of 1890 and 1938 are the only ones in England ever to have been abandoned without a ball being bowled.

Old Trafford is an impressive ground which has undergone an almost constant programme of improvement in recent years. The most unusual aspect is the siting of the pavilion, square of the wicket.

If this is unsatisfactory for the connoisseur, it does at least provide good facilities for players, is something of a sun trap when it is not raining, and has an unusual floral touch – hanging baskets outside the Long Room.

On the field, two early Tests stand out. In 1896 Ranjitsinhji, on his debut for England, made 154 not out after his side had been made to follow on. Then, needing only 125 to win, Australia nearly came unstuck. Richardson took six wickets as the visitors just got home with three wickets to spare.

In 1902 the Australian victory was even tighter, by just three runs. It was to remain the closest margin in a Test match for eighty years. Set 124 to win on a bad wicket, England were 92 for 3 but then collapsed, leaving the last pair needing 8 to win.

In true Manchester fashion, rain then held up proceedings for just under an hour, before England failed to reach the required target.

The 1934 Test against Australia was a high-scoring draw but will always be remembered for O'Reilly's leg-spin accounting for three top England batsmen, Walters, Wyatt and Hammond, in just four balls.

It was also the year when Jack Hobbs, in his final season, was greeted on his return to the pavilion, after making a century in a benefit match, to the strains of Auld Lang Syne.

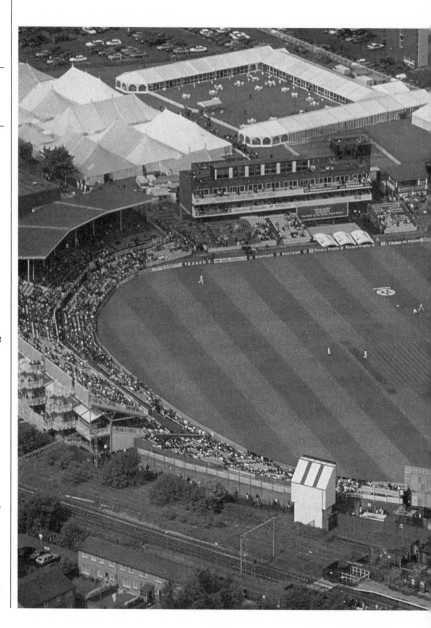

The Second World War saw Old Trafford take more punishment than any other English Test ground. It was used as a transit camp for soldiers to get some rest after Dunkirk. There was severe air raid damage, with one sentry on the gate being killed, the pavilion being hit, and craters formed on the field of play.

The Old Trafford Test of 1956 proved to be the most remarkable on the ground, and one of the most talked about matches of all time.

This was 'Laker's match', as the Surrey off-spinner took nineteen wickets – all from the Stretford end – against Australia, who were dismissed for 84 and 205 in reply to England's 459.

Much was written about the wicket as Laker made the ball lift and turn. However, the Australians were full of praise for his achievement. No one has ever matched it, and it is unlikely anyone ever will.

An aerial view of Old Trafford in 1993, showing the pavilion square of the wicket (right).

Australia had their revenge in 1961, when an Old Trafford record of 133,000 people attended the five days' play. Richie Benaud's leg-spin accounted for five wickets in 25 balls on the last afternoon as England fell to 201 all out when chasing 256 in 230 minutes to win.

There was uproar in 1975 when Old Trafford was not allotted a Test against Australia. Falling attendances was the reason given as Mancunians were told they would have to take their place on the rota with Edgbaston and Trent Bridge.

Certainly, the Manchester public had been turning up in greater numbers to the one-day game, with Lancashire drawing big crowds during their spell as masters of that particular form of cricket.

The record crowd for a single day at Old Trafford, though, was neither for a Test nor a one-day game. It came in 1926 when 46,000 people crammed in to see play on a Bank Holiday in the Roses match, a fixture that still excites great interest in the north of England.

THE OVAL

LORD'S MAY BE ENGLAND'S premier Test ground, but it is the Oval that is the country's oldest. The first two home Tests against Australia in 1880 and 1882 were staged there.

Kennington Oval, currently called the Foster's Oval following sponsorship from the brewing company, began life as a market garden. The Montpelier CC took a lease on the land in 1844, the first match taking place the following year.

Now the home of Surrey County Cricket Club, the ground is owned by the Duchy of Cornwall. In addition to cricket, it has also staged F.A. Cup finals and rugby union matches.

Few could describe the Oval, with its huge playing area, as a pretty ground, but it is an oasis of green amid the urban sprawl of South

London. With its famous gasometers to one side, it is encircled by traffic.

At its entrance stand the famous Hobbs Gates, erected in 1934 and which bear the simple legend 'In Honour of a Great Surrey and England Cricketer'.

Open terracing surrounding the playing area is a principal feature, with the famous old pavilion still standing proudly alongside a new £4 million structure that now provides the players' dressing-rooms and other facilities. The Oval also boasts what is generally regarded as the most efficient and fastest-changing scoreboard in the country.

As the ground that traditionally stages the final Test match of an English summer, the Oval has naturally witnessed some of the most dramatic moments in international cricket.

That first defeat by Australia on home soil in 1882 sparked the famous 'death notice' of English cricket in the Sporting Times. However, England won five Tests in succession leading up to the turn of the century before a memorable one-wicket victory over Australia in 1902, thanks mostly to a century from Jessop in just over an hour.

The Oval staged England's first timeless Test in 1938 when Hutton scored 364, then a record, in 13 hours and 17 minutes. At tea on the third day England eventually declared at 903 for 7 – the highest score ever in Test cricket. It is unlikely to be beaten.

It is said that 'Bosser' Martin, the groundsman, having produced such a perfect wicket, was disgusted England did not continue past the 1,000 mark!

The war years took their toll on the Oval. The ground was requisitioned as a prisoner-of-war camp, although it never actually received a prisoner. Barbed wire, weeds and concrete posts took their toll, while air raids during the Blitz damaged the pavilion and stands and left craters at the Vauxhall end.

Amazingly, about six months after the end of the war the ground was ready again to host a Test match – England drew with India.

The Oval's famous gasometer dominates the skyline as England entertain South Africa in the final Test of the 1994 series. The south London ground is the traditional venue for the last Test of the English summer.

In 1948 Bradman was the star attraction, playing his final Test match at the Oval. The great man failed. After being cheered all the way to the wicket, he was bowled second ball by Hollies. Just four runs would have given him 7,000 Test runs in all, for an average of 100.

After four drawn Tests, in 1953 the Oval was to be the stage for wild celebrations as England, led by Hutton, their first professional captain, regained the Ashes for the first time since 1932/33.

More than 115,000 people saw the four days' play and there were highly emotional scenes after the Middlesex pair of Compton and Edrich saw England home.

Although it is often regarded as the best batting wicket in the country, many bowlers have achieved milestones at the Oval. The Surrey spin twins of Laker and Lock reigned supreme during the 1950s; Fred Trueman became the first bowler to take 300 Test wickets when he dismissed Neil Hawke of Australia there in 1964; and Derek Underwood finished with 7 for 50 against Australia in 1968 when, after a downpour, he had just enough time to collect four wickets in 27 balls on a wet wicket that made him almost unplayable.

In 1994, England's Devon Malcolm took 9 for 57 from 16.3 overs to give his side a famous win over South Africa. It was the sixth best analysis ever recorded in Test cricket.

However, visiting teams have also enjoyed success at the Oval. In 1971 India achieved their first victory in England, and eight years later, thanks largely to 221 from Gavaskar, came within nine runs of a target of 438 to win. In 1992 Pakistan won by ten wickets to take the series 2–1.

OXFORD UNIVERSITY

LIKE THE STUDENTS OF Cambridge, Oxford nowadays struggle to provide much in the way of serious opposition to the first-class counties who make regular visits to their attractive ground at the Parks, their home since 1881.

However, 1992 provided them with a highlight in the form of a win over Middlesex, thanks largely to a

THE GUINNESS

sporting declaration by Mike Gatting. It was the University's first first-class win since 1974 – a measure of how the demands of modern academic life have taken their toll on achievements on the cricket field.

The debate may continue over how long the two universities can maintain their first-class status, but Oxford have had their moments over their long history.

In 1884, captained by M.C. Kemp, they won seven of their eight matches played. Among their victims were the touring Australians,

Surrey, the MCC (twice) and Lancashire (twice).

A number of fine England players have come from the ranks of Oxford graduates, among them M.J.K. Smith and Sir Colin Cowdrey, who both scored centuries in the Varsity match and went on to captain their country.

In more recent times, such players as Chris Tavaré, Vic Marks and Derek Pringle have gone on to play for England.

Leading overseas players have also represented the university. They include Abbas Ali Baig, who

made a century for India in 1959 while still an undergraduate, and Imran Khan, the Pakistani captain and one of the game's greatest all-rounders.

The Nawab of Pataudi senior, from India, was a fine batsman who recorded the highest individual score in the match with Cambridge – 238 not out in 1931.

His son also scored a century, 131, in the match in 1960. He might have gone on to become a better batsman than his father but for a car accident the following year that damaged his eyesight.

PAKISTAN

PAKISTAN MADE A commanding entrance into Test cricket and have in recent years challenged West Indies for the unofficial title of best in the world.

They have produced some of the finest players the game has seen, such as Hanif Mohammad, Imran Khan and Javed Miandad.

Pakistan were elected members of the International Cricket Conference in July 1952, and their impact on the world stage was quite extraordinary.

Within five years, they had achieved Test victories over England, Australia, New Zealand and India. However, that start was always going to be hard to maintain, and they failed to win a Test either at home or away between 1959 and 1964/65.

In the early days, cricket in Pakistan was played principally on matting wickets, turf being hard to grow in such a dry climate. Pakistan were almost invincible on matting, their only defeat coming at the hands of the Australians in Dacca in 1959/60.

Administrators realised that grass pitches had to come, as their players would increasingly be at a severe disadvantage against other nations. But since grass pitches have been introduced, positive results have invariably been hard to come by on slow wickets. Some dull Test matches have resulted, and few bowlers relish the prospect of touring Pakistan.

Despite some tension between the two neighbours, it was India which had proposed Pakistan for full membership of the ICC. But after some tedious series between them in 1954/55 and 1960/61, politics intervened and they did not meet for another eighteen years.

Cricket in Pakistan has also been dogged by frequent crowd disturbances as political protests and watching cricket have often gone hand in hand. The England tour of 1968/69 was disrupted and the final Test unfinished after anti-government students marched onto the ground at Karachi.

As for the game itself, the three Mohammad brothers, Hanif, Mushtaq and Sadiq, loom large in the history of Pakistani cricket. Hanif in the early years often held the batting together with his remarkable powers of concentration and ability to play long innings.

Mushtaq could play with more panache, and was also a more than useful leg-spin bowler. He went on to play for Northamptonshire in the County Championship. If Sadiq didn't quite have the international stature of the other two, he was nonetheless a fine opening batsman both for his country and for Gloucestershire.

Other notable batsmen have been Majid Khan, Zaheer Abbas and Javed Miandad, while Pakistan has regularly produced some of the very best leg-spinners, such as Intikhab Alam, Abdul Qadir and Mushtaq Ahmed.

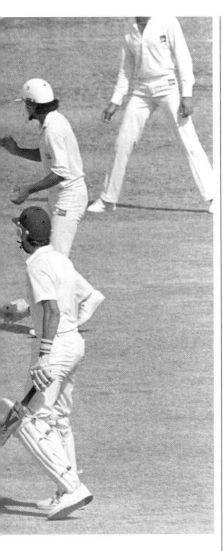

It was the influence of one particular player which in the modern era brought a greater sense of stability and purpose to Pakistani cricket. Imran Khan became a national hero. Apart from being a great all-rounder, this was a man of considerable intelligence both on and off the cricket field.

Much of Pakistan's recent success in world cricket has come about as a result of Imran's captaincy and the exploits of two superb fast bowlers. Wasim Akram, a left-armer who plays for Lancashire in the County Championship, and Waqar Younis of Surrey are a potent pair.

Pakistan's often flamboyant style of play has brought them success in one-day cricket, culminating in their

Abdul Qadir dismisses England's captain Gower at Karachi in 1984.

1992 World Cup triumph in Australia. They came close to being eliminated in the preliminary round but got stronger as the tournament progressed and eventually beat England in the final.

PAKISTAN
V
SRI LANKA

SRI LANKA PLAYED THEIR first three-Test series overseas against Pakistan in 1981/82. They lost 2–0 but were not disgraced.

Disputes over the Pakistani captaincy meant that a number of major names were missing in the first Test at Karachi. Nonetheless Pakistan won by 204 runs, with Salim Malik scoring a century on his debut.

A draw followed in Faisalabad before Pakistan won by an innings and 102 runs in the third Test at Lahore, when Pakistan were back to full strength. Imran Khan made the telling contribution, taking 14 for 116.

Pakistan repeated the same margin of victory in the next series, also played in Pakistan, in 1985/86. Sri Lanka went into the rubber having just beaten India, but it was once again the bowling of Imran that was to be a deciding factor.

The first Test was drawn, but Sri Lanka, batting first in all three Tests, were dismissed in the next two for 157 and 162 and were always struggling, as Pakistan recorded victories by eight wickets and ten wickets.

Sri Lanka recorded their first win over Pakistan, and with it a shared series, at home in the latter part of 1985/86. Having been heavily defeated in the first Test, when they could make only 109 and 101, they hit back at Colombo to win by eight wickets.

Pakistan then won the next series,

1–0 in Pakistan in 1991/92, thanks to a closely fought victory by three wickets at Faisalabad, in which Sri Lanka very nearly achieved their first win on foreign soil.

In Sri Lanka in 1994/95, Pakistan easily won two Tests of what should have been a three-test series. The second Test, scheduled for Colombo, was called off due to political unrest surrounding the Sri Lankan elections.

Season	Ven	Tests	Winner	Res
1981/82	Pak	3	Pakistan	2–0
1985/86	Pak	3	Pakistan	2–0
1985/86	SL	3	–	1–1
1991/92	Pak	3	Pakistan	1–0
1994/95	SL	2	Pakistan	2–0

PAKISTAN
V
ZIMBABWE

ZIMBABWE TOURED Pakistan for the first time in 1993/94. Facing one of the strongest teams in the world, the Test rookies could be satisfied with the outcome, despite losing 2–0.

At a new Test venue in Karachi, the Defence Stadium, Pakistan won by 131 runs. Zimbabwe found the pace of Waqar Younis too much too handle, the fast bowler finishing with match figures of 13 for 135.

It was Waqar who dominated again in the second Test, taking nine wickets. But Pakistan had to fight for their victory by 52 runs. Zimbabwe looked in a good position to cause a real upset at 135 for 1 in their second innings, chasing 240 to win. Sadly for them, they lost their final nine wickets for just 52 runs.

Rain spoiled the final Test, but Zimbabwe again acquitted themselves well, dismissing Pakistan for 147 and going on to build a first innings lead of 83.

It turned out to be a tour from which the Zimbabwe side learned a great deal.

Season	Ven	Tests	Winner	Res
1993/94	Pak	3	Pakistan	2–0

PERTH

THE WACA GROUND
(pronounced Wacker) in Perth,
Western Australia, was only added
to the Test rota during the MCC tour
of 1970/71. A stadium that was once
nothing more than a swamp now
boasts some fine facilities and has a
reputation for having one of the
quickest wickets in the world.

Much work has been carried out
in recent years to extend
grandstands and catering
arrangements, with a view to
increasing the ground capacity to
around 35,000 spectators.

It is a ground cricketers enjoy

*The WACA ground at Perth is now
instantly recognisable by the
huge floodlight pylons installed
for night cricket.*

playing on. The field is large, even
by Australian standards, the light is
good, and the heat is usually
tempered by the 'Fremantle Doctor',
a strong wind that blows off the sea
most afternoons.

Sited on reclaimed land on the
shores of the Swan River, the
Western Australia Cricket
Association ground was officially
opened in 1892/93, with turf wickets
laid the following year. Matches
were regularly held with touring
teams, England parties often getting
off the boat in Perth and making it
their first stop on a tour of Australia.

The first Test to be played at the
WACA was on 11 December 1970,
and although it ended in a draw it
was notable for Greg Chappell
making a century in his first Test
innings.

Many fine Australians have
graced the ground for Western
Australia, among them Dennis Lillee,
Rodney Marsh and Graham
McKenzie.

GRAEME POLLOCK
South Africa
Born 1944
*Eastern Province and
Transvaal*

POLITICS DETERMINED
that Graeme Pollock's Test
career should end at the age of 26.
Yet in a short, seven-year
international career, he established
himself as South Africa's finest post-
war batsman and was rivalled only
by Sir Garfield Sobers as the best
left-hander of his generation.

His father claims that Graeme was
walking by the time he was eight
months old. At nine years of age,
playing for his school, Graeme
scored his first century and took all
ten wickets in the match for good
measure.

At sixteen, representing Eastern
Province, he became the youngest

THE GUINNESS

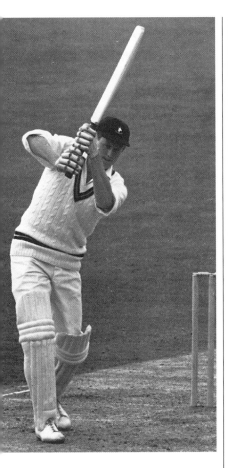

Graeme Pollock's magnificent left-handed batting was perhaps the most lamented sporting casualty of South Africa's politics. He continued to play Currie Cup cricket for Eastern Province and, from 1978, Transvaal.

player to score a century in Currie Cup cricket. Two years later he became the youngest South African to make a double century, and for good measure scored his first Test hundred against Australia. It was a phenomenal start.

Pollock made his mark in England at Trent Bridge in 1965. The South African first innings was in tatters at 43 for 4 on a cloudy morning with the ball moving around. His response was a brilliant 125 in 2 hours 20 minutes out of 160 runs scored. His brother Peter took ten wickets in the match, and South Africa won with a day to spare.

Graeme continued to score

heavily throughout his career, and in his final Test series in 1969/70 he punished the Australian bowlers, scoring 517 runs at an average of 73.85. In the Durban Test he made 274, South Africa's highest individual Test score. The series was won by four matches to nil.

Continuing his career in domestic cricket, he later showed his skill in unofficial Tests against 'rebel' West Indies sides, scoring centuries in 1983 and 1984.

Graeme Pollock's was a cricketing career that was never allowed to run its full term. Who knows how much more he might have achieved?

First Class Career:
Runs – 20,940. Average 65.18 (64 centuries)

Test Match Career:
Tests – 23
Runs – 2,256. Average 60.97 (7 centuries)

PETER POLLOCK
South Africa
Born 1941
Eastern Province

PETER POLLOCK, THE elder of the two cricketing brothers, was a genuinely fast bowler in his prime. In the 1960s, before South Africa were thrown out of Test cricket, he made his mark as a tall man bowling off a long, straight run. He was his country's most potent strike weapon in that decade.

Pollock made his Test debut as a 20-year-old, taking nine wickets in the match against New Zealand at Durban. His most memorable Test performance came at Trent Bridge

The elder of the Pollock brothers, fast bowler Peter played five more Tests than Graeme. Their father was also a cricketer; he kept wicket for Orange Free State in domestic cricket in South Africa.

in 1965, when he took 5 for 53 and 5 for 34 to win the match and, as it proved, the series. His brother Graeme scored a century in the match to make it a real 'family affair'.

At the end of the sixties, Peter formed a formidable opening attack with a young Mike Procter – a partnership that could have flourished had South Africa remained in the Test fold.

First Class Career:
Runs – 3,028. Average 22.59
Wickets – 485. Average 21.89

Test Match Career:
Tests – 28
Runs – 607. Average 21.67
Wickets – 116. Average 24.18

PORT ELIZABETH

ST GEORGE'S PARK IN Port Elizabeth holds a unique place in South African sporting history. It was the venue for the first cricket Test in 1889 and the first rugby international in 1891.

It may be a little charitable to call that first cricket fixture a Test. It lasted only two days, with a modest England team of only county strength defeating their hosts with some ease.

Despite its important place in history, St George's Park has been used only sparingly as a Test venue. No Tests were played there between the wars, and the ground only came onto the regular Test circuit from 1948/49.

South Africa's first win on the ground came against New Zealand in 1953/54, and three years later they won by 58 runs against an England side led by Peter May.

St George's Park was a ground much loved by Graeme Pollock. He scored centuries in two of the three Tests he played there, his side winning two, against Australia, and drawing the other, against England.

The ground has been much improved in recent years. Never one of the more attractive venues, thanks to cricket having to share facilities with rugby, it now has an impressive indoor cricket school and better facilities for players, administrators and spectators alike.

MIKE PROCTER
South Africa
Born 1946
Natal, Western Province,
Rhodesia and Gloucestershire

MIKE PROCTER WAS ONE of cricket's greatest all-rounders and captains, and but for South Africa's exclusion from world cricket he would have become a giant on the international stage. As it was, he had to be content with just seven Test appearances.

Six feet tall and powerfully built, Procter was a very fast but unorthodox bowler. He came in off a straight run and delivered the ball chest-on, and off the wrong foot. He would move the ball into a right-hander amid what appeared to be a mass of swirling arms.

He was an orthodox middle-order

batsman who could alter the course of a match in a matter of minutes with some belligerent hitting. Whether batting or bowling, spectators were guaranteed that Procter would never give less than one hundred per cent.

In his Test career, he faced the Australians in 1966/67 and again in 1969/70, when he made up a potent new-ball partnership with Peter Pollock. In that series he took 26 wickets at an average of 13.57 and was largely responsible for South Africa's emphatic 4–0 win.

He played county cricket for Gloucestershire, passing 1000 runs in a season nine times and twice collecting more than 100 wickets. It was no wonder he became highly popular with the West Country supporters.

In his first year as captain, 1977, he led Gloucestershire to a Benson and Hedges Cup triumph. It was only their second one-day success. He came close to taking them to the County Championship title in both 1976 and 1977.

However, Procter will best be remembered for some outstanding individual performances. In 1970/71 he equalled a world record by

Procter was another South African lost to international cricket, but he starred in the county game with his performances for Gloucestershire.

scoring six centuries in consecutive innings, and he is the only player to have scored a century and taken a hat-trick in the same match twice – against Essex in 1972 (all his victims were trapped lbw) and Leicestershire in 1979. Another hat-trick, against Yorkshire in 1979, also saw the trio of batsmen all depart lbw.

Procter's retirement did not signal an exit from the county scene, as he returned to England to become director of cricket at Northamptonshire. He later became manager of the South African side that toured England in 1994.

First Class Career:
Runs – 21,904. Average 36.15
(48 centuries)
Wickets – 1,407. Average 19.37

Test Match Career:
Tests – 7
Runs – 226. Average 25.11
Wickets – 41. Average 15.02

BCCP PATRON'S TROPHY WINNERS			
1970/71	PIA	1982/83*	PACO
1971/72	PIA	1983/84	Karachi Blues
1972/73	Karachi Blues	1984/85	Karachi Whites
1973/74	Railways	1985/86	Karachi Whites
1974/75	National Bank	1986/87	National Bank
1975/76	National Bank	1987/88	Habib Bank
1976/77	Habib Bank	1988/89	Karachi
1977/78	Habib Bank	1989/90	Karachi Whites
1978/79	National Bank	1990/91	ADBP
1979/80*	IDBP	1991/92	Habib Bank
1980/81*	Rawalpindi	1992/93	Habib Bank
1981/82*	Allied Bank		

* Not first class. Competition used as qualifying for the Quaid-e-Azam Trophy.

Hanif Mohammed represented Bahawalpur, Karachi and PIA in the Quaid-e-Azam Trophy. It was batting for Karachi against Bahawalpur that Hanif, aged 24, made his record-breaking first-class score of 499.

QUAID-E-AZAM TROPHY

THE QUAID-E-AZAM Trophy, the national championship of Pakistan, was inaugurated in 1953/54, when players were competing for places to tour England.

Bahawalpur were the first winners, thanks in no small measure to the efforts of Hanif Mohammad, who scored two centuries.

It was Hanif who made the highest individual first-class score, 499, while batting for Karachi against Bahawalpur in 1958/59. His record lasted until 1994 when it was broken by Brian Lara, playing for Warwickshire against Durham in England.

In recent years, Karachi Whites brought off a notable hat-trick of wins between 1990/91 and 1992/93.

In 1970/71 a second first-class competition was created – the BCCP Patron's Trophy. It is now contested in the earlier part of the Pakistan season.

QUAID-E-AZAM TROPHY WINNERS	
1953/54	Bahawalpur
1954/55	Karachi
1955/56	Punjab
1956/57	Bahawalpur
1958/59	Karachi
1959/60	Karachi
1961/62	Karachi Blues
1962/63	Karachi A
1963/64	Karachi Blues
1964/65	Karachi Blues
1966/67	Karachi
1968/69	Lahore
1969/70	PIA
1970/71	Karachi Blues
1972/73	Railways
1973/74	Railways
1974/75	Punjab A
1975/76	National Bank
1976/77	United Bank
1977/78	Habib Bank
1978/79	National Bank
1979/80	PIA
1980/81	United Bank
1981/82	National Bank
1982/83	United Bank
1983/84	National Bank
1984/85	United Bank
1985/86	Karachi
1986/87	National Bank
1987/88	PIA
1988/89	ADBP
1989/90	PIA
1990/91	Karachi Whites
1991/92	Karachi Whites
1992/93	Karachi Whites

SONNY RAMADHIN

West Indies

Born 1929
Trinidad and Lancashire

SONNY RAMADHIN formed one half of a spin attack that brought the West Indies their first series win in England in 1950. In harness with Alf Valentine, Ramadhin bamboozled the English batsmen that summer, taking 135 wickets on the tour – more than any other West Indies bowler had ever captured in England.

Spin bowlers, it is said, need years of experience to learn their craft. Yet Ramadhin arrived in England that summer as a 20-year-old with just two trial games back home as his only first-class experience.

His orthodox delivery was the off-break, with the middle finger down the seam. His leg-break was bowled with the fingers rather than the wrist. Wicket-keepers as well as batsmen had great difficulty spotting the difference.

It was, to put it mildly, a bold gamble to bring Ramadhin, a friendless orphan, on that 1950 tour, but he quickly set about repaying the bet handsomely.

He took 26 wickets in four Tests at an average of 23.23. The West

Indies recorded their first win at Lord's, with Ramadhin recording match figures of 115 overs, 50 maidens, 152 runs, 11 wickets. With Valentine taking seven wickets, it was no wonder the two became calypso heroes: 'Those two little pals of mine, Ramadhin and Valentine.'

Ramadhin became a regular member of the West Indies side for the rest of the decade, touring all the other Test-playing countries. His best figures invariably came in his

Ramadhin pictured at the start of the 1950 tour of England. Ironically, his best Test analysis, 7–49 in the first innings of the 1957 Edgbaston Test, was immediately followed by the May/Cowdrey stand of 411 which thwarted him.

debut series against other countries, although batsmen from Pakistan and New Zealand never got the better of him.

On his second tour of England in

● THE GUINNESS

1957 Ramadhin again mesmerised batsmen, taking 119 wickets. However, he came in for some punishment when, in the first Test at Edgbaston, Peter May and Colin Cowdrey put on 411, and he never proved as effective again.

Ramadhin played Lancashire League cricket for many years and also represented the county side with some success in 1964 and 1965, before going on to play for Lincolnshire.

First Class Career:
Wickets – 758. Average 20.24

Test Match Career:
Tests – 43
Wickets – 158. Average 28.98

RANJI TROPHY

THE RANJI TROPHY IS THE main first-class competition in India. It is perhaps ironic that it is named after a man who played most of his cricket in England.

The competition began two years after India appeared on the Test scene, and unlike domestic cricket in most other countries it was played right the way through the Second World War. The 1940s saw a decade of high scoring as India developed some fine batsmen.

The city of Bombay totally dominated the competition from 1958, winning it for 15 seasons in succession. However, in recent years the competition has been a very much more open affair. Teams such as Punjab, Delhi, Tamil Nadu and Bengal have all taken the trophy.

For all the Ranji Trophy's history, the other first-class competition, the Duleep Trophy, started in the 1960s and played on a zonal basis, is nowadays a better guide to judging the best players in India.

As in other countries, Test match claims take precedence over domestic first-class cricket in India and often it is second-string players who have a big say in the outcome of trophies.

Like other countries, too, the demands of one-day cricket have had a bearing, with sponsors keener to support the brand of the game that nowadays pulls in the biggest crowds.

Mohammed Azharuddin inspired Hyderabad to only their second ever Ranji Trophy success in 1987/88, in a tournament until recently dominated by the mighty Bombay.

1934/35	Bombay	1954/55	Madras	1974/75	Bombay
1935/36	Bombay	1955/56	Bombay	1975/76	Bombay
1936/37	Nawanagar	1956/57	Bombay	1976/77	Bombay
1937/38	Hyderabad	1957/58	Baroda	1977/78	Karnataka
1938/39	Bengal	1958/59	Bombay	1978/79	Delhi
1939/40	Maharashtra	1959/60	Bombay	1979/80	Delhi
1940/41	Maharashtra	1960/61	Bombay	1980/81	Bombay
1941/42	Bombay	1961/62	Bombay	1981/82	Delhi
1942/43	Baroda	1962/63	Bombay	1982/83	Karnataka
1943/44	Western India	1963/64	Bombay	1983/84	Bombay
1944/45	Bombay	1964/65	Bombay	1984/85	Bombay
1945/46	Holkar	1965/66	Bombay	1985/86	Delhi
1946/47	Baroda	1966/67	Bombay	1986/87	Hyderabad
1947/48	Holkar	1967/68	Bombay	1987/88	Tamil Nadu
1948/49	Bombay	1968/69	Bombay	1988/89	Delhi
1949/50	Baroda	1969/70	Bombay	1989/90	Bengal
1950/51	Holkar	1970/71	Bombay	1990/91	Haryana
1951/52	Bombay	1971/72	Bombay	1991/92	Delhi
1952/53	Holkar	1972/73	Bombay	1992/93	Punjab
1953/54	Bombay	1973/74	Karnataka	1993/94	Bombay

RED STRIPE CUP/SHELL SHIELD WINNERS

The Shell Shield was replaced by the Red Stripe Cup in the 1987/88 season.

1965/66	Barbados
1966/67	Barbados
1968/69	Jamaica
1969/70	Trinidad
1970/71	Trinidad
1971/72	Barbados
1972/73	Guyana
1973/74	Barbados
1974/75	Guyana
1975/76	Trinidad/Barbados
1976/77	Barbados
1977/78	Barbados
1978/79	Barbados
1979/80	Barbados
1980/81	Combined Islands
1981/82	Barbados
1982/83	Guyana
1983/84	Barbados
1984/85	Trinidad & Tobago
1985/86	Barbados
1986/87	Guyana
1987/88	Jamaica
1988/89	Jamaica
1989/90	Leeward Islands
1990/91	Barbados
1991/92	Jamaica
1992/93	Guyana
1993/94	Leeward Islands

RED STRIPE CUP/ SHELL SHIELD

THE RED STRIPE CUP, formerly the Shell Shield, is the first-class domestic competition in the West Indies.

Prior to its introduction, tournaments between the main islands of Barbados, Trinidad and Jamaica and British Guiana used to be known as the 'Inter-colonials'. These ended after the Second World War, but the current format was developed only from the mid-1960s.

The Shell Shield took its title from the sponsors, the Shell Oil company. They were subsequently replaced by Red Stripe beer.

Barbados, home of the great Sir Garfield Sobers, has traditionally been the strongest West Indies island. Indeed so many great players has the island produced, Barbados could probably have held its own against Test countries.

In recent years, however, other islands have emerged as strong challengers, particularly the Leeward Islands who have taken the title twice in five years.

JOHN REID
New Zealand
Born 1928
Wellington and Otago

JOHN REID WAS THE captain who led New Zealand to their first victories in Test cricket. He was a fine all-rounder who had the unique record of never missing a Test match, his international career covering the 58 consecutive appearances he made from his debut. He captained his country 34 times.

Immensely strong, Reid was a powerful batsman who believed in scoring as quickly as possible. He was a medium-pace swing bowler and a magnificent fielder. On top of that, he occasionally served as a stand-in wicket-keeper.

Such were his abilities that at one time he was the New Zealand record holder for scoring most runs, taking most wickets, holding most catches and scoring most hundreds.

He scored a half century in his first Test, against England at Old Trafford in 1949. He subsequently recorded four centuries on tours to England.

In 1953/54 he made history on his country's tour of South Africa, becoming the first player to score 1,000 runs and take fifty wickets in a South African season. He scored his first Test century that winter at Cape Town.

Reid had a particularly successful tour of India and Pakistan in 1955/56. It was in that season that he led New Zealand to their first Test victory, against the West Indies at Auckland. Appropriately enough, he was top scorer with 84.

His other Test victories as captain came against South Africa in 1961/62. That tour saw him score almost 2,000 runs at an average of 68.39, including seven centuries.

His highest score in first-class cricket was 296 for Wellington against Northern Districts in 1962/63. His best bowling was 7 for 20 for Otago against Central Districts in 1956/57.

In recent years he has become a Test match referee, showing himself to be a tough disciplinarian in the 1994/95 Ashes series.

First Class Career:
Runs – 16,128. Average 41.35
(39 centuries)
Wickets – 466. Average 22.60

Test Match Career:
Tests – 58
Runs – 3,428. Average 33.28
(6 centuries)
Wickets – 85. Average 33.41

BARRY RICHARDS
South Africa

Born 1945
Natal, South Australia,
Gloucestershire and
Hampshire

OF EVER A PLAYER suffered from being denied the opportunity to display his talents at the highest level, that player was Barry Richards.

South Africa's expulsion from world cricket left Richards, one of the finest batsmen in cricket history, to travel the world as a mercenary, playing mostly in England and Australia. But without the incentive of international cricket, he often looked bored with the daily grind on the county circuit.

Perhaps his biggest gift as a batsman was time. A tall, fair-haired opener, his style was right out of the coaching manuals – a model for any schoolboy. But he could improvise too, and his love of the unorthodox frequently left opposing captains unable to set fields to contain him.

His four Test matches were in the 1969/70 series against Australia. In seven innings he scored two centuries.

Richards first came to England as captain of the 1963 South African Schools side and two years later had a short spell with Gloucestershire. But it was with Hampshire that he made his presence felt.

From 1968, he scored 1,000 runs in a season in England nine times and formed a successful opening partnership for the county with Gordon Greenidge. It was one of the

In three different domestic arenas, Richards proved himself a batsman who would score runs wherever he played. He followed his 356 for South Australia in 1970/71 by becoming the first player ever to score 1000 runs in a Currie Cup season the following year.

great ironies of the seventies – a South African and a West Indian playing in harmony and proving such a potent force in English county cricket.

Australian pitches proved to his liking too. Playing for South Australia, he once scored 356 against Western Australia, 325 of them on the first day. He had further success down under when playing in Kerry Packer's World Series Cricket.

Having lost his appetite for the game, Richards quit county cricket in 1978 and later became coach to Natal.

First Class Career:
Runs – 28,358. Average 54.74 (80 centuries)

Test Match Career:
Tests – 4
Runs – 508 runs. Average 72.57 (2 centuries)

VIVIAN RICHARDS
West Indies
Born 1952
Leeward Islands, Somerset, Queensland and Glamorgan

VIV RICHARDS WAS unquestionably the finest batsman of his generation. From the mid-1970s and through much of the 1980s, there was no one in the world who could so dominate an attack.

He will surely go down in cricket history as one of the greatest batsmen of all time.

In true West Indian fashion, Richards always looked to attack from the very start of his innings. He struck the ball with terrific power and yet always timed it sweetly. In one-day games he was often the match-winner.

Perhaps more than anyone else, he brought the Caribbean island of Antigua to public attention. Born into a keen sporting family – his father was a fast bowler and his two brothers also played for the island –

With the minimum of ceremony, Richards smashes the England bowling out of the ground in the Barbados Test of 1985/86. In the final match of the series, in his native Antigua, Richards handed out an even more painful lesson as he reached 100 off an incredible 56 balls.

Viv made his first-class debut in 1972 and came early to British attention when he joined Somerset in 1974.

He scored more than 1,000 runs a season in England each year and helped the county to success in one-day competitions. Then in 1986, after much loyal service, Richards was stunned when Somerset decided to release both him and Joel Garner. The decision split the county, and Ian Botham, a close friend of Richard's, quit in protest.

Richards' Test career, which began in India, Sri Lanka and Pakistan in 1974/75, was one of almost unparalleled success. He is the highest run-scorer in West Indies history, with 8,540 runs in his 121 Tests at an average of 50.23. He made 24 hundreds, his top score being a memorable 291 off 386 balls against England at the Oval in 1976.

In just eight months of that year, he scored 1,710 Test runs at an average of 90.00, a record for a calendar year. They were scored against Australia, featuring Lillee and Thomson, India in the Caribbean, and England, where he made an average of 71.83 on a wonderful tour.

He took over the captaincy of the West Indies from Clive Lloyd and continued the remarkable run of success by humiliating England 5-0 in 1985/86 and 4–0 in 1988.

Richards has played many memorable one-day innings, including a match-winning 138 not out in the Prudential World Cup final against England in 1979, but none greater than his incredible 189 not out from 170 balls against a good England attack at Old Trafford in 1984 – the highest one-day score.

One should not forget either that Richards was also a useful off-spin/medium-pace bowler who took many valuable wickets.

In 1989 he joined Glamorgan but illness prevented him from playing until the following season. Far from just playing out his final days with the friendly Welsh county, Richards became an inspiration to developing younger players.

He bowed out by helping Glamorgan enjoy their finest season

Richards, a fellow Antiguan.

Despite his brilliant strokeplay, Richardson often found it hard to emerge from Richards' shadow, but captaincy appeared to bring him out of his shell.

With his distinctive maroon sun hat, Richardson is now regarded as one of the world's top batsmen, particularly on hard, fast wickets. In 1993 he decided to widen his experience of playing in England by joining Yorkshire as only their second ever overseas player, after Sachin Tendulkar had led the way. Richardson returned home for family reasons mid-way through his second season.

For such an attacking batsman, it is perhaps surprising that Richardson was regarded as a defensive player with a sound technique during his schooldays.

In 1983/84 he was lbw for a duck on his first Test appearance against India in Bombay but enjoyed a fine series against Australia in the Caribbean, averaging 81.75 with centuries at Bridgetown and in his native Antigua.

Later in the year, in England, he failed to win a place in the Test team, the West Indies preferring the consistency of Larry Gomes. Richardson fared little better in 1988, when injury ruled him out of the final two Tests.

But in 1991 he finally came good in England, scoring two centuries in his 495 Test runs, the highest on either side, and finishing the series with an average of 55.00. He scored 1,290 runs on the tour, including six centuries.

By at last mastering English wickets, he showed he had arrived as a world-class batsman. He then faced a tough task in leading the West Indies as other sides, most notably Pakistan, aimed to topple them as the world's top Test team.

But Richardson successfully led his side to a win against them in the Caribbean in 1992/93 and some months later the West Indies won by a similar score in Australia.

They returned home to beat England 3–1, as Richardson showed the years of success under Lloyd and Richards could be

for years in 1993, culminating in the Sunday Axa/Equity and Law League title.

First Class Career:
Runs – 36,212. Average 49.33
(114 centuries)
Wickets – 223. Average 45.15

Test Match Career:
Tests – 121
Runs – 8,540. Average 50.23
(24 centuries)

RICHIE RICHARDSON
West Indies
Born 1962
Leeward Islands and Yorkshire

A DASHING AND BRILLIANT right-hand batsman, Richie Richardson took over the captaincy of the West Indies from Viv

Richie Richardson, who succeeded his fellow Antiguan Viv Richards as West Indies captain.

maintained under his captaincy.

First Class Career:
Runs – 12,280. Average 41.91
(32 centuries)

Test Match Career:
Tests – 76
Runs – 5,445. Average 45.75
(15 centuries)

ANDY ROBERTS

West Indies

Born 1951
*Leeward Islands, Hampshire,
New South Wales and
Leicestershire*

IN THE LATE 1970s, ANDY Roberts was the fast bowler who struck most fear into the hearts of opposition batsmen.

His expression never betrayed his feelings, but he was an intelligent cricketer who would gain wickets by more than just pace alone.

The first man from Antigua to play for the West Indies, Roberts made his Test debut against England in Barbados in 1974, taking only three wickets on a good pitch. He was omitted for the rest of that series.

However, that summer in England he took 119 wickets for Hampshire and then had a successful winter, taking 44 wickets in seven Tests in India and Pakistan. In 1975/76 he took 22 wickets in Australia and followed that with 28 wickets on the successful West Indies tour of England in the summer of 1976.

Such was his consistency that he reached 100 wickets in just 19 Tests, in just over two years.

The effort of county cricket began to take its toll on him and he left Hampshire during the 1978 season to join Kerry Packer's World Series Cricket. He won his Test place back later, becoming Michael Holding's opening partner for two series in Australia and another in England.

Another Antiguan, indeed the first ever to play for the West Indies: Andy Roberts.

Roberts was in and out of the side in the early eighties, but against India in the Caribbean in 1982/83 he proved he was still a force to be reckoned with, claiming 24 victims to make him the leading wicket-taker in the series.

He reached his 200th wicket in his 46th Test, against India in 1983/84, also recording his highest score (68) while creating a record ninth-wicket stand of 161 with Clive Lloyd.

First Class Career:
Wickets – 889. Average 21.01

Test Match Career:
Tests – 47
Wickets – 202. Average 25.61

SHEFFIELD SHIELD

THE SHEFFIELD SHIELD IS Australia's first-class competition. The six states – New South Wales, Queensland, Tasmania, Western Australia, South Australia and Victoria – compete each year for a trophy named after the third Earl of Sheffield, who took a team to Australia in 1891/92.

The following year three states, New South Wales, Victoria and South Australia, competed for the shield, which measures 46 inches by 30 inches. Queensland joined in 1926/27, followed by Western Australia in 1947/48 and Tasmania in 1977/78.

Interest in the Sheffield Shield has flagged among the Australian public since the advent of the one-day game through World Series Cricket. While limited-overs cricket pulls in the crowds, the longer first-class version attracts a poor following.

The demands of international cricket have often meant that the best players have missed vital matches for their states.

The Australian authorities are trying to make the Sheffield Shield more attractive to watch. In November 1994, they experimented with play under floodlights – the first time a first-class match had been played under artificial light.

The most notable feature over the years has been the lack of success for Queensland. They have never won the Shield, a dismal statistic that has become part of Australian folklore.

New South Wales have been the most successful state. It is often said that when New South Wales are strong, Australia is strong. They have had two particular purple patches, taking the title six years in succession between 1901/02 and 1906/07 and nine years in succession between 1953/54 and 1961/62.

SHEFFIELD SHIELD WINNERS			
1892/93	Victoria	1947/48	Western Australia
1893/94	South Australia	1948/49	New South Wales
1894/95	Victoria	1949/50	New South Wales
1895/96	New South Wales	1950/51	Victoria
1896/97	New South Wales	1951/52	New South Wales
1897/98	Victoria	1952/53	South Australia
1898/99	Victoria	1953/54	New South Wales
1899/1900	New South Wales	1954/55	New South Wales
1900/01	Victoria	1955/56	New South Wales
1901/02	New South Wales	1956/57	New South Wales
1902/03	New South Wales	1957/58	New South Wales
1903/04	New South Wales	1958/59	New South Wales
1904/05	New South Wales	1959/60	New South Wales
1905/06	New South Wales	1960/61	New South Wales
1906/07	New South Wales	1961/62	New South Wales
1907/08	Victoria	1962/63	Victoria
1908/09	New South Wales	1963/64	South Australia
1909/10	South Australia	1964/65	New South Wales
1910/11	New South Wales	1965/66	New South Wales
1911/12	New South Wales	1966/67	Victoria
1912/13	South Australia	1967/68	Western Australia
1913/14	New South Wales	1968/69	South Australia
1914/15	Victoria	1969/70	Victoria
1915–1919	*No Competition*	1970/71	South Australia
1919/20	New South Wales	1971/72	Western Australia
1920/21	New South Wales	1972/73	Western Australia
1921/22	Victoria	1973/74	Victoria
1922/23	New South Wales	1974/75	Western Australia
1923/24	Victoria	1975/76	South Australia
1924/25	Victoria	1976/77	Western Australia
1925/26	New South Wales	1977/78	Western Australia
1926/27	South Australia	1978/79	Victoria
1927/28	Victoria	1979/80	Victoria
1928/29	New South Wales	1980/81	Western Australia
1929/30	Victoria	1981/82	South Australia
1930/31	Victoria	1982/83	New South Wales
1931/32	New South Wales	1983/84	Western Australia
1932/33	New South Wales	1984/85	New South Wales
1933/34	Victoria	1985/86	New South Wales
1934/35	Victoria	1986/87	Western Australia
1935/36	South Australia	1987/88	Western Australia
1936/37	Victoria	1988/89	Western Australia
1937/38	New South Wales	1989/90	New South Wales
1938/39	South Australia	1990/91	Victoria
1939/40	New South Wales	1991/92	Western Australia
1940–1946	*No Competition*	1992/93	New South Wales
1946/47	Victoria	1993/94	New South Wales

South Australia celebrate victory in the 1981/82 Sheffield Shield, their last success in the competition to date. With twelve wins, they now trail Western Australia (13), Victoria (25) and New South Wales (42) in the all-time list.

SHELL TROPHY/ PLUNKETT SHIELD

THE SHELL TROPHY IS THE prize for the leading province in New Zealand's first-class competition.

Its predecessor, the Plunkett Shield, first appeared in 1906. It was presented by Lord Plunkett, the Governor General, and first awarded to Canterbury.

Until 1921 it was played for on a challenge basis, before a proper points system was introduced for a competition that for many years had just four participants – Auckland, Otago, Wellington and Canterbury. Central Districts joined in 1950/51 and Northern Districts followed in 1956/57.

The Shell Series heralded a new first-class programme, made up of an initial round of matches on a points system for the Shell Cup. Teams were then divided into two divisions for a second round of matches, the two top teams playing a final for the Shell Trophy.

The Shell Trophy is now a straightforward first-class competition, with the Cup a 50 overs a-side one-day competition.

Over the years, Wellington have generally been the most successful side, although more recently the two newcomers Central Districts and Northern Districts have come into their own.

SHELL TROPHY/PLUNKETT SHIELD WINNERS	
The Shell Trophy replaced the Plunkett Shield in the 1975/76 season.	
1921/22	Auckland
1922/23	Canterbury
1923/24	Wellington
1924/25	Otago
1925/26	Wellington
1926/27	Auckland
1927/28	Wellington
1928/29	Auckland
1929/30	Wellington
1930/31	Canterbury
1931/32	Wellington

1932/33	Otago
1933/34	Auckland
1934/35	Canterbury
1935/36	Wellington
1936/37	Auckland
1937/38	Auckland
1938/39	Auckland
1939/40	Auckland
1940–1945	No Competition
1945/46	Canterbury
1946/47	Auckland
1947/48	Otago
1948/49	Canterbury
1949/50	Wellington
1950/51	Otago
1951/52	Canterbury
1952/53	Otago
1953/54	Central Districts
1954/55	Wellington
1955/56	Canterbury
1956/57	Wellington
1957/58	Otago
1958/59	Auckland
1959/60	Canterbury
1960/61	Wellington
1961/62	Wellington
1962/63	Northern Districts
1963/64	Auckland
1964/65	Canterbury
1965/66	Wellington
1966/67	Central Districts
1967/68	Central Districts
1968/69	Auckland
1969/70	Otago
1970/71	Central Districts
1971/72	Otago
1972/73	Wellington
1973/74	Wellington
1974/75	Otago
1975/76	Canterbury
1976/77	Otago
1977/78	Auckland
1978/79	Otago
1979/80	Northern Districts
1980/81	Auckland
1981/82	Wellington
1982/83	Wellington
1983/84	Canterbury
1984/85	Wellington
1985/86	Otago
1986/87	Central Districts
1987/88	Otago
1988/89	Auckland
1989/90	Wellington
1990/91	Auckland
1991/92	Central Districts/ Northern Districts
1992/93	Northern Districts
1993/94	Canterbury

RT. REVEREND DAVID SHEPPARD

England

Born 1929
Cambridge University and Sussex

DAVID SHEPPARD WAS AN outstanding schoolboy and university right-hand batsman who went on to become the first ordained minister to play Test cricket.

In 1950 he shared in two opening partnerships of more than 300 for Cambridge University against County sides. His form led him to be chosen for England in the final Test that summer against the West Indies.

He went on to captain Cambridge in the 1952 Varsity match, scoring 127, and came top of the national averages that season with 64.62 – his 2,262 runs including 239 not out for the University at Worcester.

The following season he led Sussex to second place in the championship and in 1954 he skippered England twice against Pakistan. Two years later, by now ordained into the Church of England, he was recalled for the fourth Test against Australia at Old Trafford, scoring a memorable 113.

He played two Tests the next season against West Indies, though he only made occasional first-class appearances thereafter. But he returned in 1962 to make a century in the last Gentlemen v Players match at Lord's and then toured Australia and New Zealand that winter, scoring a century in England's victory in the third Test at Melbourne.

His Church career has kept him in the public spotlight, first as an inspirational leader of the Mayflower Family Centre in London and more recently as Bishop of Liverpool, where he has regularly spoken out on the particular problems of that city and social issues in general.

First Class Career:
Runs – 15,838. Average 43.51 (45 centuries)

Test Match Career:
Tests – 22
Runs – 1,172. Average 37.80 (3 centuries)

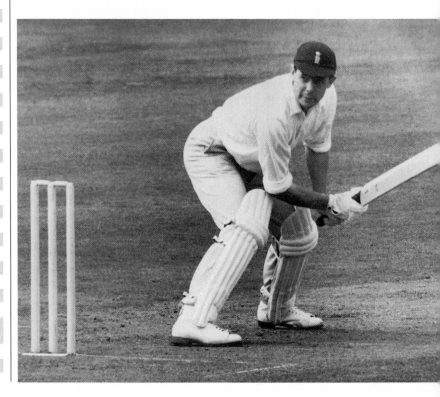

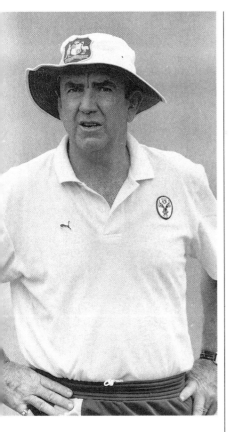

BOBBY SIMPSON

Australia

Born 1936
New South Wales and Western Australia

BOBBY SIMPSON HAS been one of the leading figures in Australian cricket since the war, serving his country as a player in 62 Tests and, after his retirement, as manager/coach.

The son of Scottish parents, Simpson was a fine all-rounder. He was a right-hand opening batsman, forming a highly effective partnership with Bill Lawry.

He was also a good leg-spin and googly bowler and one of the best

Already ordained into the Church of England, Rev. David Sheppard is pictured here on his return to the Test team of England, against Pakistan at Trent Bridge in 1962.

Simpson in his latter-day role as manager of Australia. A tough disciplinarian, he was something of a pioneer in that position.

slip fielders ever to play Test cricket.

Simpson possessed the great concentration needed to amass big scores. He made 359 for New South Wales against Queensland in 1963/64 and 311 for Australia against England at Old Trafford in 1964. The latter was a painstaking effort, taking 762 minutes, but it made sure Australia retained the Ashes.

He also made history when compiling 382 for the first wicket with Bill Lawry against the West Indies at Bridgetown in 1965. Simpson made 201 in a record first-wicket partnership for Australia that saw both openers make double centuries for the first time in Test cricket.

Simpson toured all the major Test-playing countries and captained Australia in 29 Tests between 1963/64 and 1967/68.

He returned to the Test arena for his 'second career' in 1977/78, coming back at the age of 41 to lead a young, inexperienced side after the Packer defections. He batted well in the series against India, but then found the going tougher in the following series against the West Indies.

His captaincy was bearing fruit on an improving side, but the Australian Board refused to promise him a place in the first Test against England in 1978/79 and he retired again to become a commentator and newspaper writer. In 1985/86 he again came back, not as a player this time but as manager of the Australian side.

In England, apart from his tours with Australia, he played Lancashire League cricket with Accrington in 1959, though he never played county cricket.

However, in 1990 and 1991 he was manager at Leicestershire, his supporters crediting him with bringing a more professional discipline to the dressing-room and

introducing a better recruitment policy.

First Class Career:
Runs – 21,029. Average 56.22 (60 centuries)
Wickets – 349. Average 38.07
Catches – 383

Test Match Career:
Tests – 62
Runs – 4,869. Average 46.81 (10 centuries)
Wickets – 71. Average 42.26
Catches – 110

M.J.K. SMITH

England

Born 1933
Oxford University, Leicestershire and Warwickshire

MIKE SMITH – ALWAYS better known by his initials M.J.K. – was an outstanding university cricketer who went on to lead county and country. Studious-looking through wearing glasses, he was an unflappable character with an astute cricket brain.

He set records in his Oxford years scoring 201 not out, 104 and 117 against Cambridge in successive seasons at Lord's. He was also a rugby blue and played once for England against Wales at outside half.

At county level he was a heavy scorer, reaching 2000 runs in six consecutive seasons between 1957 and 1962. Twenty times he exceeded 1000 runs.

For all that ability, his Test career never matched his county achievements. He was an uncertain starter, often trapped by the yorker early in his innings. He toured Australia, South Africa, New Zealand, the West Indies, India and Pakistan, captaining England on 25 occasions.

He had the misfortune to be dismissed four times in the nineties, but perhaps his best Test innings was at Port of Spain in 1959/60 when he made 108.

He was also a fine fielder, where his lightning reactions at short leg helped him to 53 Test catches.

Now chairman of Warwickshire, he was manager of the England party on their most recent tours in the West Indies and Australia.

First Class Career:
Runs – 39,832. Average 41.84 (69 centuries)

Test Match Career:
Tests – 50
Runs – 2,278. Average 31.63 (3 centuries)

Smith playing for Warwickshire in 1971. Also a fine rugby player, he was England's last dual international in the two sports.

JOHN SNOW
England
Born 1941
Sussex and Warwickshire

THE SON OF A clergyman, John Snow lived up to the title of his autobiography and was unquestionably a 'Cricket Rebel'. Moody, often with a look of disinterest, he was nevertheless England's most potent fast bowler in the late sixties and early seventies.

Snow had an easy, loping approach to the wicket, spearing the ball into the right-hander but also cutting it away off the wicket.

Opposite: At almost 40 years of age, John Snow shows Sir Garfield Sobers the old magic in this match for Old England at the Oval in 1980.

He could be particularly aggressive and bowled a dangerous bouncer – a weapon he never overused.

He originally joined Sussex as a batsman but quickly established himself as a bowler. He made his Test debut in 1965 and his first match-winning performance came on the 1967/68 tour of the West Indies when he took 7 for 49 in the second Test. He took 27 wickets in four Tests that winter and outshone the potent home attack.

His finest hour, however, came on the 1970/71 tour of Australia as he took 31 wickets in six Tests – a telling contribution as Ray Illingworth's side regained the Ashes.

His batting in the lower order was often effective. In 1966 he shared a last-wicket stand of 128 with Ken Higgs against West Indies at the Oval.

Snow often fell foul of authority. He was dropped from the England team in 1971 after knocking Sunil Gavaskar off his feet as the tiny Indian opener took a quick single. At Sussex he was once dropped for not trying.

A complex man, he had two books of poetry published. He was also one of the first to join Kerry Packer's revolution, and had some particularly harsh things to say about the cricket establishment.

Domestically he finished his career at Warwickshire, playing in the side that won the John Player League title in 1980. He has recently been welcomed back into the fold as one of the bowling coaches to the England senior side.

First Class Career:
Runs – 4,832. Average 14.17
Wickets – 1,174. Average 22.72

Test Match Career:
Tests – 49
Runs – 772. Average 13.54
Wickets – 202. Average 26.66

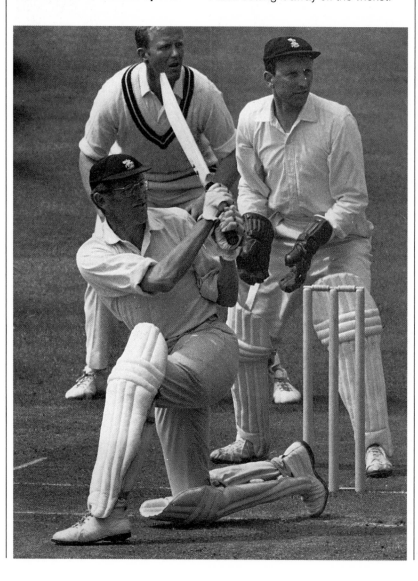

SIR GARFIELD SOBERS

West Indies

Born 1936

Barbados, South Australia and Nottinghamshire

GARY SOBERS, LATER TO become Sir Garfield, was simply the greatest all-rounder ever to have played cricket. Ian Botham, Imran Khan and Sir Richard Hadlee are among the elite as all-rounders, but few would question Sobers' position as the number one.

It seemed there was nothing Sobers could not do on a cricket field. A left-hander, he was one of the greatest batsmen the world has seen. He was a brilliant fast-medium bowler who could then switch effortlessly to bowling either orthodox slow left-arm or chinamen and googlies. Add to that his brilliance in the field, often close in at leg slip, and you have the complete cricketer.

His whole demeanour exuded authority and enjoyment. His strange, loping, knees-bent walk was instantly recognisable and a smile was never far from his lips. Despite the pressures of being the man the crowd always came to watch, and the constant publicity, he managed to maintain a high standard of performance and convey his enjoyment of the game to the spectators.

Sobers was born in Barbados with an extra finger on each hand. They were amputated early in his life. He was a natural all-round sportsman, playing golf, football and basketball for the island.

He first played cricket for Barbados as a 16-year-old and then a year later in 1954 he made his Test debut as a slow left-arm bowler against England, taking 4 for 75 in the first innings.

He had by now already started to develop his batting and his first Test century came in dramatic style against Pakistan at Kingston, Jamaica in 1957/58. He scored 365 not out – one more than the then

Test record set by Sir Len Hutton in 1938. Sobers' record stood for over 35 years before being overtaken by Brian Lara in 1993/94.

Sobers made 824 runs in that series at an average of 137.33, making two further centuries. He topped 500 runs in five other series.

He was a natural leader and his captaincy, unlike so many at Test level, was bold and imaginative. That sometimes brought its own problems and led to criticism.

In 1967/68 in the fourth Test against England, after three draws, he declared the West Indies second innings and set England a target of 215 in 165 minutes. They reached it, and Sobers, having gambled to try to win the game, was heavily blamed for losing it.

He captained the West Indies from 1965 until 1974. By then his appetite for the game was on the wane, with his damaged knees restricting his movements.

He was an inspirational leader, too, in domestic cricket for both Nottinghamshire and South Australia. And although records meant little to him, making them seemed second nature.

Against Glamorgan at Swansea in 1968, he hit Malcolm Nash, bowling slow left-arm spinners, for six 6's in an over. During his period with South Australia, he twice achieved the Australian double of 1,000 runs and 50 wickets in a season.

In 1975, a year after his retirement from the game, he was knighted by the Queen in his native Barbados. His fellow islanders rejoiced in his richly deserved award.

With the almost constant demands of top international cricket today, it seems unlikely we will see a player of Sobers' like again.

First Class Career:

Runs – 28,315. Average 54.87
(86 centuries)
Wickets – 1,043. Average 27.74
Catches – 407

Test Match Career:

Tests – 93
Runs – 8,032. Average 57.78
(26 centuries)
Wickets – 235. Average 34.03
Catches – 109

A much younger Gary Sobers bravely takes the game to England in 1957 at the Oval. He certainly showed his more experienced colleagues the way in this match, top-scoring in both innings with 39 and 42 as the West Indies were bowled out by Laker and Lock for 89 and 86.

SOMERSET

Founded: 1875

Entered Official Championship: 1891

Honours:

Gillette Cup – 1979
NatWest Trophy – 1983
Benson and Hedges Cup – 1981, 1982
John Player League – 1979

SOMERSET MAY NEVER have won the County Championship, but they have brought much fun and character to the first-class game. They have often been a team of surprises, frequently upsetting mighty opponents.

Their trophies have come in the one-day competitions. All three were won in a five-year period that was unquestionably the highlight of the club's history.

It is perhaps typical of Somerset that the club was actually formed at a meeting at Sidmouth in Devon, following a match between the Gentlemen of Devonshire and the Gentlemen of Somersetshire. Among the resolutions passed, it was decided that there should be no county ground and the club would depend entirely on voluntary contributions.

However, in 1886 the club took out a lease on their present ground in Taunton. The freehold was purchased ten years later.

It was on this ground in 1895 that Archie MacLaren scored 424 in 470 minutes for Lancashire against Somerset – the highest individual score made in English first-class cricket. Thirty years later Jack Hobbs hit two centuries in a match there for Surrey to overtake W.G. Grace's record of 126 hundreds.

Somerset's introduction to the first-class ranks in 1891 was not easy – they went down by an innings and 375 runs to Surrey after twice being dismissed for 37. However, they had their revenge later in the season and finished fifth in the table.

Somerset's love of upsetting the big boys began as cricket moved into the 20th century. Between 1900 and 1902, Yorkshire, in winning three championships, lost just two matches – both to Somerset.

In 1901 Somerset, 238 behind on first innings having been all out for just 87, scored 630 in the second and then dismissed Yorkshire for 113 to win by 279 runs – one of the greatest ever turnarounds in a cricket match.

Sammy Woods, Australian by birth, was captain of the side at the time. He was a fast bowler and big hitter who played for Australia against England, and for England against South Africa. He also played rugby for England, winning thirteen caps between 1890 and 1895.

Just before the First World War, the county finished bottom three times in four years. They improved to fifth in 1919, but in the twenties, the non-availability for long spells of talented amateurs regularly left them in the bottom half of the table.

In the 1930s two outstanding players emerged. Arthur Wellard, a big hitter and fast bowler who was similar in style to Woods, joined Somerset from his native Kent. He took 131 wickets in his first season, and went on to take 1,500 wickets and score more than 11,000 runs in his career.

In 1935 Harold Gimblett, a 21-year-old, made his first appearance, scoring 123 in just 63 minutes after going in with his side in trouble at 107 for 6. A star was born. He went on to become the county's top run-scorer with more than 20,000, yet was unfortunate to play just three times for England – twice against India and once against the West Indies.

After the Second World War, Maurice Tremlett established himself as a natural all-rounder, and in 1956 he became Somerset's first professional captain. After four seasons at the bottom prior to his appointment, the club were lifted to third in 1958.

Concern among members had forced Somerset to look for new talent, and players such as Bill Alley, who came into county cricket at the age of 38, Brian Langford and Ken Palmer brought more stability to the side.

From then on the county cleverly brought in players from other counties or from overseas. In 1968 a young Greg Chappell came from Australia to learn his craft on English wickets. Tom Cartwright from Warwickshire and Derek Taylor, a wicket-keeper from Surrey, were two others recruited before in 1971 the committee took the bold step of signing the former Yorkshire and England captain Brian Close.

The following year Close took over the captaincy and although he upset a few people, he had a tremendous influence, bringing a greater discipline to the side. Young players like Brian Rose, Peter Denning, Peter Roebuck, Vic Marks and Ian Botham all developed under Close.

In 1974 came the greatest signing of them all when the club's vice-chairman brought Viv Richards from the West Indies. Richards' impact was immediate, as his first innings for the club saw him win a gold award for scoring 81 not out in a Benson and Hedges Cup match.

The quarter-finals of the competition that year saw 18-year-old Ian Botham score a masterly 45 not out to win the match.

Rose took over the captaincy and the side that Close had built began to win trophies. The 1979 season was to be their greatest year, although it began on a sour note.

Having won three qualifying zonal matches in the Benson and Hedges Cup, Somerset declared at 1 for no wicket in a rain-affected match at Worcester. Conceding the match in this way meant they were assured of qualification for the quarter-finals, having secured enough points and achieved a high enough wicket-taking rate.

But the Test and County Cricket Board took a dim view, and although no rule had been broken they decided to expel Somerset from the competition.

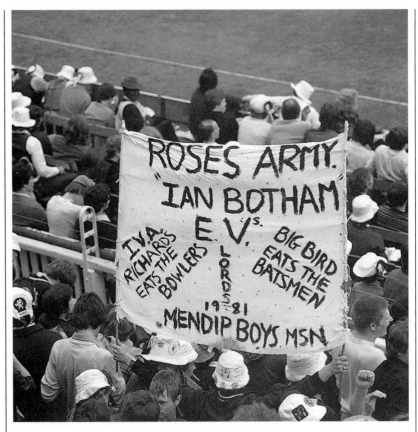

Somerset supporters in confident mood at the 1981 Benson & Hedges Cup final. Their team did not disappoint them, beating Surrey by 7 wickets.

However, all came right over the weekend of 8th–9th September. On the Saturday a century from Richards and six wickets from the mighty Joel Garner brought victory in the Gillette Cup, and the following day at Trent Bridge they beat Nottinghamshire to take the John Player League title – their first two trophies in one weekend, after 88 years of trying.

Benson and Hedges Cup triumphs followed in 1981 and 1982, with Richards scoring a century against Surrey and a half century against Nottinghamshire in successive finals. Somerset were back at Lord's the following year to beat Kent in the NatWest Trophy final.

But the bubble was soon to burst.

In 1986 Botham was suspended for much of the season after admitting in a newspaper article to smoking cannabis.

Then in August, the Somerset committee decided not to renew the contracts of Richards and Garner, and Botham said he would not stay without them.

The county was hit by furious internal strife, quite out of keeping with its usual happy-go-lucky attitude.

At a Special General Meeting the members backed the committee and the three stars departed – Botham for Worcestershire, Richards, eventually, to Glamorgan, and Garner out of county cricket.

Another foreign import, Jimmy Cook, proved to be an inspired signing. The South African opener scored heavily in three seasons with the club from 1989 to 1992.

Another period of rebuilding is currently under way, but there are some talented batsmen emerging in Lathwell and Trescothick.

SOUTH AFRICA

SOUTH AFRICA'S YEARS of international isolation have come to an end, with Test matches now being played at home and abroad. But their time in the wilderness, beginning with the 'D'Oliveira Affair' in 1968, cost the country dear and blighted the careers of some world-class players.

British soldiers stationed in South Africa are credited with having introduced cricket there around the beginning of the 19th century. Test cricket began in 1888/89 when C.A. Smith led England to two victories at Port Elizabeth.

It was not until 1905/06 that South Africa first achieved success, winning the series against England by four matches to one.

South Africa then joined England and Australia in forming the Imperial Cricket Conference, as the International Cricket Council was then known, in June 1909. It was an elite club, with membership restricted to countries in the British Commonwealth where Test cricket was played.

Domestically, the Currie Cup, now called the Castle Cup, was from 1889/90 the main first-class competition within the country. It always had the reputation of producing a particularly high standard of cricket.

It was just prior to the Second World War that a great boost was given to the development of the game with the introduction of grass wickets, and in 1938/39 Walter Hammond led an England touring party that for the first time was fully representative of English cricket.

The tour also contained the first timeless Test. It was not a success. Played over ten days, it was never finished, with rain curtailing play on the last day before the tourists were due to return home.

South Africa's tour of England in 1960 saw them defeated by three matches to nil, but will always be remembered for other reasons. The storm clouds over apartheid were gathering and there were regular demonstrations against the team.

On the field there was the depressing sight of fast bowler Geoff Griffin being forced to bowl underarm at Lord's after umpire Syd Buller had repeatedly called him for throwing. It was to be the end of Griffin's career.

South Africa were a stronger proposition on the 1965 tour, when they won the series. In Graeme and Peter Pollock and Eddie Barlow they had the nucleus of a fine side, well led by Peter van der Merwe.

They went on to record two big series wins over Australia with two young players, Mike Procter and Barry Richards, seemingly destined for long and illustrious Test careers.

Sadly for them, international opinion was hardening against South Africa and the Republic's years of isolation began with their refusal to accept Basil D'Oliveira, a Cape coloured, as part of the England team for the proposed tour of 1968/69.

D'Oliveira had, to the general indignation, been left out of the England touring party despite scoring a century against Australia at the Oval in the final Test of the summer. Then he was controversially called up after Tom Cartwright pulled out with an injury. The South African president, Mr Vorster, accused England of mixing sport and politics and the tour was cancelled.

Incredibly, the South African tour to England in 1970 was due to go ahead regardless, but it had to be called off at the last minute in the face of overwhelming political protest. South Africa's isolation began, with the authorities there warned that no resumption of matches would be possible until one national body administered cricket, with selection on merit being introduced.

With Test cricket closed to them, many of South Africa's best players joined English county clubs. Procter joined Gloucestershire, Clive Rice went to Nottinghamshire and Richards to Hampshire, ironically to form a talented opening partnership with Gordon Greenidge, the black West Indian Test star.

In South Africa a number of tours were arranged, the most notable being the 'rebel tours' involving Test players attracted by large sums of money.

In 1982, amid great secrecy, England's Geoffrey Boycott was the top name in an English party that was captained by Graham Gooch and also included John Emburey. The cricket world was shocked and the offending Englishmen were given three-year Test bans.

Other rebel tours followed, first from Sri Lanka and then from the West Indies, led by former Test batsman Lawrence Rowe and featuring a mixture of former Test stars and young hopefuls.

Another tour of Englishmen, this time led by former England captain Mike Gatting and including Test regulars such as Emburey, Foster, Dilley, Broad and Robinson, took place in January 1990 and again led

South Africa's dream of a return to international cricket was finally realised in 1991 when they lined up for this one-day match against India at Calcutta. Dr Ali Bacher is flanked by Clive Rice and Mike Procter.

to lengthy bans for all concerned, which were eventually rescinded as South Africa returned to the fold.

That they did so swiftly in the wake of a political settlement being realised in the Republic owed much to Dr Ali Bacher. It was largely through his efforts that the Indian-dominated South African Cricket Board and the whites' South African Cricket Union came together to form the non-racial United Cricket Board of South Africa.

The ICC meeting in July 1991 decided to readmit South Africa. They duly took part in the 1992 World Cup in Australia and followed that with their first Test for more than a decade, and their first ever against the West Indies, in April 1992.

The return of Test cricket to South African soil came with a series against India the following November. The first Test was marked by the release of doves of peace. It also made history with a third umpire seated in the pavilion giving a player run out after watching a video replay.

In 1994 South Africa's return to the international fold was completed with a tour to England. There were some emotional scenes as openers Andrew Hudson and Gary Kirsten stepped out onto the field at Lord's to begin the match.

The game ended with champagne on the dressing-room balcony as the visitors completed an overwhelming win by 356 runs, dismissing England for 99 in their second innings. The series was eventually drawn, providing South Africa with a thoroughly satisfactory return to cricket in England.

SOUTH AFRICA
v
INDIA

THESE TWO COUNTRIES met for the first time ever in 1992/93 in a series marking the return of Test cricket to South Africa after 23 years.

It was an historic occasion, although sadly some slow scoring and unimaginative captaincy on both sides, together with the lifeless pitches, produced rather dull cricket.

India finished the tour without a win in 25 matches outside their own country.

The first Test at Durban was drawn after the fourth day was washed out by rain. There were centuries from South Africa's captain Kepler Wessels and from P.K. Amre on his Indian debut.

But most significantly the game saw the debut of Omar Henry, South Africa's oldest debutant at 40 years and 295 days, and the first non-white player to represent South Africa.

It was also the first Test to use television replays to settle difficult run-out and stumping decisions, India's Tendulkar becoming the first man to be given out by reference to a slow-motion replay.

The second Test was also drawn, with neither captain, Wessels or Azharuddin, prepared to risk anything.

However, after winning a one-day series 5–2, South Africa went on to take the third Test by nine wickets. India had no answer to the hostile fast bowling of Allan Donald who recorded match figures of 12 for 139.

Season	Ven	Tests	Winner	Res
1992/93	SA	4	S. Africa	1–0

SOUTH AFRICA
v
NEW ZEALAND

SERIES BETWEEN SOUTH Africa and New Zealand were few and far between even before the Republic was frozen out of international cricket.

In 1931/32 H.B. Cameron's South African party played two Tests in New Zealand after their tour of Australia. They won both matches

conclusively, the first by an innings and 12 runs, the second by eight wickets despite a century by H.G. Vivian, who at 19 years and 121 days became New Zealand's youngest centurion.

It was 21 years before they met again, once more in New Zealand. A commanding 255 by Jackie McGlew set up a South African first innings total of 524 for 8 declared and an eventual victory by an innings and 180 runs. The other match was drawn.

The following season New Zealand made their first visit to South Africa for a five-match series but suffered the same sort of reverse they were used to at home, this time going down 4–0. The speed of Neil Adcock and the spin of Hugh Tayfield proved too strong for the Kiwis' batting.

It was in 1961/62 that New Zealand's fortunes changed. They recorded their first victories on foreign soil in enjoying a drawn series 2–2. John Reid led New Zealand, his batting providing a

great example to his side as he scored 546 in the series at an average of 60.64. His counterpart McGlew also proved to be his side's leading batsman, with two centuries.

South Africa went one up in the first Test before New Zealand hit back in the third. South Africa's innings win in the next looked to have settled the series, but New Zealand showed resilience to win the final match at Port Elizabeth by 40 runs, Reid this time distinguishing himself with the ball, taking 4 for 44.

The last series before South Africa's isolation, in New Zealand in 1963/64, proved to be an anti-climax with three drawn games as bad weather often thwarted the stronger South African side.

However, the resumption of matches in South Africa in 1994/95 was an altogether more entertaining affair. The visitors won the first Test, raising hopes of recording their first ever series win against South Africa, only for the home side to hit back and take the second Test by eight

South Africa took on the West Indies for the first time ever in 1992. Captains Kepler Wessels (SA, left) and Richie Richardson go out for the toss.

wickets in a match dominated by their fast bowlers.

Then South Africa made history by becoming the only side this century to come from behind to win a three-Test series, with victory in the final Test at Cape Town by seven wickets.

Season	Ven	Tests	Winners	Res
1931/32	NZ	2	S. Africa	2–0
1952/53	NZ	2	S. Africa	1–0
1953/54	SA	5	S. Africa	4–0
1961/62	SA	5	—	2–2
1963/64	NZ	3	—	0–0
1994/95	SA	3	S. Africa	2–1

SOUTH AFRICA
v
SRI LANKA

SOUTH AFRICA continued their return to the international arena with a three-Test series in Sri Lanka in 1993/94. The home side were buoyed by their series win over England and had the better of a drawn first Test.

Jonty Rhodes made his maiden Test century to save South Africa from possible defeat after they slumped to 138 for 6, chasing 365 for victory. They ended on 251 for 7.

South Africa totally dominated the second match to win by an innings and 208 runs – their biggest Test win. The Sri Lankan batsmen had no answer to the bowling of Donald, Schultz and Snell.

South Africa made sure of their series win with a draw in the final match at Colombo. It was an evenly matched contest, spoilt by the loss of the final day's play due to rain.

Season	Ven	Tests	Winner	Res
1993/94	SL	3	S. Africa	1–0

SOUTH AFRICA
v
WEST INDIES

IT WAS NOT UNTIL SOUTH Africa's return to international competition that they first faced the West Indies. It proved to be an emotional match, played at Bridgetown, Barbados. The new South Africa, apartheid behind them, taking on the might of the most formidable side in world cricket.

For much of the game South Africa had the better of things, first dismissing the West Indies and then batting well to take a first innings lead of 83, thanks largely to opener Andrew Hudson's fine 163 on his Test debut.

Set a modest 201 to win, South Africa finished the fourth day at 122 for 2 with victory in sight. But then Courtney Walsh and Curtley Ambrose took over as South Africa crashed to 148 all out – their last eight wickets falling for 26 runs in 95 minutes.

It was a huge disappointment for South Africa, tempered only by Hudson sharing the man of the match award with Ambrose.

Season	Ven	Tests	Winner	Res
1991/92	WI	1	W. Indies	1–0

F. R. SPOFFORTH
Australia
Born 1853. Died 1926
New South Wales, Victoria and Derbyshire

FREDERICK ROBERT Spofforth was the most famous bowler from the early days of cricket in Australia. He was given the nickname 'The Demon' – it was richly deserved – for his magnificent wicket-taking feats.

What made him different from his peers was the thought he gave to his craft. A fast-medium bowler who

could achieve movement both through the air and off the pitch, he went to great lengths to study his opponents' weaknesses, as well as making the most of his own abilities. He was also a natural athlete, being a fine sprinter.

In England in 1878 he took 11 wickets in a day at Lord's as the Australians embarrassed the MCC.

Spofforth did not play in the first ever Test in 1876/77, being angered over the selection of the wicket-keeper. However, he joined the fold in time for the second match.

In 1878/79 his thirteen wickets at Melbourne secured victory for Australia. He made five tours of England, improving his wicket-taking records all the while. In 1884 he took 216 wickets at an average of 12.23, and might have done better two years later but for injury.

He moved to England and played for Derbyshire for three seasons (1889–91). His most notable achievement was to take 15 for 81 against Yorkshire in his first season.

First Class Career:
Wickets – 853. Average 14.95

Test Match Career:
Tests – 18
Wickets – 94. Average 18.41

SRI LANKA

SRI LANKA, FORMERLY Ceylon, was elected to full membership of the then International Cricket Conference in July 1981 and the team played their first Test match against the touring England team in February the following year.

They have traditionally lacked true fast bowlers, but have often more than made up for that with enterprising spin bowlers. They invariably possess good strokemaking batsmen, play attractive cricket, and have merited their Test status.

The first cricket club in Ceylon – the 97th Regiment – was believed to have been formed in 1832, with the first home Ceylonese club being created 41 years later.

It was an Englishman, George Vanderpar, who really created serious interest in cricket in Ceylon. In the 1880s, he arranged for touring teams from England and Australia to play a game in Colombo.

The Ceylon Cricket Association was founded in 1922, ninety years after that first club was formed. The MCC made their first serious tour in 1927, and then an Indian side led by the Maharaj Kumar of Vizianagram played in Ceylon in 1930. The visit was notable because it featured, by special invitation, the great England opening pair of Jack Hobbs and Herbert Sutcliffe.

Ceylon made their debut tour to India in 1932/33, losing only one of their ten matches. Unofficial 'Tests'

against teams touring India and Pakistan became commonplace and in 1975 Sri Lanka did particularly well to hold the strong West Indies team to two draws. That year the Sri Lankans also played in the first World Cup in England, but lost all three matches.

Sri Lanka made a first official tour of England in 1979, winning the inaugural ICC Trophy and hence qualifying to take part in the second World Cup. This time they achieved a notable victory in Group B, beating India at Old Trafford by 47 runs.

Their performance that summer gave fresh impetus to their claims for full Test status and they became a welcome addition to the fold two years later.

Sri Lanka's first ever victory over England at Colombo in 1993 included a fine innings of 80 from Aravinda de Silva (opposite).

They achieved notable Test victories against India and Pakistan in Sri Lanka in 1985/86, and recorded their third Test win against New Zealand, also in Sri Lanka, in December 1992.

Their proudest moment, however, came three months later when they beat a demoralised England team by five wickets at Colombo – England having come fresh from a miserable tour of India. It was Sri Lanka's first Test victory over England, eleven years after that inaugural Test. They also recorded two one-day international victories to reduce England to as low an ebb as followers could remember.

SRI LANKA
V
ZIMBABWE

THE YOUNGEST TEST-playing countries met for the first time in a three-match series in Zimbabwe in October 1994.

The first Test at Harare suffered from the loss of the final day's play through rain, but the match was already heading towards a draw, Sri Lanka taking 179.5 overs to amass 383 runs when batting first.

The second Test saw Zimbabwe denied their first victory by disciplined Sri Lankan batting in their second innings.

The visitors were forced to follow on 244 behind, but an undefeated century by Ranatunga, who reached three figures off the final ball of the match, earned his side a draw.

The match was most notable for a superb 266 – the highest Test score by a Zimbabwean – by former captain David Houghton, who batted for more than eleven hours.

Rain again spoilt the final Test, washing out the last day's play, but again a draw seemed certain in any case. Zimbabwe could justifiably claim to have had the better of the series.

Season	Ven	Tests	Winner	Res
1994/95	Zim	3	—	0–0

BRIAN STATHAM
England
Born 1930
Lancashire

FAST BOWLERS, IT IS said, hunt in pairs. Brian Statham was part of two quite outstanding pairs over the course of a decade.

First he teamed up with Frank Tyson to tear through the Australians in the 1954/55 series. Then after Tyson's retirement he teamed up with Fred Trueman to provide an opening attack as good as any seen in the post-war years.

While Tyson and Trueman were fast and furious, Statham, in keeping with his personality, was the model of consistency – the perfect foil. He bowled fast and straight with the ability to move the ball both ways off the seam.

He was an undemonstrative bowler with a smooth action and never complained at ill-luck or a long day's work in the field.

Opposition batsmen often feared him more than Tyson and Trueman.

He first played for England against New Zealand in 1950/51. He toured Australia four times, and also represented his country in India, South Africa and the West Indies.

Apart from his bowling, he could also be a useful left-hand tail end batsman.

He twice took fifteen wickets in a match for Lancashire, and three times performed the hat-trick. He captained the county between 1965 and 1967.

First Class Career:
Wickets – 2,260. Average 16.36

Test Match Career:
Tests – 70
Wickets – 252. Average 24.82

Brian Statham of Lancashire and England. He briefly held the record for the most wickets in Tests before his partner Fred Trueman overtook him.

ALEC STEWART
England
Born 1963
Surrey

ALTHOUGH AT FIRST saddled with the unfair suspicion that he was only in the England side because his father Micky was the manager, Alec Stewart has through hard work and

dedication become one of the world's top batsmen.

His strength has been his adaptability. Opening batsman, middle-order batsman, fine fielder, competent wicket-keeper, one almost expected him to be called upon to bowl for his country.

Named after his godfather Alec Bedser, Stewart followed in his father's footsteps to the Oval after leaving school. Winters were spent in grade cricket in Australia where his hard, competitive edge was undoubtedly sharpened.

His tough attitude to the game, and sometimes to his opponents, occasionally went over the top, but now as captain of Surrey and vice-captain of England he has developed a more statesman-like approach.

In his first ten years of first-class cricket he managed only 16 centuries. He had the reputation of being an attractive player but without the concentration required to make big scores.

He worked hard to put things right, but it was thanks to his abilities as a wicket-keeper that he established himself in the international arena.

He was dropped from the side after the Australian tour of 1990/91 but surprisingly recalled for the final Test against the West Indies that summer as wicket-keeper/batsman. He seized his chance with two good innings and a sound performance behind the stumps to help England to a memorable victory.

Two weeks later he scored his first Test century against Sri Lanka, followed that in the winter with good innings in New Zealand and has since been a permanent fixture.

He suffered cruel luck on the 1994/95 Ashes tour, breaking a finger right at the start of the trip, and then again in the Sydney Test after Christmas. His experience and

Originally earning selection for the versatility provided by his wicket-keeping, Alec Stewart has developed into a fine attacking batsman in his own right, too often called upon to lift English spirits.

THE GUINNESS

determination against the Australian attack was sorely missed.

First Class Career:
Runs – 15,815. Average 39.64
(31 centuries)

Test Match Career:
Tests – 45
Runs – 3,055. Average 40.20
(7 centuries)
Catches – 53. Stumpings – 4

MICKY STEWART
England
Born 1932
Surrey

MICKY STEWART PLAYED only eight Tests for England, but became better known as

England's first full-time team manager. His period in charge produced an emphasis on hard effort and fitness which his critics derided as almost football-like. They claimed it led him to favour solid workers rather than truly gifted players such as David Gower.

Stewart was a highly accomplished opening batsman and brilliant short-leg fielder who

In tandem with skipper Graham Gooch, Stewart (left) brought a new work ethic to the England Test side and for a while it proved a success: on this tour of the Caribbean in 1990 they ran the West Indies very close.

came into the Surrey side towards the end of their great championship seasons in the 1950s. In 1957 he set a world record of seven catches in an innings against Northants.

He scored 1,000 runs in a season 15 times and captained Surrey from 1963 to 1972, leading them to the County Championship title in 1971.

His Test appearances, between 1962 and 1964, came against the West Indies, India and Pakistan. He often opened the batting with his Surrey colleague John Edrich.

Stewart was also a fine footballer, playing for a number of clubs in the London area, most notably Charlton Athletic and Corinthian Casuals.

Having managed the Surrey side after retiring as a player, he was appointed assistant manager of England in 1986, his duties to cover planning, fitness, and coaching. That led to him becoming full-time team manager until he was succeeded by Keith Fletcher, who took over for the tour to India and Sri Lanka in 1992/93.

Test performances during his period of office were largely disappointing, although England did show fighting qualities in sharing a series against the West Indies in 1991.

He also had the satisfaction of seeing England reach the final of the World Cup in Australia in 1992.

Like all good managers, he showed great loyalty to his players and dealt well with the introduction of his own son Alec into the team. Now he has been given responsibility for developing the game at youth level.

First Class Career:
*Runs – 26,492. Average 32.90
(49 centuries)*

Test Match Career:
*Tests – 8
Runs – 385. Average 35.00*

SUNDAY LEAGUE

SIX YEARS AFTER THE introduction of the first one-day competition, the Gillette Cup, a Sunday League of limited-overs matches was started.

The Gillette Cup had proved a crowd-puller. But for some years previously, Sunday cricket had been covered on television featuring matches involving the International Cavaliers, where some of the best players in the world displayed their skills in fairly light-hearted games against county sides, often in aid of players enjoying benefit seasons.

The matches brought the name of the sponsors, the cigarette company Rothmans, to the fore, and it was another such company, John Player, that suggested a Sunday League to the cricket authorities.

The League gave each county sixteen matches each of 40 overs per side, and although the purists may have initially dismissed it, it proved to be a hit with the spectators, producing the kind of excited atmosphere more usually seen at football grounds.

There were other changes to the game that made the John Player League unique. Forty overs each meant the game could take place over about five hours on a Sunday afternoon. No bowler could bowl more than eight overs, and bowlers' run-ups were restricted to 15 yards.

Television covered one match each week and attracted big audiences, but did not appear to affect the size of the crowds at other matches.

The critics of the competition argued that it was little more than a batsmen's thrash-about. Restrictions on run-ups reduced fast bowlers to medium-pacers and spinners had less chance to play than in the Gillette Cup, although Brian Langford of Somerset once achieved the remarkable figures of 8–8–0–0.

On the plus side, the league is credited with having raised fielding standards throughout the game, and many batsmen have developed into more fluent strokemakers.

At the end of 1986, with matches no longer having the BBC2 Sunday afternoon airwaves to themselves, John Player withdrew their sponsorship. The unpredictable nature of the competition was demonstrated by the fact that ten counties had won the title over the eighteen years.

Refuge Assurance took over in 1987, when Worcestershire, 16th in the final John Player League, took the title. The company continued to back the league for a further four years, but when they pulled out at the end of the 1991 season, no sponsor could be found for the following year.

Crowds had dwindled and television coverage had moved to the satellite channel, BSkyB. Then for 1993, a major revamp was announced.

Sponsored by the insurance

Brian Lara holds the Axa/Equity & Law League trophy as Warwickshire complete the third leg of their historic tilt at all four major competitions in 1994. It was only their second ever success in the Sunday league.

company Axa Equity & Law, the format was changed to 50 overs per side, with an earlier start and no restrictions on bowlers' run-ups. The extra ten overs, it was hoped, would result in higher quality one-day cricket.

There was a more visible change, though, with the introduction of coloured clothing, with counties dressed in a variety of shades of blue, red, green and yellow. It was hoped this would prompt commercial activity and create revenue through the sale of replica shirts, hats, and sweaters.

However, the players found the new format harder work and there was no appreciable increase in attendances. As a result, the competition returned to 40 overs a-side in 1994 when Warwickshire took the title as part of their unique treble.

SUNDAY LEAGUE

JOHN PLAYER LEAGUE

1969	Lancashire
1970	Lancashire
1971	Worcestershire
1972	Kent
1973	Kent
1974	Leicestershire
1975	Hampshire
1976	Kent
1977	Leicestershire
1978	Hampshire
1979	Somerset
1980	Warwickshire
1981	Essex
1982	Sussex
1983	Yorkshire
1984	Essex
1985	Essex
1986	Hampshire

REFUGE ASSURANCE LEAGUE

1987	Worcestershire
1988	Worcestershire
1989	Lancashire
1990	Derbyshire
1991	Nottinghamshire

SUNDAY LEAGUE

1992	Middlesex

AXA/EQUITY AND LAW LEAGUE

1993	Glamorgan
1994	Warwickshire

SURREY

Founded: 1845

Entered Official Championship: 1890

Honours:

County Champions – 1890, 1891, 1892, 1894, 1895, 1899, 1914, 1950 (joint), 1952, 1953, 1954, 1955, 1956, 1957, 1958, 1971

NatWest Trophy – 1982

Benson and Hedges Cup – 1974

ONE OF THE 'BIG' CLUBS in county cricket, Surrey will forever be remembered for their exploits in the 1950s when they won the Championship for seven consecutive seasons – a record.

But that record has proved to be a curse on the teams that have followed. Surrey's record over the past thirty years has been modest for a club which has always produced fine players, particularly batsmen, with four of them, the legendary Jack Hobbs, Tom Hayward, Andy Sandham and John Edrich, scoring 100 hundreds.

In the spring of 1845, what is now the Oval was transformed from a market garden into a cricket ground for the newly formed Surrey club. They would often play an England XI in those days and beat them, and were without doubt the premier club in those early years before the official championship began.

They dominated the first seasons of that competition too, winning the title the first three years and on three other occasions before the turn of the century. Led first by John Shuter and then by K.J. Key, Surrey were particularly strong in all departments of the game.

Bobby Abel formed an impressive opening partnership with William Brockwell, and his 357 not out against Somerset at the Oval in 1899 remains the highest innings by a Surrey cricketer.

Tom Hayward was another batsman of great class. For twenty years he scored more than 1,000 runs in a season, and he is second behind Sir Jack Hobbs as Surrey's highest run-scorer.

Peter May leads his team out at the Oval in 1958 after Surrey had claimed the County Championship title outright for a record seventh successive time. From left: Eric Bedser, May, Barrington, McIntyre, Constable, Gibson, Laker, Loader and Fletcher.

The bowling attack during this period was led by Tom Richardson, a very fast bowler who could sustain his speed for long spells. He took more than 1,500 wickets for Surrey in the championship, which was a record for over thirty years. He died prematurely from a heart attack at the age of 42 in 1912.

The Oval has long been known as one of the best batting wickets in the country, and while Surrey batsmen flourished it was probably their bowlers' inability to dismiss teams twice in three days that meant they won the title just once in the first fifty years of the 20th century.

Their 1914 title-winning side owed much to the batting of Hobbs, Ducat, Abel and Sandham. They were supported well in the field by Herbert Strudwick, a fine wicket-keeper who gave valuable service over thirty years behind the stumps.

It is the batting of Jack Hobbs, however, that dominates Surrey history from 1905 until just before the Second World War. His records are recorded elsewhere, but his ability was such that advancing years took nothing away from his strokeplay.

In 1925 he finally overtook W.G. Grace's record of 126 centuries. He equalled that feat on 16th August when he scored 101 against Somerset, and the celebrations continued the next day when he surpassed it with an undefeated century in the second innings.

Hobbs eventually retired in his 52nd year with 197 centuries to his credit and a total of 61,237 runs. The Hobbs Gates at the Oval will serve as a reminder of his greatness to future generations.

Andrew Sandham's achievements as Hobbs' regular opening partner are naturally overshadowed in comparison. But Sandham, who was with the county for sixty years as player, coach and scorer, played 14 times for England, and scored more than 30,000 runs. Perhaps his most memorable innings was his 219 for Surrey against the Australians in 1934.

After the Second World War, Surrey began to build up the formidable team that was to bring them total domination of the championship in the fifties. They shared the title with Lancashire in 1950, but then had a complete command of domestic cricket which is unlikely to be bettered.

A crucial element was the decision by the Surrey committee to appoint Stuart Surridge as captain in succession to Michael Barton in 1952. His record was unique – five seasons as captain, five championships.

Under his leadership, Surrey won 63.7 per cent of all matches played – an extraordinarily high figure. At a time when the number of drawn games was worrying administrators, Surrey only drew one in five. Indeed, in 1955 they drew no matches at all, winning 23 and losing 5.

As good a captain as he was, Surridge unquestionably had a superb team to lead. The Oval pitches became more helpful to the bowlers, and the Surrey attack, in particular pace bowlers Peter Loader and Alec Bedser and spinners Jim Laker and Tony Lock, enjoyed themselves to the full.

In championship matches in the 1950s, Lock took 1,070 wickets, Laker 957, Bedser 855 and Loader 595. All of them averaged under 20. They were well supported by Bedser's identical twin bother Eric, and Surridge himself.

The batting featured the elegant Peter May, who succeeded Surridge as captain for the final two championship titles in 1957 and 1958. He topped the county averages both years. Under his leadership, young talent came through, most notably the batsmen Mickey Stewart and Ken Barrington.

SURREY'S RECORD 1952–58					
	P	W	L	D	ND
1952	28	20	3	5	0
1953	28	13	4	10	1
1954	28	15	3	8	2
1955	28	23	5	0	0
1956	28	15	5	6	2
1957	28	21	3	3	1
1958	28	14	5	8	1

The successful years ended as May devoted more time to business, Lock emigrated to Australia and other players reached the end of their careers.

The batting, however, remained strong as John Edrich joined Barrington and Stewart, who took over the captaincy from May and proved himself a brilliant close-to-the wicket fielder.

Stewart led an attractive side in the 1960s, with bowlers Geoff Arnold and Pat Pocock winning Test places and Stewart Storey in 1966 becoming the first Surrey player to do the double since Freddie Brown in 1932.

The championship returned to the Oval in 1971 when the club finished equal on points with Warwickshire but won by virtue of their eleven victories to Warwickshire's nine. Edrich, Graham Roope and Younis Ahmed made up a formidable and attractive batting line-up, with Robin Jackman and the popular Pakistani Intikhab Alam supporting Pocock and Arnold as the main bowlers.

But tension was growing between committee and players, and dressing-room disharmony became a feature of Surrey's cricket.

Quality players were allowed to slip away to other counties, among them Bob Willis to Warwickshire, after he was denied his county cap following a successful tour of Australia; Roger Knight to Gloucestershire; and Mike Selvey and John Emburey to Middlesex.

Furthermore, the decision to go outside the county to find captains, shown in the return of Knight and the summoning from Australia of Ian Greig, led to other players leaving as their leadership claims were passed over.

After years of fairly poor achievement in the championship and one-day competitions, hopes were higher at the Oval at the start of the 1990s that a young side developing under the leadership of England vice-captain Alec Stewart, Mickey's son might reverse the slide.

The talent of the Bicknell brothers Darren and Martin, Graham Thorpe and Alistair Brown, together with the explosive bowling of Waqar Younis, suggested better times might be coming for Surrey, but as yet the Oval trophy cabinet remains bare.

SUSSEX
Founded: 1839

Entered Official Championship: 1890

Honours:

Gillette Cup – 1963, 1964, 1978

NatWest Trophy – 1986

John Player League – 1982

THEY HAVE NEVER WON the County Championship despite finishing runners-up seven times, but Sussex were the initial kings of one-day cricket, winning the Gillette Cup in its first two years.

Throughout their history, it has been Sussex's lack of a penetrating bowling attack that has denied them the domestic game's top honour. Their batting has been more effective, however, with a number of dashing strokemakers produced.

At the end of the 19th century, it was the 'lob' bowling of Walter Humphreys that was responsible for most of the county's wickets. He played until he was 47 years old, taking 767 wickets, and it owed much to his efforts that Sussex beat the Australians in 1888 and the South Africans in 1894.

Sussex finished bottom of the table in three of the first seven seasons of the official championship, but matters improved after the turn of the century. They were runners-up in 1902 and 1903, albeit finishing some distance behind the respective winners, Yorkshire and Middlesex.

The bowling of Albert Relf, as good an all-rounder as the county has produced, was largely responsible for the improvement in their fortunes. He was ably supported by George Cox, a slow left-arm bowler who went on to become Sussex's second highest wicket-taker.

The side was captained at this time by Ranjitsinhji, who together with C.B. Fry led a powerful batting line-up. In 1902 Sussex made their highest ever total, 705 for 8 against Surrey at Hastings, with Ranji scoring 275 and Fry 139. They were well supported by J. Vine and Relf.

Ranji and Fry were very much the Compton and Edrich of Sussex. Ranji, in particular, seemed able to make big scores on any type of wicket. He eventually left the county on becoming the ruler of Nawanagar.

The club then slipped back in the pre-First World War period and although comfortably placed, never seriously challenged for honours. Eighteen wins from thirty matches in 1920 suggested Sussex might be about to regain the form of the early 1900s, but inconsistency was to dog them between the wars.

It was individual rather than team success that marked the club's

Ted Dexter cuts his way powerfully to a century against the Australians at Hove in 1964. Sussex owed much to the all-round ability of their skipper.

fortunes. After making his first appearance for the county in 1912, Maurice Tate suddenly became a devastating bowler in 1923. Over three seasons he took 652 wickets and went on to play 39 times for England.

He was given strong support by Arthur Gilligan and the pair could cause havoc against the best of batsmen. In 1924, in just a fortnight, they dismissed Surrey for 53, Middlesex for 41, and the South Africans for 30.

Gilligan's captaincy also created a greater sense of purpose, and Sussex became arguably the best fielding side in the country.

Although he had by then retired, it was the foundation laid by Gilligan that was to lead to Sussex's most successful championship period as they were runners-up three times in succession from 1932 to 1934.

Duleepsinhji, a brilliant batsman who scored Sussex's highest

individual total of 333 at a run a minute against Northants in 1930, took the county to the verge of their first championship in 1932. Sadly the illness that was to end his career struck as the season's climax approached and the chance was lost.

The county was blessed at that time with some fine batsmen such as E.H. Bowley, A. Melville, John Langridge and Harry Parks. The bowling was made up mainly of Tate, James Langridge and Wensley. But as players began to age, replacements were not found and a gradual decline had already begun by the time hostilities broke out again in 1939.

In 1946, Sussex finished bottom and never rose out of the lower half of the table in the next six seasons. Yet after a disappointing 13th place in 1952, they suddenly rose to become runners-up to Surrey in 1953.

THE GUINNESS

Under the captaincy of the amateur David Sheppard, the bowling of Robin Marlar, an off-spinner, and Ian Thomson, an intelligent fast bowler, took them to within sixteen points of the champions, losing only three matches. Marlar, Thomson and A.E. James all took more than 100 wickets, and Sheppard himself was the prominent batsman, averaging over 55.

Such success was again short-lived, as the bowling declined. But there emerged in the fifties a fine young batsman who was to become a prominent figure in English cricket, first as a player and later as chairman of the selectors – Ted Dexter.

A fluent batsman who could hit the ball with great power, Dexter was also a useful medium-pace bowler. He took over the Sussex captaincy in 1960 and at last brought the county some success, following the introduction of one-day cricket.

In the first Gillette Cup final in 1963, Buss and a young John Snow dismissed Worcestershire for 154 as they chased a modest Sussex score. Dexter, who captained the side with great skill, having such a small total to defend, led them to victory by fourteen runs.

The following year they had a more commanding win, beating Warwickshire by eight wickets. Sussex were unquestionably the masters of the one-day game.

Warwickshire would have their revenge in 1968, and Sussex were also beaten finalists in 1970 and 1973.

In something of a surprise, they took the trophy again in 1978. Tony Greig, a forthright captain of the county and of England, had gone to join Kerry Packer, and Snow had retired. But under the canny guidance of wicket-keeper Arnold Long, who had joined Sussex after a long career with Surrey, they beat the mighty Somerset in the final.

The team now promised better things. Geoff Arnold had followed Long from Surrey and young players such as Parker, Mendis and Barclay were establishing themselves, supported by such foreign imports

as Kepler Wessels from South Africa and Javed Miandad and Imran Khan from Pakistan.

With Barclay now captain, Sussex came agonisingly close to taking the County Championship in 1981, finishing just two points behind the champions Nottinghamshire. Imran and Garth Le Roux, supported by the steady Ian Greig, provided a powerful seam attack that took Sussex to eleven championship victories.

The club have not mounted a serious challenge since. But after that near miss, they had the consolation of taking the John Player League in 1982, losing only one match, and the NatWest Trophy four years later.

It was in the final of that competition in 1993 that Sussex played their full part in perhaps the most remarkable one-day game ever seen at Lord's. Batting first, they reached the seemingly unassailable total of 321 for 6 off their 60 overs. But incredibly, Warwickshire matched them and took victory by five wickets off the final ball.

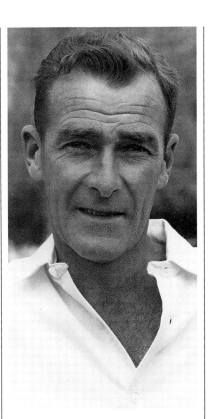

The most prolific run-scorer in New Zealand cricket: Sutcliffe on the 1965 tour of England.

BERT SUTCLIFFE
New Zealand

Born 1923
Auckland, Otago and Northern Districts

BERT SUTCLIFFE WAS A top class left-handed batsman, arguably the best of his generation. He was most noted for the stylish way he played. An opening bat who later moved to the middle order, he had every shot in the book.

Over a period of 25 years he was New Zealand's leading batsman, consistently setting new records.

Sutcliffe first caught the eye in 1946/47 when, playing for Otago against the MCC, he scored 197 and 128. On his Test debut a week later he made a half century.

His 385 against Canterbury in 1952/53 is the highest ever score by a New Zealander in first-class

cricket. For 35 years, his magnificent 230 not out against India at New Delhi in 1955/56 was the highest Test score for New Zealand. It was beaten only by Martin Crowe scoring 299 against Sri Lanka.

In England, in 1949 he scored 2,627 runs at an average of 59.70, but in 1958 he sustained a broken wrist at Lord's and was unable to emulate that achievement. He was picked for the 1965 England tour after coming out of retirement, but after being hit on the head by a ball from Fred Trueman he played little part in the rest of the tour.

After his retirement, Sutcliffe went on to become a successful coach.

First Class Career:
Runs – 17,283. Average 47.44
(44 centuries)

Test Match Career:
Tests – 42
Runs – 2,727. Average 40.10
(5 centuries)

HERBERT SUTCLIFFE

England

Born 1894. Died 1978
Yorkshire

ERBERT SUTCLIFFE WAS simply one of the greatest batsmen to play cricket. A Yorkshireman with a huge passion for scoring runs, he is best known for his England opening partnership with Surrey's Jack Hobbs.

Sutcliffe was a batsman of great concentration as well as courage and dedication, qualities mirrored in more recent times by another Yorkshire opening bat, Geoffrey Boycott.

With Hobbs for England and with Percy Holmes for Yorkshire, Sutcliffe shared in a remarkable 145 first-wicket partnerships in three figures.

In the first two Tests they opened together, against South Africa in 1924, Sutcliffe and Hobbs put on 136 at Edgbaston and 268 at Lord's.

In Australia in 1924/25, Sutcliffe finished top of the averages, having scored 734 runs at 81.55. Australia invariably brought out the best in him, as he averaged 50.57 against them in 1928/29 and 87.20 in 1930. His highest Test score, 194, came at Sydney in 1932/33.

Sutcliffe set many records in domestic cricket as well. His partnership of 555 with Holmes for Yorkshire against Essex in 1932 was a world record that stood for 45 years. His own score of 313 in the match was his highest in first-class cricket.

That 1932 season was his best, as he scored 3,336 runs, including 14 centuries, at an average of 74.13. In his career he passed the 1,000 runs total 24 times – three of them abroad.

Sutcliffe looks to be well on top of the Surrey bowling at the Oval in 1934. He topped the County Championship averages four times in his career as Yorkshire in that period carried off no fewer than 12 titles.

He rejected the offer of becoming captain of Yorkshire as he was a professional, although his son did have the honour.

After his retirement from the game, Herbert Sutcliffe became a successful businessman and for a time served as an England selector

First Class Career:
Runs – 50,138. Average 51.95
(149 centuries)

Test Match Career:
Tests – 54
Runs – 4,555. Average 60.73
(16 centuries)

THE GUINNESS

SYDNEY

UNTIL RECENTLY, THE Sydney Cricket Ground (SCG) was universally considered to be the finest in Australia and, for many, the finest in the world.

However, the changes that have been made to the ground have upset many of the game's traditionalists, and it was the arrival of Kerry Packer's World Series Cricket that sparked an enormous upheaval.

It began with the erection of giant floodlight pylons, followed in later years by an enormous electronic scoreboard. New concrete stands have been built with many private boxes for business use. *Wisden* has recorded that it is now more of a coliseum than a cricket ground.

Perhaps the saddest thing of all amid this new concrete jungle has been the almost total elimination of the Hill, a large grassy slope where those who knew their cricket would gather to dispense sparkling wit and caustic comments. It was what gave the ground its atmosphere and made Sydney unique for spectators and players alike.

But if the nature of the SCG has changed in recent years, it still remains one of the top grounds to play on. Many memorable matches have been staged there since its opening in 1878.

Naturally, Sir Don Bradman features in its history – he made his highest score there, 452 not out for New South Wales against Queensland in 1929–30. That achievement remains third in the all-time list behind Brian Lara's 501 and Hanif Mohammad's 499.

Regulars at the Sydney ground have had many heroes to cheer over the years. Famous names such as Miller, Benaud and Davidson are just three, while Doug Walters, often dubbed the 'new Bradman', was so popular among fans on the Hill that they made a banner proclaiming it the 'Doug Walters Stand'.

Sydney has been the most successful ground for England in Australia – they have won 20 of the 49 Tests played there. Only seven matches between the oldest Test rivals at Sydney have been drawn.

A spectacular view of Sydney under lights during the 1992 World Cup match between Australia and South Africa. The SCG has enjoyed many thrilling night finishes to limited-overs fixtures in recent years, when the drama of the occasion is somehow enhanced by the floodlit arena. English supporters tend to remember the Benson & Hedges World Series Cup match in 1987 when Allan Lamb, needing 18 off the last over, struck 44624 off Bruce Reid to give England an improbable victory by three wickets.

SACHIN TENDULKAR

India

Born 1973
Bombay and Yorkshire

THIS YOUNG, TALENTED batsman has already achieved two notable landmarks in his short career, being the youngest man to play Test cricket for India and the first ever overseas player to play for Yorkshire.

Tendulkar made his first-class debut at the age of 15 and scored a century. He had already made a name for himself at schoolboy level when he shared a stand of more than 600 with his Indian team-mate Vinod Kambli, both players scoring 300.

In 1989/90, at the age of just 16 years and 205 days, Tendulkar played for India against Pakistan at Karachi. His first Test century (119 not out) came against England at Old Trafford in 1990.

At the age of 19 he became the youngest player to score 1,000 Test runs during India's tour of South Africa in 1992/93.

He accepted a one-year contract to play for Yorkshire in 1992, after the White Rose county's first choice of overseas player, Australian fast bowler Craig McDermott, pulled out with an injury.

Tendulkar's arrival brought the county improved commercial success and stemmed a drop in membership. He quickly became popular with the Yorkshire cricket public and his new team-mates.

He scored runs quickly in the one-day competitions and showed good application in the County Championship, although his lack of experience at such a young age often counted against him.

Nevertheless he scored 1,070 runs in first-class matches, passing 50 eight times, with his only century effectively winning the match for the Tykes against Durham.

His stature at Test level has grown; in a three-Test series against West Indies in 1994/95 he made a century and two fifties, topping the Indian averages with 67.00. He seems certain to be one of the leading batsmen in world cricket for many years to come.

First Class Career:
Runs – 6,449. Average 55.16
(41 centuries)

Test Match Career:
Tests – 32
Runs – 2,023. Average 50.57
(7 centuries)

TEST AND COUNTY CRICKET BOARD

THE TEST AND COUNTY Cricket Board (TCCB), which runs professional cricket in England, was formed in 1968 when for the first time the game was given a clearly defined constitution.

At the head of the game is the Cricket Council, with the TCCB its principal constituent body. The National Cricket Association and the MCC make up the other parts.

The voting members of the TCCB are the eighteen First-Class Counties, the MCC and the Minor Counties' Cricket Association. Oxford University and Cambridge University, together with the Scottish and Irish Cricket Unions, are non-voting members.

The Board, based at Lord's, administers the County Championship, all other competitions concerning the First-Class Counties, and the organisation, administration and promotion of all Test, International

As a teenager Sachin Tendulkar set a host of records but even at just 17 years 112 days he was not quite the youngest to score a Test century: he was 20 days too late to match Mushtaq Mohammed's mark set for Pakistan in 1961.

and Trial matches in the United Kingdom. It is also responsible for tours to and from this country.

The TCCB is funded by income from Tests and one-day internationals, receipts from knock-out competitions including the NatWest Trophy and Benson & Hedges Cup finals at Lord's, sponsorship fees and revenue from television and radio coverage.

Most of that income is then distributed to the Board's members, the majority going to the counties. A small amount is kept to fund the administration.

The Board is largely staffed by ex-senior players, with Alan Smith, formerly of Warwickshire and England, being the current chief executive. The England team manager is also an employee.

JEFF THOMSON

Australia

Born 1950
New South Wales, Queensland and Middlesex

FEW FAST BOWLERS HAVE made quite such a dramatic impact on Test cricket as Jeff Thomson.

His opening partnership with Dennis Lillee was too much for most batsmen to handle, and made Australia a force to be reckoned with in the 1970s.

There was certainly nothing conventional about Thomson's style. Strong, and with the ability to make the ball lift sharply off a good length, he had a slinging action, similar to that of a javelin thrower. He brought the ball from behind his back, twisting his body in the delivery stride.

Ten years years after he was unleashed on the unsuspecting English batsmen, Thomson, the familiar 'slinging' action still in evidence, is pictured on his last tour of England in 1985, when he took his 200th Test wicket and his 100th against 'the Poms'.

It was effective but it also took its toll, with persistent shoulder trouble being the price he had to pay later on in his career.

Thomson made little impression on his first Test appearance against Pakistan in 1972/73. It was later discovered he had a broken bone in his foot.

However, after moving to Queensland he was picked for the first Test against England in 1974/75, going on to dominate the series. He took 33 wickets at an average of 17.93 in the first five Tests, no England batsman being able to tame him.

He missed the final Test and when Lillee also broke down soon after the start of the match, England went on to win by an innings. There was no clearer evidence of Thomson and his partner's value to the team.

The slower pitches in England the following summer blunted his threat, but he still managed to take 16 wickets in the series.

He withdrew from joining World Series Cricket after it was discovered it contravened another contract he had signed, but later accepted a second offer and so missed the 1978/79 Ashes series when England won five Tests.

When he was recalled to Test cricket in 1979/80, the fire was gone and it seemed time for Australia to look elsewhere for a fast bowler. He was left out of the 1981 touring party to England and instead played for Middlesex, only to be forced out of the action by an appendix operation.

His Test career seemed to be over, but injuries to Lillee and Alderman provided Thomson with another chance against England in 1982/83, and he repaid the selectors' faith by taking 22 wickets in four Tests.

He was chosen for the 1985 tour of England where he reached 200 Test wickets, and 100 against England. He played just one more season in Australia before retiring.

First Class Career:
Wickets : 675. Average 26.46

Test Match Career:
Tests – 51
Wickets – 200. Average 28.00

THROWING

FOR ALL THE complexities of the bowling action, remarkably few bowlers have ever been 'called' for throwing. Perhaps that is because, as Sir Don Bradman put it, 'It is not a matter of fact, but of opinion and interpretation.'

THE GUINNESS

Famously, doubts were often raised about the bowling actions of two of the best-known international bowlers of the post-war years, Tony Lock of England and Charlie Griffith of the West Indies.

In 1952 Lock, a slow left-arm bowler, was no-balled in a county match for Surrey just after he made the first of 47 appearances for England. He was called again in a Test match in Jamaica two years later, yet his career continued unchecked.

Many respected cricketing judges considered that Griffith, who formed a potent new-ball strikeforce with Wesley Hall in the 1960s, threw his faster ball. He was called against India in 1961/62, when Nari Contractor came close to death after ducking into a ball. English umpire Arthur Fagg also no-balled him once in a match against Lancashire at Old Trafford in 1966.

Yet if there were 'doubts' about those two players, there were none about two international cricketers who were forced out of the game, sad and disillusioned figures.

Australia's Ian Meckiff was a strong, genuinely quick bowler who toured South Africa, India and Pakistan, and played in home series against England, West Indies and South Africa.

The controversy over his action escalated after he returned figures of 9 for 107 against England in the Second Test at Melbourne in 1958/59. Meckiff maintained he was not a thrower, but he received merciless treatment from the cricket media.

Eventually he was called against South Africa at Brisbane in 1963/64 when umpire Colin Egar judged that he threw his second, third, fifth and ninth balls. His first over of the match was to be his last in Test or any other first-class cricket.

South Africa's Geoff Griffin, a tall, blond fast bowler, suffered an accident at school that left him unable to straighten his right elbow. Critics at home cast doubt about his action, and when he toured England in 1960 he was no-balled in three matches before the second Test at Lord's, where at first things went well for Griffin. He became the first

South African to complete the hat-trick in Test cricket, and the first player to do so in Test cricket at the game's headquarters.

However, he was called eleven times by umpire Frank Lee during the match and again, repeatedly, by Syd Buller during an exhibition game at the end of the Test match proper. He completed the over bowling underarm, and that was the end of his two-Test career. He finished the tour as a batsman.

Umpire Syd Buller, who no-balled South Africa's Geoff Griffin for throwing in 1960, watches closely as Charlie Griffith bowls for West Indies against England at Old Trafford in 1966.

TRENT BRIDGE

NOTTINGHAM'S TEST match ground was created by William Clarke, who married the landlady of the Trent Bridge Inn and turned the neighbouring field into a cricket pitch.

A larger than life character, it was Clarke, as manager of the itinerant All England XI in the middle of the 19th century, who brought matches of national significance to the ground so that it had become a natural Test venue by the time it staged its first international match in 1899.

Trent Bridge's ten acres give a

feeling of spaciousness and Test wickets usually favour the batsmen. The ground's current pavilion was built in 1886 and is now home to a library and small museum. More than 130 historic bats are dotted around the building.

After that debut Test was drawn, England beat Australia in the second Test on the ground in 1905, Bosanquet's leg breaks earning him eight wickets and bringing the team victory by 213 runs.

After the First World War, Trent Bridge became established as the traditional home of the first Test in a series, before it lost its automatic right to a Test with the elevation of Edgbaston.

Trent Bridge seen from the Radcliffe Road end during the first Test between England and New Zealand in 1994. The ground has now staged over 40 Test matches.

It was at Trent Bridge in 1930 that Don Bradman scored a century in his first Test in England, though on that occasion it was not enough to prevent a home victory.

In 1950 the feature that made the ground unique in England was erected – an Australian-style scoreboard that listed the players in both teams, and detailed scores and bowling figures. However, it was expensive to run, both in terms of manpower and electricity, and was not used after 1972.

In a break with tradition, the ground in 1950 staged the third Test of the series against West Indies. Worrell (261) and Weekes (129) with the bat, and Ramadhin and Valentine with the ball, ensured the visitors a comfortable ten-wicket win.

There have been a number of impressive individual scores on the ground in addition to Worrell's fine achievement. Denis Compton in 1954 made the highest Test score

there, 278 against Pakistan, and Tom Graveney was only twenty short of that figure against the West Indies three years later.

Perhaps the most dramatic innings, however, came from Stan McCabe of Australia in 1938, Trent Bridge's centenary season. He made 232 in just 235 minutes while wickets tumbled steadily at the other end. His final 72 runs came in just 28 minutes.

In 1977 the Queen, celebrating her Silver Jubilee Year, visited the ground during the third Test against Australia and the match saw England's first win over the old enemy there since 1930, thanks largely to a century from a relieved Geoffrey Boycott after he had run out local favourite Derek Randall.

Other landmarks involving England and Australia at Trent Bridge include the first Test in England to include Sunday play in 1981, and the record opening stand of 329 by Australia's Geoff Marsh

and Mark Taylor that led to a convincing innings victory in 1989.

TRINIDAD

TRINIDAD'S QUEEN'S Park Oval is one of the world's prettiest grounds. It used to be the venue for two Tests in each West Indies home series until St John's, Antigua was added to the list.

Credit for the development of the ground should go to the Queen's Park Cricket Club, although responsibility for the upkeep now rests with the Trinidad and Tobago Cricket Association, as agents for the West Indies Board.

Situated adjacent to open parkland, the ground can hold 25,000 spectators, considerably more than any other ground in the Caribbean. It has also been used for other sporting events, including football – the great Pele has played there – hockey, cycling and boxing.

Problems with producing grass meant that matting had to be used at the Queens's Park Oval, first made of coconut fibre and then later of jute. Jute wickets were ideal for batsmen, and no match played on the surface ever produced a definite result. Turf wickets had to come after the Test against England in 1954 produced 1,528 runs for just 24 wickets.

The run of high-scoring draws ended during Pakistan's 1958 tour, and since that time the wicket has favoured spin bowling more than most in the Caribbean, although a number of top-class fast bowlers have been produced on the island.

The Trinidad supporters are a knowledgeable and excitable crowd. The blowing of conch-shell horns whenever the home side are on top has become a part of the folklore of the Oval.

FRED TRUEMAN
England
Born 1931
Yorkshire and Derbyshire

'FIERY FRED' WAS unquestionably one of the greatest fast bowlers cricket has seen and one of its greatest characters. Some of his off-the-cuff remarks about the game are now legendary.

Fred was a Yorkshireman through and through. At five foot ten tall he was not particularly tall for a fast

Trueman faces the cameras after being selected to play for England in the 1953 home series against Australia. He had made an explosive start to Test cricket against India the previous summer.

VICTOR TRUMPER
Australia
Born 1877. Died 1915
New South Wales

BEFORE THE DAYS OF Bradman, Victor Trumper was unquestionably the greatest Australian batsman. His records are legendary, and might have been even finer but for his untimely death at the age of just 37.

He was known for being a stylish batsman, an impressive reputation, given that so many of his best innings were played on difficult wickets.

His records make stirring reading. His first innings in three figures was his 292 not out for New South Wales against Tasmania in 1898/99.

In only his second Test match, at Lord's in 1899, he scored 135 not out and went on to make more than 1,500 runs on the tour.

On his next tour in 1902, an especially wet English summer, he scored 2,570 runs, almost 1,000 more than his nearest team-mate. One particularly great innings was in the Old Trafford Test, where his 104 on an 'impossible' wicket helped Australia to victory by three runs.

It was not only England who felt the full force of his strokemaking at Test level. In the 1910/11 series against South Africa he made 661 runs for an average of 94.42, including his highest Test score, 214 not out at Adelaide.

Sadly, Trumper died from Bright's disease in 1915 and cricket after the First World War was robbed of a man who still had plenty to give.

First Class Career:
*Runs – 16,939. Average 44.57
(42 centuries)*

Test Match Career:
*Tests – 48
Runs – 3,163. Average 39.04
(8 centuries)*

bowler, but he had the perfect build – strong shoulders and legs. Unlike his modern counterparts, he thrived on bowling and seemed rarely to be affected by injuries during his career.

He made his Yorkshire debut in 1949 at the age of eighteen, and his committed approach impressed more senior figures. His Test debut came three years later and he made an immediate impact .

In three Tests against India he took 24 wickets. At Headingley he took 8 for 31 as the visitors were bowled out for just 58. Many of the Indian batsmen were quite unable to cope with his pace.

His forthright views occasionally upset selectors, especially early in his career, but he became an England regular in the late fifties and early sixties, forming a highly effective new ball partnership with Lancashire's Brian Statham.

In 1964 at the Oval he took the wicket of Australia's Neil Hawke to become the first man to take 300 wickets in Test cricket. When asked afterwards if he thought anyone would ever beat that achievement, he replied: 'Aye, but whoever does will be bloody tired.' It is claimed he can remember every victim.

He gave long and loyal service to Yorkshire, but when he retired in 1968 he went to Derbyshire where he played in some one-day games.

He is now a famous raconteur, being much in demand on the after-dinner circuit. He is best-known, though, for his work on BBC Radio's Test Match Special. His trenchant, no-nonsense views still come over loud and clear.

First Class Career:
Wickets – 2,304. Average 18.29

Test Match Career:
*Tests – 67
Wickets – 307. Average 21.57*

GLENN TURNER

New Zealand

Born 1947
Otago and Worcestershire

Glenn Turner was New Zealand's most prolific batsman, creating records both at club and international level. A mass accumulator of runs, he was a true professional and totally single-minded in his attitude to the game.

Turner was a very correct right-hander with all the qualities demanded of an opening batsman. He had a solid technique, played a straight bat, and as he matured, developed a full repertoire of shots.

After making his debut for Otago in 1964/65, he came to England at the invitation of Warwickshire, only to discover on arrival that they had their full complement of overseas players.

Turner went instead to Worcestershire and there began a career of remarkable consistency. He made more centuries in a career and a season than anyone else for the county.

Among his many achievements was an innings of 141 not out in 1977 against Glamorgan at Swansea out of a Worcester score of 169, at 83.4 per cent of the total a world record for first-class cricket.

In 1982 Turner became only the second non-Englishman, and the 19th overall, to score 100 first-class hundreds. Typically he reached that milestone making 311 not out at Worcester against the county who could find no room for him, Warwickshire.

He began his Test career with a duck against the West Indies in 1969, but went on to establish himself and made seven Test centuries, two of them in the match at Christchurch in 1974 when New Zealand beat Australia for the first time.

Turner captained New Zealand in ten Tests but quit the job after a row with officials. After retiring, he managed New Zealand sides on overseas tours.

First Class Career:
Runs – 34,346. Average 49.71
(103 centuries)

Test Match Career:
Tests – 41
Runs – 2,991. Average 44.64
(7 centuries)

Turner leg-glances Graeme Dilley (England) during a 1983 World Cup match at the Oval. Sadly, it was only the briefest of returns to New Zealand's colours for him.

UMPIRES

IT IS PERHAPS A SAD reflection on modern cricket that the pressure on umpires has never been greater. Vociferous appealing from fielders surrounding the batsman, hostile, short-pitched bowling, players' dissent, ball-tampering and television scrutiny have all contributed to make the umpire's job one for men with steely nerves and thick skins.

Yet through the years, while the game has been graced by great players, it has also been well served by some great umpires. Cricket in England, unlike a number of other sports such as football, has always employed former players as umpires.

This has meant that cricket umpires have a greater knowledge of the way players think and also builds up better trust and respect. There have been a number of honourable exceptions, however. Nigel Plews, a first-class umpire, came into the game after a career as a police officer.

Umpires are the sole arbiters. Their decisions on everything concerning the game are final, whether it be the state of the wicket, the quality of the light, or the shape of the ball.

Nowadays, at Test level, they are given more support, with a match referee, usually a retired senior Test player, sitting in the pavilion monitoring the game and, in particular, the behaviour of the players.

In England, there are currently some fine umpires who have

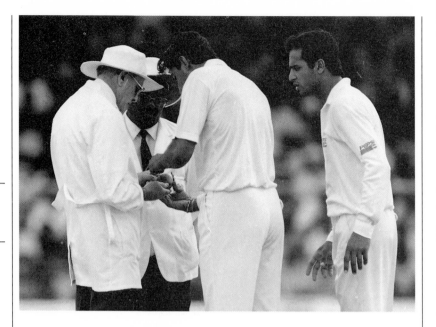

become as well known as the players. Dickie Bird and David Shepherd may be regarded as the best, but others such as David Constant, Barry Meyer, Mervyn Kitchen, Ken Palmer and Roy Palmer have stood regularly in Tests.

Touring teams the world over have always held grave suspicions about 'home' umpires and the move towards neutral umpires in Test matches gained momentum. Incidents such as England skipper Mike Gatting's angry confrontation with Pakistani umpire Shakoor Rana in 1987 graphically demonstrated the mistrust that had built up.

Relationships between the Pakistani tourists and umpires in England in the summer of 1992 all but broke down, while the pressure exerted by the Australian team in 1993 led to them receiving a warning during the third Test at Trent Bridge.

David Constant once wrote: 'They can appeal as much as they like, but if I think the appeals are getting ridiculous, the tone of my voice when dismissing the appeal will make my opinions quite clear.'

For all that, pressure does sometimes sway an umpire into giving an incorrect decision, and the media are now quicker to comment on any doubtful ones.

Recent years have seen various

The umpires examine the ball with Pakistan captain Wasim Akram during the 1993 series in the Caribbean. Dickie Bird (left) is the international, or 'neutral', umpire.

experiments. In Zimbabwe and South Africa, they have tried 'turn and turn about' systems, with three umpires controlling the game. But the biggest innovation in the history of umpiring came in November 1992 during the first Test match in South Africa for 22 years.

For the first time, a third umpire sat in the pavilion with a television monitor to decide on line decisions such as run outs and stumpings, if called upon by the umpires on the field.

The Indian batsman Sachin Tendulkar made history as the first batsman to be given run out by reference to a slow-motion replay.

The experiment was introduced in England in 1993, with Robin Smith the first to be similarly given out in an English Test. The ICC at its meeting in July 1993 ruled that the video replay should now be used in Tests around the world, where such facilities exist.

These new moves have not proved universally popular. The editor of *Wisden*, Matthew Engel, was moved to write in the 1993 edition: 'The world umpiring system is now a shambles.'

In his opposition to TV replays, he said it was something that could grow to be thoroughly pernicious. He added: 'If cricket has contributed anything to society as a whole, it is the notion that the umpire's decision is final and that cricketers do not argue with it.'

In December 1993, the ICC decided to try to reduce the pressures by setting up a panel of 20 international umpires to officiate at all Tests for three years, starting in February 1994.

Helped by sponsorship from the National Grid, each country nominates two umpires except England who, having such a large pool of experienced officials, provide four.

An international umpire now joins a home umpire in each match, with referees and captains providing their views on an umpire's performance to the ICC.

DEREK UNDERWOOD
England
Born 1945
Kent

DEREK UNDERWOOD brought a new dimension to the art of left-arm spin bowling. His pace varied from slow-medium to medium, and his consistency of line and length frustrated the very best of batsmen.

He burst upon the county scene with Kent in 1963 when at the age of seventeen he took one hundred wickets in his first season. Confounding those critics who suggested his long run-up and flat trajectory would soon be mastered, his success continued and he had taken 1,000 wickets by the time he was 25.

He made his Test debut in 1966, and often bowled England to victory. In 1968 at the Oval he took 7 for 50 to defeat Australia after a thunderstorm had produced a wet wicket that made him almost unplayable. In 1974 at Lord's, again on a damp wicket, he took 8 for 51 against Pakistan.

Underwood was a bowler who studied his craft, and as his career developed he learned to bowl an effective slower delivery and arm ball. Yet all the time he was determined never to give away unnecessary runs.

Having been a regular member of the England team and with 265 Test wickets to his credit, he joined World Series Cricket in 1977. He returned to the England side two years later and played twelve more Tests.

His England career over, he reached another personal landmark in 1984 when at the age of 39 he scored his first ever first-class

'Deadly' Derek Underwood was a consistently outstanding performer for Kent and England in a first-class career which spanned 25 years.

hundred, against Sussex at Hastings.

First Class Career:
Wickets – 2,465. Average 20.28

Test Match Career:
Tests – 86
Wickets – 297. Average 25.83

UNIVERSITY MATCH

THE ANNUAL UNIVERSITY match between Oxford and Cambridge may no longer be played in front of a packed house at Lord's each year, but it holds a special place in English cricket history as the oldest first-class fixture.

It was first played in 1827 and has continued unbroken, with the exception of the war years, since 1838. That first match, spoilt by bad weather, was played at Lord's, but cricket's headquarters only became its regular home from 1851.

In the early years there were very few draws, thanks largely to a decision to continue playing until a result was achieved, but more recently there have been 24 in the last 32 matches.

Altogether there have been 147 official matches before 1993, Cambridge winning 55 and Oxford 46, with 46 drawn. Only one match, in 1988, has been abandoned without a ball being bowled.

The highest total ever recorded in the game is 500 by Oxford in 1900. They also hold the record for the lowest, a mere 32 in 1878 against a Cambridge side considered one of the strongest that university has ever fielded, having previously beaten the Australians that year.

One of the most convincing wins came in 1972, when Cambridge were the victors by an innings and 25 runs. Majid Khan, later to be captain of Pakistan, led a side that also included future England spin bowler Phil Edmonds. However, such was their superiority that he was never called upon to bowl.

ALFRED VALENTINE

West Indies

Born 1930
Jamaica

THE OTHER HALF OF what many consider the greatest spin-bowling pair in history, Alf Valentine was, at his best, possibly the finest slow left-arm bowler since the war.

Like his partner Sonny Ramadhin, Valentine arrived in England in 1950 as a raw 20-year-old. The youngest member of the touring party, he had just two first-class wickets to his name. But his performance in a summer that saw the West Indies record their first series win in England was dramatic.

Tall, slim and bespectacled, his slow deliveries of immaculate length were rewarded with 33 Test wickets that summer at an average of 20.42. Three times he dismissed Hutton when the Yorkshireman looked set for a big score.

His most impressive performances in those Tests were taking seven wickets in the historic first West Indies victory at Lord's (Ramadhin took eleven) and 10 for 160 at the Oval.

The two spinners became heroes in the Caribbean, immortalised in the calypso refrain, 'Those two little pals of mine, Ramadhin and Valentine.'

Valentine toured England twice more – in 1957, when he suffered from much ill health, and 1963, when he failed to make the Test team as Sobers and Gibbs provided the spin attack.

He also toured New Zealand and Australia. It took him just three years and 263 days to record his 100th Test victim.

First Class Career:
Wickets – 475. Average 26.20

Test Match Career:
Tests – 36
Wickets – 139. Average 30.32

VILLAGE CRICKET

THE INFLUENCE AND excitement of one-day cricket runs from international level right down to the village green, as is clearly demonstrated by the success of the National Village Cricket Championship, which culminates each year at Lord's in a final of 40 overs a side.

The competition, organised by the *Cricketer* magazine, was first introduced in 1972. It now attracts about 650 clubs each year, and is limited to rural communities 'surrounded on all sides by open country and consisting of not more than 2,500 inhabitants.'

There are also strict rules regarding the players. For example, no one who has played in more than one first-class match is eligible, unless he is over the age of sixty.

The early stages of the competition are played in county groups – the group winners going through to the last 32, who then play a simple knock-out tournament.

Troon from Cornwall were the early kings of the village game, winning the Lord's final in the first two years, 1972 and 1973, and again in 1976.

The only other village to take the title three times is St Fagans, a village on the outskirts of Cardiff that may be small in terms of inhabitants but is regarded as one of the strongest club teams in Wales.

Indeed, Welsh clubs have a fine record in the competition, with Marchwiel, near Wrexham, winning twice, in 1980 and 1984, Gowerton winning one final and losing another, and Ynysygwern twice beaten finalists.

THE GUINNESS

The competition has produced some remarkable records, with the highest team score being 440 for 5 by Barkisland against Old Sharlston in 1989. The lowest was just 6, by the unfortunate Marston St Lawrence when they played Abthorpe in 1978.

Perhaps the most exciting final came in 1993 when Kington, of Herefordshire, beat near neighbours Frocester, from Gloucestershire, by just two runs.

A classic scene of village cricket in rural England, which was dramatised in the Central Television series Outside Edge. Oddly enough, the batsman here bears a passing resemblance to one of the stars of that series, Robert Daws.

NATIONAL VILLAGE CRICKET CHAMPIONSHIP

	Winners	Runners-up	
1972	Troon	Astwood Bank	7 wickets
1973	Troon	Gowerton	12 runs
1974	Bomarsund	Collingham	3 wickets
1975	Gowerton	Isleham	6 wickets
1976	Troon	Sessay	18 runs
1977	Cookley	Lindal Moor	28 runs
1978	Linton Park	Toft	4 wickets
1979	East Bierley	Ynysygerwn	92 runs
1980	Marchwiel	Hursley Park	8 runs
1981	St Fagans	Broad Oak	22 runs
1982	St Fagans	Collingham	6 wickets
1983	Quarndon	Troon	8 wickets
1984	Marchwiel	Hursley Park	8 runs
1985	Freuchie	Rowledge	*Lost fewer wickets*
1986	Forge Valley	Ynysygerwn	5 runs
1987	Longparish	Treeton Welfare	76 runs
1988	Goatacre	Himley	4 wickets
1989	Toft	Hambledon	6 wickets
1990	Goatacre	Dunstall	50 runs
1991	St Fagans	Harome	17 runs
1992	Hursley Park	Methley	6 wickets
1993	Kington	Frocester	2 runs
1994	Elvaston	Werrington	55 runs

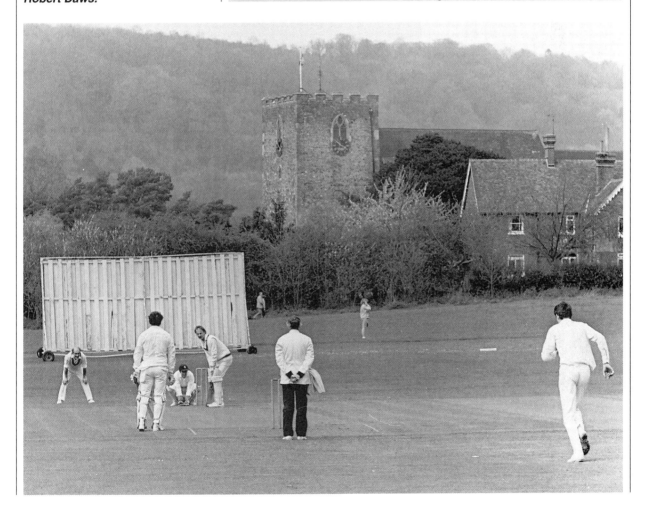

THE THREE W'S

West Indies

THREE PLAYERS, BORN IN Barbados within seventeen months of each other, went on to have a profound effect on the development of the West Indies in Test cricket. The three made their Test debuts within a fortnight of one another in 1948, and all went on to become major Test batsmen. The similarities were so striking, they quickly became known as the three W's.

CLYDE WALCOTT

Born 1926
Barbados and British Guiana

Clyde Walcott was a commanding player. At six foot two inches tall, and about fifteen stone, this right-handed batsman hit the ball with immense power, especially through the off side.

Despite making his debut for Barbados at the age of sixteen, Walcott found batting difficult in his early days and took up wicket-keeping to keep his place.

At the age of twenty, in 1946, he

shared an unbroken partnership of 574 with Frank Worrell for Barbados against Trinidad. It is a West Indian record stand for any wicket, and Walcott's 314 not out was his highest first-class score.

In 1950, when the West Indies won their first series in England by three matches to one, Walcott's 168 not out clinched victory at Lord's, their first Test win in England.

In 1954–55, in a home series against Australia, Walcott twice scored two centuries in a Test match, and scored five centuries in the series overall. He scored a total of 827 runs at an average of 82.70.

His highest Test score, 220, came at Bridgetown, against England in 1953/54, in a series that saw him score 698 runs at 87.25.

At one stage in his career he scored twelve centuries in twelve consecutive Tests.

He was out for a duck just once – falling lbw to Ray Lindwall at Brisbane in 1951.

Apart from his Test appearances in England, he was also extremely popular in the Lancashire League in the early fifties. He managed a number of West Indies touring

Walcott, the most powerful batsman of the Ws trio, pictured in action for the West Indies in England in 1957.

parties, and was awarded the OBE for his services to cricket.

First Class Career:
Runs – 11,820. Average 56.55 (40 centuries)
Catches – 175. Stumpings – 33

Test Match Career:
Tests – 44
Runs – 3,798. Average 56.88 (15 centuries)
Catches – 53. Stumpings – 11

EVERTON WEEKES

Born 1925
Barbados

Ⓐ short but powerful batsman, Everton Weekes possessed a wide range of shots. He made a dramatic appearance in England in 1950, his performances drawing comparisons with the great Don Bradman.

On that historic tour, he had scored five double centuries by mid-July. His 304 not out against Cambridge at Fenner's was the highest score of his career.

He also made the highest number of runs in a sequence before being dismissed. His run began with 246 not out against Hampshire, then 200 not out against Leicestershire and finally 129 in the third Test – 575 runs before he was out.

His form before arriving in England had already created a stir. In 1948/49 he hit 779 runs in India, including four centuries in succession. He missed a fifth by being run out for 90.

If he failed to live up to that form in subsequent tours of Australia in 1951/52 and England in 1957, he continued to accumulate a lot of runs at home.

In 1952/53 against India he made 716 runs at an average of 102.28.

Weekes starred in Tests for the West Indies for over a decade. He twice averaged over 100 in a series: on both occasions India were the unfortunate opponents.

The following year he averaged just under seventy against England, scoring 206 at Port of Spain as he and Worrell added 338 for the third wicket – a record for any wicket against England.

In England, like Walcott and Worrell, he also played league cricket. He toured with a number of Commonwealth sides and was awarded the OBE.

First Class Career:
Runs – 12,010. Average 52.90 (36 centuries)

Test Match Career:
Tests – 48
Runs – 4,455. Average 58.61 (15 centuries)

SIR FRANK WORRELL

Born 1924. Died 1967
Barbados and Jamaica

Ⓢir Frank Worrell was more than just a great cricketer. He was a fine ambassador for the Caribbean, and had he not died so early, at the age of 42, he would in all probability have become a major statesman.

Originally a slow left-arm bowler, he went on to bowl medium pace, taking 69 Test wickets. But it was as a right-handed batsman that he set

records and became a joy to watch.

In 1943/44, as a nineteen-year-old, he scored 308 not out, the best of his career, as he and John Goddard put on an undefeated partnership of 502 in just under six and a half hours for Barbados against Trinidad.

That world record for the fourth wicket was broken when he made 255 not out to amass 574 with Walcott against Trinidad in 1945/46. It remains a West Indies record for any wicket.

He scored 97 on his Test debut against England in 1947/48 and on the historic 1950 tour he made 539 Test runs at an average of 89.93. He made his highest score in Test cricket, 261, in just over five and a half hours at Trent Bridge. It included a partnership of 283 with Weekes for the fourth wicket.

Worrell went on to captain his country in fifteen Tests between 1960 and 1963, winning nine of them. He was a calm and authoritative leader – a great man-manager, never allowing splits to develop within the ranks.

Two Tests particularly stand out under his leadership. On the tour of Australia in 1960/61 there was the memorable tied Test at Brisbane. As captains in that series, Worrell and Benaud did much to revive flagging interest in the game in Australia.

Then in 1963, at Lord's, in one of the most dramatic Tests ever seen in England, the match ended in a draw only after Colin Cowdrey had come to the wicket with a broken arm. At the start of the final over, any one of four results was possible. Eventually David Allen held out, England finished on 228 for 9, six runs short of victory, and the match was drawn. Worrell retired from regular first-class cricket at the end of that tour.

In 1964 he was knighted. He went on to become Warden of the

University College of the West Indies and was elected a senator in the Jamaican Parliament.

Sadly, with so much still to offer, Sir Frank died of leukaemia in 1967. There were moving scenes at his funeral in the West Indies, and he was the first cricketer to be honoured with a memorial service at Westminster Abbey.

First Class Career:
Runs – 15,025. Average 54.24 (39 centuries)
Wickets – 349. Average 29.03

Test Match Career:
Tests – 51
Runs – 3,860. Average 49.48 (9 centuries)
Wickets – 69. Average 38.73

DOUG WALTERS
Australia
Born 1945
New South Wales

DOUG WALTERS WAS ONE of the finest batsmen to play for Australia, although English crowds never saw the best of him. He flourished on hard, true pitches, where he would transform a game by taking a bowling attack apart.

Walters had all the shots of a top batsman. He was a powerful driver of the ball, a strong cutter, and was never afraid to take on short bowling with the hook. He was a useful medium-pace bowler, often

Worrell plays an elegant on-drive. His appointment as West Indies captain in 1960 represented a significant breakthrough, as he became the first black cricketer to lead the team on a regular basis.

THE GUINNESS

chipping in with wickets to break awkward stands. He was also a cover fieldsman of the very highest order.

Saddled, as other Australian batsmen inevitably have been, with the tag the 'second Bradman', Walters quickly established himself on the first-class scene, scoring 253 and taking seven wickets in one Sheffield Shield game.

He made his Test debut against England in 1965/66 and scored two centuries, 155 and 115, in his first two appearances. He then undertook his National Service before touring England in 1968, where he suffered the first of his setbacks.

It was a wet summer, but a player of Walters' class was expected to do better than make just 223 runs in the five Tests. As his career progressed, English bowlers – John Snow particularly – detected a weakness against the short ball outside the off stump, and he regularly fell to catches in the gully.

However, against other countries he reigned supreme. Both at home and in the Caribbean, he scored heavily against the West Indies, once scoring 242 at Sydney, another time making a century between lunch and tea at Port of Spain. A second Test double century was achieved against New Zealand in Christchurch.

Walters signed up with World Series Cricket but, never coming to terms with the fast bowling there, returned to Test cricket in 1980/81, scoring a century against New Zealand.

He was to suffer a final disappointment, though, when he was omitted from the party to tour England in 1981. It would have been his fifth tour. After hearing of the decision he retired from the game.

First Class Career:
*Runs – 16,180. Average – 43.84
(45 centuries)
Wickets – 190. Average – 35.69*

Test Match Career:
*Tests – 74
Runs – 5,357. Average – 48.26
(15 centuries)
Wickets – 49. Average – 29.08*

Doug Walters, hero of the Hill.

WAQAR YOUNIS
Pakistan
*Born 1971
Multan, UBL and Surrey*

FOR A MAN STILL IN HIS early twenties, Waqar Younis has achieved a remarkable amount in world cricket. There can be few more dangerous quick bowlers, with the fast, inswinging yorker being his most effective weapon.

Controversy has dogged him, however, with allegations of ball-tampering being levelled against him and his fellow Pakistani opening bowler Wasim Akram during the tour of England in 1992. It has been a remarkable feature of his game that he often achieves considerably more swing with an old ball than at the start of an innings.

However he does it, it is quite astonishing just how many of his victims are either bowled or lbw. It shows the importance he places on bowling straight. He also has the ability to get life out of a wicket other bowlers will find docile.

The former Pakistani captain Imran Khan was Waqar's initial inspiration. The great all-rounder was watching television in hospital while recovering from an operation when he spotted Waqar bowling in a local knockout match. Waqar went on to make his Test debut as a 17-year-old against India in 1989/90.

In 1990/91 he totally dominated the touring New Zealand party, taking 10 for 106 in the Test at Lahore, and then following it with 12 for 130 in the next Test at Faisalabad.

Surrey realised his potential after just one net session and he was

Waqar Younis, the leading fast bowler in world cricket.

quickly signed up during the 1990 season. In 1991 there was no stopping him. He took 113 wickets for Surrey in 582 overs at an average of just 14.65. He is believed to be the highest paid overseas player in English county cricket.

In 1992 he was Pakistan's leading wicket-taker with 22 in the Test series in England, and took 37 wickets in 287 overs on the tour.

His nine wickets in the match helped Pakistan to a win over New Zealand in January 1993, and he went on to enjoy a good tour of the West Indies shortly afterwards.

Waqar has suffered from injuries more recently but he bounced back on Pakistan's tour of Sri Lanka in 1994/95, taking 11 for 119 in the third Test. He took seven wickets in the first Test against Australia soon afterwards before another injury forced him out of the series.

However, with a long career likely to be ahead of him, Waqar Younis is expected to be a force in world cricket for some years to come.

Test Match Career:
Tests – 29
Wickets – 166. Average 18.98

SHANE WARNE

Australia

Born 1969
Victoria

OF, IN THE MODERN GAME, fast bowlers win matches, then Shane Warne is a delightful exception to the rule. Since the Australian leg-spinner burst onto the Test scene in the early 1990s, few batsmen have been able to master him.

Warne has gone from being a rather overweight, bottle-blond, extrovert who started in a club's fourth XI, to being without doubt the foremost slow bowler in the world.

He chose cricket when his

Warne pictured during the 1994/95 series in Pakistan: few batsmen can read him properly.

'Ball of the Century' so extraordinary was the amount of turn.

He took 34 wickets in the series and no batsman ever looked confident against him. In the 1993 calendar year he took 72 wickets, a remarkable achievement for a spinner. He went on to take 15 wickets in three Tests in South Africa and 18 in Pakistan.

It seemed as if he would dominate the 1994/95 Ashes series after taking 20 wickets in the first two Tests. However, in the final three he took just seven, amid rumours about his fitness.

Warne is still developing his craft, although the amount of spin he puts on the ball places heavy demands on his body. If he can stay fit and retain his enthusiasm, he looks likely to be an integral part of the Australian team for many years ahead.

First Class Career:
Wickets – 270. Average 25.28

Test Match Career:
Tests – 34
Wickets – 161. Average 24.50

WARWICKSHIRE
Founded: 1882
Entered Official Championship: 1895
Honours:
County Champions – 1911, 1951, 1972, 1994
Gillette Cup – 1966, 1968
NatWest Trophy – 1989, 1993
Benson and Hedges Cup – 1994
John Player League – 1980
Axa/Equity and Law League – 1994

WARWICKSHIRE'S success throughout almost a century of participation in the County Championship had been spasmodic. Three Championships

dreams of stardom in Aussie Rules football were dashed. Yet his indiscipline as a youngster nearly cost him his cricket career – he left the prestigious Australian Cricket Academy under a cloud.

However, Australia's selectors chose him first at the start of 1992 after just four Sheffield Shield games. His figures of 1 for 228 against India suggested the gamble had failed.

He went back to the Academy, trained hard, lost weight, and then was chosen to tour Sri Lanka. He made steady progress and then took 7 for 52 against the West Indies at Melbourne and 17 wickets in three matches in New Zealand.

It was the Ashes series in 1993 that made him a household name. His first ball in Test cricket in England accounted for Mike Gatting, a delivery given the title

and four one-day titles represented a modest return from a county that had produced some fine England players and recruited to its ranks some top overseas stars.

However, all that changed in a remarkable 1994 season. A side that was looked upon as being made up of 'journeymen' added the world's top batsman, Brian Lara, and no one could rival them.

The County Championship was won by a clear 42 points. A tight finish saw them take the Axa/Equity & Law League, and they overwhelmed Worcestershire in the Benson and Hedges Cup final.

They came close to completing the clean sweep of all four titles but Worcestershire had their revenge in the NatWest Trophy final. A record-breaking treble, though, was no more than Warwickshire deserved, and 1994 will go down as the greatest year in their history.

William Ansell was the man who almost single-handedly created

Warwickshire County Cricket Club. He founded the club, won its first-class status, and helped to develop the Edgbaston ground that is now one of the finest in world cricket.

Warwickshire's formation was not something that immediately fired interest in the Midlands. It was not until the ground was opened four years later that membership numbers improved.

In 1894 the club was given first-class status and joined the official championship the following year, enjoying only modest results for the first decade or so. In 1896 Warwickshire had to toil in the field as Yorkshire scored 887 at Birmingham, the highest score ever by a county.

It came as a major surprise when Warwickshire won the Championship in 1911, when a new system was introduced of five points for a win and three points for a first innings lead in a drawn game. The county were led by Frank

Warwickshire's annus mirabilis, 1994, saw them launch an assault on every major domestic trophy. The first to fall was the Benson & Hedges Cup in July: Brian Lara holds the trophy.

Rowbotham Foster, a dashing all-rounder who transformed their fortunes in that hot summer.

Half-way through the season, Warwickshire were one place from the bottom. Then victory followed victory and the title was secured in the final game against Northants. Foster, at the age of 22, had played the major role, with a batting average of 44.61 and 124 wickets.

Wisden recorded: 'Not since W.G. Grace in the early days of Gloucestershire has so young a captain been such a match-winning force. He proved himself a truly inspirational leader.' Sadly, a motorcycle accident in 1915 ended his career at the age of 25.

Another player to enjoy all too short a career was Percy Jeeves, a fast-medium bowler who burst onto the scene in 1913 with more than 100 wickets. A glittering prospect, he was killed in action in 1916, although his name lives on. P.G. Wodehouse, after seeing him play, took the name Jeeves for the butler in his famous Bertie Wooster stories.

After the war, Warwickshire were led by the Honourable F.S.G. Calthorpe through the twenties, and then R.E.S. Wyatt through much of the thirties. This was a period spent mostly in the lower half of the table, with fourth place in 1934 being as close as they came to another title.

In 1922 the club took part in one of cricket's most extraordinary matches, when having dismissed Hampshire for just 15 they then allowed them to score 521 following on! Calthorpe, it was said, was told that his committee wanted to see some cricket and he should make more of a game of it by delaying the taking of the new ball.

That decision helped Hampshire add 247 for the last two wickets, and when Warwickshire were bowled out for 158, losing by 155 runs, Calthorpe was admonished by the committee.

Rebuilding after the Second World War, Warwickshire were fourth in both 1949 and 1950 before taking their second Championship in 1951. As before, it was an enterprising captain, Tom Dollery, who was responsible for getting the best out of what he described as 'an extraordinary team of ordinary cricketers playing purposeful cricket'.

There followed twenty years of inconsistency, during which time the county produced some fine players, notably under eleven years of leadership from M.J.K. Smith. Bob Barber joined from Lancashire, A.C. Smith was wicket-keeper, and the bowling was led by David Brown and the ever dependable Tom Cartwright. All played for England.

Always known by his initials, M.J.K. led Warwickshire to a Gillette Cup victory by five wickets over neighbours Worcestershire in 1966.

His namesake A.C. took over the captaincy with the aim of building a championship team. Lance Gibbs and Rohan Kanhai were recruited from the West Indies, and Smith led the side to another Gillette Cup success in 1968.

Having suffered the loss of Cartwright, who wanted to find a county with better prospects of a job after his playing days were over, Warwickshire perhaps surprised themselves when they tied with Surrey at the top of the table in 1971, Surrey winning the title by virtue of having won eleven games to Warwickshire's nine.

That disappointment was quickly eradicated by outright victory the following season. A powerful batting line-up was led by the county's record run-scorer, Dennis Amiss, and also featured Kanhai and Alvin Kallicharran, who was to enjoy two decades of success at Edgbaston.

The bowling had been strengthened by Bob Willis' defection from Surrey. With Gibbs and the steady Norman McVicker regularly taking wickets, Warwickshire ended the season a comfortable 36 points ahead of their nearest challengers, Kent.

They were also in the Gillette Cup final again, going down to Lancashire, and were beaten semi-finalists in the new Benson and Hedges Cup.

As with previous title wins, however, the success was short-lived. The Packer affair caused internal strife, with Kallicharran signing then withdrawing, Willis refusing and becoming an outspoken critic, and Amiss, as loyal a servant as the club had ever had, joining. His team-mates demanded that he be sacked. Attitudes eventually changed in both England and Australia and Amiss was welcomed back into the fold.

The John Player League title in 1981 and NatWest Trophy wins in 1989 and 1993, when they beat Sussex in a memorable final, were rare achievements among some dismal seasons that followed.

But in 1994, Dermot Reeve led a side that consistently made the most of their abilities. It was generally asscepted that the sum total was very much greater than the constituent parts. In the absence of their fearsome South African fast bowler Allan Donald, England Test players Gladstone Small and Tim Munton provided a potent attack.

Lara naturally led the way with the bat, but both Twose and Moles also averaged over 50. Warwickshire had taken domestic cricket by storm, and no one could begrudge them their success.

WASIM AKRAM
Pakistan
*Born 1966
Lahore, PACO, PNSC, PIA and
Lancashire*

WASIM AKRAM IS currently the best left-arm fast bowler in the world, and with his particularly useful middle-order batting he is arguably the world's best all-rounder. His ability to swing the ball in to a right-handed batsmen late in its flight has brought him many wickets.

With Wasim and Waqar Younis bowling in harness, Pakistan have the most potent opening attack in Test cricket.

Wasim displayed a natural ability from a young age. At 12 years of age he opened the batting and bowling for his school team, and he was captain at 15.

He took 7 for 50 on his first-class debut as a 17-year-old against the touring New Zealand team. He wasn't selected for that Test series but was in the Pakistan party for the return tour to New Zealand. In his second Test, at Dunedin, he took 10 for 128.

Imran Khan advised him to gain experience in England, and after playing in the Durham League he eventually signed a six-year contract for Lancashire during Pakistan's 1987 tour of England.

He immediately made his mark in county cricket the following season, demonstrating against Surrey at Southport just what a fine all-rounder he is. He took five wickets

Then in 1994/95 he took 8 for 138 as Pakistan recorded a memorable one-wicket win over Australia, a Test which decided the series.

First Class Career:
Runs – 3,982. Average 23.01
  (4 centuries)
Wickets – 616. Average 21.87

Test Match Career:
Tests – 53
Runs – 1,153. Average 19.54
  (1 century)
Wickets – 222. Average 23.43

WELLINGTON

THE QUAINTLY NAMED Basin Reserve ground in Wellington will forever be remembered as the venue where New Zealand finally chalked up their first Test win over England in1977/78.

The ground takes its name from the fact that it was originally a lake, which planners at one time decided to transform into a harbour. However, in 1853 an earthquake turned the lake into a swamp and permission was given to develop it into a cricket ground.

Much redevelopment work has gone on in recent years. New stands and improved landscaping have given the Basin Reserve a new look and a more attractive feel.

But if the ground looks good, it could rarely be said to be quiet. With busy roads surrounding the perimeter, it has been described as the largest traffic island in the world.

The Basin Reserve's other main claim to fame is its reputation for being one of the breeziest playing arenas in the world. Indeed, that famous victory over England was largely as a result of Sir Richard Hadlee taking ten wickets with the

The Basin Reserve pictured during the third Test of England's tour in 1992. The ground has staged the most Test matches in New Zealand.

Wasim Akram has for years been regarded as Imran Khan's natural successor thanks to a series of outstanding all-round performances for Pakistan.

in the first innings, including a hat-trick, made a half century when Lancashire batted and then scored 98 off 78 balls in the second innings.

In 1989/90 Wasim scored a century and took five wickets against Australia at Adelaide. He has now taken more than 250 Test wickets, and was perhaps at his most dominant against England in 1992.

He took 21 wickets in four Tests, his best figures being 6 for 67 in the first innings at the Oval. He took 82 wickets on the tour overall at an average of 16.21, finishing second in the national averages.

In 1992/93 he became captain of Pakistan, but his form deserted him on a disappointing tour of the West Indies. However, he came back well the following winter, taking 25 wickets in three Tests in New Zealand.

help of a gusting wind.

Unlike other grounds in New Zealand, no rugby is played at the Basin Reserve, although football is played in the winter months.

KEPLER WESSELS

South Africa and Australia

Born 1957

Orange Free State, Western Province, Northern Transvaal, Eastern Province, Sussex and Queensland

KEPLER WESSELS IS ONE of a rare breed – a man who has played Test cricket for two different countries, and the only man to score a century for both.

A talented, left-hand opening bat, he was compared in his early days to Barry Richards. But though he had the concentration to play big innings, he never dominated an attack quite like his fellow countryman. Wessels was a particularly gutsy player.

He began his career in South Africa in 1973/74 before coming to England to play for Sussex from 1976 to 1980. He played World Series Cricket in Australia in 1978/79 and decided to settle there, seeing little hope of South Africa returning to Test cricket.

After scoring heavily for Queensland, he was chosen for Australia when he became eligible in the 1982/83 season. He made an immediate impact, scoring 162 and 46 on his debut against England.

After making 70 and 3 in Australia's defeat by New Zealand in 1985/86, he retired from Test cricket and returned to South Africa.

In 1986/87 Wessels played for an unofficial Australian team in South Africa. But with the country of his birth readmitted to the international fold, he returned to Test cricket in April 1992, captaining South Africa in their historic match against West Indies in Barbados, scoring 59 and 74.

He followed that by leading the side in their first home Test for 22 years, against India at Durban in November 1992. In difficult conditions Wessels scored 118 in South Africa's first innings total of 254.

He captained South Africa on their historic tour of England in 1994, his proudest moment coming in their victory in the first Test at Lord's. His typically gritty innings of 105 was largely responsible for the victory, and earned him the man of the match award.

He announced his retirement from Test cricket on 20 December 1994, the effects of a chronic knee injury finally taking their toll. He led South Africa in 16 Tests and never lost a

Wessels in action for Australia in 1985. He retired from Test cricket the following year but returned to captain his native South Africa.

series – a proud record for a side new to international cricket.

First Class Career:
Runs – 21,318. Average 49.80
  (55 centuries)

Test Match Career: South Africa
Tests – 16
Runs – 1,027. Average 38.04

Test Match Career: Australia
Tests – 24
Runs – 1,761. Average 42.95
  (4 centuries)

WEST INDIES

THE CARIBBEAN ISLANDS that make up the West Indies have become famous the world over for the quality of the cricketers they have produced. Since gaining Test status in 1926, at the same time as India and New Zealand, the West Indies have regularly proved themselves the best side in the world, never more so than over the past twenty years.

The two islands of Barbados and Jamaica have been the heart of West Indies cricket. Trinidad, Guyana, on the coast of South America, and Antigua have also produced a number of star players.

In their early days, the West Indies charmed cricket lovers everywhere with their brand of so-called 'Calypso Cricket', a happy-go-lucky attitude to the game played by fluent batsmen and bowlers of great craft.

Their entrance into Test cricket was marked by three defeats against England in 1928 and the 1930s saw a period of

With astute captaincy, outstanding batsmanship and devastatingly quick fast bowling, the West Indies teams have dominated Test cricket for the last twenty years. Here skipper Viv Richards gives Curtly Ambrose his instructions.

consolidation, as valuable international experience was gained.

It could be said that West Indies cricket really came of age during the 1950 tour of England. This was when the three W's, Worrell, Walcott and Weekes, all from Barbados and born within a few miles and a few months of each other, totally dominated English bowlers that summer.

Their runs opened the way for spin bowlers Ramadhin and Valentine to take over, their efforts being directly responsible for the three West Indies wins in a four-Test series.

Surprisingly the success of that tour was short-lived, with England tieing a series in the Caribbean in 1953/54 and then winning comfortably at home. West Indies had little success against Australia at that time either, losing heavily at home and away.

Their tour of Australia in 1960/61 will long be remembered not just for the first tied Test, at Brisbane, but for the wonderful spirit in which the series was played as the captains Richie Benaud and Frank Worrell orchestrated attractive, attacking cricket.

The 1963 tour in England produced equally absorbing matches, with fast bowlers Wesley Hall and Charlie Griffith proving an awesome attack. They were well backed up by off-spinner Lance Gibbs and the great all-rounder Garfield Sobers.

Sobers went on to succeed Worrell as captain and in due course they were both knighted, not just for their efforts on the cricket field but for their wonderful work as ambassadors for the islands.

It was under the captaincy of Clive Lloyd, panther-like in the field and a particularly powerful left-handed batsman, that the West Indies established their domination of world cricket. Lloyd captained the side in 74 Tests and under his leadership they recorded 11 successive victories in 1984, including a 5–0 'blackwash' in England. He also led West Indies to victory in the first two cricket World Cups, in 1975 and 1979.

Lloyd had a wonderful line-up of batsmen, such as the opening pair of Greenidge and Haynes, the steady Kallicharran and Gomes, and above all the brilliant Viv Richards.

The supply of fast bowlers just kept coming, with such names as Roberts, Holding, Marshall and Garner all match-winners. In recent years they have been succeeded by Ambrose, Croft, Patterson and Bishop.

But it has been the very dominance of those bowlers that has upset many cricket administrators and aficionados. While the pace attack invariably brought convincing victories for West Indies teams, it also meant slow over-rates and a succession of short-pitched, hostile deliveries bordering on intimidation.

Efforts to redress the balance by imposing minimum numbers of overs to be bowled in a day and limits on bouncers were regularly blocked by West Indies officials.

The West Indies were badly affected by the Kerry Packer incursion into world cricket, most of their top names opting to join World Series Cricket.

Not surprisingly they were also at the forefront of South Africa's exclusion from the international scene over apartheid. There was much controversy over a 'rebel' tour of the Republic made in 1982/83 by West Indies players, who were later given life bans at home.

But with the return of South Africa to Test cricket came the first ever meeting between them and the West Indies at Bridgetown in 1991/92.

Despite leading by 83 runs on first innings, South Africa collapsed to 148 all out in their second, with Ambrose taking six wickets and Walsh four, to give the home side victory by 52 runs.

In domestic cricket, the Red

Malcolm Marshall has Ravi Shastri beaten all ends up in the fifth Test at Calcutta in 1983/84. India were skittled out for just 80 in their second innings.

Stripe Cup has now replaced the Shell Shield as the major competition, with Jamaica, Barbados, Guyana, Trinidad & Tobago, the Leeward Islands and the Windward Islands competing.

While cricket continues to be a way of life in the West Indies, there are growing worries about North American influence, with the

THE GUINNESS

increasing popularity of basketball and baseball seen as a possible threat to the continued development of cricket.

However, while the production line continues to produce players of the calibre of Brian Lara, the world's best batsman, administrators in the West Indies would seem to have little to worry about.

WEST INDIES
V
INDIA

THE WEST INDIES AND India have played each other in no fewer than fourteen series since they first met in 1948/49. India's record overall is a dismal one – they have recorded just a handful of wins – but it includes two series victories.

The West Indies batsmen found conditions to their liking when they first visited India in 1948/49. Their bowling, though, failed to win them matches except in the one positive result of the five-match series, at Madras. There the West Indies pacemen, Trim and Jones, dismissed India twice to produce a victory by an innings and 193 runs.

There was a similar outcome in the Caribbean in 1952/53 with four draws and just one victory for West Indies, thanks to the spin of Ramadhin and Valentine at Bridgetown, Barbados.

West Indies dominated the next three series, two of them in India, with their fast bowlers too strong for the Indian batting. In 1961/62, when they won all five Tests, Wesley Hall took 27 wickets at 15.74.

Against all the odds, India won their first match against the West Indies, and the series, when they visited the Caribbean in 1970/71. The crucial victory came in the second Test at Port of Spain. Gavaskar made 65 and 67 on his debut, but it was the subtle off-spin of Prasanna and Venkataraghavan that produced the seven-wicket win.

Normal service was resumed as the West Indies won 3–2 in India in 1974/75, although India did come back to level matters after going two Tests down before losing the final encounter at Bombay.

Sadly, the next series in the Caribbean in 1975/76 was marred by intimidatory West Indies bowling which led to protests by the Indian captain Bishen Bedi. With the series level at 1–1, the decider at Kingston, Jamaica was played on an unsatisfactory pitch of uneven bounce. Viswanath suffered a broken hand, Gaekwad spent two days in hospital after being hit on the ear, and Patel retired with stitches in a cut mouth.

In anger, Bedi declared at 306 for 6 as a protest and to protect his tail-enders from injury. India's second innings closed at 97 with only six men having batted. It was a highly unsatisfactory outcome.

With many of the top West Indies players having defected to World Series Cricket, India won the next series in India in 1978/79 thanks again to a single victory, at Madras, with Kapil Dev and Venkataraghavan taking important wickets.

The West Indies enjoyed a notable 3–0 win in India in 1983/84 – a series that saw Gavaskar break Geoffrey Boycott's record number of Test runs in scoring 90 at Ahmedabad. He also recorded India's highest individual Test score, 236 in the final Test at Madras. In all Gavaskar scored thirteen Test centuries against the West Indies.

Richards and Vengsarkar then took over the captaincy of their respective countries and shared a series in India in 1987/88 before the West Indies re-established their superiority in the Caribbean in 1988/89, winning 3–0.

West Indies held on to their record of being undefeated in a series for 15 years when they shared their next meeting 1–1 in India in 1994/95. They lost the first Test but won the third at Chandigarh to level the series and maintain that proud record.

Season	Ven	Tests	Winner	Res
1948/49	Ind	5	W. Indies	1–0
1952/53	WI	5	W. Indies	1–0
1958/59	Ind	5	W. Indies	3–0
1961/62	WI	5	W. Indies	5–0
1966/67	Ind	3	W. Indies	2–0
1970/71	WI	5	India	1–0
1974/75	Ind	5	W. Indies	3–2
1975/76	WI	4	W. Indies	2–1
1978/79	Ind	6	India	1–0
1982/83	WI	5	W. Indies	2–0
1983/84	Ind	6	W. Indies	3–0
1987/88	Ind	4	–	1–1
1988/89	WI	4	W. Indies	3–0
1994/95	Ind	3	–	1–1

WEST INDIES
v
NEW ZEALAND

FOR ONE OF THE WEAKER Test playing nations, New Zealand have a remarkably successful record against the mighty West Indies. Half of the 24 matches between them have ended in draws, but New Zealand's four victories have been significant ones.

The West Indies were by far the stronger side when they first toured New Zealand in 1951/52 after a series in Australia. They won by five wickets at Christchurch, with Ramadhin taking nine wickets in the match, and they looked to be heading for an innings victory at Auckland, thanks to centuries from Worrell, Stollmeyer and Walcott, until rain washed out the final day.

It was much the same story in New Zealand four years later. Two innings wins in the first two Tests, and a nine-wicket victory in the third, set the visitors up for a whitewash. But New Zealand surprised them in the fourth Test at Auckland, dismissing the West Indians for just 77 after they had been set 268 to win.

Honours were shared 1–1 when the West Indies made their third visit to New Zealand in 1968/69. Sobers' side went one up at Auckland in the first Test before New Zealand took the second by six wickets. That game saw a magnificent innings of 258 by Seymour Nurse in his last Test.

New Zealand embarked on their first tour of the Caribbean in 1971/72 very much as underdogs. In the event the series saw five drawn Tests, as the batsmen on both sides held the upper hand. Fourteen centuries were scored.

Back in New Zealand in 1979/80, New Zealand, led by Geoff Howarth, recorded a historic first series win thanks to a narrow one-wicket victory at Christchurch. For the West Indies, Desmond Haynes top-scored in each innings and was last man out each time – the only player

to bat through two complete Test innings. Needing 104 to win, New Zealand just scraped home.

West Indies had their revenge at home five years later, chalking up ten-wicket victories in the last two Tests of a four-match series, thanks largely to some hostile short-pitched bowling, which resulted in Jeremy Coney having his arm broken.

It was Coney who led New Zealand in a three-match series at home in 1986/87 which finished with honours even. West Indies won at Auckland, helped by a brilliant 213 by Gordon Greenidge, and New Zealand, inspired by Hadlee's bowling, levelled the series in Christchurch.

Season	Ven	Tests	Winner	Res
1951/52	NZ	2	W. Indies	1–0
1955/56	NZ	4	W. Indies	3–1
1968/69	NZ	3	–	1–1
1971/72	WI	5	–	0–0
1979/80	NZ	3	N. Zealand	1–0
1984/85	WI	4	W. Indies	2–0
1986/87	NZ	3	–	1–1

WEST INDIES
v
PAKISTAN

PAKISTAN HAVE WON just one of the nine series between these two. For the most part, the West Indies' stronger firepower has been the determining factor.

It was a series of records when the sides first met in the Caribbean in 1957/58. In the first Test at Barbados, Pakistan's Nasim-ul-Ghani, at 16 years 248 days, became the youngest ever Test cricketer at that time.

Having scored 579 for 9, with debutant Conrad Hunte scoring a century, West Indies dismissed Pakistan for 106 and an innings victory seemed assured. But Hanif Mohammad then scored 337 in 16 hours 10 minutes – the longest innings in first-class cricket – to steer his side to the safety of 657 for 8.

Courtney Walsh appeals for the wicket of Inzamam-ul-Haq in the first Test between Pakistan and West Indies at the Queen's Park Oval, Trinidad in 1993.

West Indies won the second Test, and then at Kingston, Jamaica a stand of 446 for the second wicket between Garfield Sobers and Conrad Hunte helped the West Indies to 790 for 3, the declaration coming after Sobers had reached 365 not out – the highest score in Test cricket at the time. They won the match and also took the fourth Test before Pakistan had the consolation of winning the final Test by an innings.

Pakistan won 2–1 at home – their only series win – when the two met in 1958/59.

This was due largely to the bowling of Fazal Mahmood, who took 21 wickets in the three Tests.

A five-Test series in the West Indies in 1976/77 saw Clive Lloyd's team win a close rubber 2–1 thanks to a win by 140 runs in the final Test. Colin Croft was the outstanding bowler on either side, taking 33 wickets.

The West Indies recorded their first series win in Pakistan in 1980/81. The only result came at Faisalabad, when Pakistan were twice dismissed for under 200.

Honours were even 1–1 in the next three series before the West Indies triumphed again, 2–0 in the Caribbean in 1992/93.

It had been billed as a battle of the giants, but Pakistan generally under-performed and lost the first two Tests, in which Desmond Haynes made centuries.

Season	Ven	Tests	Winner	Res
1957/58	WI	5	W. Indies	3–1
1958/59	Pak	3	Pakistan	2–1
1974/75	Pak	2	–	0–0
1976/77	WI	5	W. Indies	2–1
1980/81	Pak	4	W. Indies	1–0
1986/87	Pak	3	–	1–1
1987/88	WI	3	–	1–1
1990/91	Pak	3	–	1–1
1992/93	WI	3	W. Indies	2–0

WEST INDIES
v
SRI LANKA

THE WEST INDIES AND SRI Lanka met for the first time at Test level in December 1993 at Moratuwa in a game ruined by wet weather.

On a pitch that looked likely to favour spinners, Sri Lanka batted first and were dismissed for 190, thanks mainly to the pace of Ambrose and Benjamin.

Prodigious turn helped Sri Lanka in the field as their visitors could muster a first innings lead of just 14 – their last six wickets falling for 36 runs.

Sri Lanka then built up a lead of 29 with eight second innings wickets in hand, before rain washed out the fourth day's play and with it the match.

Season	Ven	Tests	Winner	Res
1993/94	SL	1	–	0–0

BOB WILLIS
England
Born 1949
Surrey, Warwickshire and Northern Transvaal

BOB WILLIS, A TALL, gangling, complex man, was England's leading fast bowler through the 1970s and early eighties, representing his country 90 times.

A determined and aggressive player, he wound himself up into intense concentration on the field, his face rarely betraying his emotions. He suffered a number of serious injuries during his career, mainly to his knees, but always bounced back. He was also dogged by insomnia, and in order to condition himself for the Test arena he would regularly turn to hypnotherapy.

Willis burst onto the international scene as a late replacement for the injured Alan Ward on the 1970/71 tour to Australia and played in four Tests, bowling well and taking some brilliant close-to-the-wicket catches. It was to be his first of six tours down under.

On his return home he was distressed at Surrey's decision not to reward his efforts with a County cap, and moved to Warwickshire in 1972. However, his figures in County cricket never matched his Test achievements, and in more than thirteen seasons with the Midlands county he took only 353 wickets.

His most memorable Test performance came at Headingley in 1981. Ian Botham had led the fightback with an innings of 149 not out after England had been forced to follow on by Australia. Willis then destroyed the Australian batting. They needed just 130 to win, but Willis took 8 for 43 as they collapsed to 111 all out.

He became captain of England in 1982, winning home series against India and Pakistan, and then led the side to Australia that winter. But the Ashes were lost, two Tests to one. His captaincy was often criticised tactically, but no one could ever fault his commitment, always leading the side by example.

Willis was awarded the MBE in 1982 and after his retirement he was assistant manager of the touring party to the West Indies in 1986. More recently he has become a familiar voice to television cricket watchers.

First Class Career:
Wickets – 899. Average 24.99

Test Match Career:
Tests – 90
Wickets – 325. Average 25.20

A study in concentration, Bob Willis was capable of generating tremendous pace in some hostile spells of bowling. He passed Fred Trueman's record of most Test wickets for England in 1984 before himself being overtaken by Ian Botham.

WISDEN

WISDEN CRICKETERS' Almanack, which was first published in 1864, is now rightly regarded as 'The Cricketer's Bible'. It is a statistical reference book without equal.

With its distinctive yellow cover, it is printed in both hardback and paperback. Publication every April tells cricket supporters that a new season is about to begin.

Each edition features the full scorecard of every first-class match played in England in the season just past, as well as in Australia. There is a full review of domestic cricket in other Test-playing countries, as well as a vast array of cricketing statistical information.

The almanack takes its name from John Wisden, one of the finest fast bowlers in England between 1845 and 1863. Born in Brighton, he played for Sussex. In 1855, together with Frederick Lillywhite, he set up a cricket and cigar business in London. His partnership with Lillywhite ended in acrimony three years later.

In 1864 the first almanack appeared. It was merely a statistical reference book – there were none of the articles and features one finds today. It cost one shilling and contained a section still found today, Births and Deaths of cricketers.

That first edition also contained a number of non-cricketing facts, such as the winners of Classic horse races and Varsity boat races and the trial of Charles I.

By 1870, reports of matches, as well as statistics, were included and two years later came the start of a review of each county's performance.

Charles Pardon, having set up the Cricket Reporting Agency, was appointed editor of Wisden in 1887, and other members of the agency, most notably his brother Sydney, worked for the publication for many years.

Sydney Pardon, until his final

edition in 1925, proved himself a superb editor, his extensive knowledge not just of cricket but also of rowing, boxing and athletics, made him a mine of information. His annual 'Notes' made compelling reading, and his views on cricketing issues gave Wisden a greater authority.

Another family closely connected with Wisden over the years were the Prestons. Hubert Preston was editor from 1944 to 1951 and was succeeded by his son Norman, who continued until his death in 1980.

John Woodcock of *The Times* and Graeme Wright then followed before Matthew Engel, a cricket writer for *The Guardian*, took over in 1993 and made some fairly far-reaching changes by Wisden standards.

The Index, for so long at the front, was moved to the back. The 'Other Matches at Lord's' section has now gone, but one of the most prestigious sections remains – Wisden's Five Cricketers of the Year.

Perhaps one of the most surprising twists in the Wisden story occurred just before the start of the 1993 season.

In its 130th year, the title was bought by the American Paul Getty, one of the richest men in the world and a keen cricket follower, who had previously donated money for the improvement of the Mound Stand at Lord's.

WOMEN'S CRICKET

THE FIRST RECORD OF A women's cricket match dates from 1745, at Gosden Common, near Guildford in Surrey, the home of Bramley Cricket Club. There, it is said, the eleven maids of Hambleton beat the eleven maids of Bramley by 127 notches to 119.

In 1986 the Women's Cricket Association celebrated their Diamond Jubilee by playing a match on that same ground.

Cricket may be considered a man's game, but there can be no

Opposite: Denise Annetts recorded the highest individual innings in women's cricket with 193 against England in 1987.

Action from the early rounds of the 1993 World Cup as New Zealand's Maia Lewis loses her wicket against England at Beckenham.

doubting that women have had a considerable effect upon it. The establishment of overarm bowling, under the revised laws adopted by the MCC in 1835, is credited to a woman.

Christina Willes, having had difficulty bowling underarm to her brother John in the barn at their home near Canterbury because of her voluminous skirt, solved the problem by bowling roundarm. John immediately saw the possibilities of this, although it was another 21 years before that style of bowling was accepted by the authorities.

The women's game flourished towards the end of the 19th century. In 1887 the first women's club – the White Heather Club – was founded at Nun Appleton in Yorkshire, and membership passed the 50 mark four years later. The club continued until 1950 and its early scorebook

was placed in the Cricket Gallery at Lord's.

By 1926, nearly two hundred years after the first women's cricket match, it was decided the game should be put on a proper footing with the setting up of an association. A number of women who played lacrosse and hockey in the winter were turning to cricket as their summer sport.

Matches at Cheltenham Ladies' College and Malvern Boys' College created such enthusiasm that it was agreed to make plans for a permanent body. Initially players joined the Women's Cricket Association as individual members until clubs could be established.

The following year the first organised cricket week took place at Colwall in Worcestershire, and apart from the war years it has been held every year since, in the same area, using a number of grounds.

In 1929 the first public match was played between London & District and the Rest of England at Beckenham. It was well received in the press and helped encourage

more women to take up the game.

It also led to women's cricket being taken seriously, with men's county grounds opening their doors to women's games three years later.

To cope with the increased interest, the WCA followed the example of the Women's Hockey Association and divided the country up into five Territories – North, South, East, West and Midlands. By 1931 the first county associations were being formed, and a match was played between Durham and a combined Cheshire and Lancashire XI.

In 1934 another landmark was reached – the first tour of Australia and New Zealand. The sixteen members of the England party had to pay their own passage (£80) and bought their own equipment for the six-month-long tour.

Despite suffering from the non-availability of several of their best players, the England team, led by Betty Archdale, was unbeaten, winning two of their three Tests in Australia and all seven matches, including one Test, in New Zealand.

Australia made their first tour of England in 1937, with the three-match Test series being drawn.

With the growth of the game internationally, the inaugural meeting of the International Women's Cricket Council was held in Melbourne in 1958, involving delegates from five countries: Australia, England, Holland, New Zealand and South Africa.

The 1960s saw a number of changes domestically. The Territorial areas were replaced by 13 Playing Areas, and a five-year development plan was drawn up in order to qualify for grants.

It was during this time that perhaps the most famous woman cricketer of them all came to prominence. Rachel Heyhoe-Flint captained England for twelve years from 1966 to 1978, leading her

country on an inaugural tour of the West Indies, and to victory in the first Women's World Cup in 1973.

She was omitted from the side for the 1977 World Cup, a move that had a major impact on the WCA. The association received, for just about the first time, a bad press and it led to splits among WCA members.

In addition to the World Cup, a European Tournament has now been established. The first was played in 1989 with the next scheduled for Ireland in 1995.

A club knockout competition has become a regular feature since 1974, an Area Championship was introduced in 1981 and a National League was created in 1988.

Women's cricket is now well established both in England and internationally. It can be an expensive pastime for its keen devotees, who often have to meet the costs of touring and take unpaid leave.

But happily it is a sport that is beginning to attract greater amounts of sponsorship.

England captain Karen Smithies (right) and player of the match Jo Chamberlain celebrate with the trophy after England's victory in the 1993 World Cup final.

WOMEN'S WORLD CUP

CHAMPIONS:
1973 – England
1977/78 – Australia
1982 – Australia
1988 – Australia
1993 – England

THE STRENGTH OF THE women's game internationally was recognised by the decision to play the final of the 1993 World Cup at the home of cricket, Lord's. The announcement of the news brought joy to the Women's Cricket Association and a sense of pride at the honour.

The first World Cup was played in

England in 1973, thanks to the initiative and sponsorship of Jack Hayward, a consistent supporter of women's cricket.

Four countries, Australia, Jamaica, New Zealand and Trinidad & Tobago, plus an International XI, were invited to take part with England and Young England.

With six matches for each team, the seedings worked out as planned, with Australia taking a one-point lead over England into the final game of the tournament at Edgbaston. A magnificent century by Enid Bakewell set the foundation for an England victory by 92 runs to make them the first world champions.

India were the hosts in 1977/78, with England, Australia and New Zealand the other countries taking part. The West Indies and Holland withdrew at the last moment, and the organisation of the tournament left a lot to be desired. Once again the round robin matches produced an England v Australia climax.

On a ground still heavy with dew, England were unlucky to lose the toss and could make only 96 for 8 in their 50 overs. Australia also struggled early on, but eventually, as conditions improved, secured a comfortable victory with 17 overs to spare.

New Zealand was the venue for the 1982 tournament, with the home nation joined by England, Australia, India and an International XI. Australia successfully defended their trophy, defeating England on three occasions.

Four countries, England, Ireland, the Netherlands and New Zealand, travelled to Australia for the 1988 World Cup. Again, the round robin tournament produced an Australia versus England final at the Melbourne Cricket Ground.

Despite having beaten the old enemy in an earlier match, England were now outclassed as they reached only 127 for 7 on a ground saturated by heavy overnight thunderstorms. Australia cruised to 129 for 2 with fifteen overs to spare.

The 1993 tournament in England attracted a record entry of eight countries: England, New Zealand, Australia, India, Ireland, West Indies, Holland and Denmark.

Australia went into the competition as firm favourites. But they were beaten first by England at Guildford – at a time when their men were comfortably beating the English in an Ashes series – and then by New Zealand and found themselves out of contention.

On 1st August, at the headquarters of cricket, England won the World Cup for the first time since that inaugural tournament in 1973, beating New Zealand by 67 runs.

In front of a noisy 5,000-strong crowd, there was a fine all-round display from Jo Chamberlain, who hit a whirlwind 38, took a vital wicket, and with a direct hit from cover ran out New Zealand's most dangerous player.

After years of limping along with little finance, it was hoped that this success, which attracted live television coverage and considerable newspaper attention, would help the women's game in England establish itself on a firmer footing.

WORCESTERSHIRE
Founded: 1865

Entered Official Championship: 1899

Honours:
County Champions – 1964, 1965, 1974, 1988, 1989
NatWest Trophy – 1994
Benson and Hedges Cup – 1991
John Player League – 1971
Refuge Assurance League – 1987, 1988

TROPHIES WERE A LONG time coming for the smallest of the first-class counties. But after recording their first Championship title in 1964, Worcestershire, with perhaps the most picturesque ground in England, have developed into one of the strongest counties of the modern era.

For all their humble origins, Worcestershire are now a firm part of the English cricket scene, traditionally providing touring teams with their first serious opposition each summer. They are a club that have always had a reputation for producing fine batsmen, with Tom Graveney, Glenn Turner and Graeme Hick just three to have made a major impact.

Two families dominate the history of the county, the Lyttletons and the Fosters. The Lyttletons, who once turned out a full XI on their own, have over the years provided presidents, chairmen, captains and players for the club.

In all, seven Foster brothers played for Worcestershire – four of them in one match. Small wonder then that the county became known as 'Fostershire'. H.K. Foster was captain when the club was given first-class status, and two others, R.E. and M.K., succeeded him. R.E. was perhaps the best of them, but H.K. and W.L. led the Worcestershire batting in 1892 while still pupils at Malvern College.

Having won the Minor Counties championship for three years, Worcester joined the County Championship just before the turn of the century. Their record was modest in the period before the First World War, with the exception of 1907 when they did the double over Yorkshire and finished runners-up to Nottinghamshire.

The club did not resume in the Championship in 1919 because of financial trouble, and when they returned the following year their record of just one win in 18 games led Wisden to comment: 'Their return to the Championship was a complete failure.'

Other failures followed. Between the wars Worcester were either bottom of the table or close to it. Among the players to represent them at this time, none was more charismatic than Fred Root. A fast-medium bowler, he developed the famous 'leg theory'. In twelve years he took more than 1,400 wickets, seven times taking more than 120 in a season.

As Root retired, Reg Perks took over his mantle. A prodigious swinger of the new ball, Perks is

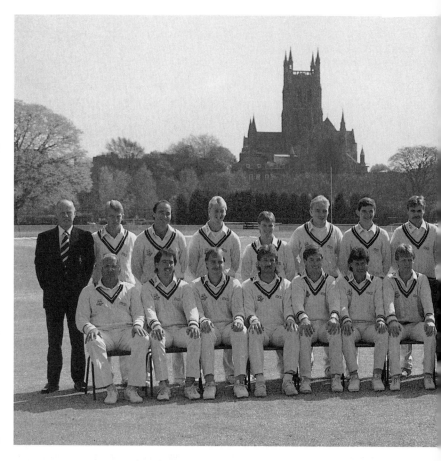

The 1989 Worcestershire side which won the County Championship for the second successive year, pictured at their New Road home with Worcester Cathedral in the background.

Worcestershire's leading wicket-taker with more than 2,000 victims to his credit in a period stretching from 1930 to 1955. He took 100 wickets in sixteen consecutive seasons.

The post-war period produced a number of false dawns as the county attempted to challenge the supremacy of the bigger clubs. But, by the early 1960s, under the captaincy of Don Kenyon, a well-balanced side had been put together.

In Flavell and Coldwell they had as good an opening attack as any in the country, well supported by other seamers Carter, Brain and Jim Standen, who also won an FA Cup winners' medal with West Ham in 1964. Gifford was a wily slow left-armer, and the batting had no shortage of talent with Tom Graveney, Ron Headley and Kenyon himself.

After coming fourth in 1961 and second in 1962, Worcestershire finally took the top spot in 1964. They dominated the Championship, winning four more matches than anyone else and finishing 41 points ahead of second-placed Warwickshire. The players celebrated their success with three matches still to play.

The fairy-tale continued the following season – their centenary year – when they retained their crown in a much closer contest, with Northamptonshire finishing just four points behind them. This was the year 34-year-old Basil D'Oliveira was awarded his County Cap.

Worcester also proved themselves adept at the one-day game, appearing in two of the first four Gillette Cup finals at Lord's.

After Graveney had presided over a period of transition, Gifford became captain in 1971 and immediately led the team to the John Player League title, edging out Essex by just 0.003 runs per over. A

Benson and Hedges final was next in 1973 before Gifford led the side to the 1974 Championship.

They may have been fortunate that bad weather robbed Hampshire on the final day of what seemed certain to be their second title on the trot, but the batting of Glenn Turner and Basil D'Oliveira, and the hostile bowling of Vanburn Holder and Brian Brain, meant the Midlands county had a team worthy of the Championship title.

It was not until the late 1980s that further success came to New Road, but when it did it returned with a bang, particularly in 1988. By now captain Phil Neale had built another fine side. Tim Curtis had replaced Turner as the steady sheet-anchor, while Damien D'Oliveira, son of Basil, formed part of the attack with Illingworth, Newport and Radford.

But three players in particular brought the crowds in wherever they played. Ian Botham chose Worcestershire after his stormy

divorce from Somerset, and England fast bowler Graham Dilley joined from Kent. But it was the unrivalled batting of Graeme Hick that attracted most attention. A score of 172 against West Indies brought him 1,000 runs by the end of May, and as the county went on to take the title by one point from Kent, Hick made ten hundreds and averaged 76.

The highlight was an outstanding 405 not out against Somerset at Taunton. It was the second highest innings in the history of the County Championship, and quite overshadowed the previous Worcester record, Glenn Turner's 311 not out against Warwickshire in 1982.

It could so easily have been a treble that year. Worcester retained the Refuge Assurance League title for a second season, but batting first on an autumnal morning at Lord's, they lost the NatWest Trophy final to Middlesex by three wickets.

The toss of a coin almost certainly prevented them from making English cricket history.

However, good fortune was on their side when they retained the Championship in 1989, thanks to the Test and County Cricket Board docking Essex 25 points for a sub-standard pitch at Southend in July. Despite injuries and Test calls Worcestershire won twelve Championship matches – two more than the previous year – to finish six points ahead of Essex. They were runners-up in the Sunday competition, and beaten semi-finalists in the two one-day knock-out tournaments.

In 1992, after six defeats in Lord's finals, Worcestershire finally broke their hoodoo by beating Lancashire

Botham and colleagues celebrate the fall of another wicket. The England all-rounder did much to revitalise the club, while he himself counted his time at New Road as the most satisfying of his county career.

by 65 runs in the Benson and Hedges Cup final. It was Hick again who led the way, striking his first ball for four in an innings of 88 that was to give him the Gold Award.

In 1994 Worcester were the only county to upset Warwickshire's march towards a clean sweep of titles as they beat their Midlands neighbours in the final of the NatWest Trophy. This time it was they who benefited from winning the toss and fielding first in conditions helpful to the bowlers.

THE WORLD CUP

1975

THE FIRST WORLD CUP, sponsored by Prudential Assurance, was held in England in June 1975. The one-day international finally came of age, and the tournament proved a great success, being blessed by fine weather and enjoyed by large crowds. Altogether there were fifteen matches played, each of 60 overs per side.

Eight countries took part, initially playing round-robin matches in two leagues of four teams. England topped Group A, winning their matches against New Zealand, India and East Africa with some ease. New Zealand qualified for the semi-finals in second place.

In Group B, the stronger group, West Indies also won all three matches but only after an extraordinary, nail-biting finish to their match with Pakistan at Edgbaston. The West Indies won by one wicket off the fourth ball of the last over, thanks to an undefeated last-wicket partnership of 64 between Deryck Murray and Andy Roberts. Australia qualified for the semi-finals as runners-up thanks to wins over Sri Lanka and Pakistan.

The two semi-finals were something of a disappointment, but produced excitement nonetheless. England lost to Australia by four wickets on a sub-standard surface at Headingley, being dismissed for just 93 off 36.2 overs. Only the captain Denness and Arnold reached double figures, as Australia's Gary Gilmour took 6 for 14.

The Australians found run-scoring no easier and lost six wickets in reaching the target, Gilmour coming to the rescue with the bat. He added 55 with Doug Walters after his side had been reduced to 39 for 6.

At the Oval, New Zealand, put in by Clive Lloyd, could manage only 158 in 52.2 overs as the West Indies pace attack took control. The West Indies reached the total with almost twenty overs to spare, Greenidge and Kallicharran scoring half centuries.

The final between Australia and the West Indies was a thrilling match, a much closer affair than their previous meeting in Group B. From eleven o'clock until just before 8.45 p.m. the sides produced wonderful entertainment.

Put in to bat, the West Indies were in trouble at 50 for 3. But their skipper Lloyd turned the game with a magnificent 102, including two 6's and twelve 4's, taking his side to 291 for 8 in their 60 overs.

Australia fought to the very end, but with five run-outs they contributed to their own downfall. There were good contributions from Ian Chappell (62) and Alan Turner (40) but the West Indies always had the edge, Australia finally being dismissed for 274 off 58.4 overs.

So Lloyd, the man of the match, received the trophy from Prince Philip as the West Indies were crowned the first one-day world champions. The tournament had taken more than £200,000 in receipts and been watched by 158,000 people.

1979

The West Indies repeated their triumph when the second World Cup, officially called the Prudential Cup, was played again in England.

Sadly, the English weather was not as kind as it had been four years previously, although only one match, the Group B game between the champions and Sri Lanka, was abandoned without a ball being bowled.

Once again eight countries took part – and again South Africa were notable absentees. To make up the numbers, a separate tournament of the associate members of the International Cricket Conference was held, with Sri Lanka and Canada winning through to compete against the Test-playing countries, who qualified automatically.

England topped Group A with three wins, Pakistan finishing runners-up thanks to an important victory over the previous beaten finalists, Australia.

In a rain-affected match over two days, Pakistan made 286 for 7 in their 60 overs, Majid Khan and Asif Iqbal both scoring 61. Australia never came close to the target, losing by 89 runs despite an impressive 72 from Hilditch.

Group B was a very much more sedate affair with the West Indies topping the table and New Zealand securing the runners-up spot thanks to a nine-wicket win over Sri Lanka and an eight-wicket victory against India.

In the semi-finals New Zealand came close to causing an upset, losing by just nine runs to England at Old Trafford in front of an almost capacity crowd of 22,000. England's batting was patchy, the best contributions coming from Gooch (71) and skipper Brearley (53). Derek Randall was at the wicket in the final scramble for runs and it was largely thanks to him that England took 25 from the last three overs to reach 221 for 8 – by no means a winning score.

With opener John Wright scoring 69, New Zealand were always in the hunt, with some sturdy hitting also from Lees and Cairns. In the end the Kiwis finished on 212 for 9, a fine effort that brought them much credit.

The West Indies scored a massive 293 for 6 in the other semi-final at the Oval, all their batsmen showing fine form. For Pakistan, Majid Khan (81) and Zaheer Abbas (93) put on 166 off 36 overs for the second wicket, but once they were out – both falling to Colin Croft – the West

Indies reasserted their grip and won by 43 runs.

It was a fine day for the final at Lord's. England, without the injured Willis, found it hard in the field after Brearley had asked the West Indies to bat. The 25,000 capacity crowd were treated to a wonderful innings of 138 by Viv Richards who with Collis King (86) added 139 for the fifth wicket in just 77 minutes, a partnership that was to turn the game. The West Indies total of 286 for 9 always looked a strong one.

Boycott and Brearley got the home side off to a sound start with a partnership of 129, but they were always behind the clock and when Brearley was out England still needed 158 from the last 22 overs.

Randall and Gooch had brief flurries, but it proved too difficult a task. England were eventually dismissed for 194, the West Indies retaining their trophy with a win by 92 runs. Richards was named man of the match.

Despite the drop in attendances, due almost entirely to the bad weather, the tournament had been another success. At their meeting shortly after it was over, the International Cricket Conference decided to make it a regular, four-yearly competition, with the 1983 event again to be staged in England.

1983

The third World Cup, and the last to be sponsored by Prudential Assurance, was a much more open affair than the previous two, producing a number of surprises, not the least in the eventual winners – India.

The matches were once again 60 overs per side, but this time the sides played each other twice in the group stages, partly to boost revenue but also to reduce the likelihood of a country being eliminated through a match being affected by bad weather.

As it turned out, the weather for the 1983 tournament was kinder than that in 1979. Only three of the 27 matches had to go into a second day. By the time the groups were completed, everyone had something to celebrate – each country won at least one match.

Group A was comfortably headed by England, who won five matches. Their only defeat came against New Zealand, who reached a target of 235 off the penultimate ball.

New Zealand themselves failed to qualify for the semi-finals, missing out to Pakistan on runs per over, both teams having recorded twelve points. A disappointing defeat at the hands of Sri Lanka was to be their undoing.

Group B was won, as expected, by the West Indies with just one defeat in their six games, that being against India who finished runners-up. For Australia it was a miserable tournament. They won just two games out of six, the biggest

Sharma grabs a stump as India celebrate what must rank as one of the all-time great upsets: their victory over West Indies in the 1983 World Cup final at Lord's. Few would have expected the Indians' total of 185 to present any sort of obstacle to Clive Lloyd's powerful team.

Mike Gatting leads his team out at the start of the 1987 World Cup final in Calcutta, followed by an apprehensive-looking John Emburey. England started as favourites, but having allowed Australia to make a brisk start, were always chasing the game.

humiliation coming in their very first match as they went down to Zimbabwe – qualifiers by winning the 1982 ICC Trophy – by 13 runs. It was the biggest shock of any World Cup.

In the semi-finals, England made a promising start against India at Old Trafford but never capitalised on it and struggled to 213 all out in

their allotted overs. India cruised to victory with more than five overs to spare, thanks to half centuries from Yashpal Sharma and Patil.

In the other semi-final, the West Indies confirmed their status of favourites with a comfortable eight-wickets victory over Pakistan at the Oval. Richards and Gomes led the way as the West Indies took only 48.4 overs to reach Pakistan's modest total of 184.

In the final, on a glorious summer's day, the Lord's crowd witnessed one of the great upsets. India, put in to bat, were all out for 183 in 54.4 overs. It did not look nearly enough.

Yet thanks to tight bowling and sensible pressure being applied by

the young Indian captain Kapil Dev, the West Indies, so full of batting talent, buckled.

They were reduced to 76 for 6, but were fighting back when Mohinder Amarnath, later named man of the match, took the vital wicket of Jeffrey Dujon. The slide continued and the West Indies were bowled out for 140, giving India, quoted at 66 to 1 before the competition, an improbable but well-deserved victory.

1987

The fourth World Cup, sponsored by Reliance, was the first to be held outside England. Despite fears that joint organisation by India and

Pakistan could lead to problems, the tournament in October and November produced very few.

The same eight countries that had participated in 1983 took part again in a similar format, the only change being that matches were reduced from 60 to 50 overs per side. The 27 matches were played in 21 different centres, which meant a lot of travelling for the teams and an extension of the tournament from 17 to 32 days.

Group A, played in India, saw easy qualification for the semi-finals for the home side and Australia, both teams winning five games and losing once, to each other –

In 1992 at Melbourne England again found the pressure of chasing 250 just a little too much to cope with: the crucial wicket of Allan Lamb fell to Wasim Akram (below). No side batting second in the World Cup final has yet won the trophy.

WORLD CUP			
	Winners	Runners-up	
1975	West Indies	Australia	17 runs
1979	West Indies	England	92 runs
1983	India	West Indies	43 runs
1987	Australia	England	7 runs
1992	Pakistan	England	22 runs

Australia beating India by one run, India later gaining their revenge by 56 runs. New Zealand, without Richard Hadlee were a poor third with just two victories to their credit.

Group B, with all but two matches played in Pakistan, saw the other host nation move comfortably through with five wins. England joined them in the semi-finals thanks to two victories over the West Indies, who were badly weakened by the absence of Malcolm Marshall.

The sub-continent was in a state of feverish excitement as it anticipated an India–Pakistan showdown for the cup. In the end, both were beaten in the semi-finals.

At Lahore, Australia always looked too strong for Pakistan. Batting first the Aussies reached 267 for 8 off their 50 overs, David Boon top scoring with 65. The task proved too hard for Pakistan, and with Craig McDermott taking 5 for 44, they were all out for 249 after 49 overs, Javed Miandad and Imran Khan making half centuries.

In Bombay the next day England were put in to bat. A magnificent 115 from Graham Gooch, and Mike Gatting with 56 off 62 balls, saw them to a total of 254 for 6. DeFreitas then took the vital wicket of Gavaskar early, and India eventually fell for 219, with Eddie Hemmings taking 4 for 52.

In the final, in front of 70,000 spectators in Calcutta, Australia chose to bat first and made 253 for 5. Despite losing Robinson for a duck, England's reply looked on course at 135 for 2. However, Gatting then fell to a reverse sweep off Allan Border's first ball, and as wickets fell the batsmen were always behind the clock. In the end Australia won by just seven runs, but the outcome looked clear well before the end.

So Border lifted the cup, the man of the match award going to David Boon, who made a steady 75 in the Australian innings.

1992

The fifth World Cup, held in Australia and New Zealand in February and March 1992, saw the return to international cricket of South Africa. Their late inclusion after 21 years of isolation meant a rescheduling of the programme, with 39 matches to be played.

The nine countries all played each other once in matches of 50 overs per side, with the top four qualifying for the semi-finals.

A new and highly controversial

rule was introduced to deal with matches affected by rain. Teams batting second who had their innings interrupted by rain would have their target altered to the number of runs scored by the side batting first from their equivalent number of highest scoring overs.

It meant, in effect, that sides fielding first would be penalised for bowling maiden overs. At first, few people saw the problems that could arise. It was a rule that came close to reducing the competition to a farce.

England's group match with Pakistan was a prime example. Having bowled Pakistan out for 74 in 40.2 overs, England appeared to have a simple task and were 17 without loss off six overs when the rain began. When the game finally got under way again, the target was 64 runs in 16 overs. Fortunately the rain came again and both sides had to settle for a point – a vital one in Pakistan's case.

New Zealand topped the group table with just one defeat. They had produced some good cricket, but were helped by playing their matches on familiar home wickets. England were runners-up, South Africa came third and Pakistan were fourth, thanks to a vital last match win over New Zealand. It meant they qualified by a point, ahead of Australia.

In the first semi-final, Pakistan again got the better of New Zealand, this time by four wickets, thanks mostly to an innings of 60 off 37 balls from Inzamam-ul-Haq. It was heartbreaking for the New Zealand captain Martin Crowe, the tournament's most consistent batsman, who hit a wonderful 91 in New Zealand's 262.

The second semi-final was a case of what might have been, the rain rule spoiling the prospect of an exciting finish. England made 252 for 6, but South Africa went well in their reply and had reached 231 for 6. They needed 22 runs from 13 balls when the umpires took the players off.

Twelve minutes were lost, and it was announced that South Africa would now need 22 off seven balls.

As they took the field, and the time lost was adjusted, that target changed to 22 off one ball. The rain rule had been made to look plain silly.

In the final, England, looking weary and hit by injuries at the end of a long tour, faced a Pakistan side who had run into form at the right time. Pakistan made 249 for 6, with 153 of those coming in their final 20 overs. England never really mounted a serious challenge after being reduced to 69 for 4, despite a brave 62 from Fairbrother. Imran Khan led his side to a win by 22 runs.

WORLD SERIES CRICKET

THE RELATIVELY SHORT existence of Kerry Packer's World Series Cricket had a profound and lasting effect on the nature of international cricket.

By signing up most of the world's top players to take part in what was derided as his 'circus', Australian media mogul Packer sent shock waves through the cricket establishment. It led to expensive court proceedings and bitter acrimony between players, administrators and cricket lovers.

World Series Cricket (WSC) was conceived amidst utmost secrecy. Then in April 1977, a newspaper in South Africa announced that four leading players had signed lucrative contracts, and the following month the story fully broke when the Packer-owned Australian magazine *Bulletin* reported that 35 of the world's top cricketers had signed for up to three years to play a series of one-day matches in Australia.

Packer's determination to set up his cricket series followed his rebuff by the Australian Board of Control over the rights to screen cricket in Australia on Channel 9, which he owned. The Board had always awarded contracts to the state-owned Australian Broadcasting Commission (ABC).

Packer worked with J.P.Sport, a promotions company that handled the interests of a number of sports stars, to recruit the top names.

In England, the leading recruitment officer for Packer was the England captain, Tony Greig. It was during the Centenary Test in Melbourne in 1977 that Greig, having just led England in India, agreed to be the contact between the players and Packer. He immediately started to discuss plans with English and Australian players, and later went to the West Indies to meet top players there.

The line-up of players, attracted by financial offers way in excess of anything they had earned before, was impressive. Among the names, from England there was Alan Knott, Derek Underwood and John Snow; from Pakistan, Mushtaq Mohammad, Imran Khan and Asif Iqbal; from the West Indies, Viv Richards, Clive Lloyd and Michael Holding; and from South Africa, Barry Richards, Mike Procter and Graeme Pollock.

The Australians naturally made up the biggest contingent, and included from their ranks were the Chappell brothers, Doug Walters and Rodney Marsh.

When the news broke on 11th May, it hit the cricket world like a bombshell. With an Ashes series just about to start, Tony Greig was immediately sacked as England captain. Greig's part in recruiting players to a rebel cause while leading the side was looked upon in many quarters as something akin to treason.

While the Ashes series was played out between players from both sides who had signed for Packer, off-the-field meetings were held between the International Cricket Conference and Packer's representatives to find a compromise. The talks failed.

The ICC at its annual meeting in July ruled that no player who had joined World Series Cricket would be eligible for Test cricket, and member countries were encouraged to apply the same restrictions in domestic first-class cricket. But Packer challenged that ruling in the

High Court in London and won a conclusive victory. It was a devastating blow for the governing body of world cricket.

All was not plain sailing, however, for World Series Cricket, which continued to have problems in Australia in the run-up to its launch in 1977/78. Packer was denied the use of certain grounds, so cricket pitches, artificially grown in greenhouses, had to be laid in showgrounds or trotting parks.

WSC had three teams: Australia, West Indies and the Rest of the World, made up of players from England, Pakistan and South Africa. The whole spectacle was geared for a television audience.

However, with a closely contested official Test series being fought out between Australia and India, the majority of television watchers shunned the WSC matches. Certainly few turned up to watch at the grounds, and Channel 9's cameramen struggled not to show the vast empty spaces.

There was disharmony in dressing-rooms around the world as Packer and non-Packer players continued to play the game together. In WSC's second year, however, things began to change.

As England played an Ashes series in Australia and won, World Series Cricket became more successful. In particular there was greatly improved television coverage of the matches, much of which has been adopted throughout the world.

WSC also marketed the game better, and their brand of one-day cricket attracted people who had never taken much interest in the game before. The climax was a game at the Sydney Cricket Ground, now adorned with enormous floodlights. It was said 50,000 people attended, and with England heavily defeating the official Australian team in the Tests, home supporters turned to the Packer Australians for success.

The Ashes series was a financial disaster for the Australian Board and they had to act – but their haste in seeking peace with Packer caused dismay among the rest of the cricket world.

On 24th April 1979, and with hardly a whisper in advance, the Australian Board effectively gave Kerry Packer all he wanted. The ICC had agreed that no individual country would do a deal with him, yet once the Board's contract with ABC came to an end, a multi-million dollar television deal was struck with Channel 9.

A month later, the Board signed a ten-year agreement with Packer, effectively giving him a big say in the running of Australian cricket in return for a large amount of money. The consensus was that the Australian Board, led by chairman Bob Parrish, so anti-Packer in the past, had capitulated, and the rest of the cricket world, through the ICC, had no option but to go along with it when they met a month later.

In time many of the WSC players resumed their roles in their national sides. It was a strong Packer condition that no player should be victimised for his association with World Series Cricket.

The name of Packer's World Series cricket survives today as an international one-day tournament staged annually in Australia. The 1994/95 competition included Zimbabwe and England, suitably attired of course. Here English cricket's rising star Darren Gough takes the wicket of Guy Whittall.

YORKSHIRE
Founded: 1863

Entered Official Championship: 1890

Honours:

County Champions – 1893, 1896, 1898, 1900, 1901, 1902, 1905, 1908, 1912, 1919, 1922, 1923, 1924, 1925, 1931, 1932, 1933, 1935, 1937, 1938, 1939, 1946, 1949, 1959, 1960, 1962, 1963, 1966, 1967, 1968

Gillette Cup – 1965, 1969

Benson and Hedges Cup – 1987

John Player League – 1983

WITH SO MUCH OF THE county's recent history dominated by internal divisions, it is perhaps hard for younger students of the game to appreciate just how Yorkshire have dominated English cricket.

With 30 Championship titles to their credit, the Tykes have been the most successful county since the formation of the official competition. But it has also been 25 years since they last won it, and the handful of one-day prizes accumulated in that time has not been enough to satisfy a demanding Yorkshire public.

No other county, however, has produced from within its own boundaries quite as many giants of the game – Hutton, Boycott, Sutcliffe, Trueman, Close, the list goes on. The proud distinction of only selecting those born in Yorkshire was put aside in 1992 when the Indian batsman Sachin Tendulkar arrived, as Yorkshire at last followed the rest and employed an overseas player.

It is perhaps ironic that the man who had the biggest single influence in the White Rose county's formative years, Lord Hawke, was actually born in Lincolnshire.

The county club was formed in Sheffield, and prior to Hawke's appointment as captain in 1883, generally played below a level that the sum of its parts would suggest.

Although never one of the great players, Hawke established the principles that were to make Yorkshire such a power in the land. Joining as a Cambridge undergraduate, he was club captain for 28 years and president for 40 years until his death in 1938. He was also an England selector and president and treasurer of the MCC.

Hawke guided Yorkshire to their first official Championship in 1893, but it was their hat-trick of triumphs in 1900, 1901 and 1902 that established their superiority. In those three seasons they played 60 matches, losing just two. Three players in particular stand out from this period.

In George Hirst and Wilfred Rhodes, Yorkshire had two supreme all-rounders. In the championship Hirst did the 'double' eight times, scoring 27,000 runs and taking more than 2,000 wickets. He also had the knack of coming up with an important contribution just when it was needed.

Rhodes managed the double seven times, scoring almost 27,000 runs and taking over 3,000 wickets. He rose in the England batting order from number eleven to opener. The Yorkshire batting was led by David Denton, a dashing player who made over 28,000 runs in his career, four times topping 2,000 in a season.

Other titles followed but it was in the period after the First World War that Yorkshire again had no equals, winning the Championship four times in succession from 1922 to 1925. Once more the side was strong in bowling and fielding, and in Holmes and Sutcliffe they had an opening pair with a reputation that stretched worldwide.

But perhaps because of this invincibility, Yorkshire won few friends on the county circuit. Everyone admired their talents, but it would be fair to say that the players would have won few popularity polls.

The next 'golden age' came in the 1930s when, under the captaincy of first F.E. Greenwood and then Brian Sellers, they won the Championship seven times in nine years.

Again their tactics were not pretty. Batting first, they would invariably secure a big score and then leave almost two days to bowl the opposition out. Bowlers such as Bill Bowes – who was sometimes accused of intimidation – and Hedley Verity ensured that the ploy generally worked.

Yet, good as they were, player for player Yorkshire were not vastly superior to other sides, didn't display any great team-spirit, and stories were told of dressing-room arguments. But despite all that, no other county could match them!

A young Len Hutton began to make an impression at this time, and it was his batting that was to dominate Yorkshire cricket in the post-war years until his retirement in 1955. He made 85 centuries for the county in his 25,000 runs.

Further championships were added in 1946 and 1949, when they shared first place with Middlesex. If the fifties were barren years, with just one title in 1959, it is worth noting that Yorkshire finished runners-up five times.

Even so, the unhappy Yorkshire members registered their disapproval when they refused to support an increase in subscriptions by way of a protest.

That 1959 triumph, secured by reaching a target of 205 in 75 minutes on the last afternoon of the season, was achieved by a young and mostly inexperienced side. It was an indication of the success that was to follow in the next decade, with six more titles coming to the county.

Vic Wilson led them to their first two in 1960 and 1962, and then began Brian Close's time as skipper. Four championships and two Gillette Cup wins bear testament to his achievements. But with the exception of the emerging talents of Geoffrey Boycott and the fiery fast bowling of Fred Trueman, the side was no more than workmanlike, and trouble was around the corner.

Internal problems began as Raymond Illingworth, a fine deputy to Close, moved to Leicestershire after being denied the long-term contract he sought.

Close caused the club to be publicly rebuked over tactics at Edgbaston in 1967, and the

Yorkshire's famous opening pair, Holmes (left) and Sutcliffe: in 1932 at Leyton they put on an incredible 555 for the first wicket.

festering atmosphere led to his removal as captain in 1970 and his subsequent departure for a second career at Somerset.

Boycott was captain through most of the seventies as Yorkshire suffered a most miserable period. He was frequently criticised for putting his own batting before team interests. Certainly Yorkshire were no longer feared. The nadir arrived in 1973 when Durham of the Minor Counties beat them in the first round of the Gillette Cup.

Another round of in-fighting broke out in 1978 as Illingworth returned as team manager and Boycott was dismissed as captain. It was a shattering week for Boycott, having been passed over as vice-captain of England for an Australian visit and suffering the death of his mother.

Discontent continued to simmer throughout the eighties. Young players considered that Boycott, his successor John Hampshire and Chris Old were receiving preferential contracts treatment.

In 1981 the feud between Illingworth and Boycott surfaced again as Boycott was suspended for remarks made about the manager, and his supporters campaigned for Illingworth to be sacked.

Illingworth survived and remarkably returned to captain the side at the age of fifty in 1983. But success in the John Player League could not hide the embarrassment of finishing bottom of the County Championship. Further strife was assured with the sacking of Boycott, still Yorkshire's best batsman, at the end of the season, the committee declaring its intention to concentrate on a youth policy. The ensuing row led to Boycott's reinstatement not just as a player but as a committee member, and Illingworth departed.

Yorkshire finally decided not to offer Boycott a further contract at the end of the 1986 season, although only on a 12–9 vote of the general committee. He had scored 29,485 Championship runs at an average of 58.27.

A Benson and Hedges Cup triumph in 1987 has been the only Yorkshire success of recent times, and still the in-fighting has continued. Boycott led criticism of the way the club was being run in 1989, and the players themselves appealed for outside help to be brought in.

Eventually, on 10th July 1991, the Yorkshire committee agreed that they would employ an overseas player, and nine days later they announced the signing of Australian fast bowler Craig McDermott.

But an injury prevented McDermott from taking up the position and instead the club hurriedly signed the young Indian batsman Sachin Tendulkar, followed in 1993 by the West Indies captain Richie Richardson.

Yorkshire's finances and general health have improved, but success on the field currently remains as elusive as ever.

ZAHEER ABBAS

Pakistan

Born 1947
Karachi, Public Works
Department, Sind, Pakistan
International Airlines and
Gloucestershire

FOR MOST OF THE 1970s, Zaheer Abbas was one of the top batsmen in the world. He played loose-wristed but very straight, and was a fine judge of line and length. Like all great players he always appeared to have time to play his shots.

Zaheer burst on the Test scene when in only his second match he scored 274 against England at Edgbaston in 1971. It was a wonderful innings, compiled with impeccable concentration over nine hours and ten minutes.

That made him a permanent fixture in the Pakistan side and he went on to make two more double centuries, 240 against England at the Oval in 1974, and 235 against India at Lahore in 1978.

In England, Zaheer chose to join Gloucestershire in 1972. After that Test innings the previous year, he could have had the pick of the counties. His time in the West Country proved to be happy and successful, highlighted by victory in the Gillette Cup in 1973.

Eight times he scored a hundred in both innings – a world record – and four times a double century and century in the same match, another world record.

Back in Pakistan in 1982/83, he became only the 20th man to reach 100 centuries, scoring 215 against India.

He went on to captain his country, leading them to their first series win over England in 1983/84.

But his Test career ended in controversy in 1985/86 when, having already announced that he would retire at the end of the series against Sri Lanka, he withdrew from the final Test, claiming senior players had forced him to stand down.

First Class Career:
Runs – 34,843. Average 51.54
(108 centuries)

Test Match Career:
Tests – 78
Runs – 5,062. Average 44.79
(12 centuries)

ZIMBABWE

FOR ZIMBABWE, THE youngest of the Test match playing nations, the date of 18th October 1992 was one to cherish.

It marked the start of their first Test match, against India at Harare Sports Club. Although the match was drawn, the debutants held the upper hand for most of the game.

Fittingly, their captain David Houghton scored a century in a first innings total of 456, easily the highest total by any country in a debut Test. Houghton has also recorded the highest score for Zimbabwe – 266 against Sri Lanka

Zaheer Abbas led Pakistan to their first series win over England in 1983/84, scoring an important 70 in the final Test at Lahore (below).

at Bulawayo, a match in which the home side just failed to record their first Test win.

They lost a one-day international against India soon after their first Test appearance, and the following month lost and drew matches in a two-Test series in Zimbabwe against New Zealand.

Their elusive first Test win came in February 1995 with a crushing innings victory over Pakistan at Harare.

For a time Rhodesia, as Zimbabwe was known until 1980, played in South Africa's domestic competition, and prior to Zimbabwe's adoption as a Test nation at a meeting of the International Cricket Council in July 1992, players mostly went south to the Republic to play international cricket.

Among them were Colin Bland and John Traicos, who returned to Zimbabwe to make his debut for his homeland in that first Test against India at the age of 45. Another

player, Graeme Hick, went on to qualify for England.

Cricket began in Rhodesia in 1890. Clubs were established as towns were created and a league was already in operation by the time the First World War began.

The quality of the cricket improved between the wars, with tours by the MCC in 1930/31 and 1938/39 giving the game a boost. The Australians also visited in 1936.

It was after the Second World War that cricket in Rhodesia became firmly established, with regular tours by the MCC, Australia and New Zealand, as well as many English counties.

Standards improved further with professional coaches employed to the benefit of club and schools cricketers.

However, Rhodesia's unilateral declaration of independence (UDI) in 1966 led to its being ostracised

On 22 October 1992 at Harare, Zimbabwean batsmen Grant Flowers and Kevin Arnott walk out to open their country's first ever innings in Test cricket against New Zealand.

by the rest of the cricket world, and the much-needed tours stopped.

However, with the creation of Zimbabwe dawned a new era, and the new country made an explosive impact on a first appearance in the World Cup in England in 1983.

Having qualified as winners of the 1982 ICC Trophy, Zimbabwe beat mighty Australia by 13 runs in a zonal match at Trent Bridge – the biggest surprise of any World Cup to that point. They also gave the West Indies a close game, with the eventual beaten finalists winning at Worcester with just one and a half overs remaining.

THE GUINNESS